T0389580

Islam, the Ancient Near East and Varieties of Godlessness

Islamic History and Civilization

STUDIES AND TEXTS

Editorial Board

Hinrich Biesterfeldt
Sebastian Günther

Honorary Editor
Wadad Kadi

VOLUME 131

The titles published in this series are listed at *brill.com/ihc*

Patricia Crone, 29 January 2004
PHOTOGRAPH BY CLIFF MOORE/INSTITUTE FOR ADVANCED STUDY, PRINCETON, NJ

Islam, the Ancient Near East and Varieties of Godlessness

Collected Studies in Three Volumes

VOLUME 3

By

Patricia Crone

Edited by

Hanna Siurua

TUTA SUB AEGIDE PALLAS · 1683 ·

BRILL

LEIDEN | BOSTON

Cover illustration: *Iraq. Kifl. Native Moslem* [*i.e., Muslim*] *village with a Jewish shrine to the prophet Ezekiel. Conical tower over Ezekiel's tomb.* Photographed by the American Colony (Jerusalem), Photo Dept. Date Created/Published: [1932]. LC-M33-4735 [P&P]. Library of Congress Prints and Photographs Division Washington, D.C. 20540 USA.

The Library of Congress Cataloging-in-Publication Data is available online at http://catalog.loc.gov
LC record available at http://lccn.loc.gov/2016010221

Want or need Open Access? Brill Open offers you the choice to make your research freely accessible online in exchange for a publication charge. Review your various options on brill.com/brill-open.

Typeface for the Latin, Greek, and Cyrillic scripts: "Brill". See and download: brill.com/brill-typeface.

ISSN 0929-2403
ISBN 978-90-04-31927-1 (hardback, volume 131)
ISBN 978-90-04-31976-9 (hardback, set, volumes 129, 130 & 131)
ISBN 978-90-04-31931-8 (e-book)

Copyright 2016 by Koninklijke Brill NV, Leiden, The Netherlands.
Koninklijke Brill NV incorporates the imprints Brill, Brill Nijhoff, Global Oriental and Hotei Publishing.
All rights reserved. No part of this publication may be reproduced, translated, stored in a retrieval system, or transmitted in any form or by any means, electronic, mechanical, photocopying, recording or otherwise, without prior written permission from the publisher.
Authorization to photocopy items for internal or personal use is granted by Koninklijke Brill NV provided that the appropriate fees are paid directly to The Copyright Clearance Center, 222 Rosewood Drive, Suite 910, Danvers, MA 01923, USA. Fees are subject to change.

This book is printed on acid-free paper and produced in a sustainable manner.

Contents

Editor's Preface IX
Remarks on Receipt of the 2014 Middle East Medievalists (MEM) Lifetime Achievement Award XI
List of Original Publications and Acknowledgments XVI

1 "Barefoot and Naked": What Did the Bedouin of the Arab Conquests Look Like? 1

2 The Ancient Near East and Islam: The Case of Lot-Casting 17

3 Idrīs, Atraḫasīs and al-Khiḍr 44

4 Abū Saʿīd al-Ḫaḍrī and the Punishment of Unbelievers 82

5 The Dahrīs According to al-Jāḥiẓ 96

6 Ungodly Cosmologies 118

7 Post-Colonialism in Tenth-Century Islam 151

8 What Are Prophets For? The Social Utility of Religion in Medieval Islamic Thought 186

9 Oral Transmission of Subversive Ideas from the Islamic World to Europe: The Case of the Three Impostors 200

10 How the Field Has Changed in My Lifetime 239

List of Patricia Crone's Publications 247
Index of Names and Terms 255

Editor's Preface

The origins of this collection of studies lie in Patricia Crone's February 2013 visit to Leiden, where she received an honorary doctorate from Leiden University and gave a lecture on how the field of Islamic studies had changed over her lifetime. Subsequent discussions between her and Petra Sijpesteijn over the possible publication of that lecture grew into the idea of compiling a collection of her recent, forthcoming and unpublished articles. Professor Crone herself selected, arranged and in some cases revised the articles to be included in the collection. Most of the articles are reprinted, but a few are published for the first time in this collection; these include articles 14 and 15 in volume 1 and articles 3, 8, 9 and 10 (the lecture mentioned above) in the present volume.

Each volume focuses on a particular theme. The first volume brings together studies on the community from which Muḥammad emerged and the book that he brought; the second volume is dedicated to Iranian religious trends both before and after the arrival of Islam; and this third volume treats Islam in the historical context of the ancient Near East, with special attention to materialists, sceptics and other 'godless' people. Each volume includes a bibliography of Professor Crone's publications.

All of the articles have been typeset anew, but the page numbers of the original publications (wherever available) are indicated in the margin. Where note numbering has changed in the reprint as a consequence of revisions, the original note numbers are given in superscript at the beginning of the affected notes.

I have edited the articles with a very light hand. Errors and misprints have been corrected, the author's revisions and additions have been incorporated, incomplete and previously forthcoming citations have been updated and the transliteration of Arabic and Persian has been standardised to follow the Arabic transliteration scheme of the *International Journal of Middle East Studies* (modified in the case of elisions). The few editorial interventions beyond these are bracketed and marked as mine ('Ed.'). Citation, punctuation and spelling practices in each article reflect those of the original publication, with only minor, silent changes.

I would like to thank Sabine Schmidtke, María Mercedes Tuya and Casey Westerman at the Institute for Advanced Study; Kathy van Vliet, Teddi Dols and Arthur Westerhof at Brill; Ahmed El Shamsy, Itamar Francez, M. Şükrü Hanioğlu, Masoud Jafari Jazi, Martin Mulsow, Bilal Orfali, Petra Sijpesteijn and Frank Stewart for help with queries; Mariam Sheibani for research assistance; Dana E. Lee for her editorial work; and especially Michael Cook, Professor

Crone's literary executor, who oversaw the finalising of the volumes once Professor Crone was no longer able to fill that role herself.

Hanna Siurua
Chicago, January 2016

Remarks on Receipt of the 2014 Middle East Medievalists (MEM) Lifetime Achievement Award iii

When I discussed with Matthew [Ed.: Gordon, then president of MEM] what I should talk about, he said he'd like to hear some manner of reflection on my work, career, books, students, and the state of the field, or some combination of these things. Well, I doubt that I shall be able to talk about all these things, but let me start by telling you a story.

One summer towards the end of my time at school, one of my sisters and I went to the theatre festival at Avignon, and there for the first time in my life, I met a live Muslim, a Moroccan. I had decided to study the Muslim world without ever knowingly having set eyes on an Arab or Persian or heard Arabic or Persian spoken. There weren't any of them in Denmark back then: it was Gilgamesh who had seduced me. I discovered him in my teens and wanted to be an ancient Near Eastern archaeologist, but for a variety of reasons I became an Islamicist instead. Anyway, I met this Moroccan in Avignon, and he told me the story of the Battle of Siffin: the Syrians were losing and responded by hoisting Qurans on their lances, the battle stopped, and so Ali lost. It never occurred to me to believe it; I smiled politely and thought to myself, "when I get to university I'll hear a different story." I got to Copenhagen University, but no Islamic history was taught there, only Semitic philology, which I did not want to do, and history, meaning European history, which I did do and enjoyed, but which was not where I wanted to stay. Eventually I got myself to England, and there I was accepted by SOAS and heard Professor Lewis lecture on early Islamic history, including the Battle of Siffin. He told the story exactly as my Moroccan friend had told it. I could not believe it. It struck me as obvious that the narrative was fiction, | and besides, everyone knows that battle accounts iv
are most unlikely to be reliable, least of all when they are told by the loser. I thought about it again many years later, in 2003, when one of Saddam Hussain's generals, Muhammad Saeed al-Sahhaf, also known as comical (not chemical) Ali, persistently asserted that the Iraqis had defeated the Americans and put them to flight, so that there weren't any American troops in Iraq any more. At the very least one would have expected Lewis to say something about the problematic nature of battle narratives, and was this really true? But no: it was a truth universally acknowledged that, during the Battle of Siffin, the Syrians hoisted Qurans on their lances and thereby stopped the battle, depriving the Iraqis of their victory.

I think this is the biggest academic shock I've ever suffered, but I didn't say anything. I never did, I was too shy. And then I encountered John Wansbrough. He read Arabic texts with us undergraduates, clearly thinking we were a hopeless lot, but he was the first person I met at SOAS who doubted the Siffin story. As it turned out, he doubted just about everything in the tradition. I was fascinated by him. I wanted to know how he thought we should go about writing about early Islamic history, so I continued reading texts with him as a graduate, but I never got an answer. Once, when we were reading Tabari's account of Ibn al-Ashʿath's revolt in the mid-Umayyad period, Wansbrough asked: "What year are we in?" I thought he simply meant "what year has Tabari put this in?," but when I replied "year 82," or whatever, he acidly retorted, "I see you have the confidence of your supervisor," meaning Bernard Lewis, my supervisor, whom he deeply disliked. I think his question was meant to be understood as, "Is all this really something that happened in year 82 (or whenever) or is it stereotyped battle scenes interspersed with poetry that could be put in any heroic account in need of amplification?" I don't know, for he did not explain. He never did. He was an *imam samit*.

From all this you can see two things. First, it was not exposure to Wansbrough that made me a sceptic or radical or whatever else they like to call me. I was a sceptic already in Avignon, years before I came to England, without being aware of it. In my own understanding I was just thinking commonsense. And secondly, Islamic history was not studied at an advanced level. I don't know how the Battle of Siffin is taught these days, but I cannot imagine it is done with the credulity of those days and, at least in England, Lewis must take part of the credit for this, for he was very keen for Islamicists to become historians.

After I'd finished my thesis, Michael Cook and I finished *Hagarism* (1977), which I assume you have heard about and don't propose to talk about; and next, in between some articles, I wrote *Slaves on Horses* (1980), which was the first third of my thesis, drastically rewritten. Then it was *Roman, Provincial and Islamic Law* (1987), which was a drastically rewritten version of my thesis part two and which I loved researching because the literature on the Greek, Roman and provincial side was so superb. The legal learning possessed by these late nineteenth- and early twentieth-century German and Italian scholars was incredible, and on top of that they were wonderfully intelligent and lucid. Then came the First World War and now it is all gone. Apparently it isn't even done
v to admire them any more. A perfectly friendly | reviewer of my book on law cautioned his readers that I was an admirer of these scholars, as if it were self-evident that they were bad people. I don't see why.

In any case, *Meccan Trade* came out in the same year. It was delayed by a report so negative that I withdrew it and sent it to Princeton University Press. The author of the negative report said that I should have my head examined, that nothing I'd written would win general acceptance and that I'd never get a job in America. This last was particularly hilarious since it had never occurred to me to apply for one there. Serjeant was also outraged by *Meccan Trade*. He wrote a furious review in which he accused me of all sorts of misdeeds. But today the book is perceived as being about the location of Mecca, to which I devote a page. I've even heard somebody introduce me as a speaker and list *Meccan Trade* among my books with the comment that it is about the location of Mecca, to which I had to say sorry, no, actually *Meccan Trade* is about Meccan trade.

After *Meccan Trade*, or at the same time (both this and other books took a long time to reach print), I published *God's Caliph* with Martin Hinds. It was a short book, but Calder nonetheless thought it was long-winded: I admit I found that hard to take seriously. It was as usual: the reviewers found fault with this, that and the other, and you let it pass. The one thing I really disliked about *God's Caliph* was the massive number of misprints, which Martin Hinds was no better at spotting than I was.

It must have been after *God's Caliph* had gone to press that I wrote *Pre-Industrial Societies*, which I hugely enjoyed doing because I had to read about all kinds of places that I didn't know much about, and also because I wrote without footnotes. It saves you masses of time. PIS, as I called it (pronouncing it Piss), was barely reviewed and took a while to gather attention, and it too was riddled with misprints, but the misprints should now have been eliminated and a fresh print-run with a new cover is on its way.

The next book I wrote was *The Book of Strangers: Medieval Arabic Graffiti on the Theme of Nostalgia* (1999), which was completely new to me when I started translating it. I inherited it from Martin Hinds and was captivated by it, but had trouble with the poetry in it. However, Shmuel Moreh came to Cambridge shortly after I'd started, and he was well versed in Arabic poetry, so I asked him if he'd help me, and he would. So we translated it together and I took responsibility for the rest.

That book almost generated another Siffin story. The author is traditionally identified as Abu 'l-Faraj al-Isfahani, but he himself says that he was in his youth in 356/967, which makes him considerably younger than Abu 'l-Faraj.[1] Yaqut, who said he did not know how to resolve the problem, noticed this already. There is only one way to resolve it: the author is not Abu 'l-Faraj. The book doesn't have much in common with Abu 'l-Faraj's works either. But a specialist in Abu 'l-Faraj insisted that it was him and came up with the explanation, also

1 Abu 'l-Faraj allegedly died in 356/967 [Ed.: noted by Antoine Borrut for MEM].

tried by older scholars, that Abu 'l-Faraj was senile when he wrote the book, so that he had forgotten when he was young. Honestly, the things that Islamicists will say!

The next book was also a joint project and also connected with Martin Hinds
vi and the so-called "Hinds-Xerox" which Martin | had received from Amr Khalifa Ennami and which Michael Cook used for his section on the Murji'a in his *Early Muslim Dogma*. Martin Hinds was working on the last section of the manuscript when he died. I could have finished that last section, but it seemed a bad idea to translate yet another fragment. What should be done was a translation of the whole epistle. But I couldn't do that on my own—there were parts of the manuscript that I simply could not decipher. So I asked my former colleague in Oxford, Fritz Zimmermann, if he would participate, and thank God, he would. So we started by writing a translation each and then amalgamating them, with long pauses over passages that seemed impossible. Fritz had some great brain waves, and somehow we managed to get a complete typescript together. Then there was all the rest, where the fun for me lay in comparing Salim and the Ibadi epistles that I had been able to buy in Oman. *The Epistle of Salim ibn Dhakwan* was published in Oxford in 2001. Very few people are interested in the Ibadis so it has not exactly been a bestseller, but I learned an extraordinary amount from writing it.

After that, I wrote *Medieval Islamic Political Thought*, which the Americans called *God's Rule*, though it is disagreeably close to *God's Caliph* and not particularly apt in my view. That book started as exam questions in Cambridge. Carole Hillenbrand was our external examiner, and when she saw the questions, she asked me if I wanted to write a volume on political thought for her Edinburgh series. I liked the idea, envisaging the book as much smaller than it actually became. I also thought I could do it fast because I thought I knew the field inside out, but that was only true of some of the subjects I wrote about. I had to do a lot of work on the Ismailis, for example, because I did not know the sources well enough. I was also acutely aware of having inadequate knowledge of the last century before the Mongol invasions and don't think I managed to get that right. I suppose I was running out of patience. I wasn't under any pressure, for I had refused a contract. I usually did until I was close to the end.

My book on political thought was the first book of mine that was uniformly well received. All the others had a controversial element to them that the reviewers didn't like, if only for my refusal to accept that Abu 'l-Faraj al-Isfahani had forgotten when he was young. Mercifully, there were also reviewers who found that a ridiculous argument. Not long afterwards they gave me the Levi della Vida medal and I also received several honorary doctorates. Altogether, it was clear that I was no longer an *enfant terrible*.

My latest, and probably also last, book is *The Nativist Prophets of Early Islamic Iran: Rural Revolt and Local Zoroastrianism* (2012), which had its roots in my teaching in Oxford and which was very exciting to write because it was about villagers, whom we rarely see in the sources, and because their form of Zoroastrianism was quite different from that of the Pahlavi books. That book was also well received; it was awarded no less than four book prizes, for its contribution to Islamic studies, to Iranian studies, to Central Asian studies, and to historical studies in general.

If I had not fallen ill, I would have started a book on the Dahris, Godless people on whom I have written some articles, and who are certainly worth a book. But I don't think I have enough time.

Patricia Crone
Princeton, November 2014

List of Original Publications and Acknowledgments

We gratefully acknowledge permission to reprint articles that originally appeared in the following publications:

'Remarks by the Recipient of the 2014 MEM Lifetime Achievement Award Written for the Annual Meeting of Middle East Medievalists and Read *in Absentia* by Matthew S. Gordon (November 22, 2014, Washington, D.C.)', *al-ʿUṣūr al-Wusṭā* 23 (2015), iii–vi. Reprinted with permission.

1. '"Barefoot and Naked": What Did the Bedouin of the Arab Conquests Look Like?', *Muqarnas* 25 ('Frontiers of Islamic Art and Architecture: Essays in Celebration of Oleg Grabar's Eightieth Birthday', ed. Gülru Necipoğlu and Julia Bailey), 2008, 1–10. © Brill.

2. 'The Ancient Near East and Islam: The Case of Lot-Casting' (with Adam Silverstein), *Journal of Semitic Studies* 55, no. 2 (2010), 423–450. Reprinted by permission of Oxford University Press on behalf of the University of Manchester.

3. 'Idrīs, Atraḫasīs and al-Khiḍr'. Previously unpublished.

4. 'Abū Saʿīd al-Ḥaḍrī and the Punishment of Unbelievers', *Jerusalem Studies in Arabic and Islam* 31 (2006), 92–106. Reprinted with permission.

5. 'The Dahrīs According to al-Jāḥiẓ', *Mélanges de l'Université Saint-Joseph* 63 (2010–2011), 63–82. Reprinted with permission.

6. '*Excursus II*: Ungodly Cosmologies', in Sabine Schmidtke (ed.), *Oxford Handbook of Islamic Theology*, Oxford: Oxford University Press, 2016. Reprinted by permission of Oxford University Press.

7. 'Post-Colonialism in Tenth-Century Islam', *Der Islam* 83, no. 1 (2006), 2–38. Reprinted with permission.

8. 'What Are Prophets For? The Social Utility of Religion in Medieval Islamic Thought'. Previously unpublished.

9. 'Oral Transmission of Subversive Ideas from the Islamic World to Europe: The Case of the Three Impostors'. Previously unpublished.

10. 'How the Field Has Changed in My Lifetime'. Previously unpublished.

CHAPTER 1

"Barefoot and Naked": What Did the Bedouin of the Arab Conquests Look Like?[*]

The Syriac churchman Bar Penkaye, who wrote about 690, held the Arab invaders to have been "naked men riding without armor or shield."[1] In the same vein Michael the Syrian (d. 1199) reports that a certain Hiran sent by the last Sasanid emperor to spy on the Arabs told his employer that the invaders were "a barefoot people, naked and weak, but very brave."[2] A Muslim text dating from, perhaps, the later eighth century similarly insists that the invaders were "barefoot and naked, without equipment, strength, weapons, or provisions."[3] In all three texts the word "naked" seems to be used in the sense of poorly equipped and lacking body armor rather than devoid of clothes, and all three depict the Arabs as poorly equipped in order to highlight the extraordinary, God-assisted nature of the Arab conquests. "I have a sharp arrowhead that penetrates iron, but it is no use against the naked," as Rustam says in the *Shāhnāma*, in his premonition of the fall of the Sasanids.[4] But precisely what *did* the Arab invaders wear? It would be the first question to spring to Oleg Grabar's mind. Under normal circumstances it would be the last to spring to mine, for as Oleg is fond of telling his colleagues, historians tend to ignore the concrete physical

* I should like to thank Michael Macdonald for invaluable help with images, inscriptions, and bibliographical references alike. Insofar as this article has any merit, it is really due to him. (The same most definitely does not apply to the shortcomings.) I am also grateful to Mika Natiff for teaching me to navigate the Index of Christian Art, to Michael Cook for reading and commenting on the paper, and to Julia Bailey for spotting visual clues that I had overlooked.

1 Bar Penkaye in A. Mingana (ed. and tr.), *Sources syriaques* (Leipzig, n.d. [1907?]), 141; trans. in S.P. Brock, "North Mesopotamia in the Late Seventh Century," *Jerusalem Studies in Arabic and Islam* 9 (1987): 58.

2 Michael the Syrian, *Chronique*, ed. and tr. J.-B. Chabot, 4 vols. (Paris, 1899–1910), 4:417, 2:421.

3 D. Sourdel, "Un pamphlet musulman anonyme d'époque ʿabbāside contre les chrétiens," *Revue des études islamiques* 34 (1966): 33 (text), 26 (trans.). For a reconstruction of the text from which the fragment comes see J.-M. Gaudeul, "The Correspondence between Leo and ʿUmar," *Islamochristiana* 10 (1984): 109–157, with the passage in question on 155. The transmitter is Ismāʿīl b. ʿAyyāsh.

4 Firdawsī, *Shāhnāma*, ed. E.E. Bertels, 9 vols. (Moscow, 1960–1971), 9:1.119 (drawn to my attention by Masoud Jafari).

© KONINKLIJKE BRILL NV, LEIDEN, 2016 | DOI: 10.1163/9789004319318_002

manifestation of things; in particular, they do not think of the way things looked and so miss an important dimension of the past. I have always pleaded guilty to that charge. Having benefited from Oleg's lively company and warm heart for over ten years, however, I shall now try to make amends, if only with a trifling offering: how should we tell a filmmaker who wanted to screen the story of the Arab conquests to depict the conquerors? More precisely, how should we tell him to depict the desert Arabs who participated in the conquests? For the bedouin will not have been dressed in the same way as the settled Arabs, and I should like to keep things simple.

Most of us would probably reply that the hypothetical filmmaker should depict the bedouin warriors as men in kaffiyehs and flowing robes, along the lines familiar from *Lawrence of Arabia* and countless Hollywood films; but as far as the bedouin of pre-Islamic Arabia are concerned, it would seem that we are wrong. Though "naked" may be a little hyperbolic, both literary and iconographic evidence suggests that it is not far from the truth.

To start with the literary evidence, Ammianus Marcellinus, commander of the eastern armies about 350 AD, tells us that the Arabs of the Syrian desert were "warriors of equal rank, half nude, clad in dyed cloaks as far as the loins."[5] The word he uses for their cloaks is *sagulum*, a short, military tunic, and one wonders how literally one should take him: were they wearing Roman army issue, passed down from relatives and friends who had served in the Roman army, or alternatively stolen from unlucky soldiers? ("When bedouin raiders in the desert encountered someone from the settled areas, it was their custom to accost him with the command, *Ishlaḥ yā walad*, 'Strip, boy!' meaning that they intended to rob him of his clothing," as Jabbur says of the Syrian bedouin many centuries later.)[6] Ammianus does not tell us what, if anything, the warriors wore on their heads, but of another Arab, this time one in Roman service at Adrianople, he says that he was long-haired and naked except for a loincloth.[7] In the same vein Malka, a fourth-century Syrian who was captured by bedouin

5 Ammianus Marcellinus, xiv, 4, 3; quoted in J.B. Segal, "Arabs in Syriac Literature before the Rise of Islam," *Jerusalem Studies in Arabic and Islam* 4 (1984): 102; also discussed in J. Matthews, *The Roman Empire of Ammianus* (London, 1989), 344, 347–348.

6 Jibrā'īl Sulaymān Jabbūr, *The Bedouins and the Desert: Aspects of Nomadic Life in the Arab East*, trans. L.I. Conrad (Albany, 1995; Arabic original 1988), 1n, with vivid illustrations on 2–3. For other examples of robbers commanding people to strip naked, see Jacob of Saroug in Khalīl Alwān, *Quatre homélies métriques sur la création* (Louvain, 1989), 43; A. Christensen, *Contes persans en langue populaire* (Copenhagen, 1918), nos. 9, 33, 42.

7 Matthews, *Roman Empire of Ammianus*, 348, with reference to Ammianus, xxxi, 16, 6.

FIGURE 1 *Ivory carving, right arm of the Chair of Maximianus. Museo Arcivescovile, Ravenna.* PHOTO: ALINARI/ART RESOURCE, NY

between Aleppo and Edessa and whose adventures were recorded by Jerome, describes how the Ishmaelites descended upon his party of about seventy travelers "with their long hair flying from under their headbands." He did not think of them as wearing turbans or kaffiyehs, then, or as shielding their heads from the sun by any kind of head cover at all. Like Ammianus, he says that they wore cloaks over their "half-naked bodies," but he adds that they wore broad military boots (*caligae*).[8] Again one wonders if they were wearing Roman army issue. They transported Malka into the desert and set him to work as a shepherd, and there he "learned to go naked," he says, presumably meaning that he learned | to cover himself with a mere skin: this seems to have been all 2
that slaves wore in pre-Islamic Arabia.[9] One would infer that he had handed over his clothes to his captors.

We now turn to the iconographic evidence, looking at it region by region.

Syria

To start in Syria, there is a representation of semi-naked bedouin in an ivory carving from a chair made in the first half of the sixth century in Antioch

---

8 Jerome, "Vita Malchi Monachi Captivi," paragraphs 4–5, in J.-P. Migne, *Patrologiae Cursus Completus, Series Latina*, 221 vols. (Paris, 1844–1864), 23: cols. 57–58, trans. in Segal, "Arabs in Syriac Literature," 103; cf. I. Shahid, *Byzantium and the Arabs in the Fourth Century* (Washington, DC, 1984), 284 ff.; Matthews, *Roman Empire of Ammianus*, 348.

9 G. Jacob, *Altarabisches Beduinenleben* (Berlin, 1897), 44 (with reference to ʿAntara's *Muʿallaqa*).

or (under Syro-Palestinian influence) Alexandria (fig. 1).[10] It depicts Joseph's brothers selling Joseph to two Saracens: the brothers are represented by the three figures on the left, Joseph stands in the middle, and two Saracens appear with two camels behind them to the right. The Saracens, who are armed with a bow and a spear respectively, have long, apparently plaited hair and wear nothing on their heads or their upper torsos, merely loose garments wrapped around their waists, which reach as far as their ankles but expose one of their legs as they walk. The brothers are also scantily clad, but in more military-looking outfits, and it is they rather than the Saracens who are wearing boots. The Saracens are shod in sandals. There is of course no guarantee that the carving is based on observation rather than artistic convention, but one point is clear: it was not as heavily clad figures in the style of *Lawrence of Arabia* that bedouin were envisaged in sixth-century Syria.

Another ivory carving on the same chair shows the Saracens selling Joseph to Potiphar (fig. 2). Here Joseph is seen twice, first on a camel (on the left) and next between Potiphar and one of the Saracens, to whom she is handing money. Potiphar is wearing classical-looking robes. The Saracens' robes also appear more flowing than in the first panel, but here as there their lower body wraps are split in the middle, exposing their legs, and their arms are bare. In fact, their entire upper torsos could be bare, though it is hard to tell. The short tunic that Joseph is wearing clearly includes a drape over one shoulder, and the adult Saracens could have a similar item on their shoulders.[11] Maybe the artist dressed his characters in classical clothes in order to conjure up a bygone age. In any case, he depicted the Saracens with the same long, apparently plaited hair as in the first panel, and he gave them sandals, too, but not any kind of headgear. One would take it to have been long hair of this kind that Malka saw flowing under headbands.

Yet another sixth-century carving, also a Syrian or Syro-Egyptian work, depicts two brothers selling Joseph to a Saracen.[12] Joseph and his brothers are wearing short tunics similar to those in which rural people are depicted on the mosaic floors of sixth-century churches in Madaba.[13] The Saracen is wearing

---

10 See O.M. Dalton, *East Christian Art: A Survey of the Monuments* (Oxford, 1925), 172, 205ff.; idem, *Byzantine Art and Archaeology* (New York, 1961; orig. publ. 1911), 203ff.

11 Cf. Dalton, *Byzantine Art and Archaeology*, 206.

12 Berlin, Staatliche Museen, inv. no. 566; cf. Dalton, *Byzantine Art and Archaeology*, 208; W.F. Volbach, *Elfenbeinarbeiten der Spätantike und des frühen Mittelalters* (Mainz, 1952), 80–81; pl. 54, no. 172.

13 M. Piccirillo and E. Alliata, *Mount Nebo: New Archaeological Excavations 1967–1997* (Jeru-

FIGURE 2 *Ivory carving, right arm of the Chair of Maximianus. Museo Arcivescovile, Ravenna.* PHOTO: ALINARI/ART RESOURCE, NY

a mantle that leaves the left part of his chest exposed, but what he is wearing underneath | is not clear. All four are barefoot and bareheaded. 3

Finally, we have the depiction a man armed with a bow, sword, and whip, leading a camel (fig. 3); this appears on the mosaic floor of the church of the monastery of Kayanos at 'Uyun Musa, at the eastern top of the Dead Sea, dated by Piccirillo to the second half of the sixth century.[14] In Piccirillo's words, the man "is half naked, wearing a long loincloth reaching beneath his knees with a cloak thrown over his left shoulder that covers his forearm." Piccirillo

salem, 1998), 333 (Church of the Deacon Thomas, whole floor); 337 (Stephanos spearing a lion, wearing "a sleeveless orbiculated tunic ... tied to the right shoulder" that seems to be identical with that of the brother on the left); 338–339 (donkey driver, soldier defending himself against a bear); 343 (date); 345, 347 (Church of Saints Lot and Procopius, whole floor).

14 M. Piccirillo, *Madaba, le chiese e i mosaici*, 207–208; Piccirillo and Alliata, *Mount Nebo*, 356–358, with a better photo (fig. 224).

FIGURE 3 *Mosaic from the church of Kaianos at 'Uyun Musa, Mount Nebo*
PHOTO COURTESY OF MICHELE PICCIRILLO

suggests that he was an auxiliary soldier and deems the representation to fit the "exaggeratedly dramatic" literary accounts of Arab soldiers given by authors such as Ammianus Marcellinus and Malka in Jerome.[15] Whether the Arab was an auxiliary soldier or not, however, the representation actually seems to be quite different. The most dramatic feature of the mosaic is the Arab's bulging chest. Neither Ammianus nor Jerome says anything about chests, but both highlight the long, flowing hair of the Arabs; though damage to the mosaic makes it impossible to say what, if anything, the soldier is wearing on his head, it is at least clear that he does not have hair (or a kaffiyeh) coming down to his shoulders. The clothes involved are quite different, too. Ammianus' Arabs were wearing short military tunics, Jerome's were dressed in cloaks and boots, but the soldier in the mosaic is wearing a waist wrap and shawl along with sandals. This could well be based on observation, for the waist wrap and shawl (*īzār* and *ridā'*) are the two chief items of male clothing in pre-Islamic poetry.[16] The main feature that the three representations have in common is the skimpiness of the outfits described. Pitched against a horsemen encased in iron, Arabs such as
4 these would indeed have come across as naked. |

In sharp contrast to these representations, an image on a piece of Coptic tapestry dating from between the sixth and eighth centuries and said to show

15 Piccirillo, in both *Madaba, le chiese e i mosaici* and *Mount Nebo*, and with reference to Ammianus and Jerome in *Madaba, le chiese e i mosaici*, 225 n. 10.

16 Jacob, *Altarabisches Beduinenleben*, 44.

Joseph and an Ishmaelite merchant on a camel depicts both Joseph and the Ishmaelite as thoroughly wrapped up.[17] But the alleged camel may well be a horse,[18] and the alleged Ishmaelite seems to be wearing trousers. So this can be left out of consideration.

South Arabia

If the inhabitants of the Roman empire envisaged the Saracens as wearing nothing on their heads and not much on their bodies, how were they seen by the Arabs themselves? We may start in the south.

Here the first image to capture one's attention is a crude relief on an alabaster incense burner from Shabwa in the Hadramawt, probably dating from around the third century AD (fig. 4). It depicts a man riding on an unsaddled camel, positioned in front of the hump; he holds a short sword or a camel stick or some such implement in his right hand and the reins in his left, and a water skin or shield is attached by a strap to the rear of the hump. He is stark naked, and, apart from the reins, the camel is as naked as he is.

The text gives the name of the person commemorated, presumably identical with the person represented, as Adhlal ibn Wahab'il but does not otherwise tells us anything about him.[19] Macdonald wonders whether the incense burner is a funerary object rather than a dedicatory one (as suggested in the catalogue of the exhibition in which it was most recently displayed[20]), for the inscription does not mention any deity, only a name and a patronym, and the vast majority of funerary stelae in both North and South Arabia only give the deceased's name and patronym. If the object is funerary, the relief might in Macdonald's opinion represent the naked soul of the deceased riding his camel on the Day

17 A. Kakovkine, "Le tissu copte des VIIe–VIIIe siècles du Musée Metropolitan," *Göttinger Miszellen* 129 (1992): 53–59. It was formerly classified as showing the flight into Egypt.

18 Presumably it was classified as a camel on the basis of its peculiar head (which mostly looks like that of a dog) and the similarity of its hooves and tail to those of the camel at Dura Europos (cf. the reference given below, n. 24). But it has no hump, and its legs and harness are those of a horse.

19 St. J. Simpson, ed., *Queen of Sheba: Treasures from Ancient Yemen* (London, 2002), 97–98, no. 110; also in W. Seipel (ed.), *Jemen: Kunst und Archäologie im Land der Königin von Saba'* (Vienna, 1998), 86 and 88, no. 20, both without comments on the absence of clothes; *Répertoire d'épigraphie sémitique*, 8 vols. (Paris, 1900–1968), 7, no. 4690.

20 Simpson, *Queen of Sheba*, 97–98, no. 110.

FIGURE 4 *Relief from an alabaster incense burner. British Museum, ANE 125682.*
REPRODUCED WITH THE PERMISSION OF THE TRUSTEES OF THE BRITISH MUSEUM

of Judgment.[21] But as Macdonald himself stresses, this is highly conjectural. Besides, did the pagans of South Arabia believe in the resurrection? There is nothing to suggest that the deceased was a Jew or a Christian. And the people depicted on other funerary reliefs are fully clothed. On the whole, it seems more likely that a bedouin of the Hadrami plateau is being depicted here, for there are plenty of naked Arabs in the rock reliefs, as will be seen. Why such a man should figure on a Shabwan incense burner is another question.

A fully clothed camel rider appears on a funerary relief, also of alabaster, dated to roughly the first | to the third century AD, with an incription identifying the deceased as Mushayqar Hamayat ibn Yashuf (fig. 5).[22] He too is holding a short spear or camel stick in his right hand and the reins in his left, and he is sitting on a fine camel saddle of a type also attested on a bronze figurine of a camel thought to be from Yemen.[23] Unlike the wild bedouin on the incense burner, this camel rider was presumably a soldier in the local army, dressed in conformity with the sense of propriety of the settled people. Of decently dressed camel-riders, presumably soldiers in the local armies, we also have an example in a relief from Dura Europos that shows such a rider seated on a saddled camel, armed with a long lance, and wearing a tunic and mantle.[24] But he is bareheaded, and maybe the South Arabian was too: Calvet and Robin interpret his apparent head cover as a hair style.[25]

In another funerary relief, a Sabaean alabaster of the second or third century AD, the lower panel shows a horseman with the north Arabian name of ʿIjl ibn Saʿdallat touching a camel with his spear, the act by which a camel raider appropriates a camel. The upper panel shows the deceased sitting at a table with his wife and child in attendance, or perhaps the deceased at a banquet, and both the stool and the table indicate that we are in a settled environment, as also suggested by the fact that the *nisba* of the deceased was Qryn: he may have come from Qaryat al-Faw or from Wadi ʾl-Qura.[26] He was not a bedouin

21 Michael Macdonald, personal communication with reference to a discussion at the recent congress "Rencontres sabéennes 10," in St. Petersburg.

22 Y. Calvet and C. Robin, *Arabie heureuse, Arabie déserte: Les antiquités arabiques du Musée du Louvre* (Paris, 1997), 109–110, no. 20, where both the image and the text are reproduced along with a transliteration, translation, discussion, and bibliography.

23 Reproduced in Simpson, *Queen of Sheba*, 99, no. 113.

24 A. Perkins, *The Art of Dura-Europos* (Oxford, 1973), fig. 40.

25 Cf. the reference given above, n. 22 ("Il porte une coiffure arrondée avec une sorte de pendant à l'arrière").

26 Louvre, AO 1029: see Calvet and Robin, *Arabie heureuse*, 107–108, no. 18 (image, text, transliteration, translation, discussion, and bibliography); A. Caubert, *Aux sources du*

FIGURE 5 *Alabaster funerary relief. Louvre, AO 1128.*
PHOTO COURTESY OF MICHAEL MACDONALD

monde arabe: L'Arabie avant l'Islam, collections du Musée du Louvre (Paris, 1990), 28 and 39, no. 3 (where the upper panel is interpreted as a banquet scene). For the meaning of the gesture with the spear see M.C.A. Macdonald, "Camel Hunting or Camel Raiding?," *Arabian Archaeology and Epigraphy* 1, no. 1 (1990): 24–28, with a reproduction of the stela on 26.

raiding camels, then, but rather a sedentary Arab engaged in what one would assume to be camel catching staged as a sport.[27] All the figures are fully clothed, the deceased in a long robe and the other two in shorter garments, and the deceased seems to be wearing some kind of head cover, though his putative wife and children are clearly bareheaded. The deceased's headgear, if it is not simply hair, looks like some sort of stiff bonnet, certainly not like a turban. South Arabian reliefs, which usually show people bareheaded, do not in fact seem to depict any turbans at all.

Moving slightly north to Qaryat al-Faw, which flourished from roughly the second century BC to roughly the fifth century AD, we find a bronze statue of a man wearing nothing but a loincloth, but he is kneeling reverently, presumably in prayer, and his outfit is more likely to be a form of *iḥrām* than bedouin dress.[28] Also at Qaryat al-Faw we find two drawings on plaster walls of horsemen hunting or raiding camels. One horseman could be naked, but the other is wearing something like a tunic or at least a skirt. Whether they have headgear is impossible to tell.[29]

The Desert

That leaves us with the countless rock drawings left by the inhabitants of the desert themselves. The most striking image among these is a drawing of a horse-
| man hunting an oryx with a short spear (fig. 6). He is wearing a waist wrap 6
similar to that of the Arab soldier in the sixth-century mosaic; the thickened lines across his shoulders could be taken to suggest that he is also wearing a *ridāʾ*, and he has bushy or kinky hair that, although quite long, sticks straight out from his head, in a style that is quite common in Safaitic drawings.[30] Unless

---

27 This seems at least as likely as that the deceased should be shown as engaged in camel-raiding, perhaps out of a desire to claim links with a real or nomadic past, as suggested by Macdonald, "Camel Hunting or Camel Raiding?," 25–26; idem, "Hunting, Fighting, and Raiding: The Horse in Pre-Islamic Arabia," in *Furusiyya*, ed. D. Alexander, 2 vols. (Riyad, 1996), 1:76. Either is compatible with the conjecture that he was a caravaneer (Calvet and Robin, *Arabie heureuse*, 108).

28 A.R. al-Ansary, *Qaryat al-Fau: A Portrait of a Pre-Islamic Civilisation in Saudi Arabia* (London, 1982), 109, no. 3.

29 Ansary, *Qaryat al-Fau*, 130–133 (where the rider called Salim b. Kaʿb seems to be hunting rather than raiding, given that the camel appears to have been speared or shot with an arrow).

30 G.M.H. King, *The Basalt Desert Rescue Survey: Safaitic Inscriptions* (forthcoming; my thanks to Dr. King for allowing me to reproduce the image).

FIGURE 6 *Rock drawing depicting a Safaitic horseman*
PHOTO COURTESY OF G.M.H. KING

we take his hair actually to be some sort of hat, he is not wearing anything on his head. Other drawings do depict headgear, sometimes very elaborate, but apparently in the form of plumes, which are hardly intended here.[31] The author of the Safaitic inscription on the same stone claims to have made the drawing, which is thus roughly datable to the period from the first century BC to the fourth century AD. By then, it would seem, the pre-Islamic "uniform" of *īzār* and *ridāʾ* was in place, but without the turban or other headgear by which it is usually taken to have been complemented.

By the standards of the rock drawings, this horseman is well dressed, for most drawings depict males as either naked or wearing skimpy clothes "mainly meant to cover the private parts," as Nayeem puts it.[32] But these drawings are difficult to date, and though some are Safaitic,[33] many of them are likely to be much older than the period under consideration here.

31 Cf. Macdonald, "Hunting, Fighting, and Raiding," 76, 77 fig. 5b, where the upper tier of the headdress looks like giant feathers.

32 M.A. Nayeem, *The Rock Art of Arabia* (Hyderabad, 2000), 337. For some striking examples of naked people see Macdonald, "Hunting, Fighting, and Raiding," 72, nos. 3, 1d, 1g, 1h. Unfortunately, these drawings are known only from hand copies, and there is no way of telling how accurately they represent the originals.

33 M.C.A. Macdonald, "Reflections on the Linguistic Map of Pre-Islamic Arabia," *Arabian Archaeology and Epigraphy* 11 (2000): 45.

FIGURE 7 *Rock drawing*
PHOTO COURTESY OF MICHAEL MACDONALD

There is an example of what the makers of rock art wore in a Thamudic drawing from the Tabuk region of northern Arabia, which depicts a horseman and two men in a chariot—a driver and an archer (fig. 7).[34] The horseman, who is riding in front of the chariot, appears to be every bit as naked as the camel on the Sabaean stela, though one should perhaps envisage him as wearing a loincloth. He also seems to have long, flowing (rather than bushy) hair. The driver could be naked, at least as far as his upper torso is concerned (the lower part of his body is hidden from view), but maybe the draftsman simply refrained from trying to depict his clothes. He could be bareheaded, but his head is pointed, perhaps to suggest the conical helmet worn by Assyrian soldiers.[35] The footsoldier who is pursuing the chariot and shooting arrows at it, however (fig. 8), is dressed in a long waist wrap, with a slit at the side or the front to allow

34 Cf. Macdonald, "Hunting, Fighting, and Raiding," 74, 76 ff., with the complete composition on 224–225.
35 Macdonald, "Hunting, Fighting, and Raiding," 78.

FIGURE 8 *Rock drawing, detail*
PHOTO COURTESY OF MICHAEL MACDONALD

freedom of movement, along the lines of those depicted on the ivory panel of Saracens buying Joseph from his brothers (see fig. 1). He too seems to have long hair.

This drawing is likely to be very old. The chariot points to ancient Near Eastern times, perhaps the seventh to fourth century BC,[36] and the footsoldier has a long, pointed thong between his legs, a feature also found on images of

36 Macdonald, "Hunting, Fighting, and Raiding," 78; idem, "Wheels in a Land of Camels: Another Look at the Chariot in Arabia," *Arabian Archaeology and Epigraphy* 20 (2009): 156–184.

FIGURE 9 *W. Boutcher, detail of an Assyrian relief, Room L of the North Palace at Nineveh.* BRITISH MUSEUM OR. DR. 28. (DRAWING REPRODUCED WITH THE PERMISSION OF THE TRUSTEES OF THE BRITISH MUSEUM)

Arabs on Assyrian reliefs (although precisely what it is meant to represent is unknown). Indeed, one wonders if the occupants of the chariot should not actually be identified as Assyrians (or perhaps Babylonians) pursuing one Arab while being shot at by another.[37]

The age of the drawing notwithstanding, the clothing and hairstyle of the Arab archer are not drastically different from those examined above, suggesting that the desert Arabs dressed in much the same way for over a millennium before the rise of Islam. In a drawing by W. Boutcher of a detail from the Assyrian reliefs showing the campaign of Ashurbanipal (688–627 BC) against the Arabs, the Arabs, with plaited hair, are shown dismounted from their camels and dressed in wraparounds, each with an opening to allow freedom of movement (fig. 9). Their wraparounds are not flowing like those of the

37 The main objection to this proposition is that the man on horseback is identified in the inscription above him as *ḥrb*, taken by Macdonald to mean *enemy* warrior on the basis of modern bedouin dialect. But this is clearly conjectural, and the word may not even have been correctly deciphered (cf. Macdonald, "Wheels in a Land of Camels," 175, no. 9).

7, 8 Saracens who purchase Joseph from his brothers (fig. 1), | | and their hair looks shorter and a good deal neater, too, but given that there are more than a thousand years between the images, the continuity is nonetheless striking. To a somewhat lesser degree, the same holds true when one compares the Assyrian representations with the Safaitic rock drawings and the Madaba mosaic.

In sum, what did the bedouin participants in the conquests wear? The answer seems to be generally not very much at all: either bits and pieces of what their settled neighbors—whether the latter were Byzantines, Arabians, or (one assumes) Iranians—wore, or a wraparound and a *ridāʾ* covering part of their upper torso, and perhaps even sandals, but rarely, insofar as one can tell, anything on their heads. It is the absence of headgear that is the most surprising. Whatever the variations, all the desert dwellers seem to have looked a good deal more like their ancestors of Assyrian times than like Musil's Rwala.[38] As far as desert clothing is concerned, Arabia on the eve of Islam seems still to have been rooted in the ancient Near East.

When and why did the desert Arabs start covering themselves up? I cannot claim to know. My guess would be that they started doing so in the centuries after the rise of Islam, and in consequence of the rise of Islam, for Islam drew the bedouin closer together to the settled people, giving them shared religious and other norms. Wrapping up was what the people who mattered did, and so the bedouin came to do so too (at least when they could afford it). According to Ibn al-Kalbi (d. 819 or later), the Tanukh who met the caliph al-Mahdi (d. 785) in Qinnasrin were wearing turbans. They were trying to look their best on this occasion.[39] A Byzantine miniature of ca. 976–1025 depicting Simeon Stylites venerated by Arabs shows Simeon in a hooded monk's habit and the three Arabs wearing turbans, now apparently as a matter of course.[40] But I had better leave this question for another birthday.

38 Cf. A. Musil, *The Manners and Customs of the Rwala Bedouins* (New York, 1928).

39 Shahid, *Byzantium and the Arabs in the Fourth Century*, 431.

40 Rome, Bibliotheca Vaticana, gr. 1613. The ninth-century miniature of Joseph's brothers selling Joseph to a Saracen is uninformative, since no attempt seems to have been made to distinguish the Saracen from the other figures: all are wearing the same long cloaks and all are bareheaded (cf. A. Grabar, *Les miniatures du Grégoire de Nazianze* [Paris, 1943], pl. LXI).

CHAPTER 2

The Ancient Near East and Islam: The Case of Lot-Casting 423

With Adam Silverstein

In 1993 classical archaeologists made an exciting discovery at Petra. This city, once the capital of the Nabataean kingdom, thereafter a major town in the Roman province of Arabia, had long been assumed to have been destroyed in an earthquake of 551 CE, but this proved to be wrong, and in the church of St Mary the archaeologists found a cache of papyri. Completely carbonized by the fire which had destroyed the church in the early seventh century, these papyri could nonetheless be read by means of sophisticated modern techniques, and an edition is in progress.[1] They contained the private archive of a major family of the city, covering the years from at least 537 to 593 CE. The papyri are in Greek but reflect a community whose native language appears to have been Arabic, and among the papyri is a record of a division of an inheritance between three brothers. The | estate, which consisted of land and 424
buildings, was divided into three equal shares and awarded to the sons by a procedure which the editors, with reference to a comparable papyrus from Nessana, take to have been lot-casting.[2] The Nessana papyrus, written in 562 CE, also records the division of an estate, here among four sons. The property, which consisted of buildings, farmland and personal articles, was divided into four shares of roughly equal value and awarded to the sons by lot in the presence of friends and relatives. Here, as at Petra, the parties concluded

---

1 For all this, see L. Koenen, R.W. Daniel and T. Gagas, 'Petra in the Sixth Century: the Evidence of the Carbonized Papyri', in G. Markoe (ed.), *Petra Rediscovered* (New York 2003), 250–261; J. Frösén, A. Arjava and M. Lehtinen (eds), *The Petra Papyri*, 1 (Amman 2002). Our thanks to Glen Bowersock for referring us to this literature.

2 Cf. Koenen, Daniel and Gagas, 'Petra in the Sixth Century', 251. The papyrus (Inv. 10, P. Petra Khaled and Suha Shoman) is still unpublished. There is no explicit mention of lots in the draft edition and translation that Crone has seen, courtesy of her colleague Glen Bowersock, but the parallels with the Nessana papyrus are certainly striking. [Ed.: The papyrus has now been published as L. Koenen, J. Kaimio, M. Kaimio and R.W. Daniel (eds), *The Petra Papyri*, 2 (Amman 2013).]

© KONINKLIJKE BRILL NV, LEIDEN, 2016 | DOI: 10.1163/9789004319318_003

the proceedings by swearing by the Trinity and the Emperor's health that they would abide by the division.[3]

The interest of this discovery to historians of the Near East lies in the fact that the procedure used for the division of the property in these two papyri is endorsed in Islamic law. It is also extremely ancient and raises the question how far, and in what way, the traditions of the ancient Near East lived on to contribute to Islamic culture. In what follows we briefly survey the attestations of lot-casting as an official practice from ancient Near Eastern to Islamic times and discuss what we see as its significance.

Assigning Land, Booty, and Other Property by Lot

In the ancient Near East (by which, for the purposes of this article, we mean the ancient Fertile Crescent), lot-casting was much used in the division of inheritances. The standard way of distributing an inheritance in Assyrian and Babylonian Mesopotamia was to divide the property into parcels and then to assign the parcels by lot to the heirs (with variations when the eldest son was privileged).[4] The gods themselves are said to have divided the world by this procedure. 'They took the box (of lots) …, cast the lots; the gods made the division': Anu acquired the sky, Enlil the earth and Enki the bolt which bars the sea.[5] This
425 is | famously one of the ancient Near Eastern myths that passed into Greek culture: Zeus, Poseidon and Hades divide the world among themselves by lot in the *Iliad*, and here as in the Akkadian myth, the three gods are brothers.[6]

The custom is well attested in the Bible, too.[7] God Himself distributed the desolate land of Edom to wild animals by lot (Isa. 34:17), and He also instructed

3 C.J. Kraemer, *Excavations at Nessana*, III (Non-Literary Papyri) (Princeton 1958), no. 21. Compare nos. 16, 31, where lots are not mentioned.

4 *A History of Ancient Near Eastern Law*, ed. R. Westbrook (Leiden 2003), 1, 57f. (general), 395f. (Old Babylonian), 542f. (middle Assyrian); 2, 939 (Neo-Babylonian).

5 *Atrahasis* in B.R. Foster, *Before the Muses: an Anthology of Akkadian Literature*[3] (Bethesda, Md., 2005), 229; also in S. Dalley (tr.), *Myths from Mesopotamia*, revised ed. (Oxford 2000), 9.

6 Cf. W. Burkert, *The Orientalizing Revolution* (Cambridge, Mass., and London 1992), 90f.; id., *Babylon, Memphis, Persepolis: Eastern Contexts of Greek Culture* (Cambridge, Mass., and London 2004), 36. For the subsequent history of this myth, see A. Silverstein, 'From Atrahasīs to Afrīdūn: on the Transmission of an Ancient Near Eastern Motif to Iran', *Jerusalem Studies in Arabic and Islam* 39 (2012), 95–108.

7 Cf. Th. Gataker, *On the Nature and Use of Lots*[2] (London 1627), modernized and updated by C. Boyle (Exeter 2008), ch. 4, § 10, an extremely learned work still worth consulting despite its age; J. Lindblom, 'Lot-Casting in the Old Testament', *Vetus Testamentum* 12 (1962), 164–178.

Moses to divide the Promised Land by lot when it had been conquered;[8] Joshua duly did so.[9] Micah seems to have envisaged conquest as the result of divine or angelic lot-casting: he prophesied that Israel would have nobody in God's assembly to cast lots for land for it (Mic. 2:5). Ezekiel added that the land would be divided up anew by means of arrows in the messianic age (Ezek. 45:1; 47:22). Land and captives taken by the Babylonians and Assyrians were apparently divided up in the same way: the Babylonians entered Israel's gate and 'cast lots for Jerusalem' (Obad. 1:11); but God would punish the nations for having divided up his land and cast lots for his people (Joel 3:3). When the Assyrians conquered Thebes in Egypt in 663 BCE, 'lots were cast for her nobles' (Nah. 3:10). The Bible does not refer to inherited land being divided by this method.

The idea of allocating new land by lots reappears in Jewish Hellenistic works. In *Jubilees*, composed by a Palestinian Jew in the second century BCE and later translated from Hebrew into Greek and Syriac, Noah divides the earth by lot between his three sons, Shem, Ham and Japheth; Canaan, the son of Ham, nonetheless settled in Shem's portion.[10] In *Maccabees*, Antiochus IV (175–163 BCE) is described as sending a Syrian commander with orders to wipe out the
residents | of Judaea and Jerusalem and to 'settle aliens in all their territory, 426
and distribute their land by lot' (1 Macc. 3:36).[11] Thereafter, leaving aside mere retelling of the Biblical passages, the theme of lot-casting for land and/or its inhabitants seems to disappear from the indigenous sources for a long time.

Lot-casting must be a universal institution, and not just as a private or *ad hoc* method of decision making: both land and fortune are things that one is 'allotted' in a great many languages. In Greek, too, a piece of land was known as a lot (*klēros*), reflecting the fact that lots were used to distribute land when colonies were set up in order to ensure that every group received an equal share. Moveable booty was distributed in the same way,[12] but whether

8 Num. 26:52 ff.; 33:50 ff. (at 54); 34:13; cf. also Josh. 21:4 ff.; 1 Chron. 6:54 ff., where priests and Levites are given certain cities to dwell in by lot.

9 Josh. 18:3 ff., 10; 19:51; cf. Josephus, *Antiquities*, book 5, ch. 1, pars. 22, 24, 26.

10 Jubilees 8:11 ff., 10:30 (tr. O.S. Wintermute in J.H. Charlesworth [ed.], *The Old Testament Pseudepigrapha* [New York 1983–1985], ii; cf. also his introduction). The detail that the division was effected by lots seems to have been lost in the later Greek, Latin and Syriac translations, but it was apparently known to the Muslims, cf. Silverstein, 'From Atrahasīs to Afrīdūn'.

11 Settling foreigners on land confiscated from the local population was an Assyrian practice later adopted by the Achaemenids and Macedonians alike, but this passage could be inspired by Obadiah on foreigners casting lots for Jerusalem.

12 Cf. G. Wissova, *Pauly's Real-Encyclopädie der classischen Altertumswissenschaft* (Stuttgart

inherited land was also divided in this way is uncertain.[13] The practice is not attested at Athens[14] nor, it would seem, anywhere else in Greek antiquity, except in a speech once attributed to Dio of Prusa (in Anatolia, d. *c.* 120), now held to be by Favorinus (d. mid-second century), a native of Arles: here we are told that 'brothers also divide their patrimony that way'.[15] Wherever the orator may have encountered the practice, it certainly sounds similar to that attested in Petra and Nessana, but it is hard to say more on the basis of a single passage.

The Romans, who took over from the Greeks, also used lots for the distribution of land, both at home and in connection with the foundation of colonies.[16] Moveable booty, too, was (or might be) distributed by lot.[17] But the evidence
427 relating to conquered land and | booty peters out in the third century, and the Romans do not seem to have used this method in connection with inherited property either, except in three specific circumstances. First, in actions for the division of an inheritance or common property, or for the regulation of boundaries, it was difficult to decide who was the plaintiff and who the defendant, but the person who appealed to the law was generally considered plaintiff; to this Ulpian (d. 223) adds that if the parties appealed at the same time, the matter was usually decided by lot.[18] Secondly, in 428 a law was passed which entitled the *curia* (city council) to claim one fourth of the estate left by a member of the council to an outsider: the estate was to be divided into four parts, of which the

---

1894–1980, hereafter Pauly-Wissova), s.v. 'Losung', col. 1463 (Ehrenberg); D. Asheri, *Distribuzioni di terra nell'antica Grecia* (Turin 1966), 13 (drawn to our attention by D. Roussel).

13 Ehrenberg categorically denies it, against earlier authors (cf. Pauly-Wissova, s.v. 'Losung', col. 1478b).

14 Cf. A.R.W. Harrison, *The Law of Athens: the Family and Property* (Oxford 1968), ch. 5 (where the possibility is not even discussed).

15 Dio Chrysostom (attrib.), *Oratio*, 64, 25, where 'that way' refers to 'by lot' (*klērōtas*). Adduced by Gataker, *Nature and Use of Lots*, ch. 4, § 12 (p. 102 of the original work, where the references are given, misprinted as 46.25); cf. *The Oxford Classical Dictionary*^{3}, ed. S. Hornblower and A. Spawforth (Oxford 1996), s.v. 'Favorinus'. We are much indebted to Glen Bowersock and Christopher Jones for help with this passage.

16 Pauly-Wissova, s.v. 'Losung', col. 1493; D.J. Gargola, *Lands, Laws, and Gods* (Chapel Hill, N.C., 1995), 95 ff. For examples, see Dionysius of Helicarnassus, *Roman Antiquities*, II, 16; II, 35; V, 60; X, 32.

17 Cf. the story of the third-century emperor Probus in *Historia Augusta, Life of Probus*, 8 (ed. and tr. D. Magie [London and Cambridge, Mass., 1932], iii, 351).

18 Justinian, *Digest*, book 5, tit. 1, 13 f. (ed. and tr. T. Mommsen, P. Krueger and A. Watson [Philadelphia 1985], i, 167).

curia would take one by lot.[19] Thirdly, in 531 Justinian ruled that when several persons had been given the option, by bequest, to pick an item such as a slave and disagreement arose, they could cast lots: the winner would pick the item and pay the others the value of their share.[20] Division of the estate among the heirs by lot as the normal procedure in intestate succession does not seem to be attested.

In line with this, it is mostly as a literary theme that lot drawing for land is attested in the Near Eastern literature (Jewish and Christian) from the second century onwards, with no sense of a live practice behind it. The gods cast lots again, this time for the nations of the earth, in the Pseudo-Clementine *Recognitions*, a Jewish Christian work of the mid-fourth century: Simon Magus, representing heresy, here argues that there are many gods, and that it was to one of the lower gods that the Jews were assigned (a gnosticizing paraphrase of Deut. 32:8 f.).[21] In the same vein, *Pirqe de Rabbi Eliezer*, a Jewish work of (perhaps) the mid-eighth century, tells us that when seventy angels descended in order to confuse the nations building the Tower of Babel, they cast lots among the nations and Israel fell to God (who is not, of course, a lower God here).[22] The nations are also divided up by lot in the *Acts of Thomas*, but now among the apostles rather | than the gods: India fell to Thomas.[23] Egypt, 428
Ethiopia, Nubia and the Pentapolis fell to St Mark by lot (*qurʿa*), as a later Christian adds.[24] The story of the father who divides the earth between his three sons by lot may have gone into the Persian tradition, though it is only in Ibn al-Kalbī (d. 204/819 or later) that we see it: according to him, the ancient king Farīdūn divided his realm (consisting of the entire world) among his three sons by writing the names of the regions on arrows and telling each son to choose an arrow.[25] There does not seem to be any attestation of this method of allocating inheritance shares in Persian law or practice, however.

19 Justinian, *Codex*, 10, 35, 2; cf. 10, 35, 1; A.H.M. Jones, *The Later Roman Empire, 284–602* (Oxford 1964), 2, 747 f.

20 Justinian, *Codex*, 6, 43, 3, 1; cf. id., *Institutes*, II, xx, 23.

21 Clement of Alexandria (attrib.), *Recognitions*, ii, 39 (tr. B.P. Pratten, M. Dods and T. Smith, *The Writings of Tatian and Thophilus and the Clementine Recognitions* [Ante-Nicene Christian Library, iii, Edinburgh 1867], 218 f.).

22 *Pirqe de Rabbi Eliezer*, tr. G. Friedlander (New York 1971), 176 f.

23 *Acts of Thomas*, 1 (tr. A.F.J. Klijn [Leiden 2003], 17).

24 Severus b. al-Muqaffaʿ, 'History of the Patriarchs of the Coptic Church of Alexandria', ed. and tr. B. Evetts, in R. Graffin and F. Nau (eds), *Patrologia Orientalis*, i (Paris 1907), 105.

25 Al-Ṭabarī, *Taʾrīkh al-rusul waʾl-mulūk*, ed. M.J. de Goeje et al. (Leiden 1879–1901), i, 226 f. (Ibn al-Kalbī), with further details in Silverstein, 'From Atrahasīs to Afrīdūn'. It is not clear

At this point one is tempted to conclude that the ancient practice of casting lots for land, whether conquered or inherited, had disappeared, except for some special cases where Roman law applied. But it had not. The rabbis discuss it, apparently as a live institution, with reference to two or three brothers dividing an inheritance among themselves in material from second-century Sephhoris (Tiberias) in Palestine onwards;[26] and it now proves to have been practised by Christians in Roman Arabia, too, at Petra and Nessana.

Apparently, it was also alive in the Prophet's Arabia, at least in connection with conquered land and booty. We are told that when the Prophet conquered Khaybar (in the year 7/628), he set aside God's fifth by lot (using arrows); the rest of the conquered land was divided into eighteen portions and subdivided, according to one tradition, into a hundred plots of roughly the same productive capacity which he distributed to his followers by lot.[27] Of the booty from the
429 campaign against B. Qurayẓa we are told that it was | divided into 3072 shares, consisting partly of land and partly of moveable booty, of which a fifth was assigned to God and the rest to the Muslims by lot.[28] The Muslims also cast lots for the captives taken at Badr.[29] ʿUthmān (644–656) instructed Muʿāwiya to single out God's fifth of the booty by writing 'God' on one of the five arrows used for their allocation.[30] When ʿAlī's followers wanted to divide the captives from the Battle of the Camel among themselves, in 36/656, ʿAlī dissuaded them by first telling them to bring the lots and next, when they brought the arrows, by asking them who might get his (spiritual) mother ʿĀʾisha in his lot.[31] On another occasion he used the lots to divide non-Muslim booty.[32] Of the Kufan ʿAbīda b.

---

whether the story should be taken to reflect Persian appropriation of the theme, either directly from Mesopotamian sources or via para-Biblical literature such as *Jubilees*, or simply Ibn al-Kalbī's own familiarity with the theme.

26 *Babylonian Talmud*, Baba Bathra, 106a. It is not found in the Jerusalem Talmud.

27 Al-Wāqidī, *Kitāb al-maghāzī*, ed. M. Jones (London 1966), ii, 680, 692; al-Māwardī, *Adab al-qāḍī*, ed. Y.H. al-Sirḥān (Baghdad 1971), ii, 196 f., no. 2715 (citing Wāqidī); al-Shāfiʿī in al-Bayhaqī, *Aḥkām al-Qurʾān*, ed. M.Z. al-Kawtharī (Cairo 1951), 163; cf. also Ibn Saʿd, *al-Ṭabaqāt*, ed. E. Sachau et al. (Leiden 1904–1940), II/1, 78, 82 f.; ed. Beirut 1957–1960, ii, 107, 113 f. (without explicit mention of lots); *EI*², s.v. 'Khaybar', col. 1141a.

28 Wāqidī, *Maghāzī*, ii, 522; cited in Māwardī, *Adab al-qāḍī*, ii, 196, no. 2714.

29 Wāqidī, *Maghāzī*, i, 100, 107, 139.

30 Al-Sarakhsī, *Sharḥ kitāb al-siyar al-kabīr li-Muḥammad b. al-Ḥasan al-Shaybānī*, ed. Ṣ.-D. al-Munajjid (Cairo 1957–1960), iii, 889.

31 Ibn Qutayba (attrib.), *al-Imāma wa'l-siyāsa* (Cairo 1969), i, 78.

32 Al-Nuwayrī, *al-Bidāya wa'l-nihāya* (Cairo 1975), xx, 219, where he divides the booty from Iṣfahān, even including a loaf, into seven portions (one for each of the sevenths into which Kufa was divided at the time) and distributes them by lot.

Qays (d. 70s/690s) we are told that he would cast lots to assign the leftover from the division of moveable booty, such as a dirham, saying that this was how it had been done in past campaigns, but this was more controversial: the point of the report is that he was persuaded to stop, on the grounds that it was more equitable to use the dirham to buy something that could be distributed (by lot or otherwise).[33]

All these reports are prescriptive and hardly to be taken at face value as historical reports. Taken as literature, however, they certainly suggest that Muslims who came out of Arabia took the use of lots for the division of conquered land and booty for granted. This is corroborated by the fact that the standard word for a share of the booty was *sahm* (literally 'arrow').

As regards inherited land, a Prophetic tradition reports that two men who had a dispute over inherited property submitted their case to the Prophet without having anything to prove their respective claims: he told them to cast lots and take whatever was assigned to them by this method.[34] The two men are not identified as brothers, | however, and the issue is their dispute in a situation 430
without proof rather than the normal procedure in intestate succession. We are also told that when Abān b. ʿUthmān was governor of Medina in the reign of ʿAbd al-Malik (685–705), a man manumitted the six slaves who were his only property on his deathbed; and since bequests were not allowed to exceed a third of the property, Abān drew lots and manumitted the two slaves who had the lucky draw.[35] The Prophet is said to have used the same solution when two earlier Medinese manumitted six slaves who were their only property, but this is presumably a simple reworking of the Umayyad report (though it was of course the Prophetic precedent which became canonical).[36] Here too the procedure diverges from that attested at Nessana and Petra, for the lots are not

---

33 Ibn Saʿd, *Ṭabaqāt*, ed. Sachau, vi, 62 f.; ed. Beirut, vi, 93. He was *ʿarīf* (paymaster) for his tribal group.

34 Abū Dāwūd, *Sunan* (Cairo 1982), ii, 295 (*K. al-qaḍā, bāb fī qaḍāʾ al-qāḍī idhā akhṭaʾa*); cited in Ibn Qayyim al-Jawziyya, *al-Ṭuruq al-ḥukmiyya fī siyāsat al-sharʿiyya*, ed. N.A. al-Ḥamad (Mecca 1428), ii, 743 (in a useful list of Prophetic traditions on *qurʿa*), where further references are given. For an Imāmī Shīʿite version, see al-Majlisī, *Biḥār al-anwār* (Tehran 1357–1392), civ, 324. Our thanks to Aron Zysow for help in connection with this tradition.

35 Al-Shāfiʿī, 'K. al-qurʿa', in his *Umm* (Beirut 1993), viii, 5; cf. J. Schacht, *The Origins of Muhammadan Jurisprudence* (Oxford 1956), 201 f. For further references, see Bayhaqī, *Aḥkām al-Qurʾān*, 162n.

36 Ibn Abī Shayba, *al-Muṣannaf*, ed. M.A. al-Nadwī (Bombay 1979–1983), xiv, 158, nos. 17934 f.; Shāfiʿī, 'K. al-qurʿa', *Umm*, viii, 5 (where one manumitter is a woman, the other an Anṣārī male); further references in Bayhaqī, *Aḥkām al-Qurʾān*, 162n.

being used to allocate equal shares, but rather to pick out two winners. Though it seems unlikely that the inhabitants of Petra and Nessana should have been the only Arabs to use lots as the normal procedure for the division of inherited land, the practice does not seem to be attested in the material on the rise of Islam. We do however find it in classical Islamic law: here we are told that once the property had been divided into parcels representing the smallest fractions to be distributed, the heirs could draw lots among themselves for the parcels; if the estate consisted of different types of property, such as houses and land, the different types had to be divided up separately; they could not be bundled together as was done at Nessana.[37]

The Near East is not the only region in which lots have been used for
431 the partition of inherited land. It crops up in Europe, too. Thomas | Aquinas (d. 1274) knew of it,[38] and English common law endorsed it for the partition of land held in coparcenary from medieval down to modern times.[39] The solution is likely to have commended itself wherever property had to be distributed among equally entitled claimants, and it could in principle turn up anywhere in unrelated forms. The Near Eastern forms come across as related in that all they treat lot-casting as a standard way of dividing land and other property, not simply as a last resort or special solution, as in Roman or common law. The same may well have been true among many other peoples in ancient times, however, especially in connection with conquered land, and the Near Eastern forms are not related etymologically: the usual term for a

---

37 Māwardī, *Adab al-qāḍī*, ii, 194 f., nos. 2709 ff., cf. also 204, nos. 2746 ff.; al-Nawawī, *Minhāj al-ṭālibīn*, ed. and tr. L.W.C. van den Berg (Batavia 1882–1884), iii, 395 ff.; Ibn Rushd, *Bidāyat al-mujtahid*, ed. M.S. al-Muḥaysin and Sh.M. Ismāʿīl (Cairo 1970–1974), ii, 298 ff.; tr. I.A. Khan Nyazee and M. Abdul Rauf (Reading 1996), ii, 319 ff. (both with further discussion); al-Marghīnānī, *al-Hidāya* (Cairo n.d.), iv, 46; tr. C. Hamilton, 2nd ed. (Lahore 1957), iv, 571 (*K. al-qisma*); *al-Mawsūʿa al-fiqhiyya*, xxxiii (Kuwait 1995), 139 (drawn to our attention by A. Zysow); A. ʿAbd al-ʿAzīz, *Fiqh al-kitāb wa'l-sunna* (Nablus 1999), iv, 2305.

38 [38] He describes it as a method used for the division of inheritances in cases of disagreement, without giving further details (Thomas Aquinas, *Commentary on the Ephesians*, tr. M.L. Lamb [Albany 1966], book 1, lecture 4, *ad* Eph. 1:11).

39 [39] An estate held in coparcenary was taken by several heirs as if they were a single person, for example when the deceased only left daughters (the principle being that there could only be one heir, normally the eldest son, who would take everything in the absence of a will). The use of lots for the partition of such estates is first described by Thomas de Littleton (d. 1481), cited in Gataker, *Nature and Use of Lots*, ch. 4, § 12 (p. 104 of the original work); it is endorsed in Great Britain, Courts, *The Legal Guide*, 1 (London 1839), 324 f., but is now obsolete.

lot in the sense of the object used in the procedure is *pūr*(*u*) in Assyrian, *isqu* in Babylonian, *goral* in Hebrew (where it also stands for the share allotted), and *qurʿa* in Arabic, with *sahm* ('arrow') as the normal word for the lot awarded. But though they may have originated separately in pre-historic times, by the time we have literary evidence, the Near Eastern institutions stand apart from those of the neighbouring lands in that they still treat lot-casting as the standard mode of division, even in connection with inheritance law, and even, after the coming of Islam, when the heirs were awarded highly unequal shares. It is with reference to this feature that we treat them as so many members of a single family, visible in the cuneiform, Jewish, Greek papyrological, and Muslim records at different times and places thanks to a combination of local conditions and the haphazard manner in which the evidence has survived.

One interesting point here is that if it had not been for the chance preservation of the two Greek papyri, one might have taken lot-casting for the distribution of land in early Islamic society and classical law to represent a case of Jewish *Fortleben* in Islam; for until the papyri were discovered, it was only in rabbinic texts that the practice seemed to be alive in connection with inheritance shares, and the rabbis would of course have had much to say about the Biblical use of lot | drawing in connection with conquered property, had they 432
been asked. But as the papyri show, the inference would have been false. Lot-casting for the allocation of inherited property had remained a live practice in Roman Arabia, too, and also, as the accounts of the Prophet's procedures suggest, in connection with conquered land and booty elsewhere in Arabia. What the striking similarity between Jewish and Islamic law reflects is not, in this particular case, Jewish *Fortleben* in Islam, but rather the shared roots of Jewish and Islamic culture in the ancient Near Eastern tradition. We seem to have here a case comparable to that of circumcision, practised by both the Jews and the Arabs (eventually Muslims), not by the one borrowing from the other, but rather by both retaining an ancient custom which had once been widespread in the Near East (notably in Egypt). In the case of circumcision, the Biblical record played a role in endowing the old Arabian practice with a new religious meaning. There is no suggestion that it did so in the case of lot-casting.

It is because the Arabs were apt to preserve ancient practices also recorded in the Jewish scripture that Old Testament scholars (Wellhausen prominent among them) used to study Arabia with such interest, with special attention to the bedouin because the ancient Israelites had been pastoralists. It is the townsmen of Arabia that we see at work at Nessana and Petra, but the bedouin continued to furnish parallels into modern times: Musil reports that in what

he called Arabia Petraea (former Roman Arabia) agricultural land belonging to the whole tribe would be divided into fields of equal size every year and distributed among the families or tribal groups by lot.[40] The continuity with ancient Near Eastern practice in Arabia should presumably be related to the forbidding nature of the peninsula. Difficult to conquer and colonize, it was the only region of the Near East to escape a millennium of Greek, Roman or Persian domination, though parts of it (including Petra and Nessana) fell under foreign rule for periods ranging from centuries to decades. We have to stress, however, that the Jews and the Arabs may not have been the only inhabitants of the Near East to use lot-casting for the division of inherited property in late antiquity, for on the Jewish side it is in rabbinic literature that it is attested, not in the Bible. This suggests that what the rabbis discussed was a practice they shared with their neighbours, or in other words that in this particular case the
433 rabbinic literature should not be seen as evidence | for the Jews alone, but also for the larger Aramaic culture of which they formed part.

Choosing People by Lot

It was not only in connection with the distribution of land and its inhabitants that lot-casting was used in the ancient Near East; people were selected for a wide variety of functions by that method, too. The Assyrians used sortition to choose the annual occupant of the 'office of the year eponym', a dignitary who had the privilege of having a calendar year named after him.[41] The king himself never seems to have been chosen by lot in ancient Mesopotamia,[42] nor do priests. But the Bible tells us that Saul was chosen as king by lot,[43] and the Samaritan Chronicle has it that the first Samaritan king was chosen by the same method.[44] In Pseudo-Philo (*c.* 50–150) the Israelites also choose Kenaz as their leader against the Philistines by lot, directed by an angel, and repeatedly try the same method to find a successor to Phinehas without success.[45] By Roman

40 A. Musil, *Arabia Petraea* (Vienna 1907–1908), 3, 294.

41 W.W. Hallo, 'The First Purim', *The Biblical Archaeologist* 46 (1983), 19 f.

42 M.T. Larsen, 'The City and Its King', in *Le palais et la royauté*, ed. P. Garelli (Paris 1971), 298 f. (against Oppenheim).

43 1 Sam. 10:19–21. But God's answer in v. 22 must have been given by a seer or prophet, cf. J. Lindblom, 'Lot-Casting in the Old Testament', 165n.

44 J. Macdonald, *The Samaritan Chronicle*, no. II (Berlin 1969), 99.

45 Latin text (originally Hebrew) and English translation in H. Jacobson, *A Commentary on Pseudo-Philo's Liber Antiquitatum Biblicarum* (Leiden 1996), 25:1 f.; 49:1.

times succession to the high priesthood of the Jews had come to be decided in the same way, with explicit reference to ancient practice.[46]

In Biblical times, lots were also used to single out the groups and individuals who were to serve as temple musicians and gate keepers in ancient Israel (1 Chron. 24:5 ff., 25:8 ff., 26:13 f.), and to allocate rotating responsibilities such as serving as priests and providing wood offerings to the temple (Neh. 10:35).[47] Zachariah was a priest chosen by lot to officiate at a particular time (Luke 1:8 f.),[48] and Peter found a replacement for the apostle Judas by selecting two men and then casting lots (Acts 1:23–26), a procedure which was to be imitated | 434
by later Christians in the Near East and the West alike.[49] Indeed, the word 'clergy' is derived from *klēros*, 'lot', the clergy being people allocated to God.[50] Lot-casting may also have been used to assist the decision who should be admitted as new members of the community at Qumran, but this is disputed.[51]

Again, the Greeks and the Romans had similar practices. In Greece lot-casting was used for the selection of magistrates, especially in democracies, where it was of fundamental importance as an egalitarian device.[52] The Romans would distribute functions among magistrates already chosen by sorti-

---

46 Josephus, *Wars*, book 4, ch. 3, pars. 7 f.

47 Cf. Josephus' amplifications, *Antiquities*, book 7, ch. 14, par. 7.

48 Compare *Protoevangelium of James*, 24:4, in W. Schneemelcher and R. McL. Wilson (eds), *New Testament Apocrypha*, 1 (Cambridge 1991), 437, where Zachariah in his turn is replaced by Simeon by lot.

49 For thirteenth-century nuns choosing an apostle (as patron saint) by lot, see G.G. Coulton (tr.), *Life in the Middle Ages*, 1 (Cambridge 1928), 69 f. Thomas Aquinas held that lot-casting could not be used for ecclesiastical office after the arrival of the Holy Spirit (*Commentary on the Ephesians*, book I, lecture 4), but the Mennonites of today choose priests by lot (personal communication from Christopher Melchert). In the Middle East known to T. Fahd, monks would decide by lot which novices should receive the habit (EI^2 [Leiden 1956–2004], s.v. 'ḳurʿa').

50 This too is discussed in Pauly-Wissova, s.v. 'Losung', cols. 1466 f. (and indeed by Aquinas, *loc. cit.*).

51 Lots figure prominently in the Dead Sea scrolls, but almost exclusively in a metaphorical sense (Y. Licht, 'The Term Goral in the Writings of the Judean Desert Cult', *Beth Miqra* 1 [1956], 90–99 [Hebrew]). For the question of its use in admissions, see W.A. Beardslee, 'The Casting of Lots at Qumran and in the Book of Acts', *Novum Testamentum* 4 (1960), 245–252; S.J. Pfann, 'The Essene Yearly Renewal Ceremony and the Baptism of Repentance', in D. Parry and E. Ulrich (eds), *The Provo International Conference on the Dead Sea Scrolls* (Leiden 1999), 337–352; P.S. Alexander, 'Predestination and Free Will in the Theology of the Dead Sea Scrolls', in J.M.G. Barday and S.J. Gathercole (eds), *Divine and Human Agency in Paul and His Cultural Environment* (London 2007), 27–49.

52 *Oxford Classical Dictionary*, s.v. 'sortition'; Pauly-Wissova, s.v. 'Losung', cols. 1475 ff.

tion. Consuls and praetors, for example, would cast lots among themselves to determine the assignment of campaigns and provinces ('What if the casting of lots had allocated you Africans or Spaniards or Gauls to rule over?', as Cicero asked his brother, then governor of Asia);[53] lots were also used to determine voting order and other sequences, to choose officials for special tasks, and in diverse other connections, including (at least on one occasion) that of selecting recruits.[54] We even hear of bandits who reputedly used lots to decide which
435 members of the gang should labour or serve the | others,[55] but whether this can count as an example of official use is another question.

On the Greek and Roman side, the official use of lots for the allocation of office and functions seems to have petered out by late antique times, and the evidence is thin on the Near Eastern side as well. Rabbinic literature does admittedly abound in discussions of temple duties and other Old Testament institutions, but it is all academic. Choosing priests, monks and other ecclesiastical personnel by lot is more likely to have continued among the Christians, thanks to the precedent set by Peter's choice of Matthew by this method. It is reflected in the *Protoevangelium of James*, where Mary is chosen by lot for the privilege of weaving a particular item,[56] but the only attestation relating to real life that we know of is modern.[57] This undoubtedly reflects our ignorance of the vast mass of relevant Syriac literature. Once again there is some ambivalent evidence on the Iranian side:[58] in the account of Ardā Virāz' journey to heaven and hell, Ardā Virāz is chosen for the journey by three lances (*nēzag*) which are thrown at him. But this procedure was in the nature of an ordeal rather than lot-casting, for the lances were meant to confirm or deny the suitability of a man already chosen; there were no other candidates.[59]

---

53 Cicero, *Ad Quintum fratrem*, 1, 9, 27.

54 Pauly-Wissova, s.v. 'Losung', cols. 1494 ff.; Gargola, *Land, Laws, and Gods*, 95; R.J.A. Talbert, *The Senate of Imperial Rome* (Princeton 1984), 61, 139, 144, 207 f., 347–353 (drawn to our attention by Nathan Rosenstein); N. Rosenstein, 'Sorting Out the Lot in Republican Rome', *American Journal of Philology* 116 (1995), 43–75, with the recruits at 44, n. 7.

55 B. Shaw, 'The Bandit', in A. Giardina (ed.), *The Romans*, tr. L.G. Cochrane (Chicago and London 1993), 330 (with ref. to Apuleius, *Metamorphoses*, 4.8).

56 *Protoevangelium of James*, 10:2, in Schneemelcher and Wilson, *New Testament Apocrypha*, 1, 430.

57 Cf. Fahd, above, note 49.

58 The Persians are envisaged as casting lots to fix the day on which the Jews were to be killed in the Book of Esther (3:7). The institution credited to them here is Akkadian, but whether it can be inferred that the Persians had adopted it is unclear.

59 Cf. P. Gignoux, 'Une ordalie par les lances en Iran', *Revue de l'Histoire des Religions* 200 (1983), 155–161. The procedure is construed as lot-casting in S. Shaked, 'Quests and

One would be inclined to conclude that the once prevalent practice of choosing people for high office and other functions by lot had died out.

Again, however, the practice must have survived in Arabia. Unfortunately, there does not seem to be any documentary evidence for this. Three pre-Islamic inscriptions, one from al-Lāt's temple at Palmyra and two from Yemen, do refer to lot-casting, but they probably refer to divination.[60] We are told, however, that the pre-Islamic Quraysh would choose men to lead them in war by lot and accept the candi|date even if he was a minor or very old;[61] and 436
the terms *qarīʿ* and *maqrūʿ* (chosen by lot) were used in the sense of chief, leader and person chosen.[62] In line with this we later hear of lot-casting for the selection of caliphs. The Christian astrologer Theophilus of Edessa, active under the caliph al-Mahdī (d. 169/785), tells us that when Yazīd I died, the future Marwān I (64/684–685) proposed to solve the succession dispute which ensued by drawing lots; this was apparently agreed, but when Marwān's name came up, his rival al-Ḍaḥḥāk b. Qays refused to accept the result, so the two of them fought it out at Marj Rāhiṭ.[63] Al-Jāḥiẓ also knew of lot-casting in connection with the choice of caliphs, though he did not think it was necessary: in his view, the rightful claimant would always be known without the need for formal procedures, just as everyone knew who was the most generous man or the best horseman among Qays in the Jāhiliyya without discussion of their merits or *shūrā* or casting lots (*al-iqrāʿ wa'l-musāhama*).[64] Lot-casting was endorsed by some jurists for situations in which two candidates for the caliphate were equally qualified, or when two of them had come to be elected by some mishap, but others disagreed.[65] 'In our opinion, lots are required by

---

Visionary Journeys in Sasanian Iran', in J. Assmann and G.G. Stroumsa (eds), *Transformations of the Inner Self in Ancient Religions* (Leiden 1999), 73.

60 R.G. Hoyland, *Arabia and the Arabs* (London 2001), 156.

61 Ibn al-Jawzī, *al-Muntaẓam* (Beirut 1992–1993), ii, 217 f., apparently from Ibn al-Kalbī.

62 Ibn Manẓūr, *Lisān al-ʿarab* (Beirut 1955–1956); Murtaḍā al-Zabīdī, *Tāj al-ʿarūs*, ed. ʿA. Shīrī (Beirut 1994), both s.v. '*qrʿ*'.

63 Theophilus as reconstituted by R.G. Hoyland, *Seeing Islam as Others Saw It* (Princeton 1997), 647, cf. 400 ff.

64 Al-Jāḥiẓ, *al-ʿUthmāniyya*, ed. ʿA.-S.M. Hārūn (Cairo 1955), 266. In Ibn Ṭāwūs, *Fatḥ al-abwāb bayna dhawī 'l-albāb wa-bayna rabb al-arbāb fī 'l-istikhārāt*, ed. Kh. al-Khaffāf (Beirut 1989), 267 ff. (chs 20–21), *musāhama* consists of drawing lots from paper with names written on them, whereas a *qurʿa* is an object such as a pebble or a rosary bead, but it was not necessarily so in Jāḥiẓ' time. (Our thanks to Etan Kohlberg for drawing Ibn Ṭāwūs' work to our attention.)

65 Abū Yaʿlā, *al-Aḥkām al-sulṭāniyya*, ed. M.Kh. al-Fiqī, second printing, Cairo 1966, 25 (where lot-casting is prescribed in the first situation and is one out of two acceptable views in the

the law to spare people's feelings, not to establish rights' (*li-taṭyīb al-qulūb dūna ithbāt al-ḥuqūq*), as al-Nasafī (d. 508/1114) observed with reference to the second situation, meaning that it could only be used for the random distribution of things to which people had a lawful claim, not to pick out winners.[66] No caliph
437 actually seems to have been chosen by this method, but | much later we hear of an Ottoman grand vizier who was chosen by lot (drawn from pieces of paper with the names of candidates written on them).[67] This was in 1204/1789 f., at the beginning of the reign of Selim III, and its relevance to our present concerns is uncertain.

There seems to have been a tradition in Arabia of choosing people for other functions by lot as well. The Prophet is said to have decided which wife should accompany him on his travels by lot-casting;[68] the Medinese are said to have used lots to determine who should have the privilege of hosting the Prophet;[69] ʿAlī is credited with using lots to settle a case in Yemen in which three men denied paternity of a child that any one of them could have fathered.[70] ʿUmar II is said to have included the wives and children of the soldiers in the *dīwān* and cast lots to decide who should receive a hundred and who forty dirhams, i.e. from the income of the immoveable booty which was paid out as stipends.[71] All these examples refer to men in official positions, but hardly to lot-casting as a regular, public institution (though all decisions recorded for the Prophet were to assume that character). We do, however, encounter lot-casting as a regular institution in connection with mobilisation.

---

second); al-Māwardī, *al-Aḥkām al-sulṭāniyya*, ed. M.J. al-Ḥadīthī (Baghdad 2001), 60.1, 62.–6; tr. W.H. Wahba (Reading 1996), 6, 8, on unnamed jurists (without verdict on the first situation, but with arguments against lot-casting in the second).

66 Abū ʾl-Muʿīn al-Nasafī, *Tabṣirāt al-adilla*, ii, 826 f., against al-Qalānisī and al-Kaʿbī. His position is Ḥanafī, cf. below.

67 Ahmed Cevdet Pasha, *Tarih-i Cevdet* (Dersaadet 1309), v, 18 (on Ruscuklu Hasan Pasha). We owe this reference to Şükrü Hanioğlu.

68 Ṭabarī, *Taʾrīkh*, i, 1519. Compare *Babylonian Talmud*, Shabbath, 149b, on how Nebuchadnezzar would cast lots to decide which of his recently acquired (male) captives to have sexual relations with.

69 Ibn Saʿd, *Ṭabaqāt*, ed. Sachau, iii/1, 288; ed. Beirut, 396 (s.v. "Uthmān b. Maẓʿūn').

70 He imposed two thirds of the blood-money (for the child) on the man picked out as the father, presumably on the reasoning that he had caused the other two men to lose a third of a child each. The Prophet found this solution uproariously funny (Ibn Ḥanbal, *Musnad* [Cairo 1313], iv, 373; Wakīʿ, *Akhbār al-quḍāḥ*, ed. ʿA.-ʿA.M. al-Marāghī [Cairo 1947–1950], i, 91). For a variant involving two men and a slave girl, see al-Majlisī, *Biḥār*, xl, 244 f., cf. also civ, 63.

71 Ṭabarī, *Taʾrīkh*, ii, 1367.

When ʿUthmān permitted Muʿāwiya to conduct campaigns by sea, he stipulated that Muʿāwiya was not to select the men himself or cast lots among them (*lā tantakhib al-nās wa-lā tuqriʿ baynahum*), but rather to let them decide themselves whether to go.[72] Sortition was apparently among the methods normally used in the army to decide who was to go on duty. Of a Syrian soldier who went on annual summer campaigns in the Byzantine empire in the reign of Muʿāwiya we are told that he had a bad dream predicting that he would be the killer of an eminent Medinese and thereby doom himself to Hell; | when people 438
were chosen by lot for Yazīd I's campaign against Medina (*ḍuriba qurʿat baʿth al-Madīna*) in 63/682 f., this man had the misfortune to be selected (*fa-aṣābatnī al-qurʿa*).[73] In these two examples it is the authorities who use lots, but there are also stories in which it is the soldiers themselves who do so, some set in the Prophet's time. A Medinese desirous of martyrdom told the Prophet that he had missed the battle of Badr because he drew lots with his son to decide which one of them should go and it was his son's lot that had come out (*kharaja sahmuhu*).[74] *Qurʿa* was used to select eighty men from a group of volunteers in connection with another expedition.[75] In these stories enlistment is envisaged as voluntary, but only one man can go because one has to stay behind to look after the family, or only eighty men are needed of the many who have volunteered. In another *ḥadīth*, Abū Hurayra invokes the example of a man who goes on campaign with some people and whose lot does not come out (*lam yakhruj sahmuhu*) because he has not said 'amen';[76] here the volunteers are already on campaign and the question is who should go on a particular expedition in the course of it. We also hear of men in the mid-Umayyad period who would cast lots among themselves when they were called up to decide who should actually go; those who won would stay at home in return for payment of a sum known as *jaʿāʾil*.[77] Here the assumption seems to be that a particular tribal group would be told to supply a specified number of men and that the men could decide

72 Ibid., i, 2824.

73 Ibn Qutayba, *al-Imāma wa'l-siyāsa*, i, 215 f.

74 Wāqidī, *Maghāzī*, i, 212, on Saʿd b. Khaythama; cited in Majlisī, *Biḥār*, xx, 125.

75 Ibid., xxi, 77 (on *ghuzāt al-silsila*).

76 Al-Haythamī, *Majmaʿ al-zawāʾid* (Beirut 1982), ii, 113 (*K. al-ṣalāh, bāb al-taʾmīn*).

77 M. Bonner, 'Jaʿāʾil and Holy War in Early Islam', *Der Islam* 68 (1991), 47 f., with reference to T. Nöldeke, *Delectus Veterum Carminum Arabicorum* (Wiesbaden 1933), 77, and other sources where the poet is said to have been called up by Muʿāwiya's governor of Kufa (but the campaigns in Khwārizm only started in the governorship of Qutayba); Ṭabarī, *Taʾrīkh*, ii, 1029, without the poem, where the expedition is despatched by ʿAbd al-Malik. Exactly how the procedure worked is not clear.

for themselves whom to send: they all wanted to stay at home rather than to be martyred. The Ottomans provide a much later parallel for the use of lots in connection with military service, too. Al-Majlisī records that when ʿUmar Pāshā (1764–1776), Mamluk governor of Iraq on behalf of the Ottomans, arrived, he 'imposed harsh lot-casting on them (*ishtadda ʿalayhim al-qurʿa*)' and took sol-
439 diers from villages and the *amṣār*, high and low, learned | and ignorant, and ʿAlids and others alike.[78] When Muḥammad ʿAlī (1805–1848) introduced conscription in Egypt, *qurʿa* was apparently also meant to be used;[79] the Ottoman conscription system of 1848 was actually known as *Qurʿa niẓamnamesi* (regulation on the drawing of lots);[80] and lots were also used to draft soldiers in Egypt under Khedive Ismail (1863–1879).[81]

We abstain from the attempt to account for the Ottoman examples. The point of interest to us is that in the period with which we can claim some familiarity (from the rise of Islam to the Mongols), references to the use of lots in an official context are clustered in the first century, where the Prophet, the Rāshidūn and the Umayyads form a continuum, to fall off rapidly thereafter, except in connection with legal procedure. No doubt more will turn up, but it seems reasonable to infer that the official use of lot-casting for the selection of persons was a practice rooted in Arabia.

The Qurʾān and the Law

Lot-casting figures in the Qurʾān, but only as a literary theme, not as a live practice or an object of legislation. Two passages are relevant. The first is Q. 3:44, concerned with Mary. Much of what the Qurʾān has to say about her

78 al-Majlisī, *Biḥār*, liii, 331.

79 Kh. Fahmy, 'The Nation and its Deserters: Conscription in Mehmed Ali's Egypt', in E.J. Zürcher (ed.), *Arming the State: Military Conscription in the Middle East and Central Asia 1775–1925* (London and New York 1999), 67, citing Sir John Bowring's report of 1840 on how men would be seized without any order, arrangement, inscription 'or lot-drawing'.

80 E.J. Zürcher, 'The Ottoman Conscription System in Theory and Practice, 1844–1918', in Zürcher, *Arming the State*, 82 f., with a description of the system. Prof. Şükrü Hanioğlu, to whom we are much indebted for help on Ottoman questions, tells us that the draw of lots for conscription was called *qurʿa-i sherʿiyye* in the vernacular, military service being a religious duty. According to Fahd, *qurʿaya girmek* came to mean 'reaching the age of military service' (*EI*², s.v. 'ḳurʿa'). See also Granquist in Lindblom, 'Lot-Casting in the Old Testament', 169n, where the system is slightly different from that described by Zürcher.

81 J.P. Dunn, *Khedive Ismail's Army* (New York 2005), 43.

life reflects the *Protoevangelium of James*, a work written in Greek some time after 150, widely read in the Christian Near East, and translated into Syriac in the sixth century. In this work we read that Mary grew up in the temple and that the priests decided to marry her off when she was twelve years old, lest she pollute the temple by having periods (this passage is strikingly reminiscent of the story of the 'Mouse-Maiden' in the *Pañcatantra/Kalīla | wa-Dimna*). The 440
priests assemble the widowers of the people and tell them to bring a rod, and when a dove flies out of Joseph's rod, they assign Mary to him.[82] In other words, it is a miracle that singles out Joseph as her husband, not lots. But lots appear in other stories in the *Protoevangelium*, and on a later occasion it even mentions that Joseph himself had won his bride by lot.[83] The Qur'ān, on the other hand, briefly declares that 'you (sg.) were not there when they threw their rods (to determine) which of them should take care of Mary' (*idh yulqūna aqlāmahum ayyuhum yakfulu Maryama*, 3:44), seemingly referring to the version with the miracle (and presenting the contest as over *kafāla*, care, rather than marriage).[84] But the exegetes generally understood the rods as 'the arrows with which the lot-drawers (*al-mustahimūn*) from among the sons of Israel cast lots (*istahama*) for the guardianship of Mary', as al-Ṭabarī puts it.[85]

The second passage is in the story of how Jonah came to be thrown overboard from the ship on which he was travelling. In the Bible, Jonah is identified by lots as the sinner on whose account the storm is sent (Jon. 1:7). In the Qur'ān there is no reference to the storm, the ship is simply overloaded, so lots are cast to determine who should be jettisoned; but Jonah is a guilty party here too, and this does seem to be what the lots indicate: he has run away (*abaqa*) and behaved shamefully (*wa-huwa mulīm*), and when he cast lots, his plea was rebutted (*fa-sāhama fa-kāna min al-mudḥaḍīn*) (37:140–142).

---

82 *Protoevangelium of James*, 8:2–9:1, in Schneemelcher and Wilson, *New Testament Apocrypha*, 1, 429 f.; in the Indian story it is her father's house that should not be polluted (cf. the six versions of the passage, including the old Syriac, in F. de Blois, *Burzōy's Voyage to India and the Origin of the Book of Kalīlah wa Dimnah* [London 1990], 7 ff.).

83 *Protoevangelium of James*, 19:1, in Schneemelcher and Wilson, *New Testament Apocrypha*, 1, 434 (Tischendorf's version).

84 The *Protoevangelium* thinks of Mary as a perpetual virgin and accounts for Jesus' brothers by casting Joseph as an old widower with children by his first marriage when he wins Mary. In the Qur'ān, the old man who wins her is Zakariyyā (cf. 3:37), the father of John the Baptist, and her husband has completely disappeared, an interesting development which must tell us something about the religious milieu reflected in the Qur'ān.

85 Ṭabarī, *Tafsīr*, *ad* 3:44; similarly Fakhr al-Dīn al-Rāzī, *Tafsīr*, ad loc., and Ibn al-ʿArabī, below, note 87.

The fact that lot-casting is mentioned in the Qurʾān in connection with venerable figures meant that the procedure had excellent legitimation. It also generated some stories in which Muḥammad's *kafāla*, like Mary's, is decided
441 by lots.[86] But since it was only in accounts of | earlier religious communities that the procedure is mentioned, it did not shape Islamic law on this topic. As Ibn al-ʿArabī observed, in the earlier *sharīʿa*, lot-casting had been sanctioned for general use, whereas it was only used in specific cases in Islamic law, and not in connection with *kafāla*; nor would using lots to throw a man overboard be acceptable under Islamic rules, as both he and others pointed out.[87]

As Ibn al-ʿArabī noted, lot-casting did, however, remain acceptable in Islam in other contexts. First, as mentioned already, the jurists accepted that inheritances (and other joint property) could be allocated by lot. They seem to have done so without any controversy, and the method is still prescribed for the partition of joint property in the Ottoman *Majalla*.[88] It is a remarkable example of continuity from the ancient to the modern Near East, if only at a fairly low level of juristic interest.

That booty could be allocated among equals by lot seems also to have been widely accepted, at least as long as it was only a method of allocation of the appropriate shares rather than the assignation of things left over. The imam was charged with concern for the feelings of his subjects (*murāʿāt qulūb al-raʿiyya*) and avoidance of preferential treatment, as al-Sarakhsī explained; for this reason division of the booty was done by *qurʿa*, both in connection with the fifth set aside for the imam and for the distribution of the remaining four fifths. The four fifths would also be assigned to the pay-masters (*ʿurafāʾ*) by lot, and each *ʿarīf* would divide the portion assigned to him among the men of whom he was in charge by *qurʿa*, too, he said (using terminology from the Umayyad period). He adduced the Prophet's choice of a wife to accompany him on his travels by lot as the paradigmatic case in that the Prophet had used lots to spare their feelings (*ṭayyiban li-qulūbihinna*).[89] In connection with partition, the Mālikī Ibn Rushd also tells us that the jurists

---

86 Al-Balādhurī, *Ansāb al-ashrāf*, ed. M. Ḥamīdallāh (Cairo 1959), 85.

87 Ibn al-ʿArabī, *Aḥkām al-Qurʾān*, ed. ʿA.M. al-Bijāwī (Cairo 1378/1958), iv, 1610 f.; al-Qurṭubī, *al-Jāmiʿ li-aḥkām al-Qurʾān* (Cairo 1967), xv, 126; and, before both of them, al-Jaṣṣāṣ, *Aḥkām al-Qurʾān* (Beirut 1994), iii, 496 f.; all *ad* 37:141.

88 *Al-Majalla* (*Mecelle-yi ahkām-i ʿadliyye*), book x, articles 1151, 1156; cf. also 1180 (available in English at www.iium.edu.my/deed/lawbase/al_majalle).

89 Sarakhsī, *Siyar*, iii, 889 f. On his handling of the Prophet's precedent in connection with wives, see also below, note 98.

accepted lot-casting *taṭyīban li-nufūs al-mutaqāsimīn*.[90] It was on the same principle that the Shāfiʿites and others accepted that one could choose prayer leaders, *naqīb*s | and other persons by sortition when the candidates were 442
equally entitled:[91] the contenders had to be *mustawīna fī ʾl-ḥujja*, as al-Shāfiʿī said.[92]

There were situations in which some jurists, above all the Ḥanafīs, deemed lot-casting to amount to gambling (*qimār*), however. If a man manumitted slaves worth more than a third of his property in death, sickness or by will, the Shāfiʿīs, Ḥanbalīs, Mālikīs and Imāmīs would draw lots and manumit however many could be accommodated within the third in accordance with the Prophetic *ḥadīth*, but the Ḥanafīs held that all the slaves should be set free and obliged to work until they had paid off the value of the unmanumitted parts.[93] Similarly, when two men claimed ownership of some property and adduced equally valid proof, the Shāfiʿīs, Ḥanbalīs and Imāmīs accepted (among various other solutions) that one could cast lots and give the disputed property to the winner, directly or by having him take the oath which settled the matter; there were *ḥadīth*s in which the Prophet and ʿAlī did so. But the Ḥanafīs (and Mālikīs) would divide the property, arguing that the *ḥadīth*s dated from the period before the prohibition of gambling.[94] There were also traditions in

90 Ibn Rushd, *Bidāya*, ii, 299.2; tr. Nyazee, i, 320 (translated 'for the satisfaction of the persons participating in the partition').

91 Māwardī, *Aḥkām*, 273 (*niqāba*), 278 (leadership of prayer), 532.ult. (order on the military roll), 589.ult. (retaliation); tr. Wahba, 109, 113, 224, 254; Nawawī, *Minhāj*, iii, 99 f., 102 (*ḥaḍāna*), 119 f. (retaliation), 379 (admission to the court room). The Mālikīs and Ḥanbalīs also accept lot-casting in such situations (*Mawsūʿa*, xvii, 138 ff., 148 f.), and the Imāmī Shīʿites list many more; see Ḥusayn al-Karīmī al-Qummī, *Qāʿidat al-qurʿa* (Qum 1420 [1999]), 20 f.; Muḥammad Jawād Ashʿarī, *Barrasī-yi ḥujjiyat-i qurʿa* (Qum 1382 [2003]), 106 ff., 120.

92 Shāfiʿī, 'K. al-qurʿa', *Umm*, viii, 3; Bayhaqī, *Aḥkām al-Qurʾān*, 158.

93 ʿAbd al-Wahhāb b. ʿAlī al-Baghdādī, *al-Ishrāf ʿalā masāʾil al-khilāf*, ed. Ḥ. Ṭāhir (Beirut 1999), ii, 990 (no. 2005); al-Ṭūsī, *al-Nihāya* (Beirut 1970), 105 ff.; Ashʿarī, *Barrasī*, 109. Some Mālikīs rejected *qurʿa* if the slaves had been freed in death sickness (Ibn Rushd, *Bidāya*, ii, 405 f. [*K. al-ʿitq*]; tr. Nyazee, ii, 450 f.). Compare the case of a man who divorces one of his four wives and marries a fifth in death sickness without it being known which of the four he had in mind: Yaḥyā b. Aktham (eventually classified as a Ḥanafī) would let all five inherit and observe the *ʿidda*, the Ḥanbalīs and some Imāmīs would cast lots for the one who had been divorced (Ibn Qayyim al-Jawziyya, *Ṭuruq*, ii, 744, 789; Karīmī, *Qāʿida*, 21; Ashʿarī, *Barrasī*, 111). Cf. *Mawsūʿa*, xvii, for the Mālikī and Shāfiʿī solutions.

94 Al-Sarakhsī, *al-Mabsūṭ* (Beirut 2001), xvii, 49 f.; al-Khaṣṣāf, *Adab al-qāḍī*, 391, no. 452;

which the Prophet cast lots to decide who should swear first (in the situation
443 in which two parties raise claims against | each other and both have to swear), but the Ḥanafīs held that the judge should decide in most such situations.[95] The reasoning is clearly that lots could not be used in situations in which all claimants were entitled, but only some could be satisfied in full, or only one person was entitled, but nobody knew who that person was: picking out the lucky winners by lots amounted to gambling with their legal rights. Al-Shāfiʿī also had reservations about lot-casting in the latter case, but Ḥanbalīs endorsed it in both.[96] Those who claimed that *qurʿa* amounted to gambling and had been abrogated were ignorant, foul, or positively evil people, Ibn Ḥanbal said; they had the temerity to label a Prophetic decision *qimār*.[97] Polemicists who credit Abū Ḥanīfa with the statement *al-qurʿa qimār* typically cast him as rejecting the use of lots altogether. The Imāmīs are among them.[98] According to them, sortition was acceptable in all matters unknown (*kullu majhūl fa-fīhi ʾl-qurʿa*), a principle they defend to this day.[99]

Attitudes to Lots

In the Old and New Testaments, too, all forms of lot-casting are consistently envisaged as an appeal to the divine: God could see differences hidden to the

---

Baghdādī, *Ishrāf*, ii, 983 (no. 1993); Nawawī, *Minhāj*, iii, 440 ff.; *Mawsūʿa*, xxxiii, 142 f.; Ṭūsī, *Nihāya*, 343 f.; Karīmī, *Qāʿida*, 105 ff.; Ashʿarī, *Barrasī*, 108; cf. F. Rosenthal, *Gambling in Islam* (Leiden 1975).

95 Cf. *Mawsūʿa*, xxxiii, 147 f.

96 Cf. Ibn Taymiyya, *Ṣiḥḥat uṣūl madhhab ahl al-Madīna* (Beirut n.d. [1980?]), 85 f. Our thanks to Aron Zysow for drawing this work to our attention.

97 Ibn Qayyim al-Jawziyya, *Ṭuruq*, 742, 744 f., 747 f.

98 Thus Karīmī, *Qāʿida*, 18. He later notes that the *Mawsūʿa* shows Abū Ḥanīfa to have accepted *qurʿa* in general, only to cite a barrage of stories in which Abu Ḥanīfa rejects the Prophet's precedent, including the latter's use of *qurʿa* for choosing a wife to accompany him on a journey (pp. 101 f.). Since the Prophet's use of lots in connection with wives is a situation in which the procedure was used to pick a winner, Abū Ḥanīfa may well in fact have disliked this *ḥadīth*, but according to Sarakhsī (above, note 89), none of the wives had any legal right to accompany him (whereas the slaves did have a legal right to such freedom as the estate allowed by virtue of the bequest).

99 Ṭūsī, *Nihāya*, 345 f.; Majlisī, *Biḥār*, x, 203; xiv, 325; Ibn Ṭāwūs, *Fatḥ al-abwāb*, 272 (citing Ṭūsī); Ashʿarī, *Barrasī*, 106; Muḥammad Ḥusayn Faḍl Allāh, *al-Qurʿa waʾl-istikhāra* (Beirut 1417/1997), 24 ff., against Abū Ḥanīfa, Ibn Abī Laylā and Ibn Shubruma at 27, 29; Karīmī, *Qāʿida*, 34 f.

human eye; there are passages in which the outcome of lot-casting is explicitly equated with His will (1Sam. 10:24; Prov. 16:33; Acts 1:23–26). The Greeks may once have thought in similar terms, though it has been argued that they never did so | in connection with divisory lot-casting.[100] Divisory lot-casting is 444
an expression coined by Thomas Aquinas for the use of lots to determine who should have or do what, as opposed to consultative and divinatory lot-casting, used to decide what to do and to obtain information about the future respectively.[101] From ancient times to late antiquity the Greeks seem to have envisaged lot-casting of the divisory kind as a matter of chance, and the same is true of the Romans.[102] It was a matter of *fortuna*, as Justinian called it in his legislation.[103] Their attitude affected their Hellenised Near Eastern subjects. Josephus, for example, famously tells how the rebels at Masada chose ten men by lot to kill the rest of them, and thereafter each other,[104] and how he himself had used lots to decide who, of his small band about to be captured by the Romans, should kill whom first (he surrendered as one of the last to survive). He too seems to think of the outcome as a matter of luck. He does put it to the reader that his own survival could have been due to God's providence rather than to chance, but it sounds like mere self-justification.[105]

The Sunnī jurists generally seem to have thought of divisory lot-casting (*qurʿa*) in much the same sober vein as their Greek and Hellenised predecessors. Their attitudes must of course have varied in place and time and we cannot claim to have studied them in any detail, but unlike Aquinas who (invoking Augustine) identified all sortition as 'a questioning concerning realities whose occurrence depends on the divine will', they convey little impression of seeing the divisory form as an appeal to God. They make no attempt to distinguish it

100 Cf. N.D. Fustel de Coulanges, *The Ancient City* (New York n.d.; originally published Paris 1864), 182f. (book III, ch. x); Pauly-Wissova, s.v. 'Losung', cols. 1461ff., mostly disagreeing with Fustel de Coulanges and claiming that the Greeks distinguished between the lot as a divine oracle and as a tool of equality from the start.

101 Thomas Aquinas, *Commentary on the Ephesians*, book 1, lecture 4, citing Proverbs 18:18 ('The lots put an end to dispute') in justification of the first. He put lot-casting for the selection of people in the consultative rather than the divisory category. For other classifications, see Gataker, *Use and Nature of Lots*, ch. 3.

102 Rosenstein, 'Sorting Out the Lot', esp. 51.

103 Cf. Justinian, above, note 20; also Favorinus (Ps.-Dio), above, note 15. Fortuna had once been a goddess, but only in the sense that everything beyond human control could be seen as divine.

104 Josephus, *Wars*, book 7, ch. 9, par. 1; cf. Y. Yadin, *Masada: Herod's Fortress and the Zealots' Last Stand* (London 1966), 201.

105 Josephus, *Wars*, book 3, ch. 8, par. 7.

from, or relate it to, consultation (*istikhāra*) or divination (*istiqsām*, *kihāna*),
445 apparently taking it for granted that they were | different; and those who classified *qurʿa* as gambling in some situations evidently thought of it as a matter of chance. Their opponents did sometimes counter this by presenting it as an appeal to the divine: one *ḥadīth* displays the Prophet as casting lots in a situation in which there would be winners and losers with the prayer, 'O God, give judgement among your servants with truth', and Ibn Ḥanbal is credited with the statement that 'the lot hits the truth' (*al-qurʿa tuṣību 'l-ḥaqq*).[106] But such statements are rare in the Sunnī material we have seen.

Even on a superficial reading, the Shīʿites come across as different. Using lots was indeed a way of delegating matters to God in their view,[107] and particularly effective if it was done by the imam: his *qurʿa* never went wrong, being in the nature of *waḥy*, they said.[108] The seventh/thirteenth-century Shīʿite scholar Ibn Ṭāwūs did think of lot-casting as a form of consultative divination, *istikhāra*;[109] and *qurʿa* and *istikhāra* are also treated together in booklets by contemporary Shīʿites, including Faḍl Allāh, who repeats that lot-casting is a way of delegating problems to God. He mentions unidentified persons who hold that only the imam can do lot-casting, on the grounds that only he knows the special prayer to be said in connection with it (an argument perhaps designed to eliminate the whole institution), but he rejects it on the grounds that no special prayer is needed. The method is only to be used when there is no other solution, he says, and its purpose is simply to solve a problem, not the unveiling (*kashf*) of anything; but God does not cheat, as he also says.[110]

By way of contemporary comment, it may be worth noting that there has been much interest in divisory lots as a political device in both England and America in recent years.[111] Most Westerners probably think of the procedure as
446 archaic, not so much because they see | it as a form of gambling or divination as

106 Saʿīd b. al-Musayyab's *ḥadīth* in Sarakhsī, *Mabsūṭ*, xvii, 49 (with *takhrīj*); Ibn Ḥanbal in Ibn Qayyim al-Jawziyya, *Ṭuruq*, ii, 745.

107 Thus several traditions in Majlisī, *Biḥār*, xci, 234; civ, 325.

108 Majlisī, *Biḥār*, ii, 177; xxvi, 32; xl, 245, 328, 363; liii, 331, 332, etc.

109 Ibn Ṭāwūs, *Fatḥ al-abwāb*, 267 ff.

110 Faḍl Allāh, *Qurʿa*, 26, 30, 33, 49, 62 f., 65. For the question whether lot-casting is the prerogative of the imam (as claimed in some traditions), see Ashʿarī, *Barrasī*, 56 ff. For lot-casting, *istikhāra* and *istiqsām* in another booklet, see Ḥusaynī, *Qāʿida*, 123 ff.

111 E. Callenbach and M. Phillips, *A Citizen Legislature* (Berkeley 1985); K. Sutherland, *The Party Is Over: Blueprint for a Very English Revolution* (Exeter 2004), revised as *A People's Parliament* (Exeter 2008); B. Goodwin, *Justice by Lottery* (Exeter 2005). Our thanks to Anthony Barnett for these references.

because they think they can do better than random chance. (In fact, this seems to have been the Ḥanafī attitude, too, but since the Prophet had endorsed sortition, it was only via his prohibition of gambling that they could reject it.)[112] Even today, however, Westerners usually accept the principle of random selection in connection with juries, which are still chosen by (computerised) lot-casting, and it is precisely this principle that is attracting attention as a way of introducing direct representation and popular control to counter what nowadays goes under the name of the 'democratic deficit'. As a democratic device, random selection is what one book on the subject calls 'the Athenian option',[113] heartily disliked by a philosopher such as Ibn Rushd because it took no account of virtue;[114] but as an antidote to partiality and special interests in general it was wholeheartedly endorsed in the Islamic legal tradition. Ancient though the practice is, it may still be in for new roles, and not just in the West.[115]

The Return of the Near East

Here, however, our interest is not in modern politics, but rather in the relationship between ancient Near Eastern and Islamic culture. The question has not been much studied, but it has received some attention of late,[116] deservedly in our view, because it amounts to asking how far we can reconstruct the cultural and religious history of the Near East as a single, continuous narrative rather
than as dis|jointed parts studied under the rubrics of Biblical, Greek, Roman, 447
ancient Iranian and Islamic history. Between them, the ancient and the Islamic

---

112 The explanation offered by Rosenthal, *Gambling*, 33, does not fit the contexts in which *qurʿa* was identified as gambling.

113 Cf. A. Barnett and P. Carty, *The Athenian Option: Radical Reform for the House of Lords* (Exeter 2008); cf. also O. Dowling, *The Political Potential of Sortition* (Exeter 2008), which examines lot-casting as a political device in both Athens and the Western tradition.

114 Cf. P. Crone, *Medieval Islamic Political Thought* (Edinburgh 2004), 280 and note 111 thereto.

115 Curiously, a ballot or election is actually *iqtirāʿ* in modern Arabic (see H. Wehr, *A Dictionary of Modern Literary Arabic* [Wiesbaden 1966], s.v.). Other words may be more common (notably *intikhāb*), but *iqtirāʿ* was used in the Iraqi election in 2005, see http://www.newsday.com/news/nationworld/nation/ny-oiraqelectiongallery,0,322603.photo gallery ?index=7 (photo 2) [Ed.: This URL is now defunct.].

116 Cf. S. Dalley (ed.), *The Legacy of Mesopotamia* (Oxford 1998); M. Levy-Rubin, 'On the Roots and Authenticity of Conquest Agreements in the Seventh Century', *Jerusalem Studies in Arabic and Islam* 34 (2008); and the MELAMMU Project (www.aakkl.helsinki.fi/melammu).

periods cover most of the history of the region, but not all of it: there is a thousand years in between the two, and this is where the problem arises.

The thousand years in question are those in which the Near East was under colonial rule, first under the Achaemenids, next under Alexander and his successors, and thereafter under the Greeks and the Romans in its western part, under the Parthians and the Sasanians in Iraq. As the foreigners moved in with their own cultural traditions, the high culture of the Near East was unseated and increasingly reduced to a local tradition of limited interest to those who mattered. The ancient Near Eastern tradition did not die, of course. It changed when it ceased to be written in cuneiform languages and was expressed instead in Aramaic, but as Aramaic culture it lived on. Unfortunately, very little of it has come down to us. We do have Jewish writings in Aramaic, and from the third century CE onwards also Christian ones, but the pagans who formed the vast majority in the region for most of the period have not left us much. By and large, we are forced to study the Near East through the eyes of its conquerors, who remained outsiders to the region in the sense that they continued to be orientated towards their own cultural centres even after having made themselves thoroughly at home in the land. As ill luck would have it, the bulk of the Persian tradition is also lost, so that for practical purposes we only have one pair of foreign eyes, those of the Greeks and the Romans. Some of those who wrote in Greek were Near Easterners by origin, and some of them did try to make their native tradition available in Greek, adapted to Greek tastes. But the bulk of these writings is also lost, and most of the Near Easterners who wrote in Greek had assimilated the hegemonic culture so thoroughly that they sound no different from people of other origin writing in that language. The Jews are again the main exception.

From the third century CE onwards, however, all this begins to change. In 211 all members of the Roman empire were granted Roman citizenship (some minor exceptions apart), with the result that all now had to live by Roman law. Since people could not change their ways overnight whatever the degree of Roman control, inevitably this meant that much of what they actually practised was a mixture of Roman and native law. Often called 'provincial law', such native law surfaced in both the eastern and the western parts of
448 the empire, and some of it came to be officially endorsed as Roman | law.[117]
What this means for us is that the indigenous tradition begins to be visible in the hegemonic culture. The two Greek papyri from Petra and Nessana

117 See J. Mélèze Modrzejewski, 'Diritto romano e diritti locali', in A. Schiavone et al. (eds), *Storia di Roma*, III/2 (Turin 1993), 985–1009.

are perfect examples: the lot-casting by which the shares were allocated was a provincial practice, not a procedure specified in Roman law.

Christianity made for even greater change. It originated as a Near Eastern religion carried by speakers of Aramaic, initially Jews, thereafter Jews and gentiles. A socially inclusive movement in which Greeks and non-Greeks, elite and masses, were brought together in a manner hitherto unknown in the Mediterranean, it gradually converted the entire empire to Near Eastern, if increasingly Hellenised, modes of thought, and in the Near East itself it allowed for a more extensive resurfacing of Aramaic culture as the Christians of Syria and Mesopotamia took to writing in Syriac (i.e. the Aramaic dialect current at Edessa). The establishment of a new capital in Constantinople also contributed to the 'Orientalisation' of the Roman empire, to use the term adopted by those who see the process from the Greek or Roman point of view. From our point of view, 'Orientalisation' is simply a way of saying that it becomes possible to see continuities outside the sphere of law as well.

The return of the Near East continued after the Arab conquest, for if Christianity was a kind of homecoming for the Near Eastern provincials, this was even truer of Islam. The Arabs were Near Easterners who definitively unseated the Greeks from their hegemonic role in the region. By then, of course, Greek culture had served as the high culture of the Near East for close to a thousand years, so that there was no way of shedding it: it had gone into the bloodstream of the local culture. But living by Greek culture under the hegemony of Greeks, who continued to see themselves as its ultimate arbiters even in its Christian form, was quite different from continuing Greek cultural ways on one's own terms, with or without awareness of their Greek origin. Initially, of course, the Arabs were much like the Greeks in that they saw themselves as arbiters of Islamic culture, and they too were prejudiced against Aramaeans. But their hegemonic position was shortlived. As converts to Islam, the Aramaeans assumed the legacy, and eventually also the ethnicity, of the Arab conquerors and became their own cultural masters. When we speak of the Arabs today, it is largely the former Aramaeans (and Copts) that we have in mind. Consequently, a great deal of Islamic culture is Aramaic culture, | brought into 449
Islam in the form in which it had developed under Greek and Persian rule, to develop in new directions thereafter.

This is the overall framework in which the connections between ancient Near Eastern and Islamic culture have to be pursued. Lot-casting as an official procedure provides us with a striking example of such a connection, with a typically uneven distribution of documentation: well attested in the cuneiform record, its only attestation in Aramaic seems to be in Jewish works. This is presumably due to the loss of the pagan Aramaic tradition rather than the disappearance of the practice, though it would help if it turned up in Syriac too. As it is, however, we do have it in Greek, and as good luck would have it, the Greek evidence comes from Petra and Nessana, which puts us in the rare situation of having conclusive evidence for pre-Islamic Arabia. Thereafter the evidence is plentiful, but only for the time of the Prophet, the Rāshidūn and the Umayyads: as the Arab conquest society wanes, so do the attestations. We do find discussion of the practice in Islamic law, but incidental references to the practice in real life seem to disappear until its curious reappearance under the Ottomans. Even the Jews eventually cease to mention it. Partition by lot-casting is still discussed in the Gaonic literature, dating from *c.* 700–1050; but there is no reference to it in the *Kitāb al-mawārīth* of Saʿadiya Gaon (d. 942), for all that it covers inheritance issues in detail, nor do we know of any in the Cairo Geniza. In short, the overall impression one gets is that what came out of Arabia was in this case an institution that no longer meshed with the way things were done in the rest of the Near East. It came and it went, leaving behind only some traces.

One may contrast this with another institution of ancient Near Eastern origin in Islamic law, the clause requiring a freed slave to remain with his or her master until the latter's death, i.e. as a servant. Known as *paramonē* ('remaining by'), it was also found as a labour contract for free people. Originating as a contract of adoption designed to provide for the manumitter in old age, it was transmitted from the Near East to Greece at an early stage, and after Alexander's conquest of the Near East the indigenous and the Greek forms of the institution interacted, to breed an amazing range of variations. The Romans accepted the validity of such contracts when they were made by non-Roman subjects under their own law, but not as part of Roman law. Inevitably, however, it came to be practised under Roman law after the universal grant of citizenship, and though the guardians of Roman law resisted this development, they may eventually have capitulated. With or without official recognition, the *paramonē* remained
450 a prominent | part of provincial practice in the Near East. It was also known in Arabia, where free slaves seem often to have been adopted very much as they had been in the ancient Near East. We encounter the *paramonē* as a free labour contract at Nessana and as an archaic requirement of staying with the master in the Ḥijāz and elsewhere. After the conquests it is reflected in a wide variety of forms in a large number of *ḥadīth*s attributed to early jurists and the Rāshidūn, and it formed the raw material of what the Muslims were to systematise as *kitāba* and *tadbīr*.[118]

118 Cf. P. Crone, *Roman, Provincial and Islamic Law* (Cambridge 1987), ch. 5, and the literature cited there.

If the contract had not been so important outside Arabia, it would presumably have had much the same history as lot-casting: it would have come and gone, leaving behind some traces. But far from receding into obscurity, it generated massive discussion and two new formal institutions. Manumission was of course of much greater practical importance in daily life than lot-casting, so the examples are not entirely comparable. For all that, it is hard not to suspect that the key transmitters of originally ancient Near Eastern culture will prove to be the inhabitants of the Fertile Crescent, now assisted by the Arabian tradition and now without it, but not usually the Arabians on their own.

CHAPTER 3

Idrīs, Atraḫasīs and al-Khiḍr*

Idrīs

Idrīs is a mysterious figure mentioned twice in the Qur'ān, in both cases in somewhat unilluminating terms. One passage says of him and two others, Ismāʿīl and Dhū 'l-Kifl, that they were among the patient (*min al-ṣābirīn*) and that 'We admitted them to Our mercy, for they were among the righteous ones (*min al-ṣāliḥīn*)' (21:85 f.). The other passage exhorts the believers to 'remember in the book Idrīs', once again mentioning him after Ismāʿīl and now identifying him as a righteous man and prophet (*ṣiddīqan nabiyyan*) whom God had 'raised to a lofty place' (*wa-rafaʿnāhu makānan ʿaliyyan*) (19:56 f.); the continuation, perhaps added later, includes him among the prophets who were of the seed (*dhurriyya*) of Adam, Noah, Abraham and Israel (19:58).[1] It is clear, then, that Idrīs was a prophet, a biblical figure and someone who had been raised up in some sense, but it hardly suggests that he was Enoch, who lived before Noah, Abraham, Israel/Jacob and Ishmael, though he was of course a descendant of Adam. Nonetheless, it is usually as Enoch (Akhnūkh, Ḥanūkh), the great-grandfather of Noah, that the exegetes identify him. Of Enoch Genesis twice tells us that he 'walked with God (*hāʾelōhîm*)' (Gen. 5:22, 24), adding on the second occasion that 'then he was no more, because God (*ʾelōhîm*) took him'. The Septuagint takes the first statement to mean that Enoch was pleasing to God and the second that he was moved to heaven without dying, and this became the standard interpretation (though there was also a tradition that he died).[2] As the Epistle to the Hebrews explains, quoting from the Septuagint,

* I should like to thank Tzvi Abusch, Michael Cook and Adam Silverstein for helpful comments on earlier drafts of this article, and Tommaso Tesei for a memorable conversation about the subject.

1 For 19:58 as an interpolation (by the Messenger himself?), see A. Neuwirth, 'Imagining Mary—Disputing Jesus', in B. Jokisch, U. Rebstock and L.I. Conrad (eds.), *Fremde, Feinde und Kurioses*, Berlin and New York 2009, pp. 383–416, at 389 f.

2 Thus *Jubilees*, 7:39, as against 4:23 (tr. O.S. Wintermute in J.H. Charlesworth (ed.), *Old Testament Pseudepigrapha*, New York 1983–1985, ii, pp. 71, 63). Targum Onqelos unambiguously declares God to have made Enoch die, though a variant denies it (the translation of J.W. Etheridge, London 1862, reflects the variant); and both Neofiti and Ps.-Jonathan say that Enoch was taken away, using a verb that can also mean to die (*ʾtngd*). For all that, both seem to

© KONINKLIJKE BRILL NV, LEIDEN, 2016 | DOI: 10.1163/9789004319318_004

'by faith Enoch was taken so that he did not experience death and *he was not found* because God had taken him. For it was attested before he was taken that *he had pleased God*'.[3] The exegetes often take Q. 19:57 to refer to Enoch's translation: the lofty place to which God had raised him was the fourth or sixth heaven; he had been moved there without having died, like Jesus, and he was immortal; Muḥammad met him in the fourth heaven during his heavenly journey.[4]

Some exegetes took the Qur'ānic statement that God had raised Idrīs to a lofty place to mean that He had raised him in terms of rank and status rather than location.[5] This was the view of al-Ḥasan al-Baṣrī (d. 110/728), al-Jubbā'ī (303/915 f.) and Abū Muslim al-Iṣfahānī (d. 322/934), for example.[6] But according to al-Ḥasan al-Baṣrī, the earliest exegete from whom this view is transmitted, it was in paradise (*fī 'l-janna*) that Idrīs' rank had been raised.[7] In other words, al-Ḥasan probably shared the belief that Idrīs had been translated to heaven (or conceivably to some inaccessible place on earth). In principle, he could have believed that Idrīs died here on earth to be first resurrected and next moved to paradise after the fashion of Jesus according to the Christians; but the Qur'ānic Jesus is not said to have been resurrected before ascending to heaven: either he died a normal death on earth and will be resurrected along with the rest of mankind (19:33, cf. 19:15) or else he was taken to heaven as soon as he died (cf. 3:55; 5:117).[8] Muslim martyrs are killed here on earth

have his translation in mind; Ps.-Jonathan even adds that Enoch ascended to the firmament to be known as Metatron (see M. Maher (tr.), *Targum Pseudo-Jonathan: Genesis*, Collegeville, MN, 1992, p. 37, n. 8; M. McNamara (tr.), *Targum Neofiti 1: Genesis*, Collegeville, MN, 1992, p. 70, n. 11; L.R. Ubigli, 'La fortuna di Enoc nel giudaismo antico: valenze e problemi', *Annali di Storia dell'Esegesi* 1, 1984, pp. 153–163, at 156 f.; J.C. VanderKam, *Enoch: a Man for All Generations*, Columbia, SC, 1995, pp. 165 ff.).

3 Hebrews 11:5; similarly Sirach 44:16; 49:14; Philo, *De mutatione nominum*, 34, 38 (with allegorical interpretation); Josephus, *Antiquities*, I, 4:85 (cf. IX, 2:28).

4 Al-Ṭabarī, *Jāmiʿ al-bayān ʿan tafsīr al-Qur'ān*, Beirut 1988, *juz'* xvi, pp. 96 f., citing al-Mujāhid, al-Ḍaḥḥāk and others; al-Ṭabrisī, *Majmaʿ al-bayān fī tafsīr al-Qur'ān*, Beirut 1995, vi, p. 430, citing the same and other authorities; al-Suyūṭī, *al-Durr al-manthūr*, Beirut 1983, v, p. 519, all *ad* 19:57. Further references in *Encyclopaedia of Islam*², Leiden 1960–2009 (hereafter *EI*²), s.v. 'Idrīs (Vajda); cf. also *Encyclopaedia of the Qur'ān*, Leiden 2001–2006 (hereafter *EQ*), s.v. 'Idrīs' (Erder).

5 Cf. al-Māturīdī, *Ta'wīlāt al-Qur'ān*, ed. B. Topaloğlu and others, Istanbul 2005–2011, ix, pp. 147 f. (*ad* 19:57), where this view is preferred.

6 Ṭabrisī, *Majmaʿ*, vi, p. 430.

7 Māturīdī, *Ta'wīlāt*, ix, p. 147, *ad* 19:57.

8 Differently N. Robinson in *EQ*, s.v. 'Jesus'.

and go straight to heaven without being resurrected first (evidently because this would have required them to be seen alive again before their transfer to heaven); but although this view is attested already in the Qurʾān (2:154; 3:169), the martyrs never seem to figure in the discussion of either Jesus or Enoch. There were certainly scholars who denied Idrīs' immortality, Ibn Isḥāq and Muqātil b. Sulaymān (both d. 150/767) among them. Ibn Isḥāq envisaged Idrīs as dying here on earth, but he says nothing about him being raised to heaven, with or without being resurrected first.[9] But Muqātil and others accepted that Idrīs was alive when he went to heaven, for in their view it was in the fourth heaven, or on the way to the fifth, that the angel of death had taken him (an idea which generated some gripping stories).[10] In short, there was almost complete agreement among the early exegetes that Idrīs was Enoch and that he had gone to heaven/paradise without dying first.

Needless to say, the agreement was not complete. Ibn Isḥāq (and others?) apart, there were also exegetes who identified Idrīs with Elijah, another prophet who had been translated to heaven (2 Kings 2:5). Ibn Masʿūd, for example, held that Idrīs' name was Elijah and read Idrīs for Elijah in two of the three passages in the Qurʾān in which Elijah (Ilyās) is mentioned.[11] (What he said about the third does not seem to be recorded.) Elijah in his turn was often identified with al-Khiḍr/al-Khaḍir, yet another mysterious figure characterised by immortality, and apparently Idrīs was sometimes held to be al-Khiḍr as well.[12] Since Enoch was believed to be a scribe in heaven no less than on the earth,[13] he also came to be identified with the heavenly scribe of the Egyptians, Thoth, under the latter's Greek name of Hermes; and though the identification of the two is likely to predate the rise of Islam, it seems to be only in Islamic sources that it is attested:

---

9 Ṭabarī, *Taʾrīkh al-rusul waʾl-mulūk*, ed. M.J. de Goeje and others, Leiden 1879–1901, ser. i, p. 176.

10 Muqātil b. Sulaymān, *Tafsīr*, ed. ʿA.M. Shiḥāta, Beirut 2002, ii, p. 631; Māturīdī, *Taʾwīlāt*, ix, p. 147; cf. the neat survey of al-Māwardī, *Tafsīr*, ed. Kh.M. Khiḍr, Kuwait 1982, ii, p. 529; Ṭabarī, *Jāmiʿ*, *juzʾ* xvi, pp. 96 f. For the gripping stories, see al-Qummī, *Tafsīr*, Beirut 1991, ii, pp. 25 f. (here combined with a version of the fallen angels theme); Suyūṭī, *Durr*, v, pp. 518 ff. (where one story also works in the fallen angels).

11 Ṭabarī, *Jāmiʿ*, *juzʾ* xxiii, p. 96, *ad* 37:130; cf. *juzʾ* vii, p. 261, *ad* 6:85; Suyūṭī, *Durr*, vii, p. 117, *ad* 37:123, where both Ibn Masʿūd and Qatāda identify Idrīs and Elijah. Further references in *Encyclopaedia of Islam*[3], Leiden 2007– (hereafter EI[3]), s.v. 'Elijah' (Rippin).

12 Cf. EI[2], s.v. 'al-K͟haḍir (al-K͟hiḍr)' (Wensinck); and EQ, s.v. 'Khaḍir/Khiḍr' (Renard). The occasional identification of Idrīs and al-Khiḍr is reported by Vajda in EI[2], s.v. 'Idrīs'.

13 Cf. D.E. Orton, *The Understanding Scribe: Matthew and the Apocalyptic Ideal*, Sheffield 1989, pp. 77 ff.; A.A. Orlov, *The Enoch-Metatron Tradition*, Tübingen 2005, pp. 50 ff.

the earliest author to mention it appears to be al-Jāḥiẓ (d. 255/869).[14] It reflects the thinking of astrologers, alchemists and others to whom Hermes counted as an authority, not that of theologians or religious scholars. To the latter, Idrīs was practically always a biblical figure, and almost always Enoch.

Modern scholars sometimes dispute that their predecessors are right. To Alexander, for example, it seems abundantly clear that the Qur'ān is not, in fact, referring to Enoch, given that the names Idrīs and Enoch have nothing in common, that no plausible link between the two figures has been proposed, and that the statement 'We raised him to a lofty place' need not refer to an ascent to heaven.[15] All Alexander's objections are right, or rather were, for the first two fall away if the argument presented here is correct; and as we have seen, even the exegetes who held God to have elevated Idrīs in terms of honour and status rather than by translation to heaven identified Idrīs as Enoch. A more serious objection might be that the Qur'ān never identifies Idrīs as an antediluvian figure, but on the contrary lists him after much later figures in sura 21:85, and after Ismāʿīl in both that passage and 19:56f. But disregard of the chronological order is quite common in the Qur'ān: 6:84–86, for example, enumerates David, Solomon, Job, Joseph, Moses, Aaron, Zakariyah, John, Jesus, Ishmael, Elisha, Jonah and Lot in that order. Another objection might be that the Qur'ān associates Idrīs with endurance or patience (*ṣabr*), as opposed to repentance, the characteristic with which Enoch had come to be associated.[16] But Idrīs does at least share his righteousness with Enoch,[17] and Reeves deems the Qur'ānic passage on his elevation to a lofty place to be arrestingly close to that used in *Jubilees* and *1Enoch* of Enoch's transfer to Eden/a lofty place.[18] Above all, the exegetes could hardly have been so united in their opinion at so early a stage if they had first encountered Idrīs as a Qur'ānic figure open

---

14 Jāḥiẓ, *K. al-tarbīʿ wa'l-tadwīr*, ed. C. Pellat, Damascus 1955, par. 40: 'Tell me about Hermes, is he Idrīs?'.

15 Cf. P.S. Alexander, 'Jewish Tradition in Early Islam: the Case of Enoch/Idrīs', in G.R. Hawting, J.A. Mojaddedi and A. Samely (eds.), *Studies in Islamic and Middle Eastern Texts and Traditions in Memory of Norman Calder*, Oxford 2000, pp. 11–29, at 23f.

16 Cf. Sirach 44:16; cf. also Philo, *De Abrahamo*, 17f.

17 E.g. Sirach 44:17; *1Clement* (The Letter of the Romans to the Corinthians, ed. and tr. in *The Apostolic Fathers*, ed. J.B. Lightfoot, ed. and rev. M.W. Holmes, Grand Rapids, MI, 1992), 9:3 (*dikaios*); *1Enoch* (Book of Parables), *passim* (*ṣādeq*), discussed in Orlov, *Enoch-Metatron Tradition*, pp. 77f.

18 J.C. Reeves, 'Some Explorations of the Intertwining of Bible and Qur'ān', in J.C. Reeves (ed.), *Bible and Qur'ān: Essays in Scriptural Intertextuality*, Atlanta 2003, pp. 43–60, at 47, with reference to *1Enoch*, 87:3; *Jubilees*, 4:23 (in Charlesworth, *Old Testament Pseudepigrapha*, ii, pp. 62f.).

to identification as any biblical prophet; on the contrary, one would in that case have expected some to dispute the identification on the grounds that the Qurʾānic description of Idrīs as 'of Abraham and Israel's seed' does not fit the antediluvian Enoch. But no early exegete makes this point; all apparently took the statement to mean no more than that Idrīs formed part of the line of biblical prophets and patriarchs from Adam to Jesus of which Abraham and Jacob/Israel were also members. They never reached any comparable agreement on the mysterious Dhū ʾl-Kifl, with whom Idrīs is mentioned in Q. 21:85,[19] and the early exegetical discussion of this verse is dominated by the problem of who he could be, not by Idrīs, whose identity with Enoch seems to be taken for granted. The commentators did not recognise Dhū ʾl-Kifl, but Idrīs they knew, presumably on the basis of the same tradition as the Qurʾān.

What then was this tradition? Our only clue is the name Idrīs under which Enoch was held to be known. The etymology of this name is an old problem. Albright thought that it was derived from Poimandrēs, the name of a Hermetic treatise and, according to Albright, also of Thoth/Hermes himself;[20] Gil, playing by philological rules all his own, derived Idrīs from the very name Hermes (Hīrmīs, Hirmis);[21] and Erder connected Idrīs with *dōresh ha-torah*, the 'expounder of the law' mentioned in the Qumran literature, noting that both the latter and Idrīs were identified with Hermes.[22] It is hard to take the first two suggestions seriously, and the third falls on the fact that *dōresh* could neither develop into Idrīs nor be translated as such. Casanova derived Idrīs from Esdras, the Greek form of Ezra, via scribal mistakes, but this does not fit the long vowel in Idrīs, nor did he explain why it was with Enoch rather than Ezra that the exegetes identified him.[23] Philologically speaking, by far the best suggestion was made back in 1903 by Nöldeke, who observed that Idrīs could easily be derived from the Syriac forms of Greek Andreas (*ʾndrys* and the like). But Nöldeke failed to explain why Andrew, one of the twelve apostles, should have been singled out

---

19 Cf. *EI*³, s.v. 'Dhū l-Kifl' (Rippin).

20 W.F. Albright, review of P. Boylan, *Thot, the Hermes of Egypt*, in *Journal of the Palestine Oriental Society* 2, 1922, pp. 197 f.; id., 'Islam and the Religions of the Ancient Orient', *Journal of the American Oriental Society* 60, 1940, pp. 283–301, p. 287n.

21 M. Gil, 'The Creed of Abū ʿĀmir', *Israel Oriental Studies* 12, 1982, pp. 9–57, at 35.

22 Y. Erder, 'The Origin of the Name Idrīs in the Qurʾān: a Study of the Influence of Qumran Literature on Early Islam', *Journal of Near Eastern Studies* 49, 1990, pp. 339–350; succinctly also in *EQ*, s.v. 'Idrīs' (Erder).

23 P. Casanova, 'Idrîs et ʿOuzaïr', *Journal Asiatique* 205, 1924, pp. 356–360. Thus also C.C. Torrey, *The Jewish Foundation of Islam*, New York 1933, p. 72; followed by Alexander, 'Jewish Tradition in Early Islam', p. 23.

for special attention as a prophet in the Qurʾān or why the exegetes should have understood this apostle as Enoch.[24] Hartmann improved on Nöldeke's suggestion by proposing that the relevant bearer of the name Andreas was not the apostle, but rather the cook who inadvertently acquires immortality in the Alexander Romance.[25] Here at last the name is associated with immortality, but Andreas the cook is a shifty character who uses his possession of the water of immortality to seduce Alexander's daughter and who is punished by transformation into a sea demon.[26] He could not have gone into the Qurʾān as a prophet and righteous Israelite, nor could he have blended with Enoch outside it. Hartmann's thesis is also open to improvement, however. The suggestion offered here is that a still unattested Aramaic name lies behind both Greek Andreas and Arabic Idrīs and that the name in question was that of Atraḫasīs, the ancient Mesopotamian king who survived the flood and acquired immortality. That Atraḫasīs is the ultimate source of the name Idrīs has in fact been suggested before, by the Aramaicist Montgomery, but he presented his case much too briefly and superficicially to carry conviction, or even to be mentioned thereafter.[27] In fact, since we do not know how 'Atraḫasīs' was rendered in Aramaic, there is no way of proving that it is in fact his name that lives on in that of Idrīs; but as this article will try to persuade the reader, it can at least be shown to be plausible.

Atraḫasīs

Atraḫasīs ('exceedingly wise') is the epithet of several ancient Mesopotamian mythological figures, including the Mesopotamian flood survivor.[28] He appears under that name in the Akkadian epic known as *Atraḫasīs*. Here we are told that humans were created to do all the hard labour of feeding, clothing and

24 Th. Nöldeke, 'Idrīs', *Zeitschrift für Assyriologie* 17, 1903, pp. 83f.

25 R. Hartmann, 'Zur Erklärung von Sūre 18, 59ff.', *Zeitschrift für Assyriologie* 24, pp. 307–315, at 314f. For the Alexander tradition in Arabic, see F. Doulfikar-Aerts, *Alexander Magnus Arabicus*, Leuven 2010.

26 Pseudo-Callisthenes, ed. C. Müller, Paris 1846, book II, chs. 39, 41; *The Greek Alexander Romance*, tr. R. Stoneman, London 1991.

27 J.A. Montgomery, 'Some Hebrew Etymologies', *Jewish Quarterly Review*, NS, 25, 1935, pp. 261–269, at 261. The only scholar to mention his idea seems to be A. Jeffery, *The Foreign Vocabulary of the Qurʾān*, Baroda 1938, p. 52.

28 *Reallexicon der Assyriologie*, ed. E. Ebeling, B. Meissner and others, Berlin and Leipzig 1931–2008, i, s.v. 'Atraḫasîs(a)' (Jensen).

housing the gods that the gods (or rather some of them) had formerly done themselves. This worked well except that humans grew so numerous that their noise became intolerable. Enlil, the chief of the gods, could not sleep. He tried to reduce their number with plagues and droughts, but eventually he and other gods decided to send a flood. On the advice of Enki, a somewhat mischievous deity, Atraḫasīs managed to escape by building a special boat, which also carried his family and animals of all kinds. In short, Atraḫasīs is here the Mesopotamian Noah, not Enoch.[29]

In the Sumerian deluge story the flood survivor is called Ziusudra (later Zisudra),[30] the name under which he also appears in one version of the Sumerian king list[31] and the *Babyloniaca* of Berossos (fl. c. 290 BC), the Babylonian priest who made his ancestral heritage available in Greek. Berossos' work is lost, but excerpts survive,[32] and Zi(u)sudra's name is here transliterated as Xisouthros,[33] Sisithros,[34] and perhaps also Sisythes.[35] Ziusudra differs from Noah in that the

29 W.G. Lambert and A.R. Millard (eds. and trs.), *Atra-ḫasîs, the Babylonian Story of the Flood*, Oxford 1969 (repr. Winona Lake, IN, 1999); also in B.R. Foster (tr.), *Before the Muses: an Anthology of Akkadian Literature*, 3rd ed., Bethesda, MD, 2005, pp. 229 ff.

30 M. Civil (ed. and tr.), 'The Sumerian Flood Story', lines 254–260, in Lambert and Millard, *Atra-ḫasîs*, p. 145; previously translated by S.N. Kramer in J.B. Pritchard (ed.), *Ancient Near Eastern Texts relating to the Old Testament*, Princeton, NJ, 1955, p. 44 (with a slightly different line numbering). For the forms of the name, see A.R. George (ed. and tr.), *The Babylonian Gilgamesh Epic*, Oxford 2003, i, p. 154n.

31 Cf. S. Langdon, 'The Chaldean Kings before the Flood', *Journal of the Royal Asiatic Society* 1923, pp. 251–259; T. Jacobsen (ed. and tr.), *The Sumerian King List*, Chicago 1939, p. 76, n. 34 (on WB 62); cf. also id., 'The Eridu Genesis', *Journal of Biblical Literature* 100, 1981, pp. 513–529, at 520 (on CT 46.5). Ziusudra was probably also mentioned in a portion of the California tablet (UCBC 9–1819), now too damaged to be read (J.J. Finkelstein, 'The Antediluvian Kings: a University of California Tablet', *Journal of Cuneiform Studies* 17, 1963, pp. 39–51).

32 They are collected in G.P. Verbrugghe and J.M. Wickersham, *Berossos and Manetho, Introduced and Translated*, Ann Arbor, MI, 2001, pp. 43 ff.

33 Verbrugghe and Wickersham, *Berossos and Manetho*, pp. 47–50. It is the form used by Apollodorus, Alexander Polyhistor and Abydenos as preserved in Eusebius' *Chronicle* (in Armenian), pp. 4–6 (also in Cyril of Alexandria, *Contre Julien*, ed. and tr. P. Burguière and P. Évieux, i, Paris 1985, book I, 6–8) and by Syncellus, *Ecloga Chronographica*, pp. 53–56.

34 This form appears in Eusebius' version of Abydenos in his *Praeparatio Evangelica*, book IX, 12, 2; but cf. above, note 33.

35 The *De Dea Syria* attributed to Lucian refers to a myth about the flood of Deukalion *ton Skythea*, 'Deukalion, the Scythian' (par. 12: Deukalion is the Greek Noah). This was emended to *ton Sisythea* by Buttmann in 1828, and the emendation has been so widely accepted that its conjectural status is often forgotten. Though 'the Scythian' is problem-

gods reward him for his role in the preservation of mankind by granting him eternal life. They do not do this by taking him up to heaven, but rather by sending down life and eternal breath 'like [that of] a god' to him and making him dwell in 'the land of the crossing, the land of Dilmun, the place where the sun rises'.[36] It is in some such mysterious place that Gilgamesh seeks him out in the Gilgamesh epic. Here the hero, who has been wandering far and wide in search of immortality, builds a boat on which he reaches the sea of death which only Shamash can traverse, but which he nonetheless succeeds in crossing. He reaches the immortalised human, who is here called Ūta-napishti (or Utnapishtim) the Faraway, except for two passages in which he appears as Atraḫasīs.[37] (Ūta-napishti is an Akkadian interpretation of Ziusudra meaning 'he [or I] found life'.)[38] Ūta-napishti, alias Atraḫasīs, imparts a mystery of the gods' to Gilgamesh, meaning knowledge normally beyond the reach of human beings, by telling him how he was divinely instructed to build the boat on which he preserved the seed of all living things and how the gods made him and his wife immortal and made them dwell 'far away, at the mouth of the rivers'. Again it is clear that to acquire immortality is to become like a god, but also that it did not amount to deification: Ūta-napishti remains a human being.[39] He tells Gilgamesh that if he too is to become immortal, he must start by staying awake for six days and seven nights, which naturally Gilgamesh fails to do. By way of consolation Ūta-napishti shares another 'mystery of the gods' with him, namely the existence of a plant that will rejuvenate him.[40] Gilgamesh dives into the deep and brings up the plant, but while he is bathing in a well a snake eats it and sloughs its skin. Gilgamesh must grow old and die like everyone else.[41]

---

atic, it is preserved in J.L. Lightfoot (ed. and tr.), *Lucian on the Syrian Goddess*, Oxford 2003, p. 252, with arguments against the emendation at pp. 342 f. It is worth nothing, however, that the form Sisythes makes sense to George, *Gilgamesh Epic*, i, p. 154n, as a reflection of the form Zisuddu. It would imply that Lucian (if he is indeed the author of the *Dea Syria*) was familiar with Ziusudra independently of Berossos.

36 Tr. Kramer in Pritchard, *Ancient Near Eastern Texts*, p. 44; cf. Civil, 'Sumerian Flood Story', in Lambert and Millard, *Atra-ḫasîs*, p. 145.

37 Gilgamesh epic (standard Babylonian version), tablet XI, lines 49, 197. My transliteration is George's.

38 Thus George, *Gilgamesh Epic*, i, p. 153.

39 Cf. Gilgamesh epic, tablet XI, lines 1–7, 204.

40 It is not clear whether the plant will confer eternal youth, and thus immortality, or rejuvenation repeatable on further ingestion, and thus immortality again, or just one rejuvenation. But the narrator probably did not have give thought to these distinctions.

41 Gilgamesh epic, tablet XI, lines 281 ff. For the snake eating the drug against old age in Greek myth, see W. Burkert, *The Orientalizing Revolution*, Cambridge, MA, 1992, p. 123.

In short, Atraḫasīs (aka Ziusudra, Ūta-napishti) is not just the Mesopotamian Noah, but also a figure who was granted immortality like Enoch. This is what could have enabled him to blend with Enoch. In fact, he may even have contributed to Enoch's genesis:[42] this is suggested above all by the fact that both Enoch and Noah are said to have 'walked with God' (Gen. 6:9), an expression which is not used of any other antediluvian figure.[43] More commonly, however, Enoch is seen as a reflection of another Mesopotamian figure, the antediluvian king Enmeduranki.[44] The Sumerian king list shares with Genesis the feature of narrating the early history of mankind as a succession of enormously long-lived worthies followed by a flood, and there are ten figures in some versions of the king list, as also in Genesis. In several versions of the king list the seventh is Enmeduranki, and in Genesis the seventh is Enoch. Of Enmeduranki we are told that he 'sat in the presence of Shamash and Adad', and that Shamash and Adad brought him into their assembly, seated him on a throne of gold and taught him the art of divination.[45] We also hear of a sage in Enmeduranki's time by the name of Utuabzu, 'who ascended to heaven' for initiation into heavenly secrets.[46] One way or the other, then, the seventh generation was associated with ascent to heaven. But the Sumerian king list and the biblical genealogies also differ in significant ways, and Enoch does not quite match his alleged Mesopotamian counterpart.[47] Enmeduranki's presence in heaven

42 For the view that he is lurking in the background, cf. J.J. Collins, *The Apocalyptic Imagination: an Introduction to Jewish Apocalyptic Literature*, 2nd ed., Grand Rapids, MI, 1998, p. 46.

43 Noted by H.S. Kvanvig, *Roots of Apocalyptic: the Mesopotamian Background of the Enoch Figure and of the Son of Man*, Neukirchen-Vluyn 1988, pp. 93, 230. For the view that Enoch could have been the flood hero in the hypothetical flood story in the J stratum, see E.G. Kraeling, 'The Earliest Hebrew Flood Story', *Journal of Biblical Literature* 66, 1947, pp. 279–293, at 291f.

44 Cf. J.C. VanderKam, *Enoch and the Growth of an Apocalyptic Tradition*, Washington, DC, 1984, pp. 33ff., with discussion of the earlier literature in ch. 1; Kvanvig, *Roots*, pp. 185ff., 230ff.; Orlov, *Enoch-Metatron Tradition*, ch. 1.

45 Untitled text dating, probably, from the time of Nebuchadnezzar I (c. 1126–1103 BC) edited and translated in W.G. Lambert, 'Enmeduranki and Related Matters', *Journal of Cuneiform Studies* 21, 1967, pp. 126–138, at 130, 132.

46 R. Borger, 'Die Beschwörungsserie Bīt Mēseri und die Himmelfahrt Henochs', *Journal of Near Eastern Studies* 33, 1974, pp. 183–196 (esp. 192f.).

47 For objections to the assumption of Mesopotamian influence, see C. Westermann, *Genesis*, Neukirchen-Vluyn 1971, pp. 474ff., 484ff. (countered in Kvanvig, *Roots*, pp. 224ff.); G.F. Hasel, 'The Genealogies of Gen 5 and 11 and Their Alleged Babylonian Background', *Andrews University Seminary Studies* 16, 1978, pp. 361–374; T.C. Hartman, 'Some Thoughts

was temporary and the same was probably true of Utuabzu's, whereas Enoch's translation to heaven was permanent. Of course we should not envisage the priests behind Genesis 5 as working directly with Mesopotamian writings, as opposed to using motifs and themes of Mesopotamian origin that they would put together as they saw fit,[48] but the motif of ascent to heaven for a visit is rather different from that of permanent translation, and it of Ūta-napishti/Atraḫasīs that we hear that the gods 'took' him.[49] As will be seen, there were Jewish readers of the Hellenistic period who took the Genesis passage on Enoch to refer to *both* temporary ascent à la Enmeduranki *and* permanent translation to a remote place on earth à la Atraḫasīs; but by their time there was a Jewish diaspora to the east of the Euphrates, and it was probably to this diaspora that they owed their views.

However we are to envisage the origin of the Enoch figure, it is with the formation of the Jewish diaspora in Mesopotamia that the development of interest to us begins. In the eighth century BC the northern tribes of Israel were deported to Assyria, and in the sixth century BC their southern counterparts followed them to Babylonia. Enoch and Atraḫasīs, two possibly related and certainly very similar figures, now came to coexist in Mesopotamia, and inevitably they interacted there. Initially it may only have been in the minds of the Jewish captives that they did so, for it was the Jews who had to find ways of harmonising their native tradition with the more prestigious culture of their imperial overlords, whereas their overlords could ignore Enoch. As will be seen, however, the interaction seems eventually to have affected the Mesopotamians themselves, and it certainly came to do so when they converted to Christianity, for now it was they who had to find ways of harmonising their own tradition with that of the Bible. In short, from the exilic period onwards the stage was set for Enoch and Atraḫasīs to merge.

Unfortunately we cannot follow the interaction between them directly. The last datable cuneiform tablet was written in 75 AD,[50] but by then the main

on the Sumerian Kinglist and Gen 5 and 11B', *Journal of Biblical Literature* 91, 1972, pp. 25–32; J.R. Davila, 'The Flood Hero as King and Priest', *Journal of Near Eastern Studies* 54, 1995, pp. 199–214.

48 Cf. George, *Gilgamesh Epic*, i, pp. 56 f. Davila, 'Flood Hero as King and Priest', p. 211, argues against direct adaptation of the Mesopotamian lists, but whether direct use has actually been advocated is not clear to me.

49 Gilgamesh epic, tablet XI, line 206. The verbal root in Akkadian is *leqû*, that of the Hebrew text *lāqah*, cf. K. Luke, 'The Patriarch Enoch', *Indian Theological Studies* 23, 1986, pp. 125–153, at 133.

50 M. Geller, 'The Last Wedge', *Zeitschrift für Assyriologie* 87, 1997, pp. 43–95, at 46.

literary language of Mesopotamia had been Aramaic for some five centuries, and the bulk of the Aramaic tradition is lost. Of the mythological literature of the pagan Aramaeans nothing survives except for occasional reflections in Greek, Jewish and Syriac works. (It undoubtedly left plenty of marks on Persian literature, but as ill luck would have it, the pre-Islamic Persian tradition is also largely lost.) These reflections do not tell us anything about Enoch or Atraḫasīs, but they do allow us to connect Atraḫasīs, Andreas the cook and al-Khiḍr. We also have Jewish sources, however, and we can observe the post-biblical transformation of Enoch in the Enoch literature, above all *1 Enoch* and *Jubilees*. Since the bulk of this literature originated on the Greek side of the Euphrates, it does not show us how Enoch and Atraḫasīs interacted in Mesopotamia, but it does allow us to see that Atraḫasīs exercised a magnetic pull on Enoch even in Palestine. One paragraph in Berossos' *Babyloniaca*, moreover, suggests that Enoch's pull on Atraḫasīs was no less significant in Mesopotamia. I shall deal with the material relating to Enoch first.

Enoch and Atraḫasīs

The texts that make up *1 (Ethiopic) Enoch* are attributed to Enoch and were composed in Aramaic at different times between the third or second century BC and the turn of the era, though they survive in full only in Ethiopic.[51] The texts are apocalypses, or in other words revelations about the past, present and future of the world, and like most apocalypses they envisage the future as a violent end to the world in which all sinners are horribly punished and the righteous rewarded. The story of the flood is repeatedly told and alluded to as a prototype of the final punishment ahead. The book expands on an enigmatic passage in Genesis 6:1–2 according to which sons of God mated with daughters of men and sired giants by them. The sons of God are understood as angels of the kind called 'watchers', and their giant offspring have such trouble satisfying their enormous appetites that they end up eating people, and even each other, and drinking their blood. God responds to these developments first by sending angels to bind the watchers and to induce the giants to destroy themselves in internecine wars, and next by unleashing the flood to cleanse the earth.[52]

51 It is used here in the translation of G.W.E. Nickelsburg and J.C. VanderKam, *1 Enoch*, Minneapolis 2004. They date its earliest part to the late *fourth* century BC, perhaps a mere slip (p. vii).

52 For the Mesopotamian antecedents of this, see S. Bhayro, 'Noah's Library: Sources for 1 Enoch 6–11', *Journal for the Study of the Pseudepigrapha* 15, 2006, pp. 163–177.

All this is told without reference to Enoch. The latter is introduced as a scribe whom God sends to the watchers with a decree ordering their punishment and whom the watchers send back again to God with a petition for forgiveness (which is rejected); and from this point onwards the texts are about Enoch and his visions.

Jubilees, on the other hand, is a work composed in Hebrew, perhaps around 125 BC,[53] and it too is extant only in Ethiopic. It is a retelling of Genesis and the beginning of Exodus presented as the full revelation received by Moses at Sinai, and it too covers both Enoch and the flood, if much more briefly than *1 Enoch*.

In these works Enoch is reshaped along the lines of Atraḫasīs in three main ways. First, he has come to be linked with the flood. He is not connected with it in Genesis, nor would one expect him to be, given that he represents the seventh rather than the tenth generation after Adam. (There is no attempt to link Enmeduranki with the flood on the Mesopotamian side.) In *1 Enoch*, however, Enoch is associated with the flood partly by participation in the story of the watchers who cause it to be unleashed and partly by repeatedly receiving advance warning of it. An angel tells him that God will open all the chambers of the waters above the heavens and all the fountains beneath the earth, and that all dwellers on the earth will be obliterated.[54] He sees in a vision that the earth will sink into the abyss and be utterly destroyed, and he reacts by imploring God together with his son Methuselah that a remnant of mankind might remain upon the earth.[55] In another passage he predicts 'the first end' (as opposed to the day of judgement), here fully aware of the fact that mankind will be saved.[56] There will be a flood and a great destruction, he predicts in yet another passage, and here he tells his son, who has been sent by his grandson to consult him about the infant Noah, that 'this child that was born to you will be left on the earth, and his three children will be saved along with him'.[57] There is also a passage in which it is Noah who sees that the destruction is near: he reacts by setting off to speak with his great-grandfather Enoch about it, and the latter explains all the secrets to him.[58] One way or the other, the immortalised human and the flood survivor are now closely linked.

---

53 For the date around 125 (as opposed to the vaguer c. 170–100 BC), see D. Mendels, *The Land of Israel as a Political Concept in Hasmonean Literature*, Tübingen 1987, pp. 57–88.

54 *1 Enoch* (Book of Parables), 54:7–9.

55 *1 Enoch* (Dream Visions), 83:3–9.

56 *1 Enoch* (Apocalypse of the Weeks), 93:4.

57 *1 Enoch* (The Birth of Noah), 106:15 f.

58 *1 Enoch* (Book of Parables), 65:1–68:1.

Secondly, Enoch has become a visionary. Again, there is no hint of this in Genesis, but it is now by revelation that he knows about the flood, and many other hidden things as well, including astronomy and other secrets of the cosmos. In some passages he is envisaged as receiving his supernatural knowledge during a visit to heaven in the style of Enmeduranki. 'The vision of heaven was shown to me, and from the words of watchers [i.e. the ones who stayed in heaven] and holy ones I have learned everything, and in the heavenly tablets I read everything', as he says before predicting the 'the first end'.[59] At other times he receives visions in his sleep. 'Dreams came upon me, and visions fell upon me', he explains with reference to an occasion on which a voice, apparently God's, commanded him to go and reprimand the wayward watchers.[60] He had two visions before he married, he informs us, one of the destruction of the earth and the other of the entire history of mankind from Adam to the day of judgement, and we are duly given an account of both.[61] Since his ascent to heaven is usually cast as a dream vision, the two modes of revelation are mostly identical.[62] In *Jubilees*, too, Enoch is a visionary who foresees the entire future of mankind down to the day of judgement in his sleep.[63] He is not a diviner like Enmeduranki. He does not interpret signs or read omens, but rather communicates directly with God and/or the angels or receives revelations in dreams, and this is a feature he shares with Atraḫasīs. Of the latter we are told that he 'would speak [with his god], and his god [would speak] with him';[64] and when Enki was under oath not to subvert Enlil's plans by speaking to Atraḫasīs, the mischievous deity would communicate with Atraḫasīs in dreams.[65] When Atraḫasīs asked Enki to explain the meaning of a dream he had received, Enki circumvented his vow by speaking to a reed wall with Atraḫasīs listening on the other side: this was how Atraḫasīs was warned of the flood.[66] 'I knew of the counsel of the great gods, I knew of their oath, though they would not reveal it to me. He repeated their word to the wall',

---

59 *1 Enoch* (Apocalypse of the Weeks), 93:2–4; also Book of Parables, 54:7–9.

60 *1 Enoch* (Book of Watchers), 13:8.

61 *1 Enoch* (Dream Visions), chs. 83–90.

62 *1 Enoch* (Book of Watchers), 13:8; 14:1, 8 ff.

63 *Jubilees*, 4:19 (in Charlesworth, *Old Testament Pseudepigrapha*, ii, p. 62).

64 *Atraḫasīs*, tablet I, lines 366 f., in Lambert and Millard, *Atra-ḫasîs*, p. 67; in Foster, *Before the Muses*, p. 239.

65 *Atraḫasīs*, tablet II, col. 3, lines 7–10, in Lambert and Millard, *Atra-ḫasîs*, p. 77; in Foster, *Before the Muses*, p. 243.

66 *Atraḫasīs*, tablet III, col. 1, lines 1 ff., in Lambert and Millard, *Atra-ḫasîs*, p. 89; in Foster, *Before the Muses*, p. 247.

as the Ugaritic version has Atraḫasīs declare.[67] The theme is present already in the Sumerian flood story.[68] In the Gilgamesh epic Enki (now known by his Akkadian name Ea) denies that it was he who told Atraḫasīs about the flood: 'I did not myself disclose the secret of the great gods; I let Atraḫasīs see a dream, and so he heard the gods' secret'.[69] Xisouthros is also warned of the flood in a dream in Berossos.[70]

Thirdly, the permanent abode to which God took Enoch is sometimes envisaged as a distant place on earth rather than heaven. As we have seen, the Bible was normally taken to say that Enoch was pleasing to God and that God took him up to heaven on a permanent basis. The Book of Parables, one of the youngest parts of *1 Enoch*, adheres to this solution, except that it has Enoch go on a temporary trip to heaven first. His first ascent was perhaps made in a dream, though the explanation that 'a whirlwind snatched me up from the face of the earth' suggests that he ascended physically.[71] In the second ascent he was raised 'on the chariots of the wind', which sounds much like the whirlwind, and though we are twice told that his spirit was taken away and ascended to heaven, he had his body with him too, for when he saw God and the angels in heaven, his flesh melted and his spirit was transformed, i.e. he became an angel; soon thereafter he is addressed as the Son of Man, apparently his heavenly double with whom he has now merged.[72] But things are less clear in the Book of Watchers, an older part of *1 Enoch*. Here the editorial comment with which Enoch is introduced says that he had been taken (by God) before the descent of the wayward watchers and that nobody knew where he was because he was with the (virtuous) watchers and holy ones, clearly in heaven. The biblical statement that Enoch 'walked with *hāʾelōhîm*' has been taken to mean that

---

67 RS 22.421 in Lambert and Millard, *Atra-ḫasîs*, p. 133; in Foster, *Before the Muses*, p. 255 (whose translation I have reproduced).

68 Civil, 'Sumerian Flood Story', lines 148–157, in Lambert and Millard, *Atra-ḫasîs*, p. 143; in Pritchard, *Ancient Near Eastern Texts*, p. 44; in Jacobsen, 'Eridu Genesis', pp. 522 f.

69 Gilgamesh epic, tablet XI, lines 196–197.

70 Berossos in Syncellus in Verbrugghe and Wickersham, *Berossos and Manetho*, p. 49; also tr. in Lambert and Millard, *Atra-ḫasîs*, pp. 135 f.

71 *1 Enoch* (Parables), 39:3; cf. 52:1.

72 *1 Enoch*, 70:2; 71:1, 5, 11, 14; cf. Orlov, *Enoch-Metatron Tradition*, pp. 167 f. and the literature cited there. One wonders if these passages were overlooked by P.S. Alexander, 'From Son of Adam to Second God: Transformations of the Biblical Enoch', in M.E. Stone and Th.A. Bergren (eds.), *Biblical Figures outside the Bible*, Harrisburg, PA, 1998, pp. 87–122, at 102 f.: according to him, the Slavonic Enoch (*2 Enoch*) marks a radical departure from the earlier Enoch literature when it unequivocally claims that Enoch ascended bodily to heaven.

he walked with the angels,[73] and the statement that 'he was no more, because God took him' is taken to explain how he had come to walk with them: God had moved him.[74] The fact that nobody knew where he was shows that he is envisaged as having ascended physically, not just in a dream, so one would assume God to have moved him to heaven on a permanent basis. But not long thereafter we see him ascend to heaven again, though we have not heard anything about his descent, and this time he ascends as an earthling who can only do so in a dream. Clearly, the editorial comment has been inserted without much attention to coherence. *Jubilees*, a later work, has tidied things up. Here too the biblical statement that Enoch 'walked with *hāʾelōhîm*' is taken to mean that he walked with angels, again for a long time, but not on a permanent basis: he did so for six jubilees of years. The statement that 'he was no more, because God took him' still refers to his permanent removal, but it is not to heaven that God removes him: rather, God places him in the garden of Eden, explicitly identified as a place on earth. There he still was, writing condemnation and judgement of the world.[75]

The idea that Enoch was removed to a remote place on earth is not limited to *Jubilees*. A text on the birth of Noah in *1Enoch* tells us that Noah's father, Lamekh, feared that Noah had been sired by an angel and did not believe his wife's protestations that the child was his own. For this reason Lamekh asked his father Methuselah to go and see Enoch about it, and Methuselah came to Enoch 'at the ends of the earth'.[76] The Book of Parables, the very part of *1Enoch* in which Enoch sees his flesh melt in heaven, likewise tells us in what is probably an older stratum that when Noah had a vision of the destruction of the earth and set off to speak with Enoch about it, it was at 'the ends of the earth' that he found him.[77] It also has Noah mention 'the garden where the chosen and righteous dwell, where my great-grandfather was taken up, the seventh from Adam'.[78] In the Genesis Apocryphon from Qumran, Methuselah goes off to find Enoch in 'Parwain',[79] an exotic, far-off country from which the gold of the temple came.[80] In the Book of Giants, of which fragments were found at

73 Cf. VanderKam, *Man for All Generations*, p. 32.

74 Cf. VanderKam, *Man for All Generations*, p. 43.

75 *Jubilees*, 4:21ff. (in Charlesworth, *Old Testament Pseudepigrapha*, ii, p. 62f.).

76 *1Enoch*, 106:8.

77 *1Enoch*, 65:1.

78 *1Enoch*, 60:8.

79 1Q20 Genesis Apocryphon, II, line 23, in G. Vermes (tr.), *The Complete Dead Sea Scrolls in English*, 4th ed., Harmondsworth 1997, p. 450.

80 2Chr. 3:6 (Parwaim); Kvanvig, *Roots*, p. 89.

Qumran, the giants send one of their own, Mahaway, to Enoch so that he can interpret a dream for them, and Mahaway finds Enoch past the wastelands, on the other side of a great desert,[81] apparently meaning in the garden of Eden.[82] According to *Jubilees*, the garden of Eden was one of the four places of the Lord on earth, and it was because of Enoch that Eden was spared inundation during the flood. Here Enoch is as close as he can get to being the flood survivor, keeping dry in Eden rather than in the ark. It is presumably on the basis of *Jubilees*, which was available in Syriac and left some marks on Islamic literature too, that al-Ḥasan al-Baṣrī envisaged Idrīs as being in the garden (*al-janna*), i.e. paradise, when God raised his rank, though whether he located the garden in heaven or on earth one cannot tell.[83]

In short, Enoch became more like Atraḫasīs. As Kvanvig observes, Noah did too: he also figures as a visionary who foresees the flood in *1Enoch*, and sometimes it is hard to tell whether it is Enoch or Noah that the book is speaking about.[84] The flood survivor and the immortalised human are flowing together, exactly as one would expect. That Mesopotamian rather than Greek culture was the engine behind these developments is nicely illustrated by the fact that although the man-eating, blood-sucking giants undoubtedly typify the Hellenistic rulers under whose control the Jews had fallen, it is the Mesopotamian Gilgamesh, not the Greek Hercules, who figures among them in the fragments of the Aramaic Book of Giants (omitted from *1Enoch*). It was presumably the Jews of Babylonia who first depicted Gilgamesh in this negative light, with reference to the rulers they had to bear with there.[85]

---

81 QG5, 5f., with identification of the speaker in QG4A, 21–23, in J.C. Reeves, *Jewish Lore in Manichaean Cosmogony*, Cincinnati 1992, pp. 63f.; corresponding to 4Q530, col. 2, 21–23; col. 3, 5f., in L.T. Stuckenbruck, *The Book of Giants from Qumran: Texts, Translation, and Commentary*, Tübingen 1997, pp. 126, 130.

82 Cf. the material in Reeves, *Jewish Lore*, p. 104.

83 For echoes of *Jubilees* in Qudāma b. Jaʿfar and in the Persian tradition, see A. Silverstein, 'From Atraḫasīs to Afrīdūn: on the Transmission of an Ancient Near Eastern Motif to Islamic Iran', *Jerusalem Studies in Arabic and Islam* 39, 2012, pp. 1–14, at 5, 8ff.

84 Cf. *1Enoch* 60:23, where the speaker refers to an event in the life of Enoch, implying that the speaker is somebody other than Enoch (presumably Noah). Nickelsburg and VanderKam, however, emend Enoch to Noah, thus retaining Enoch as the speaker.

85 For the polemical nature of the appearance of Gilgamesh and other figures from the Gilgamesh epic in the Book of Giants, see Reeves, *Jewish Lore*, p. 126. According to D.R. Jackson, 'Demonising Gilgameš', in J. Azize and N. Weeks (eds.), *Gilgameš and the World of Assyria*, Leuven 2007, pp. 107–114, at 113, the author(s) chose Gilgamesh rather than a Greek figure in order to hide his significance from their opponents, while M. Goff, 'Gilgameš the Giant: the Qumran Book of Giants' Appropriation of Gilgameš Motifs', *Dead Sea Discover-*

A passage from the lost work of Berossos suggests that by the third century BC the interaction between Jewish and Babylonian models had affected not only the Jewish understanding of Enoch, but also the Babylonian understanding of Atraḫasīs. The passage concerns the grant of immortality to the flood survivor, which Berossos narrates in wording quite different from that of the two earlier works known to us, the Sumerian deluge story and the Gilgamesh epic. According to the Sumerian account, when the flood was over, Ziusudra sacrificed and prostrated himself to An and Enlil, who responded favourably: 'Life like [that of] a god they give him, breath eternal like [that of] a god they bring down for him. Then Ziusudra, the king, the preserver of the name of vegetation [and] of the seed of mankind, in the land of crossing, the land of Dilmun, the place where the sun rises, they caused to dwell'.[86] In the Gilgamesh epic Ūta-napishti sacrifices while still in the boat; we then hear of a dispute between the gods about Ea's role in Ūta-napishti's survival and the questionable merits of Enlil's use of so drastic a remedy as the flood; Enlil then enters the boat and touches the foreheads of Ūta-napishti and his wife, who are kneeling before him, and declares that 'In the past Ūta-napishti was (one of) mankind, but now he and his wife shall be like us gods! Ūta-napishti shall dwell far away, at the mouth of the rivers'. Ūta-napishti reports, 'They took me and settled me far away, at the mouth of the rivers'.[87] Berossos' account is initially similar. Xisouthros disembarks together with his wife and daughter, prostrates himself and sacrifices to the gods. But the continuation says that 'after this he disappeared together with those who had left the ship with him. Those who remained on the ship and had not gone out with Xisouthros ... searched for him and called out for him by name all about. But Xisouthros from then on was seen no more, and then the sound of a voice that came from the air gave the instruction that ... Xisouthros, because of the great honour he had shown the gods, had gone to the dwelling place of the gods'.[88]

There are several noteworthy changes in Berossos' account. First, the gods who are present in person in the two earlier Mesopotamian accounts are here

---

ies 16, 2009, pp. 221–253, sees more 'creative appropriation' than polemics here; and I. Fröhlig, 'Enmeduranki and Gilgamesh: Mesopotamian Figures in Aramaic Enoch Traditions', in E.F. Mason and others (eds.), *A Teacher for All Generations: Essays in Honor of James C. VanderKam*, Leiden 2012, ii, pp. 637–653, at 652 f., denies that Gilgamesh is envisaged as a giant.

86 Sumerian flood story, final lines, in Pritchard, *Ancient Near Eastern Texts*, p. 44; slightly differently (and less powerfully) in Lambert and Millard, *Atra-ḫasîs*, p. 145; Jacobsen, 'Eridu Genesis', p. 525.

87 Gilgamesh epic, tablet XI, lines 157 ff., 199–206.

88 Syncellus in Verbrugghe and Wickersham, *Berossos and Manetho*, p. 50.

replaced by a disembodied voice: the concept of the divine had drastically changed.[89] Secondly, it is not clear that the immortalised Atraḫasīs is being moved to a remote place on earth: he goes to the dwelling of the gods, probably meaning heaven rather than Dilmun.[90] Finally, Berossos tells the story of Xisouthros' reward from the point of view of those left behind: those on the boat could not find him, 'Xisouthros from then on was seen no more'. The wording here is strikingly similar to the biblical 'he was no more' and *1 Enoch*'s more expansive 'none of the sons of men knew where he had been taken or what had happened to him'.[91] This has been noticed before,[92] but the assumption has been that Berossos may show us the source of the biblical formulation, though he wrote around 290 BC. It is possible, of course, that Berossos here preserves an ancient Akkadian formulation that passed into Genesis even though it happens not to have come down to us. It could even be argued that Berossos is giving us the missing Mesopotamian source for Enoch's permanent translation to heaven, assuming his 'dwelling place of the gods' to be ancient too. But given that Berossos freely departs from the tradition to accommodate a new concept of the divine, it seems more likely that the other unprecedented elements are also new, or in other words that they reflect exposure to Enoch. Berossos would not, of course, have read the Bible or any other Jewish writings, but Jews would have retold the story of Enoch along lines that fused Enoch and Atraḫasīs, and these versions could easily have passed to Babylonian priests and scribes, especially in the Persian and Hellenistic periods, when the Babylonians lost their hegemonic status and the position of the Jews improved.

---

89 Differently E.G. Kraeling, 'Xisouthros, Deucalion and the Flood Traditions', *Journal of the American Oriental Society* 67, 1947, pp. 177–183, at 178, 179, according to whom Berossos is covering up the polytheism of the original narrative out of consideration for enlightened Greek taste. Why the polytheist Greeks should be more enlightened than the polytheist Babylonians, or indeed why polytheism should be unenlightened, is not explained.

90 Luke, 'The Patriarch Enoch', pp. 132, 135, takes Dilmun to be the abode of the gods in the Gilgamesh epic with reference to Gilgamesh's question to Ūta-napishti: '(Tell me) how you joined the assembly of all the gods in your quest for life' (Gilgamesh epic, tablet XI, line 7; cf. the translation by Speiser in Pritchard, *Ancient Near Eastern Texts*, p. 93). But George translates, 'How was it you attended the gods' assembly, and found life?', which suggests a temporary meeting with the gods (presumably when he came out of the boat), not permanent residence in their midst. There is no suggestion in the Gilgamesh epic that Ūta-napishti was surrounded by gods.

91 *1 Enoch*, 12:1.

92 C. Westermann, *Genesis 1–11, a Continental Commentary*, Minneapolis 1994 (German original 1974); Kvanvig, *Roots*, pp. 226, 228.

In short, in the Hellenistic period there were Jews who cast Enoch as a figure connected with the flood, a visionary who received communications from the divine, and a recipient of immortality who was removed to a remote place on earth. All three features assimilated Enoch to Atraḫasīs. Conversely, there were Babylonians who thought of Atraḫasīs as a figure who had disappeared, apparently by being taken to heaven, when he was granted immortality, a feature which assimilated him to Enoch (or alternatively reveals him as one of the sources of this figure). Either way, Enoch and Atraḫasīs were now difficult to tell apart. The learned will hardly have gone so far as to identify them, but it is no wonder if Atraḫasīs came to be regarded as simply another name for Enoch at a popular level in Babylonia.

The Name

At this point the reader may be ready with two objections. First, how could the Mesopotamian flood hero have blended with Enoch under the name of Atraḫasīs rather than Ziusudra or Ūta-napishti when, with the exception of two passages in the Gilgamesh epic, it is only under the name of Ziusudra (and variants) or Ūta-napishti that the flood hero is associated with immortality in the Akkadian literature known to date? The most obvious response is that although the immortality theme is absent from the Atraḫasīs epic as it has come down to us, it must in fact have been present there too. We do not have a complete version. There is a lacuna of 34 lines at the end of tablet III, containing the final part of the epic. Here Enlil, after first being enraged by Atraḫasīs' survival, institutes new measures of population control that will not wipe out mankind, and this is where one would expect to hear that he also granted immortality to Atraḫasīs and his wife and moved them to a distant place. 'The apotheosis of the flood hero could have been contained in the damaged ending of *Atra-ḫasīs*', as Lambert and Millard remark.[93] That this was actually the case is further suggested by the fact that the flood survivor is granted immortality both in the earlier Sumerian flood story and in the later Akkadian Gilgamesh epic: how could these themes have been absent from the Atraḫasīs epic in between? It is a version of this very epic that is being retold in the Gilgamesh epic.[94] In short, the flood hero was probably granted immortality under all three names under which he appears in the tradition. This does not, of course,

93 Lambert and Millard, *Atra-ḫasīs*, p. 137.

94 Lambert and Millard, *Atra-ḫasīs*, p. 11.

explain why the name Atraḫasīs was preferred over the other two. The reason could be that it stressed the great wisdom of the hero. But at all events, there is nothing particularly problematic about the use of this rather than the other two names.

It has been suggested that Enoch also came to be known as Ūta-napishti in circles which surface in Manichaeism. Mani's Book of Giants mentioned a figure called At(a)nabīsh (*'tnbysh*), a name which Reeves tentatively explained as derived from Ūta-napishti. In Reeves' view the book downgraded Ūta-napishti and other figures from the Gilgamesh epic to the status of iniquitous giants.[95] Huggins provisionally accepts the derivation of At(a)nabīsh from Ūta-napishti, but he denies the downgrading. He sees a parallel between a passage in the Qumran Book of Giants and a line in Mani's Book of Giants (both known only from fragments) which would identify At(a)nabīsh as Enoch.[96] If so, Enoch appears both under his own name and as At(a)nabīsh in the Manichaean book. *Pace* Stuckenbruck, this is hardly a problem, given that Ūta-napishti himself appears both under his own name and that of Atraḫasīs in the Gilgamesh epic;[97] but there simply is not enough information in the fragment to clinch the reality of the parallel, and both the form of his name and another two fragments suggest that At(a)nabīsh was indeed a giant.[98]

95 J.C. Reeves, 'Utnapishtim in the Book of Giants?', *Journal of Biblical Literature* 112, 1993, pp. 110–115; id., *Jewish Lore*, pp. 126, 159, n. 373 (using the form Atambīsh).

96 R.V. Huggins, 'Noah and the Giants: a Response to John C. Reeves', *Journal of Biblical Literature* 114, 1995, pp. 103–110. In the Qumran Book of Giants the giant Mahaway is sent to ask Enoch for the interpretation of a dream. In the Manichaean Book of Giants 'Māhawai went to Atambīsh (and) related everything' (Reeves, 'Utnapishtim in the Book of Giants?', p. 114).

97 Cf. Stuckenbruck, *Book of Giants*, p. 73n; id., 'Giant Mythology and Demonology: from the Ancient Near East to the Dead Sea Scrolls', in A. Lange, H. Lichtenberger and K.F.D. Römheld (eds.), *Die Dämonen: die Dämonologie der israelitisch-jüdischen und frühchristlichen Literatur im Kontext ihrer Umwelt*, Tübingen 2003, pp. 318–338, at 334.

98 Similarly Stuckenbruck, *Book of Giants*, p. 73n; id., 'Giant Mythology', pp. 333ff. There are two figures presumed to come from the Gilgamesh epic in the Qumran Book of Giants, Gilgames(h) and Ḥobabis(h), both written now with a *šin* and now with a *samek*; there are also two in the fragments of the Manichaean book, Ḥobabīsh (thus written in Manichaean Middle Persian) and At(a)nabīsh. The name Ḥobabis(h) is generally held to be derived from Ḫumbaba, the monstrous guardian of the cedar forest, and the *-ish* ending, which has generated much learned speculation, was presumably just stuck on to make the names rhyme (for more learned explanations, see Stuckenbruck, 'Giant Mythology', pp. 327f.). The fact that At(a)nabīsh fits the rhyming pattern strengthens the case for his identification as Ūta-napishti, and also for his status as a giant rather than as Enoch.

The second objection perhaps present in the reader's mind is philological. In order for Atraḫasīs to turn into Idrīs the velar fricative *ḫ* would have to disappear, but how could it? Needless to say, we lack the material with which to follow a gradual transformation of the name, but the development postulated does at least have to be plausible, and *ḫ* (or *kh* in the common Islamicist transliteration) is not a sound that is easily elided. Nonetheless, its disappearance is not a problem. Aramaic did once distinguish between the pharyngeal *ḥ* and the velar fricative *ḫ*, though it used the same letter to express them in writing; but by about 200 BC the velar fricative *ḫ* had turned into the pharyngeal *ḥ*.[99] In the subsequent development the pharyngeal *ḥ* was weakened in several Aramaic dialects (as also the *ʿayn*), and it completely disappeared in Babylonian Aramaic as known from the Talmud and Mandaic: *ḥ* was reduced to *h* or eliminated.[100] Transmission through Pahlavi also reduced *ḥ* to *h*.[101] In Babylonian Aramaic and Pahlavi, then, Atraḫasīs would have become something like Atra(ha)sīs. Transformation of the *t* into *d* and contraction would have done the rest. A form such as *Addarasīs, easily shortened to Idrīs, could have turned into *Andarasīs by dissimilation of gemination in Pahlavi (well attested in connection with other Aramaic words) and thus yield the Andreas of the Alexander Romance.[102] Perhaps even an ungeminated form such as Adrasīs could yield Idrīs and Andreas alike. If not, we evidently need to explain how *Addarasīs got to be geminated in the first place, but though I do not have an answer, it is hardly an insuperable problem.

---

99 E. Lipinski, *Semitic Languages: Outline of a Comparative Grammar*, Leuven 1997, p. 146; K. Beyer, *Die aramäischen Texte vom Toten Meer*, Göttingen 1984, i, p. 102 (my thanks to Kevin van Bladel for drawing the second work to my attention).

100 S. Weninger and others (eds.), *The Semitic Languages*, Berlin and Boston 2011, pp. 612, 624 f., 633 f. (Jewish Palestinian, Samaritan and Christian Palestinian Aramaic), 662 (Jewish Babylonian Aramaic), 674 (Mandaic); M. Morgenstern, *Studies in Jewish Babylonian Aramaic*, Winona Lake, IN, 2011, pp. 73 ff. (Jewish Babylonian Aramaic).

101 In fact the development seems usually to be explained with reference to the influence of Iranian languages in the east, of Greek in the west. The mystery is how Syriac escaped.

102 For such dissimilation, compare the transformation of Syriac *guddā* into Middle Persian *gond*, *shabbta* into *shamba*, and Manichaean Aramaic *zaddīq* into Middle Persian *zindīk* (all adduced by F. de Blois in *EI*^{2}, s.v. 'Zindīḳ').

The Reflections of Gilgamesh's Search for Immortality

We may now turn to the reflections of pagan Aramaic mythology in the literature of the neighbours that take us to al-Khiḍr. All are reflections of Gilgamesh, an enormously popular figure who lived on under both his own name and those of others; indeed, thanks to the conservatism of magic his name appears in an amazingly faithful form even in a work attributed to al-Suyūṭī (d. 911/1505), who reproduces an incantation of Solomon that includes Gilgamesh (Jiljamīsh) among the spiritual beings. As Reeves observes, this reflects the use of Gilgamesh's name in incantations, a practice well attested in Akkadian times.[103] Outside the domain of magic Gilgamesh may appear twice in a list of ancient kings in Theodore Bar Koni (fl. late 8th century AD), but no information is offered about these figures.[104] The last author to mention him by his own name (Gilgamos) with some information about him is the Greek Aelian (d. c. 235), but most of what he says about him was originally told about others.[105]

103 Reeves, *Jewish Lore*, pp. 120 f. and 159, n. 370; cf. George, *Gilgamesh Epic*, i, pp. 112 ff., 130 ff.; T. Abusch, 'Ishtar's Proposal and Gilgamesh's Refusal: an Interpretation of "the Gilgamesh Epic", Tablet 6, Lines 1–79', *History of Religions* 26, 1986, pp. 143–187, at 150 f. and the literature cited there; M. Schwartz, 'Qumran, Turfan, Arabic Magic, and Noah's Name', in R. Gyselen (ed.), *Charmes et sortilèges, magie et magiciens*, Bures-sur-Yvette 2002, pp. 231–238.

104 Theodore Bar Koni, *Livre des scolies (recension de Séert)*, ed. A. Scher, *Liber Scholiorum* (CSCO 55, 69/Syr. 19, 26), Paris 1910, 1912; tr. R. Hespel and R. Draguet (CSCO 431–432/Syr. 187–188), Louvain 1981–1982, *mimrā* II, par. 120 (Gamigos and Ganmagos).

105 Aelian, *De natura animalium*, XII, 21. Gilgamos, son of the daughter of the king of Babylon, was hurled from a tower by the king who had been warned that the son of his daughter would oust him; saved by an eagle, he was brought up by a gardener and eventually became king of Babylon. Not much of this fits Gilgamesh (cf. George, *Gilgamesh Epic*, i, pp. 61, 106 ff.). For the gardener, compare Sargon of Akkad (3rd millennium BC), whose father or foster-father is said to have been a gardener, cf. B. Lewis, *The Sargon Legend*, Cambridge, MA, 1980; S. Dalley and A.T. Reyes, 'Mesopotamian Contact and Influence in the Greek World: 2. Persia, Alexander, and Rome', in S. Dalley (ed.), *The Legacy of Mesopotamia*, Oxford 1998, pp. 107–124, at 119. By Aelian's time the motifs had also been transferred to the Achaemenids: Achaemenes was supposedly nursed by an eagle, as Aelian himself mentions, while Cyrus was supposedly brought up by a Median cowherd for the same reason that Gilgamesh was brought up by a gardener, cf. Herodotus, *Histories*, I, 107 ff. Cf. also W.F.M. Henkelman, 'Beware of Dim Cooks and Cunning Snakes: Gilgameš, Alexander, and the Loss of Immortality', in R. Rollinger and others (eds.), *Interkulturalität in der alten Welt*, Wiesbaden 2010, pp. 323–358, at 323 f. (my thanks to Tommaso Tesei for drawing this splendid study to my attention); id., 'The Birth of Gilgameš (Ael. NA XII.21):

In the material reflecting Gilgamesh's search for immortality, by contrast, it is the names of other people that have been affixed to a story originally told about him. The earliest reflection is in a narrative found in some recensions of the Greek Alexander Romance.[106] The role of Gilgamesh is here played by Alexander the Great.[107] Alexander goes off with his troops to the land of perpetual darkness with the intention of reaching the Land of the Blessed. Unlike Gilgamesh he does not find an immortal human resident on the other side: there is no Atraḫasīs/Ūta-napishti in this version. (A wise old man does appear, but he is an ordinary human being and a member of Alexander's own camp.) On the way, however, Alexander and his troops come to a spring with twinkling water, and when Alexander's cook Andreas (whose name is not given in β) goes to wash a dried fish in it, the fish comes alive and swims away.[108]

The cook does not tell anyone about this, but drinks of the water himself and fills a silver vessel with it, which he later gives to Alexander's daughter in order to seduce her. Alexander, who reaches the Land of the Blessed without being able to enter it, only hears the story of the fish on his way back and never gets to drink of the life-giving water. He reacts by angrily turning Andreas into a *daimōn* of the sea, while his own daughter becomes a *daimōn* of the desert.[109]

---

a Case Study in Literary Receptivity', in R. Rollinger and B. Truschnegg (eds.), *Altertum und Mittelmeersraum: die antike Welt diesseis und jenseits der Levante. Festschrift für Peter W. Haider*, Stuttgart 2006, pp. 807–856.

106 For the recensions in question (β, the expanded version of β contained in a Leiden manuscript L, and the versions of β known as λ), see Henkelman, 'Dim Cooks', pp. 325–328.

107 This is denied by R. Stoneman, 'Oriental Motifs in the Alexander Romance', *Antichthon* 25, 1992, pp. 95–113, at 99, to whom the similarity between the Gilgamesh epic and the Alexander Romance is slight and superficial. His views are ably countered by Henkelman, 'Dim Cooks', pp. 342f.

108 The cook is nameless in the regular manuscripts of β. The name Andreas first appears in L (the Leiden MS containing an expanded version of β) at II, 41 in a passage explaining the name of the Adriatic as derived from his, and also once in the margin (II, 39); two later versions have the name in the text in both passages, cf. Henkelman, 'Dim Cooks', n. 68. The folk etymology of the name of the Adriatic is presumably based on knowledge that the cook who became a sea demon was called Andreas in some circles. The narrator can hardly have invented Andreas' name to explain that of the Adriatic, which is incidental to the story.

109 Pseudo-Callisthenes, book II, 39ff.; tr. Stoneman, *Greek Alexander Romance*, pp. 119–122, cf. 8ff., 28f., for the dates; cf. T. Tesei, 'Survival and Christianization of the Gilgamesh Quest for Immortality in the Tale of Alexander and the Fountain of Life', *Rivista degli Studi Orientali*, NS, 83, 2011, pp. 417–440.

Andreas the cook is playing the role of the snake in the Gilgamesh epic: it is he who robs Alexander of his immortality (the dried fish is just a passive beneficiary of the cook's action). The substitution of a human being for the snake, as also the transformation of this human into a maritime *daimōn*, reflects the presence in the narrator's mind of a Greek mythological figure, Glaukos, who achieved immortality as a sea god or sea monster after eating grass brought up from the sea.[110] The intrusion of this figure meant that there came to be a second immortalised human in the story originally told of Gilgamesh and Ūta-napishti (Alexander's daughter, in principle the third, is treated in too perfunctory a manner to count), but the story is only designed to have one, and this may be why Atraḫasīs/Ūta-napishti has disappeared from the version in the Alexander Romance. The immortal human who remained in the story, however, seems to have inherited Atraḫasīs' name, in an Aramaic version that sounded somewhat like Andreas to a Greek ear.

The story of the cook who washes the fish in the spring of life is not found in the Syriac version of the Alexander Romance, but it appears in the Syriac Alexander Poem (or Song, or metrical Homily) which is attributed to Jacob of Sarug (d. 521) but was actually composed between 628 and 636.[111] In this work Alexander does meet a wise old man after traversing the land of darkness. Alexander tells him he has come to find the spring of life, and the wise old man advises him to let his cook test the diverse springs in the area by washing a salted fish in them; if the fish comes alive, he has found it. When the cook comes to the spring of life, the fish swims away and the cook jumps into the water to catch it, without success. He then tells Alexander about it, but Alexander does not succeed in bathing in the spring, apparently because he cannot find it in the darkness. The wise old man consoles him, and thereafter the story shifts to questions asked by Alexander and the wise man's answers. The momentous fact that the cook has become immortal by jumping into the water is left unmentioned. The focus is on the old man and the wisdom he imparts to

110 *Pauly's Real-Encyclopädie der classischen Altertumswissenschaft*, ed. G. Wissova, Stuttgart 1894–1963, vii/1, s.v. 'Glaukos' (no. 8).

111 Thus G.J. Reinink's introduction to his translation of the work, *Das syrische Alexanderlied: die drei Rezensionen*, Louvain 1983, p. 12; also tr. E.A.W. Budge, *The History of Alexander the Great*, Cambridge 1889, repr. 2003, pp. 163–200, at 172 ff. (lines 170 ff.). Cf. also Henkelman, 'Dim Cooks', pp. 328 f.; and the further references in Tesei, 'Survival and Christianization', p. 419n. The otherwise interesting study by S. Dalley, 'Gilgamesh in the Arabian Nights', *Journal of the Royal Asiatic Society*, 3rd series, 1, 1991, pp. 1–17, at 9, summarises this story in a mongrel form in which al-Khiḍr is Alexander's servant, supposedly on the basis of the version in Budge, *History*, p. 168.

Alexander with his answers. That the old man himself is immortal is also left unmentioned, and neither he nor the cook is given a name.

The fish episode also went into the Babylonian Talmud, where Alexander once more travels through the land of darkness, but here both the cook and the wise old man have disappeared. It is Alexander himself who washes the fish that comes alive, and we are told that according to some he responded by washing his face in the water: the significance of this is left unspecified. Others said that Alexander responded by tracing the water to its source at the entrance to the garden of Eden, where he clamoured to be let in on the grounds that he was a king, unsuccessfully of course.[112] Here the garden of Eden to which Enoch was moved reappears as the Jewish version of the Land of the Blessed.[113]

There is also a reflection of Gilgamesh's search for immortality in an obscure account of the origins of Zoroastrianism in the Syriac *Cave of Treasures*. Here we are told that Nimrod was the first to worship fire and that he went to Yoqdora in Nod, where he found Yonṭon (or Maniton), son of Noah, by the sea of Aṭras (or Ukaras or the like). Nimrod bathed in that sea and then went and prostrated before Yonṭon, saying he had come for his sake. Yonṭon taught Nimrod wisdom and the writing of the revelations (or just the revelations) and told him not to come any more; and when Nimrod came up from the east, he astounded people with his wisdom.[114] The identification of Nimrod as the first to worship fire and/or as Zoroaster is a late antique commonplace, but the rest is distinctly unusual. Nimrod is playing the role of Gilgamesh while Yonṭon plays Atraḫasīs/Ūta-napishti. The latter lives in the land of Nod, located to the east of Eden according to Genesis 4:16, and it is duly

112 *Babylonian Talmud*, Tamid 32b. The spring of life also originates in paradise in 'Umāra's Alexander story in I. Friedlaender, I. Friedlaender, *Die Chadirlegende und der Alexanderroman*, Berlin 1913, pp. 135, 309.20.

113 For other features shared by *1 Enoch* and the Gilgamesh epic, see Tesei, 'Survival and Christianization', p. 425 and the literature cited there.

114 The passage is translated S.M. Ri, *Commentaire de la Caverne des Trésors*, Louvain 2000, pp. 341f., on the basis of ch. 27.6–12 of his edition and translation of the text (*La Caverne des Trésors*, Louvain 1987). For further comments on the passage, including variants, see his *Commentaire*, esp. pp. 79–81, 319 ff., 327 ff.; 355. The variant versions of the names in the Syriac manuscripts are listed at p. 341n. The passage is also cited with a partial translation in M. Lidzbarski, 'Wer ist Chadhir?', *Zeitschrift für Assyriologie* 7, 1892, p. 115; and with a full translation by R.H. Gottheil, 'References to Zoroaster in Syriac and Arabic Literature', *Classical Studies in Honour of Henry Drisler*, New York and London 1894, pp. 25f., with reference to C. Bezold (ed. and tr.), *Die Schatzhöhle*, Leipzig 1833, 1888, p. 230 = 136f.

from the east that Nimrod returns.[115] As the cook jumps into the water in the Alexander poem and Alexander washes his face in the life-giving water in the Talmud, so Nimrod bathes in the Sea of Aṭras, but in all three cases the significance of the act is left unidentified; and although Nimrod worships Yonṭon, we are given to understand that this was for his wisdom, not for his immortality (or quasi-divinity), which is not mentioned. There is no sign of the ancient names either, unless we take Aṭras to be another version of the name Atraḫasīs.

Finally, the fish episode appears in the Qurʾān (18:60–64). Here the role of Gilgamesh is played by Moses, who vows not to give up until he reaches the confluence of the two seas. When he and his servant (*fatā*, lit. young man) get there, they 'forget' the fish, which swims away. Later Moses is hungry and asks his servant for food; the servant, who is clearly his cook, replies that he (not they) forgot the fish, thanks to Satan, and that the fish has swum away. Moses realises that this water is what they are seeking and they retrace their steps, with what degree of success we are not told. Instead, the text shifts to an account of an enigmatic superior being, identified only as a servant (*ʿabd*, lit. slave) of God, who imparts wisdom to the hero. The nature of the wisdom relates to theodicy: the anonymous servant of God justifies God's seemingly unjust ways by engaging in seemingly evil acts. This is quite different from the wisdom imparted by the old man to the hero in the Alexander Poem,[116] to which

115 For a different explanation of Nod, see Ri, *Commentaire*, p. 322; but cf. also 350f. Ri does not seem to be aware of the longer roots of this passage in the Gilgamesh epic, and this the main reason why his understanding of Nod and other aspects of the passage differs from mine.

116 It is a version of the folktale motif 'God's justice vindicated' (type 759 in the Aarne-Thompson motif index), and many hold the Qurʾānic story to be based on a midrash concerning Rabbi Joshua b. Levi and Elijah. This theory was apparently first proposed by Zunz, but it was endorsed by Geiger and so came to be accepted by luminaries such as Friedlaender and Wensinck among many others. As Jellinek and others pointed out long ago, however, and as Wheeler has stressed again more recently, the rabbinic story is not attested until the eleventh century; it was originally written in Arabic, and it is more likely to be dependent on the Qurʾān than the other way round (cf. H. Schwarzbaum, 'Some Theodicy Legends', in his *Jewish Folklore between East and West*, ed. E. Yassif, Beersheva 1989, pp. 75–125; B.M. Wheeler, 'The Jewish Origins of Qurʾān 18:65–82? Re-examining Arent Jan Wensinck's Theory', *Journal of the American Oriental Society* 118, 1998, pp. 153–171). The pre-Islamic version closest to the Qurʾān that has been found to date is in John Moschus' *Leimon*, where Moses' role is taken by a monk and the superior being is an angel (R. Paret, 'Un parallèle byzantin à Coran XVIII, 58–81', *Revue des Études Byzantines* 26, 1968, pp. 137–159).

the Qur'ānic passage is otherwise closely related;[117] but here as there, neither the servant of Moses nor the servant of God is given a name.

All in all, then, the only name of interest yielded by all these accounts is Andreas. That apart, the most striking feature of the stories is the virtual disappearance of the immortality theme, presumably due to Christianisation. The only human to become immortal is Andreas (if we discount Alexander's daughter); nothing is said about the acquisition of immortality by the nameless cooks in later versions of the story. The wise old man, where he appears, is not said to be immortal either. It is still to find the spring of life that Alexander seeks him out in the Syriac Alexander Poem, but it is from his wisdom that he benefits, and wisdom is also what the enigmatic sage imparts to Nimrod and Moses. The association of the waters of life with wisdom is found already in the Bible, both Jewish and Christian, and thereafter in the *Odes of Solomon* and Gnostic literature.[118] It is also the association we find in the Qur'ān.

Al-Khiḍr

The exegetes read the immortality back into the Qur'ānic story by identifying the enigmatic servant of God in sura 18:65–82 as al-Khiḍr, an immortal figure first encountered in the commentaries on this passage. He is introduced as a character familiar to the reader, without any sign of disagreement over the identification until we reach the rationalising theologians (*mutakallims*).

117 It is identified as the direct source in Th. Nöldeke, *Beiträge zur Geschichte des Alexanderromans*, Vienna 1890, p. 32, and again in Friedlaender, *Chadirlegende*, p. 61. But this is unlikely if it dates from the 630s, as proposed by Reinink, *Syrische Alexanderlied*, p. 12; id., 'Alexander the Great in 7th-Century "Apocalyptic" Texts', *Byzantinorossika* 2, 2003, pp. 150–178, at 165. The shared features are unduly minimised by B.M. Wheeler, *Moses in the Qur'ān and Islamic Exegesis*, London 2002, pp. 11–19.

118 Tesei, 'Survival and Christianization', pp. 428 f. As he notes, the living waters were also associated with baptism and resurrection, and the substitution of a fish (a symbol of Christ) for the snake certainly resonates with Christian concepts. But though the editor of recension β was a Christian who did his best to eliminate the most pagan features of the Alexander Romance (Tesei, op. cit., p. 432), it is difficult to see the fish as a symbol of Christ here, or even in the Alexander Poem attributed to Jacob of Sarug. There is no special interest in or sympathy for the fish in either version, the emphasis is on its revival at Alexander's expense, and it does not stand for us even in the version attributed to Jacob of Sarug (contrast the Infancy Gospel of Thomas and the Apocryphal Acts of Peter, where Christ and Peter revive a salted fish). But the resonance with Christianity may have mattered to Christian readers even if it did not fit the story line.

Al-Jubbāʾī (d. 303/915 f.), for example, objected that al-Khiḍr was sent as a prophet after Moses and so could not be the servant of God that Moses encountered (he is probably identifying al-Khiḍr with Elijah); and Fakhr al-Dīn al-Rāzī (d. 606/1209) adds that if the servant of God was al-Khiḍr, then al-Khiḍr must have been a more important person in the Torah than Moses, who plays the role of pupil here, and this he deems to be impossible.[119] But we can leave these developments aside. The earliest material is narrative rather than analytical and takes the form of a story narrated in different versions with different *isnād*s that all go back to Ibn ʿAbbās. According to this story, God rebuked Moses for declaring himself to have greater knowledge than anyone else on earth and told him that He had a servant who knew more than he did. When Moses asked how he could find this servant, God replied that he would have reached his destination when a salted fish came alive in the water. Moses and his servant (identified as Joshua) duly set off, the fish came alive, but the servant forgot to tell Moses; he remembered when Moses became hungry and asked for food, so they retraced their steps and found al-Khiḍr, the man of superior knowledge that Moses had set out to locate.[120] Like the earlier narrators, these exegetes saw the hero as searching for wisdom rather than immortality; but unlike them, they knew the dispenser of wisdom to be immortal.

Who then was this al-Khiḍr? In the long run there were to be many answers to this question, for al-Khiḍr was a popular figure, and a massive amount of material accumulated around him.[121] The bulk of it is irrelevant to us, however, because it is not tied to the story of Moses and the waters of life in sura 18. In the non-exegetical tradition the predominant image of al-Khiḍr is that of a wanderer who turns up in unexpected places to offer his help.[122] This was an idea was of great appeal to both the popular and the Sufi imagination, and it is still current today,[123] but there is no mention of it in the early interpretations of the Qurʾānic passage. In fact, though the early exegetes took familiarity with

119 Fakhr al-Dīn al-Rāzī, *al-Tafsīr al-kabīr*, Tehran 1413, xxi, p. 149, *ad* 18:65.

120 See the exegetes ad loc., e.g. Ṭabarī, *Jāmiʿ*, xv, pp. 277–279, 281, 282; also id., *Taʾrīkh*, ser. i, pp. 417 ff.; al-Kisāʾī, *Qiṣaṣ al-anbiyāʾ*, ed. I. Eisenberg, Leiden 1922, pp. 230 ff.; tr. W.M. Thackston, *Tales of the Prophets*, Chicago 1997, pp. 247 f.; Friedlaender, *Chadirlegende*, pp. 75 ff. For the *ḥadīth* collections, see *EI*², s.v. 'al-Khaḍir (al-Khiḍr)' (Wensinck), bibliography.

121 There is a helpful survey of all this material in *EI*², s.v. 'al-Khaḍir (al-Khiḍr)' (Wensinck).

122 For this feature see K. Vollers, 'Chidher', *Archiv für Religionswissenschaft* 12, 1909, pp. 235 ff., with the proverb *asyaru min al-Khiḍr*, 'more of a traveller than al-Khiḍr', recorded by al-Maydānī (d. 518/1124).

123 Cf. P. Franke, *Begegnung mit Khidr: Quellenstudien zum Imaginären im traditionellen Islam*, Beirut and Stuttgart 2000.

al-Khiḍr for granted, they were not sure who he was. Some said that he was an angel sent by God to Moses and others that he was a human being who had lived a long time ago, such as a figure connected with Alexander, or someone mentioned in the Bible, or he was a Babylonian or a Persian rather than an Israelite. The idea of al-Khiḍr as an angel fits John Moschus' version of the theodicy motif. It is admittedly also an angel who justifies God's ways (to a monk rather than to Moses) in John Moschus' version of the theodicy motif, but this solution is rare in the Islamic tradition: all we are told is that God sent an angel to teach Moses,[124] or that al-Khiḍr was transformed into an angel, not in heaven after the fashion of Enoch, but here on earth.[125]

As regards the explanations of al-Khiḍr as a historical figure, the exegetical attempt to connect al-Khiḍr with Alexander reflects recognition of the fact that the Qur'ān was retelling a story familiar from the Alexander Romance; but it was hampered by the fact that there was no immortal sage in this version of the story. Ibn Isḥāq tells us (on the authority of Ibn 'Abbās, needless to say) that Moses' servant drank of the water of life and so became immortal, and that since he had no right to drink this water, the learned man (i.e. the servant of God or al-Khiḍr) punished him by sending him out to sea, where he would remain until the day of judgement.[126] This is a remarkably faithful version of the cook Andreas who turned into a sea *daimōn*, and it is explicitly told in response to a question about Moses' cook rather than the servant of God. But it obviously could not explain how the servant of God had become immortal.[127] According to other scholars, al-Khiḍr was a commander in charge of Dhū 'l-Qarnayn's vanguard who reached the river of life and drank of it, with the result that he became immortal and remained alive to this day. He drank of it inadvertently, or without having set out to do so, or because he and Dhū 'l-Qarnayn had been searching for it, and he found it when a salted fish came

124 For attestations, see Māwardī, *Tafsīr*, ii, p. 495; Friedlaender, *Chadirlegende*, p. 274. The idea that al-Khiḍr was an angel did not find many takers, but it was taken up by Mawdūdī (Franke, *Begegnung mit Khidr*, pp. 366 ff.).

125 Thus 'Umāra (fl. 2nd/8th century) in Friedlaender, *Chadirlegende*, pp. 135 f., 145, 146 f.; Arabic text pp. 309, 313 f., 314 f.

126 Ṭabarī, *Ta'rīkh*, ser. i, p. 428; Friedlaender, *Chadirlegende*, pp. 105 f.

127 Friedlaender nonetheless thinks that al-Khiḍr's origins are to be sought in the wayward cook (*Chadhirlegende*, p. 108). But the two are properly distinguished even in the much later story of Bulūqiyā in the *Arabian Nights*. Here the cook/servant is not just a demon but king of the entire demon world, and we are told that he would never grow old or die because he had drunk from the fount of immortality guarded by the sage al-Khiḍr (Dalley, 'Gilgamesh in the Arabian Nights', p. 5, on the basis of Mardrus' version).

alive, but in any case his behaviour was morally impeccable.[128] Here the servant has been upgraded to the status of upright sage, suggesting that the exegetes did not know of Alexander stories in which the sage was still present: the cook was the only figure they had to work with. It was not easy, and there was also a problem of chronology in that Moses lived long before Dhū ʾl-Qarnayn in the sense of Alexander the Great. Some responded by asserting that the Moses who was associated with Dhū ʾl-Qarnayn was not the Moses who had led the Israelites out of Egypt, an idea against which Ibn ʿAbbās is said to have protested vigorously.[129] Accordingly, al-Ṭabarī places the Dhū ʾl-Qarnayn connected with al-Khiḍr in the time of Abraham and calls him 'Dhū ʾl-Qarnayn the Elder', perhaps meaning Nimrod or perhaps just creating a doublet of Alexander the Great sufficiently old for things to fit.[130] This was the best one could do with the Alexander material.

No wonder, then, that others tried to find al-Khiḍr in the biblical tradition. He really ought to be mentioned there, given his exalted status as somebody more knowledgeable than Moses, but who was he? Muqātil and ʿUmāra identified him as Elisha (al-Yasaʿ).[131] For a figure connected with Moses this was an odd choice, perhaps suggested to them by a comparison of the two verses of the Qurʾān that mention Dhū ʾl-Kifl. One says of Ismāʿīl, *Elisha* and Dhū ʾl-Kifl that all of them were among the good (38:48; cf. 6:86), and another says of Ismāʿīl, *Idrīs* and Dhū ʾl-Kifl that all of them were among the patient and the righteous (21:85 f.). This could obviously be taken to imply that Elisha was identical with Idrīs, and the latter in his turn was easily identified with al-Khiḍr. According to Ibn Isḥāq citing Wahb b. Munabbih, however, al-Khiḍr was a prophet sent to the Israelites in the days of Josiah, namely the Aaronid called Jeremiah, son of Hilkiah.[132] Jeremiah is also the biblical equivalent of al-Khiḍr in a passage

128 Ṭabarī, *Taʾrīkh*, ser. i, p. 414; Ibn Bābawayh, ʿUmāra, al-Thaʿlabī and Ibn Hishām citing Wahb b. Munabbih, and in Friedlaender, *Chadhirlegende*, pp. 125 ff., 143 ff., 169 f., 199 f.

129 E.g. Ṭabarī, *Taʾrīkh*, ser. i, p. 424, cf. 417, 419 f.

130 Ṭabarī, *Taʾrīkh*, ser. i, pp. 414, 416. Lidzbarski, 'Wer ist Chadhir?', p. 115n.

131 Muqātil, *Tafsīr*, ii, p. 594; ʿUmāra in Friedlaender, *Chadirlegende*, p. 137, with the Arabic text at p. 310. The identification is maintained in what follows, and Elisha/al-Khiḍr is Dhū ʾl-Qarnayn's cousin and *wazīr*.

132 Ṭabarī, *Taʾrīkh*, ser. i, pp. 415 f., 657 f., 661; Friedlaender, *Chadirlegende*, pp. 269 f. The association of Josiah and al-Khiḍr is preserved even in al-Thaʿālibī's version of the Bulūqiyā story, though Jeremiah himself has fallen by the wayside here (S. Dalley, 'The Tale of Bulūqiyā and the *Alexander Romance* in Jewish and Sufi Mystical Circles', in J.C. Reeves (ed.), *Tracing the Threads: Studies in Jewish Pseudepigrapha*, Atlanta 1994, pp. 239–269, at 248; more briefly also ead., 'Gilgamesh in the Arabian Nights', pp. 6 f.).

in al-Jāḥiẓ' *Tarbīʿ* in which a number of identifications are paraded as open to doubt.[133] This too is an odd choice for a figure associated with Moses. Maybe it is rooted in Matthew 16:13 f., where Jesus asks his disciples, 'Who do people say the Son of Man is?', and the disciples reply, 'Some say John the Baptist, others say Elijah, and still others Jeremiah or one of the prophets'. All these figures are seen as alive in some sense and capable of coming back as the 'Son of Man'. John the Baptist and Elijah were often identified (Mark 9:12 f.; similarly Matthew 11:13 f.), and it is still John the Baptist who is Elijah in al-Jāḥiẓ' passage; only Jeremiah, then, was free for candidacy as al-Khiḍr. The underlying assumption would be that al-Khiḍr was the Son of Man, a heavenly being identified with Enoch in the Parables of Enoch[134] and with Jesus in the Gospels.

A fair number of other biblical figures were to be suggested,[135] and the winner in the long run proved to be Elijah. Like Idrīs, he possessed the requisite immortality, but he too was an odd choice for a figure in the time of Moses, for he was not credited with pre-existence. The reasons he won out do not seem to have anything to do with the exegesis of sura 18, however.[136]

Al-Ṭabarī did not like the identification of al-Khiḍr as Elijah, which he does not even mention, though he cites a tradition that rules it out,[137] and he explicitly argues against the theory that al-Khiḍr was Jeremiah. He held al-Khiḍr to be a much earlier figure, as indeed he would have to be if he was the instructor of Moses. The only biblical figure before Elijah to achieve immortality was the antediluvian Enoch/Idrīs, but al-Ṭabarī does not propose him, perhaps because he envisages Enoch as Idrīs ensconced in heaven or perhaps because he did not think that Enoch could have been known under two names in Arabic. Instead, he cites a nameless scholar or scholars who claimed that al-Khiḍr was the offspring of a Babylonian who lived in the reign of the mythical Persian king Farīdūn, corresponding to the time of Abraham, and who emigrated to

133 Al-Jāḥiẓ, *al-Tarbīʿ wa'l-tadwīr*, ed. C. Pellat, Damascus 1955, §40, asks whether Jeremiah (Armiyā) is al-Khiḍr, reserving Elijah for John the Baptist.

134 *1 Enoch*, 71:14 ff.

135 Friedlaender, *Chadirlegende*, pp. 258 ff., 268 ff., 272 ff., on Melchizedek (Malkān), Job and others.

136 The same is true when we are told that some held al-Khiḍr's mother to be a daughter of Pharaoh, or that he was a pure Arab, or that he descended from Cain (Ibn Ḥajar, *al-Iṣāba fī tamyīz al-ṣaḥāba*, Cairo 1328, i, p. 429; all ten suggestions are reproduced in Vollers, 'Chidher', p. 258).

137 Ṭabarī, *Taʾrīkh*, ser. i, p. 415: al-Khiḍr was a Persian, Elijah an Israelite, and they used to meet every year. For other traditions to the same effect, see U. Rubin, *Between Bible and Qurʾān: the Children of Israel and the Islamic Self-Image*, Princeton, NJ, 1999, p. 42.

Palestine together with Abraham.[138] This made al-Khiḍr a monotheist without requiring him to be mentioned by name in the Bible. It also made him come from Babel, whether as an Aramaean, an Israelite or a Persian settled there. Al-Ṭabarī held him to be a Persian, apparently in the third sense (*min wuld al-furs*, as he says shortly thereafter).[139] There were also some who held that his father was a Persian and his mother a Byzantine, or the other way round, but this looks like mere embroidery.[140]

What is so interesting about al-Ṭabarī's suggestions is that he seems to have believed al-Khiḍr to belong in Mesopotamia, but lacked a framework of Mesopotamian history in terms of which to position him. He and his likes wrote at a time when ancient history was either Persian or biblical. Practically nothing was known of the civilisations behind the tablets strewn all over Iraq. Pagan Aramaic culture was almost extinct, and whereas ancient Mesopotamia is nowadays seen as the background to the Bible, in al-Ṭabarī's time it conjured up Hellenised magic, astrology, alchemy and other esoteric wisdom of the type that could be credited to Hermes and envisaged as written on tablets in antediluvian times. Respectable religious scholars could not attach al-Khiḍr to that tradition. Yet their sense that he belonged in Babylonia was right. As Lenormant, Guyard and Lidzbarski recognised long ago, al-Khiḍr in his role as the instructor of Moses is a late descendant of Atraḫasīs/Ūta-napishti, the exceedingly wise and immortal flood survivor who is the instructor of Gilgamesh, Alexander, Nimrod and Moses in Akkadian and Syriac literature and the Qurʾān.[141] One takes it that stories about a famous hero's search for immortality had been told by story-tellers in Aramaic and Arabic, and that the immortal human in these versions bore a name that was Arabised as al-Khiḍr.

138 Ṭabarī, *Taʾrīkh*, ser. i, pp. 414 f.; mentioned by Ibn Ḥajar, *Iṣāba*, i, p. 429. Some identified him as Abraham's nephew or simply as Lot (cf. Friedlaender, *Chadirlegende*, p. 273).

139 Ṭabarī, *Taʾrīkh*, ser. i, p. 415.

140 Ibn Ḥajar, *Iṣāba*, i, pp. 429 f.

141 Lidzbarski, 'Wer ist Chadhir?' (cf. also id., 'Zu den arabischen Alexandergeschichten', *Zeitschrift für Assyriologie* 8, 1893, pp. 263–312); S. Guyard, 'Bulletin critique de la religion assyro-babylonienne', *Revue de l'Histoire des Religions* 1, 1880, pp. 327–345, at 344 f., with the observation that Lenormant had noted the parallel before him (he does not say where); cf. also Henkelman, 'Dim Cooks', pp. 334 ff.

Ancient Mesopotamia

The reason that European scholars of the late nineteenth and early twentieth centuries could do better than the early exegetes is that they could read Akkadian. In 1857 the language was declared to have been deciphered; in 1872 George Smith announced the existence of a Babylonian flood story; and by 1880 Guyard had connected the Babylonian flood survivor with al-Khiḍr, if only as a hunch.[142] The documentation soon followed. The link between the Qurʾān and the Alexander material was established by Nöldeke in 1890, that between the Alexander Romance and the Gilgamesh epic by Meissner in 1892 and 1894, and it was also in 1892 that Lidzbarski documented the link between the Babylonian flood survivor and al-Khiḍr.[143] Al-Khiḍr was the object of intense Orientalist discussion, with some scholars tracing his roots to Glaukos and others accepting his descent from Atraḫasīs. Friedlaender made as good a case for al-Khiḍr's Greek origins as could be made,[144] but though his book is a most impressive piece of scholarship that can still be consulted with profit, it is the 'Babylonianist' thesis that carries conviction today.[145]

What, then, is the name al-Khiḍr? It is often explained as meaning 'Mr Evergreen', the eternally young man,[146] but as Lidzbarski noted, this is unlikely to be right, for no early source associates his name with either eternal youth or immortality. One early explanation is that he was called green because he sat on white fur that gave off a green sheen; another is that he was so called because of his shining beauty, or because he wore green clothes, or because everything turned green around him, or under him.[147] Only the fourth explana-

---

142 Cf Guyard, 'Bulletin critique', pp. 344 f.

143 Nöldeke, *Beiträge*; B. Meissner, 'De servitute babylonico-assyriaca', dissertation, University of Berlin, defended in 1892; id., *Alexander und Gilgamos*, Leipzig 1894 (neither seen); Lidzbarski, 'Wer ist Chadhir?'. Lidzbarski refers to Meissner's thesis at p. 109n.

144 K. Dyroff, 'Wer ist Chadir?', *Zeitschrift für Assyriologie* 7, 1892, pp. 319–327; Friedlaender, *Chadirlegende*, pp. 113 ff., 241 ff., with arguments against his roots in the Gilgamesh epic at pp. 37 f.

145 Lidzbarski's thesis was accepted already by K. Vollers, 'Chidher', *Archiv für Religionswissenschaft* 12, 1909, pp. 234–284, at 274, though he cites Lidzbarski only to disagree with him (pp. 281 f.). It is Lidzbarski's thesis that is immortalised by Wensinck's entry 'al-Khaḍir (al-Khiḍr)' in EI². For fair criticism of Friedlaender's thesis, see Henkelman, 'Dim Cooks', pp. 336 ff.

146 E.g. Vollers, 'Chidher', p. 235; EI², s.v. 'al-Khaḍir (al-Khiḍr)'; EQ, s.v. 'Khaḍir/Khiḍr'.

147 Cf. Friedlaender, *Chadirlegende*, pp. 110 ff. The Abū 'l-Fatḥ he cites at p. 112n as explaining the name with reference to al-Khiḍr's immortality flourished in the tenth/sixteenth century.

tion fits 'Mr Evergreen', and then only just, for it is not he who is evergreen, but rather the vegetation that becomes green (again) thanks to him.[148] Clermont-Ganneau, writing in 1877, held the name al-Khaḍir to be a simple translation of Glaukos, the Greek mythological figure who became an immortal sea *daimōn*; Dyroff independently reached the same conclusion in 1892, and Friedlaender agreed.[149] But even granting that the colour designations may correspond (which Lidzbarski disputed) and that al-Khiḍr has a maritime side to him, this is extremely unlikely, for Glaukos is not actually mentioned in any version of the heroic quest for immortality: he was merely present in the narrator's mind as the latter reshaped his material.[150] And more importantly, Glaukos fused with Andreas, the wayward cook, not with the immortal sage who lived on as al-Khiḍr, the instructor of Moses.

It may well be by accident that the name of the immortal sage acquired a form that happened to mean green. Lidzbarski derived al-Khiḍr from 'Chasisadra', an inversion of Atraḫasīs' name assumed at the time to lie behind Berossos' Xisouthros: Arabs doing their best to reduce foreign words to three radicals could only end up with al-Khaḍir, he claimed, carried away by youthful exuberance (he was twenty-four at the time).[151] In fact, as we now know, Berossos' Xisouthros reflects the Sumerian Zisudra and the form Khasīsadra is a chimaera (retained in the second edition of the *Encyclopaedia of Islam*!).[152] Given that al-Khiḍr may have been a multifaceted figure already in the second/eighth century, we cannot be sure that his name originated in the context of stories descended from Gilgamesh's search for immortality. If it did, it would have to be derived from Zisudra. This has in effect been proposed,[153] but it requires the sibilant *z* to turn into the velar fricative *ḫ*, which sounds impossible. It is noteworthy, though, that Berossos transliterated Zisudra as Xisouthros, with a *xī* rather than a *zēta*. Did he hear the initial letter as a palatalised velar fricative? I have not seen a discussion of Berossos' transliteration and would prefer to leave the question for the experts in Sumerian and Semitic languages to decide.

---

148 For this aspect of him, see Franke, *Begegnung mit Khidr*, pp. 80 ff.

149 Cf. the references given above, note 144.

150 Both Dyroff ('Wer ist Chadir?', p. 327) and Friedlaender (*Chadirlegende*, pp. 116, 242) held that there must have been versions in which the cook was called Glaukos. For al-Khiḍr as a maritime figure, see Friedlaender, op. cit., pp. 116 ff.

151 Lidzbarski, 'Wer ist Chadhir?', pp. 109 f.

152 The explanation is that Wensinck's entry 'al-Khaḍir (al-Khiḍr)' is a reprint from the first edition of the *EI*, published in 1913–1936.

153 Guyard, 'Bulletin critique', pp. 344 f.

Conclusion

As noted already, the hypothesis presented in this paper is not amenable to proof. It is a fact that Enoch had come to be identified with somebody known as Idrīs by the time the exegetes were active, and there is no doubt that Atraḫasīs and Enoch were similar, perhaps related, figures who grew even more alike in the course of time. But that they actually fused at a popular level cannot be demonstrated in the present state of the evidence, and the same is true of the claim that the name Atraḫasīs lives on in that of Idrīs. Both propositions have a fair degree of plausibility, however.

Whether the speaker of the Qur'ān himself had Enoch in mind when he spoke of Idrīs is a good deal more uncertain. Obviously, if the name 'Idrīs' is derived from 'Atraḫasīs', the answer has to be yes, regardless of whether God had raised him to heaven or to an exalted position; but it cannot be ruled out that the reference is to another figure. That Atraḫasīs (alias Zisudra and Ūtanapishti) lived on, without any sign of fusion with Enoch, as the figure known to the exegetes as al-Khiḍr is not in doubt. It is one out of several cases in which the Muslim material preserves features of Akkadian origin not found in the Alexander Romance.[154] But it is impossible to tell whether the speaker of the Qur'ān had the same figure in mind as did the exegetes. All that can be said is that the exegetes are drawing on an ultimately Mesopotamian tradition on which the Qur'ān itself may be drawing as well. This is also what they are doing when they explain the angels Hārūt and Mārūt (2:102) as angels who came down to earth in Enoch's time and sinned, though these angels are not easy to recognize in their Qur'ānic version. Modern scholars probably would not have been able to identify them on the basis of the Qur'ān alone, though in this particular case the Qur'ān and the exegetes are certainly drawing on the same tradition. The ease with which the exegetes identified figures from the Enoch literature contrasts strongly with their handling of other passages, where they plainly do not know whom or what the Qur'ān is talking about and so resort to guessing (as they do in connection with Dhū 'l-Kifl, for example).

Why there should be such a high degree of continuity between the Qur'ān and exegesis in connection with the Enoch material is hard to say, but it may have something to do with the fact that the material originated in Iraq, where most of the early exegetes were active. For it was evidently in Iraq, not Ethiopia,

154 Cf. Tesei, 'Survival and Christianization', pp. 418, n. 2; 426, n. 27 (citing Wensinck, 'al-Khaḍir (al-Khiḍr)', and D. Bodi, 'Les mille et une nuits et l'épopée de Gilgamesh', in A. Chraïbi (ed.), *Les mille et une nuits en partage*, Paris 2004, pp. 407 f., on Bulūqiyā).

that Enoch acquired the Babylonian name under which he appears in the Qurʾān, if the thesis advanced here is accepted; and it was also in Iraq rather than Ethiopia that the fallen watchers were reduced to two and endowed with the Zoroastrian names of Haurvatāt and Ameretāt, to pass into the Qurʾān as Hārūt and Mārūt.[155] The Slavonic Enoch book (*2 Enoch*) must have some connection with Iraq as well, since there are Zoroastrian features in its views on animals and time;[156] and the Hebrew Enoch book (*3 Enoch*, alias *Sefer Hekhalot*) is assumed to have reached its final shape in Iraq in the sixth or seventh century. In short, the Enoch literature was well known in Iraq and probably more familiar to the exegetes active there than Qurʾānic material of other provenance.

It is noteworthy that the Enoch literature continued to be read on the Sasanian side of the Euphrates, for on the Greek side the Jews and Christians had ceased to regard it as authoritative in the course of the third and fourth centuries. Both had come to dislike the story of angels mating with humans and now interpreted the biblical 'sons of God' as humans of elevated status.[157] The rabbis were also wary of the idea of Enoch's translation to heaven, which they associated with heretics.[158] They rarely mention Enoch, and they take a poor view of him when they do. In a famous passage in *Genesis Rabba* one rabbi interprets the biblical statement that 'he was not' to mean that Enoch was not inscribed in the scroll of the righteous; another passage declares that Enoch was sometimes righteous, sometimes wicked and that God took him in a righteous phase (to save him from further sins); or what the Bible means when it says

---

155 See P.J. de Ménasce, 'Une légende indo-iranienne dans l'angélologie judéo-musulmane: à propos de Hārūt et Mārūt', *Études Asiatiques* 1, 1947, pp. 10–18; P. Crone, 'The *Book of Watchers* in the Qurʾān', in H. Ben-Shammai, S. Shaked and S. Stroumsa (eds.), *Exchange and Transmission across Cultural Boundaries: Philosophy, Mysticism and Science in the Mediterranean*, Jerusalem 2013 [Ed.: reprinted in P. Crone, *The Qurʾānic Pagans and Related Matters*, vol. 1 of *Collected Studies in Three Volumes*, ed. H. Siurua, Leiden 2016, art. 7], pp. 16–51.

156 S. Pines, 'Eschatology and the Concept of Time in the Slavonic Book of Enoch', in R.J. Zwi Werblowsky and C.J. Bleeker (eds.), *Types of Redemption*, Leiden 1970, pp. 72–87; cf. F.I. Anderson's introduction to his translation of *2 Enoch* in Charlesworth, *Old Testament Pseudepigrapha*, i, esp. p. 95.

157 Judges according to the rabbis, sons of Seth as opposed to descendants of Cain according to the Christians; see for example B.J. Bamberger, *Fallen Angels*, Philadelphia 1952, pp. 78 ff., 91, 149 ff.; A.Y. Reed, *Fallen Angels and the History of Judaism and Christianity: the Reception of Enochic Literature*, Cambridge 2005. Further literature is cited in Crone, 'Book of Watchers', nn. 11–20.

158 *Genesis Rabba*, 25:1: heretics asked R. Abbahu why they did not find any mention of Enoch's death (in Genesis).

that God took him is simply that he died, as we are also told.[159] Around 600 AD the circles viewed with suspicion by the rabbis surface in *3 Enoch*, alias *Sefer Hekhalot*, in which Enoch is the angel Metatron and the 'lesser YHWH', second only to God himself.[160]

The Christians did not turn against Enoch as a person. They continued to mention him in connection with the two eschatological witnesses of Revelation 11 (where John predicts that at the end of times, between the sixth and seventh trumpets, two witnesses will come forth to give testimony, to be killed by the beast of the abyss, revived after three and a half days, and then translated to heaven). The witnesses are unnamed, but they were usually held to be Enoch and Elijah, the two biblical figures who had not died.[161] Other Christian works, however, presented Enoch as living in paradise right now: thus for example the much read *Apocalypse of Paul*, composed in Greek in probably the mid-third century and translated into Syriac, Coptic and many other languages thereafter (like Muḥammad, Paul met Enoch in heaven).[162] That Enoch was translated is also affirmed, for example, by Epiphanius (d. 403),[163] Ephraem of Amida (patriarch of Antioch under Justinian), Theodosius of Alexandria (d. 566) and Timothy of Antioch (sixth/seventh century).[164] Byzantine historians continued to quote from the Enoch book as well, though not without warning their readers

159 *Genesis Rabba*, 25:1; VanderKam, *Man for All Generations*, pp. 161 ff.; Alexander, 'Jewish Tradition in Early Islam' (above, note 15), p. 17; M. Himmelfarb, 'A Report on Enoch in Rabbinic Literature', in P.J. Achtemeier (ed.), *Society of Biblical Literature 1978 Seminar Papers*, i, Missoula, MT, 1978, pp. 259–269.

160 Tr. P.S. Alexander in Charlesworth, *Old Testament Pseudepigrapha*, i, pp. 223–315. He ascends to heaven and turns into Metatron, the great scribe, in Targum Ps.-Jonathan, too, but not in the other targums (VanderKam, *Man for All Generations*, pp. 165–168; Orlov, *Enoch-Metatron Tradition*).

161 VanderKam, *Man for All Generations*, pp. 180 ff.; id. and W. Adler, *The Jewish Apocalyptic Heritage in Early Christianity*, Assen, MN, 1996, pp. 89 ff.; cf. the *History of Joseph the Carpenter* in J.K. Elliott (tr.), *The Apocryphal New Testament*, Oxford 1993, p. 115, pars. 31–32 (4th–5th century); Oecumenius (6th century?), *Commentary on the Apocalypse*, tr. J.N. Suggit, Washington, DC, 2006, ch. 6, 4 (p. 102); Andrew of Caesarea (early 7th century), *Commentary on the Apocalypse*, tr. E.S. Constantinou, Washington, DC, 2011, ch. 30, *ad* 11:3–4 (pp. 131 f.); W. Bousset, *The Antichrist Legend*, Atlanta 1999, pp. 203 ff.

162 In Elliott, *Apocryphal New Testament*, p. 628.

163 Epiphanius, *Panarion*, tr. F. Williams, Leiden 1987–1994, ii, p. 622 (heresy 79, 2:4).

164 Cf. D. Krausmüller, 'Timothy of Antioch: Byzantine Concepts of the Resurrection, Part 2', *Gouden Hoorn* 5, no. 2 (1997–1998), http://goudenhoorn.com/2011/11/28/timothy-of-antioch-byzantine-concepts-of-the-resurrection-part-2/ (unpaginated), at note markers 71, 85 (Timothy himself), 87 ff. (Ephraem of Amida) and 114 (Theodosius).

of corruptions 'by Jews and heretics'. According to Jacob of Edessa, however, the Enoch book had been unjustly anathematised. It was a genuine antediluvian work in his view, and the only reason Athanasius (d. 373) had proscribed it was that heretics in his time had incorporated the work into their library of secret books.[165]

There is no sign in either the Qurʾān or the early exegetical tradition of the rabbinic denigration of Enoch or of the Christian view of him as an eschatological witness; but here as in the Christian tradition, Enoch is a prophet,[166] and the Qurʾānic association of Idrīs with *ṣabr* (endurance, patience), for which there is no precedent in either the Bible or the Enoch literature, is perhaps also rooted in the Christian tradition.[167] Hārūt and Mārūt are still angels in the Qurʾān, however, not human beings of elevated status, as both the Jews and the Christians had come to affirm; so if we assume the Qurʾānic material on Enoch and these two angels to have been transmitted by the same circles (which is not certain), the circles in question would seem to be Iraqis who had parted ways with mainstream Christianity by the third or fourth century, to develop along lines of their own. This fits the Manichaeans, who certainly liked Enoch and read books ascribed to him, but the Qurʾānic material is not likely to go back to them.[168] In fact, the circles in question were not necessarily sectarian at all, as opposed to simply poorly policed by the rabbis, churchmen or Zoroastrian priests. It may be that just as the Arab conquerors inadvertently turned the social map of the Near East upside down,[169] so they inadvertently elevated marginal traditions to high cultural status.

---

165 W. Adler, 'Jacob of Edessa and the Jewish Pseudepigrapha in Syriac Chronography', in Reeves, *Tracing the Threads*, p. 145.

166 Cf. Reed, *Fallen Angels*, pp. 152 f.

167 Cf. the *Apocalypse of Paul* in Elliott, *Apocryphal New Testament*, p. 644; in E.A.W. Budge, tr., *Miscellaneous Coptic Texts*, London 1915, p. 1076, where Enoch declares that 'the sufferings which a man endures for the sake of God God will not afflict him with when he leaves the world'.

168 My reasons for doubting that there is thought of Manichaean origin in the Qurʾān are presented in P. Crone, 'Jewish Christianity and the Qurʾān (Part Two)', *Journal of Near Eastern Studies* 75, 2016 [Ed.: reprinted in P. Crone, *The Qurʾānic Pagans and Related Matters*, vol. 1 of *Collected Studies in Three Volumes*, ed. H. Siurua, Leiden 2016, art. 10], section no. 10.

169 Cf. P. Crone, *The Nativist Prophets of Early Islamic Iran: Rural Revolt and Local Zoroastrianism*, New York 2012, p. 17.

CHAPTER 4

92 Abū Saʿīd al-Ḥaḍrī and the Punishment of Unbelievers*

In his *al-Imtāʿ waʾl-muʾānasa*, the littérateur al-Tawḥīdī (d. 414/1023) tells of a theologian called Abū Saʿīd al-Ḥaḍrī/Ḥuṣrī/Ḥaṣīrī/Ḥuḍarī/Ḥaḍramī who held that God would admit all human beings to Paradise. This passage, which is of considerable interest for the intellectual climate of ninth-century Baghdad, has been translated and discussed by Van Ess, who has also assembled the little we know about the theologian:[1] his *ism* was al-Ḥasan b. ʿAlī and he was a Basran Shīʿī of the mid to late ninth century; originally he was a Muʿtazilī of the Ṣūfī variety; later, according to Ibn al-Nadīm, his mind became unhinged and he struck out of his own (*khulliṭa wa-abdaʿa*).[2] The passage, which must refer to Abū Saʿīd's unorthodox phase, goes as follows:[3]

> Abū Saʿīd al-Ḥaḍramī, one of the clever theologians (*ḥudhdhāq al-mutakallimīn*) in Baghdad and the one who openly professed belief in the equipollence of proofs (*wa-huwa ʾlladhī taẓāhara biʾl-qawl bi-takāfuʾ al-adilla*),[4] said that if God is just, generous, munificent, omniscient, kind and merciful, He will admit all human beings (*jamīʿ khalqihi*) to Paradise, for all in their different ways endeavour to seek His pleasure and avoid His anger as far as their knowledge and intelligence allows. They only fail to follow His command because they have been deceived. Falsehood has been decked out as truth for them. They are like a man carrying a gift to
> 93 a king who | was stopped on the way by people engaging in deception, trickery and theft. They set up a man and called him by the name of the king he was travelling to, so he handed the gift to them. If the king he

---

* I should like to thank Fritz Zimmermann for reading an early draft of this article and Michael Cook for reading the final version.

1 Van Ess, *TG*, vol. 4, pp. 91–93, 333, with the translation at vol. 5, p. 344; see also Monnot, *Penseurs musulmans et religions iraniennes*, pp. 61–63.

2 Van Ess' translation reads *khallaṭa*, "spread confusion", which is also possible, but cf. *TG*, vol. 2, p. 4, note 1. My thanks to F. Zimmermann for the reading adopted here.

3 Tawḥīdī, *Imtāʿ*, vol. 3, pp. 192 f.

4 Not everyone who believed in *takāfuʾ* was willing to say so openly (cf. Tawḥīdī, *Muqābasāt*, nos. 35, 54, pp. 159, 227).

© KONINKLIJKE BRILL NV, LEIDEN, 2016 | DOI: 10.1163/9789004319318_005

meant to see was generous, he would excuse him and have mercy on him and treat him with extra generosity and kindness when he learnt of what had happened to him. That would be more proper to him (*awlā bihi*) than getting angry and punishing him.

In brief, God as normally conceived was mean: He punished people who failed to worship Him even though He knew full well that they were innocent victims of deception. Abū Saʿīd does not seem to think that God really *is* mean or that therefore there must be a higher God above Him, but rather that God really *is* generous and merciful and that therefore He cannot engage in the behaviour imputed to Him. His statement is one out of many arguments mounted by ninth-century theologians from a dualist background against the punitive God of the Judaic tradition. But who are the tricksters and precisely whom are they deceiving?

According to Van Ess, the tricksters are theologians and their victims are sinners: Abū Saʿīd's message is that God will admit all human beings in the sense of all Muslims to Paradise, even sinners, because all would worship the true God if only they followed reason, but they are misled by the theologians, who offer lies and enrich themselves at the expense of simple folk. Van Ess does wonder whether Abū Saʿīd meant to include unbelievers along with the sinners, but he leaves it uncertain. He also observes that one could read the tricksters as false prophets, noting that Abū Saʿīd's parable would in that case give us something approaching the "three impostors" thesis, i.e., the idea that Moses, Jesus and Muhammad were tricksters who used religion to accumulate worldly power.[5] He does not accept this reading, however. In what follows I shall argue that the victims are indeed unbelievers, but that the tricksters are neither theologians nor false prophets; rather, they are demons. I shall conclude with some further thoughts on Abū Saʿīd's views.

Who Were the Tricksters?

The tricksters are unlikely to be theologians because Abū Saʿīd's parable is plainly about false religions, not theological fabrications. The traveller is made
to honour a man impersonating the king, i.e. a false deity; he | is misled into wor- 94
shipping somebody other than God, not simply into having some wrong ideas about him. One could hardly blame the *mutakallimūn* for the existence of false

5 Van Ess, *TG*, vol. 4, pp. 93, 333 (small print).

religions. It does not even come easily to see them as corrupting the beliefs of simple folk, for they were normally accused of doing the very opposite, namely making religion so abstruse that simple folk could not understand them. They were guilty of *takfīr al-ʿawāmm*, holding ordinary people to be unbelievers for taking their religion on trust even in respect of fundamentals. Abū Saʿīd may have written against *takfīr al-ʿawāmm*, for he is credited with a book denying the superiority of theologians over the common people (*fī taswiyat aṣḥāb al-kalām biʾl-ʿawāmm*).[6] That he saw them as corrupting the common people is not implied. If the choice is between understanding the tricksters as theologians or as false prophets, it surely comes much more naturally to see them as prophets. As Van Ess notes, some later readers may actually have understood them as such,[7] perhaps even ʿAbd al-Jabbār (d. 415/1025), who repeatedly mentions Abū Saʿīd along with Abū ʿĪsā al-Warrāq, Ibn al-Rāwandī and their likes as Shīʿites guilty of slandering God and the prophets.[8] But since ʿAbd al-Jabbār on one occasion includes Hishām b. al-Ḥakam in the list of slanderers, he is probably indulging in polemical exaggeration.[9] Van Ess is in any case right that the tricksters are unlikely to be false prophets, for they are envisaged as operating as a team rather than following one another. Unlike both pseudo-prophets and theologians, moreover, they enrich themselves at God's expense, not at that of the traveller.

By Abū Saʿīd's time, however, there was a long tradition in the eastern Mediterranean of comparing God with a human king in order to illustrate His relationship with other celestial beings, usually angels, but in the case of the Christians also demons. This tradition was shared by monotheists of both the pagan and the Biblical type, and it is above all in polemics between them that it is attested. I shall now give a brief aperçu of how the different groups used the imagery to show that Abū Saʿīd's parable continues the usage of the Christians.

Late antique pagans liked to defend their polytheist heritage by casting God as a king who ruled with the assistance of largely autonomous governors after the fashion of such monarchs as the Persian emperor. Zeus had appointed the lesser gods to the various regions of the world and they were like his governors and satraps, Aelius Aristides (d. 181 or later) said.[10] One God was king of all and
95 many gods ruled together | with him, according to Maximus of Tyre (d. 185).[11]

---

6 Van Ess, *TG*, vol. 5, p. 344 (from ʿAbd al-Jabbār, *Tathbīt*, p. 51.–6).
7 Van Ess, *TG*, p. 333 (small print), in the context of the three impostors thesis.
8 ʿAbd al-Jabbār, *Tathbīt*, pp. 51, 129.
9 ʿAbd al-Jabbār, *Tathbīt*, p. 232, *supra*.
10 *Orations*, xliii, 18.
11 Maximus of Tyre, *Orations*, xxxix, 5.

God had allotted different parts of the earth to different overseers, Celsus (c. 180) and Julian (d. 361) agreed in polemics against the Christians.[12] Celsus added that one should pay due reverence to all beings who had been allotted control by God over earthly things: for just as the satrap or sub-governor of the Persian or the Roman emperor and other officials, including lesser ones, could do one much damage if they were slighted, so it went without saying that all God's underlings could cause much harm if they were insulted.[13] Ambrosiaster, writing in fourth-century North Africa, tells us that if one asked a pagan how he could worship a whole lot of gods, he would reply that they were like dignitaries interceding with the sovereign on his behalf.[14] God delegated matters to such dignitaries because it would be unseemly for him to attend to the details of petty administration, just as it was below the dignity of a human king such as Xerxes to do so, according to the first-century Pseudo-Aristotelian *De Mundo*, where the comparison between God and the Persian emperor is developed at length.[15] In the same vein a fragment attributed to the Zoroastrian Mazdak (d. 530s) depicts God as seated on his throne as Khusraw sits on his in the lower world; in front of God and Khusraw alike are four powers, who rule through seven powers, and so on.[16]

The pagans never seem to envisage God as a king in connection with malicious powers. They did see a link between such powers and false religious claims: thus Celsus entertained the possibility that Jesus and other wonder-workers were "wicked men possessed by an evil demon",[17] while the *mushrikūn* immortalized in the Qur'ān asked themselves whether there was a spirit (*jinna*) in the man who claimed to have been sent to them, when they did not simply dismiss him as mad (*majnūn*).[18] But the demons are not cast as usurpers of the prerogatives of the supreme God in these examples, nor is there any suggestion that they took possession of their victims with a deliberate intention to mislead mankind.

The combination of God as king and demons as usurpers also seems to be missing on the Gnostic side, though evil powers actively seeking to | trick 96

12 Celsus in Origen, *C. Celsum*, v, 25; Julian, *Against the Galilaeans*, p. 402 (= Cyril, *Pro Christiana Religione*, 290E).

13 In Origen, *C. Celsum*, viii, 33, 35; cf. also vii, 68.

14 Cumont, "Polémique", pp. 426 f. Compare Celsus in Origen, *C. Celsum*, viii, 2. The *mushrikūn* say much the same in Qur'ān 39:3, but without the governmental imagery.

15 Aristotle (attrib.), *De Mundo*, ch. 6, pp. 398a–b.

16 Shahrastānī, *Milal*, p. 193.

17 Origen, *C. Celsum*, i, 68.

18 Qur'ān 15:6; 34:8; 37:36; 44:14; cf. 26:27, where Pharaoh dismisses Moses as *majnūn*.

people into worshipping false deities are extremely common here. In fact, it is typically the evil powers that are cast as rulers (prince of darkness, archons, and so on), not the hidden God, who was apparently too pure and too transcendent to be conceived in terms relating to government.

The governmental image reappears when we turn to the Jews, however. According to Philo (died ca. 50 CE), it would be most unwise to give the same tribute to the creatures as to their maker, just as it would be most unwise to give subordinate satraps the honour due to the great king.[19] A famous rabbinic vignette conveys much the same message by depicting a king as sitting in a chariot together with a governor: when the subjects mistakenly greet the governor as lord, the king pushes the governor out of the chariot. The rabbis mention this in illustration of God's response when the angels mistook Adam for a divine being: God pushed Adam out of the chariot by putting him to sleep, thereby demonstrating that he was a mere mortal.[20] Humans were all too prone to casting Adam or a principal angel such as Metatron as God's vice-regent and magnifying his position to the point where it rivalled God's. A famous story tells of a third-century rabbi who made a mystic ascent to heaven, where he mistook the angel Metatron in all his glory for God. On this occasion, too, God pushed the governor out of his chariot, this time by having Metatron whipped and the rabbi excommunicated.[21] In all three examples, the lesser beings are legitimate subordinates of God, however, and though humans sometimes overdo their worship of them, there is no suggestion that the subordinates are trying to mislead them.

The Jews were also familiar with malicious celestial powers, and like the pagans they would invoke them in explanation of false religious claims. In the Gospels, for example, they sometimes react to Jesus by dismissing him as possessed: "he has a demon and is out of his mind", as many of them said with reference to his presumptuous statements (John 10:19); "you have a demon", they insisted when he denied it (John 8:48 f., 52); "he has Beelzebub, and by the ruler of the demons he casts out demons", the scribes said (Mark 3:22). In fact, fallen angels and demons had played a major role in the explanation of evil among Jews in the Greek and Roman periods, and in the *Book of Watchers* (part of the Book of Enoch), perhaps dating from the third century BCE, it is demons who are responsible for the existence of idolatry: the fallen angels here generate evil spirits which lead people into error by inducing them to

19 Philo, *De Decalogo*, p. 61.

20 *Genesis Rabba*, VIII, 10; for a translation and further references, see Schäfer, *Rivalität zwischen Engeln und Menschen*, p. 82.

21 Deutsch, *Guardians of the Gate*, chs. 3–4.

offer sacrifices to these spirits themselves in the mistaken belief | that they are 97
gods.[22] The idea that the gods venerated by the pagans were actually demons is also encountered in the Septuagint.[23] But the Jews did not to my knowledge cast the demons who led mankind astray as usurpers of the prerogatives of the true king; and in any case the rabbis played down the idea of demonic powers as it rose to prominence in Gnosticism and Christianity.[24]

It is among the Christians that we find the right combination of God as king and demons as usurpers of His prerogatives. According to the Christians, the analogy between divine and human kingship did not serve to vindicate polytheism, as the pagans claimed; rather, it refuted it, for monarchy was the best constitution: polyarchy meant anarchy, so that if there were many gods, all things would go to pieces.[25] (This argument also appears in the Qurʾān.)[26] A pagan philosopher, perhaps Porphyry (d. c. 305 CE), retorted that a monarch is unique in being a ruler, not in being a human: on the contrary, one would not call him a king at all if he did not rule over other human beings, only over beasts; it followed that God would not be king at all if he did not rule over other gods, only over humans.[27] To this and other pagan arguments the Christians responded, much like Philo, that if a servant of the king allowed himself to be called Caesar, both he and those who had called him by that name would perish.[28] It was quite wrong to claim that God's underlings would harm those who slighted them by refusing to call them gods, Origen (d. 254 or 255 CE) explained in refutation of Celsus, for the angels were true satraps, subordinate governors and officers of God. If demons had the ability to hurt people, it was

---

22 1 Enoch 19 (in Charlesworth, ed., *Old Testament Pseudepigrapha*, vol. 1, p. 23).

23 Psalms 96:5 declares that "the gods of the nations are idols". The Septuagint (95:5) rendered this as "the gods of the nations are demons".

24 Cf. Bamberger, *Fallen Angels*, ch. 16.

25 Lactantius, *Divine Institutes*, i, 3; Eusebius, *Laus Constantini*, III.6 (trans. Drake, *In Praise of Constantine*, p. 87); Gregory of Nazianzus, *Discours*, no. 29, 2; Gregory of Nyssa, *Poemata*, in Dvornik, *Early Christian and Byzantine Political Philosophy*, vol. 2, p. 689 (*MPG*, vol. 37, p. 414); cf. also the tenth-century Moses Bar Kepha, *Hexaemeronkommentar*, ch. 3, 9 (trans. Schlimme, p. 101).

26 Qurʾān 21:22; cf. also 17:42 (here with echoes of the old combat myth, cf. Forsyth, *Satan and the Combat Myth*).

27 Macarius Magnes, *Apocriticus*, iv, 20, 2 (English trans. Hoffmann, *Porphyry's Against the Christians*, pp. 83 f.). For a thorough discussion of this work and the philosopher it refutes, see Goulet's edition and French translation, vol. i.

28 Ambrosiaster and Pseudo-Maximus of Tyre in Cumont, "Polémique", p. 427. The philosopher in Macarius Magnes disagrees again (*Apocriticus*, iv, 23, 3; trans. Hoffmann, *Porphyry's Against the Christians*, p. 88).

precisely because they had not received any appointment from God, but were evil powers who would cause suffering to those who submitted to them. Origen
98 implies that even Christians were known to submit themselves "to the demon | of the locality"; a real Christian, however, meaning one who submitted himself to God alone and His Logos, would be safe from such powers, for the angel of the Lord would be with him.[29]

Here the demons seem to be envisaged as local power-holders of an illegitimate kind, such as barbarian usurpers, warlords, or robbers; and though Origen does not say so, the Christians held such usurpers to be trying actively to lead people astray. The demonic offspring of the fallen angels had enslaved the human race, among other things by teaching people how to offer sacrifices, incense and libations to them, as Justin Martyr (d. 160s CE) said, developing the theme from the *Book of Watchers*.[30] That demons were the forces behind paganism became the standard Christian view: evil spirits lurked behind the idols, coming out in all their hideousness when the idols were cut down (as they were to do in Muhammad's Arabia too; early Muslims also held that it was demons [*al-jinn*] who made infidels worship idols and ascribe partners to God).[31] According to Eusebius (d. 340 CE), "spirits and demons, also called principalities, powers, world-rulers, spiritual hosts of wickedness", hate God so much that "they wish themselves to be proclaimed gods and steal away for themselves the honours intended for God, and attempt to entice the simple by divinations and oracles as lures and baits".[32] Here the imagery is very close indeed to Abū Saʿīd's, though it is only implicitly that God is cast as king.

The imagery reappears in a work by the Christian *mutakallim* Theodore Abū Qurra (d. ca. 825 CE) on how to identify the true religion. Like Abū Saʿīd al-Ḥaḍrī, he uses a parable: a king had a son who went away on a journey and fell ill; the king sent a messenger with a prescription that would cure him, but the king's enemies heard of this and sent their own messengers with harmful prescriptions, hoping to harm the king and his son; their plot was foiled by a wise physician accompanying the son: he told him to scrutinize all the messages to determine which was the right one, and only one proved to be true.[33] The king was God, the son was Adam/mankind, and the wise

29 Origen, *C. Celsum*, viii, 36, cf. also 33.

30 *Second Apology*, 5 (trans. Barnard, pp. 76 f.). Cf. 1 Enoch 19 (above, note 22); Reed, *Fallen Angels*, p. 164.

31 Thus, for example, al-Ḥasan al-Baṣrī in Fakhr al-Dīn al-Rāzī, *Tafsīr*, vol. 13, p. 115, *ad* 6:100.

32 Eusebius, *Praeparatio Evangelica*, vii, 16.9 f.

33 Griffith, "Faith and Reason in Christian Kalām", pp. 34 f., citing Abū Qurra, *Traité de l'existence du créateur et de la vraie religion*, viii.

physician was reason, Abū Qurra explains, adding that God's enemies were the demons (*al-shayāṭīn*).[34] In both his and Abū Saʿīd's parable, the demons interfere with communications between the king and his subjects, in the one by | sending false messages to the travellers, in the other by falsely giving them 99
to understand that they have arrived at their destination. In both, the object of the exercise is to divert royal prerogatives to the illegal operators, stealing honours intended for God as Eusebius puts it. In short, it comes naturally to read the evil-doers in both as demons.

By the ninth century, idolatry was no longer a problem. What troubled people now was the existence of rival scriptural religions, and Abū Qurra's demons no longer operated as they did in Eusebius' time: instead of seducing people into worshipping idols they now sent messengers in imitation of the true God. Their behaviour is shaped by the rise of Islam, in other words; the paradigmatic bearer of a false message is clearly Muhammad, whom Abū Qurra characterizes as a false prophet possessed by a demon elsewhere as well.[35] It cannot be said that the adaptation of the old imagery to the new conditions is entirely felicitous, however, for the demonic explanation only works in connection with false religions, not when we add superseded ones. Abū Qurra inadvertently suggests that even Moses was an impostor, given that all the messengers other than the one true one are sent by the enemies of God. In Abū Saʿīd's parable the demons even operate in the old style by setting up one of themselves as a rival god, which is hardly a good characterization of any of the religions with which Islam was in competition; and again no distinction is made between false religions and superseded ones, so that Moses and Jesus are implicitly put on a par with figures such as Mani or Zoroaster. Maybe both authors were using the old imagery in an offhand manner, or maybe they would have explained that demons worked through many kinds of people: pseudo-prophets in some cases, rabbis and priests or the obstinate infidels themselves in others. But both parables would have worked better if the demons had been envisaged as working in the same way in all cases.

When we meet the demonic explanation again, it is precisely in connection with the view that all prophets were victims of demonic trickery. According to Abū Bakr al-Rāzī (d. 313/925), "the souls of evildoers who have turned into demons show themselves in the form of angels, who come to people and command them to go and tell people that an angel has appeared to them and told them that God has given them prophethood … with the result that discord

34 Abū Qurra, *Traité*, viii, 33 (p. 217).

35 Meyendorff, "Byzantine Views of Islam", p. 120.

appears among people".[36] Here the demons are imitating Gabriel, the paradigmatic prophet being Muhammad yet again. Al-Rāzī hardly meant the explanation literally; rather, he was using mythical language for didactic purposes to
100 show how | his view of the prophets, above all the Prophet, fitted in with the historical record and to bring out that he took them to believe in their own mission even though he did not believe in it himself. Demons were no longer routinely invoked in explanation of evil by his time, however; they sound curiously out of date even here. Once they had been discarded, the explanation of false prophets had to be that they were cynical manipulators rather than innocent victims of deception, for now they were acting on their own, yet every bit as evil as before. In effect, the removal of the demons simply secularised the explanation: the pseudo-prophets turned into demons stripped of their supernatural status. It was in this guise, smacking of conspiracy theory, that the concept of the three impostors was exported to Europe.[37]

Abū Saʿīd's Position

Even if Abū Saʿīd's tricksters had been false prophets, his parable would not have been an early version of the "three impostors" thesis, for like Abū Qurra's, it is based on the assumption that there was a true religion, centered on worship of the real king. At least one revealed religion is right, and one assumes it to be Abū Saʿīd's own. In keeping with this, his parable is not in fact concerned with the question how far people can reach God by rational means, unaided by prophets (or for that matter theologians), but rather with the importance of their intentions: all humans do their best to please God in their very different ways (*ʿalā ikhtilāfihim*), he says, presumably meaning that all try to please Him even though they belong to different religious communities. The issue he is addressing is whether God is being fair to those of them who are in the wrong communities. Since Abū Saʿīd openly professed belief in the doctrine of *takāfuʾ al-adilla*, the sceptical view that an argument in favour of a particular proposition could always be matched by another of equal weight to the contrary,[38] he plainly cannot have regarded reason as a better guide to truth than prophethood.

---

36 Nāṣir-i Khusraw, *Jāmiʿ al-ḥikmatayn*, in Kraus, *Rasāʾil*, p. 177; also translated in Stroumsa, *Freethinkers*, p. 106.

37 Cf. Van Ess, *TG*, vol. 4, p. 333, for literature.

38 Cf. Hankinson, *The Sceptics*, p. 27; Van Ess, *Erkenntnislehre*, pp. 221 ff.

On the contrary, his problem must have arisen from the very fact that reason did not offer any guidance here. In Abū Qurra's parable the wise physician shows the prince how to tell the difference between healing and harmful prescriptions: one could tell a true revelation from a false one by rational means. This is precisely what Abū Saʿīd denied with his doctrine of *takāfuʾ*.
What his parable is saying is surely that it would be | unfair of God to punish 101
those who have been duped by demons, for all would follow the truth, if only they knew what it was. All have the best of intentions, all are trying to please Him to the best of their ability; it is precisely their reason which is deficient. How were people to guard themselves against tricksters if they did not even know when they were being deluded? Their sharpened intellects notwithstanding, theologians were not in fact in a better position than anyone else, for their attempts to establish criteria of judgement came to grief on the equipollence of proofs. One would assume this to be what Abū Saʿīd said in his book *Fī taswiyat aṣḥāb al-kalām biʾl-ʿawāmm*. It would certainly do something to explain why ʿAbd al-Jabbār found it deeply offensive.[39]

If one could not tell a true religion from a false one, what was Abū Saʿīd's own faith? Al-Tawḥīdī has a wonderful vignette of a sceptic who decides to stay in the religion he has grown up in on the grounds that if one does not know where the truth is, one may as well stay where one is.[40] This was also a well-known reaction of sceptics in antiquity: entertaining a rational distrust of reason, they practised suspension of judgement and so were apt to cope with the problem of what to do and think by following tradition.[41] One would assume Abū Saʿīd to have reacted similarly, for there is no suggestion that he abandoned Islam.[42] In fact, he seems to have remained not only a Muslim, but also a Muʿtazilī.

That he remained a Muʿtazilī is suggested by a comparison of his presentation of the problem of God's justice with that of his contemporary, the Zoroastrian Martān Farrūkh. What the latter disliked about the Muslim conception of God was not just that He punished unbelievers, but also that He punished people for evil that He Himself had created and made them follow. Martān Farrūkh could not see how such a God could possibly be called just, merciful or wise. If God was just and wise, as he believed Him to be, He could not be omnipotent: evil had to have autonomous existence. Martān Farrūkh mentions omniscience

39 Cf. his *Tathbīt*, 51.–6.

40 *Imtāʿ*, vol. 3, pp. 193 f.; cf. Van Ess, "Skepticism", pp. 6 f.

41 Burnyeat, "Can the Sceptic Live his Scepticism?", p. 33; Schofield, "Cicero for and against Divination", pp. 55 f. (my formulation reflects his).

42 There was a Manichaean Abū Saʿīd about the same time, but he does not seem to be identical with ours (Van Ess, *TG*, vol. 4, p. 92).

as a problem too, but it is the incompatibility of omnipotence and justice that he stresses time and again.[43] By contrast, Abū Saʿīd makes no reference to God's omnipotence at all, only to His omniscience. That God should punish people for evil that He Himself had created and made His servants prone to follow did not apparently trouble him: he does not ask how the tricksters came into being
102 or why God allows them to mislead people. | He may of course have done so in other works of his, but apparently he had found an answer, for it would not otherwise have made sense for him to worry about the subsidiary problem of God's punishment of infidels on its own. This is explicable on the assumption that he was still a Muʿtazilī: God did indeed have power over all things, but this did not make Him unfair, for He had given people free will; what was unfair was only that He should punish them even when their free will could not help them, i.e., when rational choice was rendered impossible by *takāfuʾ al-adilla.*

According to Ibn Ḥazm, believers in the equipollence of proofs fell into three groups. The first took the doctrine to mean that one could neither prove nor disprove the existence of God or anything that followed from it. The second accepted the existence of God and affirmed that the truth was available in some belief system or other, but held *takāfuʾ* to rule out certainty as regards the rest. The third accepted that the true religion was Islam and so limited the applicability of *takāfuʾ* to inner-Islamic divisions (an anti-sectarian use of scepticism of the type first attempted by the Murjiʾīs).[44] Abū Saʿīd appears to belong in the second group, for although his parable is based on the assumption that Islam is the true religion, he does not limit his *takāfuʾ* to inner-Islamic divisions. This was what made him heterodox: only one religion was true, but given the inability of human reason to tell which one it was, he held that one could be saved in all of them. No doubt he said this too in his book *Fī taswiyat aṣḥāb al-kalām biʾl-ʿawāmm*, and it was probably this feature that struck Ibn al-Nadīm as *bidʿa*:[45] it overstressed the importance of good intentions.

Though Abū Saʿīd was far less radical than Abū ʿĪsā al-Warrāq and Ibn al-Rāwandī, with whom ʿAbd al-Jabbār associates him and with whom he seems to have been personally acquainted too,[46] he shared with them the feature of being a Muʿtazilī *mutakallim* with strong Shīʿī sympathies who fell into *zandaqa*, which in a ninth-century context meant heresy of a vaguely Iranian

43 Martān Farrūkh, *Škand-Gumānīk Vičār*, ch. 11.

44 Ibn Ḥazm, *Faṣl*, vol. 5, pp. 118 f. For the Murjiʾīs and scepticism, see Cook, *Early Muslim Dogma*, ch. 7.

45 Cf. above, note 2.

46 Ashʿarī knew them to have participated in a debate together in Baghdad (Van Ess, *TG*, vol. 6, p. 364 [no. 43]).

and thoroughly rationalist kind. All three were troubled by the behaviour of an all-powerful God who declared Himself to be just and merciful, but who nonetheless inflicted eternal pain on tiny beings that He had made Himself; and all three allowed reason to sit in judgement of the revelation, though they did not all go so far as to reject it altogether. Unlike his associates, however, Abū Saʿīd does not seem to have impressed other *mutakallims*. The view that
God | would not punish infidels, or anyone, or that at least He would not do so 103
for ever, is aired at some length in al-Qirqisānī (10th century) and Fakhr al-Dīn al-Rāzī (d. 606/1209).[47] Neither mentions any names, but both reproduce the objections of Abū ʿĪsā and Ibn al-Rāwandī to divine punishment, namely that it would amount to inflicting harm of no benefit to either God or the victims, which was morally repugnant (*qabīḥ*),[48] and that God knew in advance that the infidel would not believe: since He created human beings for beneficial rather than harmful purposes, He could not have given them obligations that He knew He would have to punish them for eternally, as the argument continues in the formulation of later *mutakallims*.[49] In Fakhr al-Dīn al-Rāzī, the opponents of divine punishment add that God is the creator of the impulses that led to sin, for the stupidity and foolishness that cause people to disobey God are not something they have chosen themselves, but rather something built into their natures (*al-aḥwāl al-gharīziyya*), so that it would be morally repugnant for God to punish them for it. ("Should the forms be ugly, whose fault is it?", as ʿUmar Khayyām asked.)[50] And even if one accepted that He would in fact punish them, why should He do so for ever?[51] The Qurʾān did of course threaten unbelievers with eternal punishment, but God was not obliged to carry out His threats, and even the sternest human master who inflicted that kind of torments on his slaves would eventually be moved to forgive them. God's words to the unbelievers in Qurʾān 2:7, "theirs is a mighty punishment" (*lahum ʿadhābun ʿaẓīm*), simply meant that they deserved such punishment,

---

47 Qirqisānī, *Anwār*, iii, 9 (vol. 2, pp. 246 ff.); Fakhr al-Dīn al-Rāzī, *Tafsīr*, vol. 2, pp. 54 ff. (*ad* Qurʾān 2:7), vol. 27, pp. 74 f. (*ad* Qurʾān 40:56–60).

48 Cf. Abū ʿĪsā al-Warrāq in Tawḥīdī, *Imtāʿ*, vol. 3, p. 192 (trans. Van Ess, *TG*, vol. 6, p. 432); Ibn al-Rāwandī in Ibn al-Jawzī, *Muntaẓam*, vol. 6, pp. 101 (*sub anno* 298).

49 The early formulation was simpler and ruder, cf. Abū ʿĪsā al-Warrāq, *loc. cit.*; Ibn al-Rāwandī in Khayyāṭ, *Intiṣār*, p. 12.5. It is also simpler in Qirqisānī, who attributes it to the Manichaeans (*Anwār*, iii, 9, 9 f.).

50 Dāya, *God's Bondsmen*, trans. Algar, p. 54.

51 Compare Ibn al-Rāwandī on how a God who condemns people who disobey or do not believe in Him to eternal, everlasting hellfire is stupid and ignorant of the right measure of punishment (*lā ʿālim bi-maqādīr al-ʿiqāb*) (Khayyāṭ, *Intiṣār*, p. 12.6).

but His magnanimity would necessarily make Him forgive them. (To all these arguments Fakhr al-Dīn al-Rāzī laconically replies that God is above human reasoning.) One wonders why Abū Saʿīd's argument has been left out. It does come across as rather Ṣūfī in its concern with the human heart where the other *mutakallims* focus on the nature of God. Maybe even those who agreed with him found him to overstress the importance of good intentions.

104 Bibliography

ʿAbd al-Jabbār. *Tathbīt dalāʾil al-nubuwwa*. ʿA.-K. ʿUthmān, ed. Beirut, 1966.

Abū Qurra. *Traité de l'existence du créateur et de la vraie religion*. I. Dick, ed. Jounieh and Rome, 1982.

Aelius Aristides. *Orations*. In C.A. Behr, trans., *The Complete Works*. Leiden, 1981–1986.

Aristotle (attrib.). *De Mundo*. J. Tricot, trans. Paris, 1949.

Bamberger, B.J. *Fallen Angels*. Philadelphia, 1952.

Burnyeat, M.F. "Can the Sceptic Live his Scepticism?". In M. Schofield, M. Burnyeat and J. Barnes, eds., *Doubts and Dogmatism*. Oxford, 1980.

Celsus, *see* Origen.

Charlesworth, J.H., ed. *The Old Testament Pseudepigrapha*. New York, 1983–1985.

Cook, M. *Early Muslim Dogma*. Cambridge, 1981.

Cumont, F. "La polémique de l'Ambrosiaster contre les paiens." *Revue d'Histoire et de Littérature Religieuse* 8 (1903): 417–440.

Dāya, Najm al-Dīn Rāzī. *The Path of God's Bondsmen*. H. Algar, trans. New York, 1982.

Deutsch, N. *Guardians of the Gate. Angelic Vice Regency in Late Antiquity*. Leiden, 1999.

Dvornik, F. *Early Christian and Byzantine Political Philosophy*. Washington, DC, 1966.

Ess, J. van. *Die Erkenntnislehre des ʿAḍudaddīn al-Īcī*. Wiesbaden, 1966.

———. "Skepticism in Islamic Religious Thought". *Al-Abḥāth* 21 (1968): 1–18.

———. TG = *Theologie und Gesellschaft im 2. und 3. Jahrhundert Hidschra*. Berlin and New York, 1991–1997.

105 Eusebius. *Laus Constantini*. H.A. Drake, trans., *In Praise of Constantine*. Berkeley, 1976.

———. *Praeparatio Evangelica*, book VII. G. Schroeder and É. des Places, eds. and trans. Paris, 1975.

Fakhr al-Dīn al-Rāzī. *Al-Tafsīr al-kabīr*. Tehran, 1413.

Forsyth, N. *The Old Enemy: Satan and the Combat Myth*. Princeton, 1987.

Gregory of Nazianzus. *Discours*. P. Gallay, ed. and trans. (nos. 27–31). Paris, 1978.

Griffith, S.H. "Faith and Reason in Christian Kalām: Theodore Abū Qurrah on Discerning the True Religion". In S.Kh. Samir and J.S. Nielsen, eds., *Christian Arabic Apologetics during the Abbasid Period*. Leiden, 1994.

Hankinson, R.J. *The Sceptics*. London and New York, 1995.

Ibn Ḥazm. *Al-Faṣl fī ʾl-milal waʾl-ahwāʾ waʾl-niḥal*. Cairo, 1317.

Ibn al-Nadīm. *Kitāb al-fihrist*. R. Tajaddud, ed. Tehran, 1971.

Ibn al-Jawzī. *Al-Muntaẓam*, vol. 6. Hyderabad, 1357.

Julian. *Against the Galilaeans*, in his *Works*. W.C. Wright, ed. and trans. Loeb Classical Library, vol. 3. Cambridge, Mass., and London, 1923.

Justin. *The First and Second Apologies*. L.W. Barnard, trans. New York, 1997.

Al-Khayyāṭ. *Kitāb al-intiṣār*. A.N. Nader, ed. and trans. Beirut, 1957.

Kraus, P., ed. *Rasāʾil falsafiyya li-Abī Bakr ... al-Rāzī*, vol. 1 (no more published). Cairo, 1939.

Lactantius. *The Divine Institutes*, books i–vii. M.F. MacDonald, trans. Washington, D.C., 1964.

Macarius Magnes. *Apocriticus*. R. Goulet, ed. and trans., *Le Monogénès*. Paris, 2003. R. Hoffmann, partial trans., *Porphyry's Against the Christians*. Amherst, 1994.

Martān Farrūkh. *Škand-Gumānīk Vičār: La solution décisive des doutes*. J.P. de Menasce, ed. and trans. Fribourg, 1945.

Maximus of Tyre. *The Philosophical Orations*. M.B. Trapp, trans. Oxford, 1997.

Meyendorff, J. "Byzantine Views of Islam," *Dumbarton Oaks Papers* 18 (1964): 113–132. 106

Monnot, G. *Penseurs musulmans et religions iraniennes: ʿAbd al-Jabbār et ses devanciers*. Paris and Beirut, 1974.

Moses Bar Kepha. *Der Hexaemeronkommentar*. L. Schlimme, trans. Wiesbaden, 1977.

Nāṣir-i Khusraw, *see* Kraus.

Origen. *Contra Celsum*. H. Chadwick, trans. Cambridge, 1953.

Philo. *De Decalogo*. In F.H. Colson, ed. and trans., *Philo*. Loeb Classical Library, vol. 7. Cambridge, Mass., and London, 1950.

Porphyry, *see* Macarius Magnes.

Al-Qirqisānī, Yaʿqūb. *Kitāb al-anwār waʾl-marāqib: Code of Karaite Law*. L. Nemoy, ed. New York, 1939.

Reed, A.Y. *Fallen Angels and the History of Judaism and Christianity: the Reception of Enochic Literature*. Cambridge, 2005.

Schofield, M. "Cicero for and against Divination." *Journal of Roman Studies* 76 (1988): 47–63.

Schäfer, P. *Rivalität zwischen Engeln und Menschen*. Berlin and New York, 1975.

Al-Shahrastānī. *Al-Milal waʾl-nihal*. W. Cureton, ed. London, 1842–1846. D. Gimaret and G. Monnot, trans., *Livre des religions et des sectes*. Paris, 1986.

Stroumsa, S. *Freethinkers of Medieval Islam*. Leiden, 1999.

Al-Tawḥīdī. *Al-Imtāʿ waʾl-muʾānasa*. A. Amīn and A. al-Zayn, eds. Cairo, 1939–1944.

———. *Al-Muqābasāt*. M.T. Ḥusayn, ed. Baghdad, 1970.

CHAPTER 5

63 The Dahrīs According to al-Jāḥiẓ*

In the third/ninth-century Islamic world we encounter people of whom it is said that they denied the existence of God, angels, prophets, spirits, the resurrection, post-mortem reward and punishment, and the afterlife altogether. In effect, they rejected the entire metaphysical realm as either false or beyond the limits of human reasoning, on the understanding that there was no point in trying to know about anything *unless* it was accessible to human reasoning. It was this understanding which made them radical even when or if they were willing to consider the possibility of a reality beyond us: they did not accept revelation as an alternative source of knowledge. They were empiricists in the sense that they held all genuine knowledge to be based on sense impressions in conjunction with reasoning. The sources call them Dahrīs, eternalists, *aṣḥāb al-hayūlā*, adherents of prime matter, and *aṣḥāb al-ṭabāʾiʿ*, adherents of the four "natures", i.e. the four elementary qualities (heat, cold, moisture, and dryness) of which they held the world to be composed. It is not in the third/ninth century alone that we hear of them: there are intimations that they existed earlier and the polemics against them continue down to at least the sixth/eleventh century. But it seems to have been in the third/ninth century that they attracted most attention.[1]

The Dahrīs sound so weirdly out of place in the early Islamic world that modern Islamicists often have trouble believing that they really existed, unless they have studied them themselves.[2] No Dahrī writings survive, most of the evidence is polemical, and with some minor exceptions no individual Dahrīs
64 are known by | name, so it comes naturally to suspect that all there is to them

* I should like to thank the participants in a graduate seminar on Dahrism I taught at Princeton University in 2006 for assisting my attempt to understand the texts we read, Everett Rowson for the generosity with which he shares his expertise, and Michael Cook and Emma Gannagé for commenting on a draft of this article.

1 See I. Goldziher and A.-M. Goichon (1965), "Dahriyya", *Encyclopaedia of Islam*, 2nd edition, Brill, Leiden, vol. II, pp. 95a sq.; M. Shaki and D. Gimaret (1993), "Dahrī", *Encyclopaedia Iranica*, http://www.iranicaonline.org; J. Van Ess (1991–1997), *Theologie und Gesellschaft im 2. und 3. Jahrhundert Hidschra, eine Geschichte des religiösen Denkens im frühen Islam*, 6 vols., De Gruyter, Berlin/New York (hereafter *TG*), esp. vol. IV, pp. 451 sqq.

2 I have never encountered any doubts about their reality in the literature on them, but suspicion of polemical invention is a common response to oral presentations of their views.

© KONINKLIJKE BRILL NV, LEIDEN, 2016 | DOI: 10.1163/9789004319318_006

is heresiographical stereotyping and construction of the "other". This makes the testimony of al-Jāḥiẓ (d. 255/869) particularly important. He is one out of many Muʿtazilites who wrote on the Dahrīs in the third/ninth century, but the others wrote refutations and heresiographical accounts of the Dahrīs, and their works are lost except for extracts in later sources.[3] Al-Jāḥiẓ, by contrast, wrote as a littérateur, most of his work is extant, and though his attitude to the Dahrīs is also polemical, he gives us a vivid picture of them as a live presence. In what follows I go through the information he provides, restraining myself from the temptation to adduce material from other ninth-century sources, so that the reader will have a clean picture of the Dahrīs as perceived by a single, contemporary author.

Overall Portrait

Most of al-Jāḥiẓ's references to Dahrīs are found in his book on animals, and the single most informative passage comes in the last volume of that work.[4] It is long and convoluted, and it starts with a relative clause of which the first part goes on for so long that it can be read either as incomplete or as completed in a way suggesting that the author (or copyist) had himself lost his sense of where he was. I have read it as incomplete and inserted some words that seem to be missing; the alternative is to remove two that would be superfluous, and the reader can construe the sentence either way, as I have underlined the words that introduce the relative cause and those that could be taken to initiate its

3 A *Kitāb al-Radd ʿalā ʾl-dahriyya* is listed for al-Aṣamm (d. 200/816 or the year after), Bishr b. al-Muʿtamir (d. 210/825), and al-Naẓẓām (d. before 232/847) (Muḥammad b. Isḥāq Ibn al-Nadīm [1971], *Kitāb al-Fihrist*, ed. R. Tajaddud, Maktabat al-Asadī, Tehran, pp. 206, 13; 214, 15; *TG*, vol. v, p. 285, no. 48). Of these, all we have are the samples of al-Naẓẓām's polemics against Dahrī cosmology preserved in al-Jāḥiẓ's animal book (cf. the references below, notes 29 sq.). The polemics against the Dahrīs by Muḥammad b. Shabīb (d. 230/840), presumably from his *Kitāb al-Tawḥīd*, survive in Muḥammad b. Muḥammad al-Māturīdī (d. 833/944) (1970), *Kitāb al-Tawḥīd*, ed. F. Kholeif, Dar al-Mashreq, Beirut, pp. 141 sqq.; *cf. TG*, vol. iv, pp. 124 sqq. on Ibn Shabīb. The section on the Dahrīs from the heresiography of the third/ninth-century Abū ʿĪsā al-Warrāq survives in Maḥmūd b. Muḥammad Ibn al-Malāḥimī (d. 536/1141) (1990), *Kitāb al-Muʿtamad fī uṣūl al-dīn*, ed. M. McDermott and W. Madelung, al-Hoda, London, pp. 548 sqq.; cf. S.M. Stern (1960), "Abū ʿĪsā al-Warrāq", *EI*[2], vol. i, p. 130.

4 Al-Jāḥiẓ (1938), *Kitāb al-Ḥayawān*, ed. ʿA.S.M. Hārūn, 7 vols., Maktabat Muṣṭafā al-Bābī al-Ḥalabī, Cairo, vol. vii, pp. 12 sqq.; also discussed in H. Daiber (1999), "Rebellion gegen Gott. Formen atheistischen Denkens im frühen Islam", in F. Niewöhner and O. Pluta (eds.), *Atheismus im Mittelalter und in der Renaissance*, Harrassowitz, Wiesbaden, pp. 23–44, pp. 24 sq.

completion. Al-Jāḥiẓ has just said that nobody who prays towards the *qibla* will
65 disagree with what he has said, and that this holds | true even of the *mulḥids* who believe in the resurrection and revealed religion/law (*al-sharāʾiʿ*), so that the only one who will disagree is the Dahrī:

> for the one who denies divinity (*al-rubūbiyya*), makes the command and prohibition something absurd, rejects the very possibility of the prophecy (*jawāz al-risāla*), holds matter (*al-ṭīna*) to be eternal, flatly denies (*yajḥadu*) reward and punishment, does not recognize the prohibited and the permitted, does not acknowledge that there is any proof in the entire world of a maker and things made or a creator and things created, and who considers the heavenly sphere—which does not know itself from others, which cannot distinguish between that which appears in time and the eternal, or between the doer of good and of evil, which cannot increase its movement or decrease its circular motion, and which cannot follow movement with rest, stand still for one moment, or deviate from its direction—to be the one[5] through which everything is held firm and destroyed, and which accounts for all things fine or great, including these marvelous, wise arrangements, perfect forms of governance, the wonderful composition and wise construction in accordance with a known computation and familiar order exhibiting the subtlest ways of wisdom and perfect workmanship [such a Dahrī cannot accept what we say], but such a Dahrī has no right to object to our book, even if it goes against his views and calls to the opposite of what he believes. For the Dahrī does not think there is any revealed religion (*dīn*) or creed (*niḥla*) or religious law (*sharīʿa*) or religious system (*milla*) on earth. He does not think the permitted has any sanctity (*ḥurma*) or know what it is, nor does he think that the forbidden has any limit or know what it is. He does not expect any punishment for evil-doing, nor does he hope for any reward for doing good. What is right in his view and true in his judgment is that he and undiscriminating quadrupeds (*al-bahīma*) are the same and that he and predatory animals (*al-sabuʿ*) are the same. Moral wrong (*al-qabīḥ*) in his opinion is simply that which goes against his inclination, moral good (*al-ḥasan*) is merely what conforms with his inclination: things turn on (*madār al-amr*) failure and success, pleasure and pain, and what is right lies simply in that which confers benefit, even killing a thousand upright

5 Daiber's translation is clearly wrong here (compare the editor's helpful gloss at *K. al-Ḥayawān*, ed. Hārūn, vol. VII, p. 13, n. 2).

> men for the sake of a bad dirham. This Dahrī does not fear that he will be punished and chastised, temporarily or for ever, if he stops criticizing the scriptures[6] or the imams, nor does he hope for any reward in this world or the next if he finds fault with them and displays hostility to them.

The Dahrī is here depicted as an atheist in the sense of someone who denies the existence of a God outside nature, or God in any sense at all. In so far as the Dahrī operates with anything that could be called a deity, it is the celestial sphere, which he sees as ruling the universe, and which he may have credited with intelligence, though al-Jāḥiẓ does not say so; he even seems to reject that possibility by having the Dahrī deny divinity (*al-rubūbiyya*) outright. To the Dahrī, the cosmos is ruled by itself, not | regulated by a being outside it, and 66
it has not been created by such a being either: there is not in his view any evidence for creation anywhere in the universe. Matter has always existed, and by implication always will, though it is only the first of these points that al-Jāḥiẓ singles out for attention. Since the Dahrī does not believe in a personal God, he also denies that there can be any such thing as a divine message, meaning one carried by a prophet, and accordingly he also rejects the possibility of "command and the prohibition", here as elsewhere in al-Jāḥiẓ meaning divine law.[7] What God has forbidden and allowed means nothing to the Dahrī: it has no inviolability and sets no limits in his view. Since there is no God, there is not any religion on earth either in his view, or in other words, he does not think that any of the many religions found on earth is true; and since it is only from the revelation that we know about rewards and punishments after death, he does not believe in them either. He is described as an outright denier, not a sceptic or agnostic. Elsewhere, al-Jāḥiẓ cites his teacher al-Naẓẓām as observing that he had engaged in disputation with two kinds of *mulḥid*s, the denier (*al-jāḥid*) and the doubter (*al-shākk*), and that he had found the latter to be better at *kalām* than the former.[8] But the term Dahrī is not used there, and al-Jāḥiẓ himself always seems to think of a Dahrī as a *jāḥid*.

What the Dahrī does believe, in al-Jāḥiẓ's presentation, seems to be that the combination of eternal matter and the motion of the celestial sphere suffices to explain everything in the world around us. Al-Jāḥiẓ highlights the absurdity of this belief by recourse to an old argument against the divinity of the planets

6 *Al-kutub*, clearly not al-Jāḥiz's own animal book, as Daiber says ("Rebellion", p. 25).

7 See for example al-Jāḥiẓ, "Al-Maʿāsh wa'l-maʿād", in ʿA.-S.M. Hārūn (ed.) (1965–1979), *Rasāʾil al-Jāḥiẓ*, 4 vols., Maktabat al-Khānjī, Cairo, vol. I, pp. 100, 1; 104, 2; id., "Maqālat al-Zaydiyya wa'l-Rāfiḍa", in ibid., vol. IV, p. 320, 1.

8 Al-Jāḥiẓ, *K. al-Ḥayawān*, ed. Hārūn, vol. VI, p. 35.

and stars. The very regularity of the motion of the heavenly bodies which had constituted proof of their divinity to the Greeks proved to the Christians that they were ruled by a higher power, and this was how al-Jāḥiẓ saw it, too: how could the heavenly bodies, which did not have the ability to vary their own movements, be the regulators of everything?[9] That the Dahrī should claim to find no evidence for a creator or maker anywhere in the world also strikes al-Jāḥiẓ as absurd in view of the wonders of nature and the exquisitely intricate
67 ways of things, clearly meant as a reference | to the wonderful things he has described in his animal book. His response to the Dahrī, in other words, is recourse to the argument from design. He is envisaged as having developed this argument at greater length in a book against deniers of God and providence which is falsely attributed to him.[10]

Though the Dahrī rejects divine law, he operates with a concept of morality and distinguishes between good and bad, *al-ḥasan wa'l-qabīḥ*, literally the beautiful and the ugly (or the nice and the nasty), the standard terms for good and bad as perceived by the human intellect, as opposed to *al-ḥalāl wa'l-ḥarām*, the forbidden and the allowed, or in other words the good and the bad as defined by divine legislation. The Dahrī thinks that humans are capable of defining good and bad themselves, with reference to concepts such as benefit or utility: to al-Jāḥiẓ, this boils down to setting moral standards to suit your own convenience. He takes it for granted that the Dahrī will set the standard with exclusive reference to his own personal advantage, so that he could in principle approve of killing a thousand good people for a bad coin. The possibility that the Dahrī thought of right and wrong in terms of collective welfare is not considered. Like so many believers, al-Jāḥiẓ cannot help thinking that an atheist must be a deeply immoral and selfish person: his moral rules are not set by an external authority higher and wiser than himself; and he does not expect to be either rewarded or punished for anything he does after death,

---

9 This argument had been disseminated in Iraq by Christians, cf. J.T. Walker (2004), "Against the Eternity of the Stars: Disputation and Christian Philosophy in Late Sasanian Mesopotamia", in G. Gnoli and A. Panaino (eds.), *La Persia e Bisanzio* (Atti dei Convegni Lincei 2001), Accademia Nazionale dei Lincei, Rome, pp. 518–535, where the Christian ʿAbdishoʿ uses it against the Zoroastrian Qardagh (who converts); id. (2006), *The Legend of Mar Qardagh: Narrative and Christian Heroism in Late Antique Iraq* (Transformation of the Classical Heritage, 40), University of California Press, Berkeley/Los Angeles/London, pp. 29; 190 sqq.

10 Cf. al-Jāḥiẓ (attrib.) (1928), *Kitāb al-Dalāʾil wa'l-iʿtibār ʿalā 'l-khalq wa'l-tadbīr*, ed. M.R. al-Tabbākh, al-Maṭbaʿa al-ʿIlmiyya, Aleppo; M.A.S. Abdel Haleem (tr.) (1995), *Chance or Creation? God's Design in the Universe*, Garnet, Reading.

so what motives could he possibly have for behaving unselfishly? The Dahrīs familiar to al-Jāḥiẓ seem to have argued that humans have it in them to manage their lives, including the determination of right and wrong, on the basis of their innate intelligence much as animals do; and al-Jāḥiẓ is on shaky grounds here, for his book is full of praise for the wonderful governance that one can see in nature, and he sometimes adduces animals as examples of the way things work in human societies too. If the wonderful general governance of the world suffices to make animals flourish, why must humans have prophets, revealed law, or beliefs in Paradise and Hell in addition? It was a good question, later taken up by Abū Bakr al-Rāzī as an argument against the idea of prophecy.[11] The Sincere Brethren, too, adduced the animals in illustration of natural as opposed to prophetic religion.[12] But al-Jāḥiẓ wriggles out of the question by simply appealing to human self-esteem: the Dahrī downgrades us to undiscriminating quadrupeds (*al-bahīma*) | and predatory animals (*al-sabuʿ*), he says. In his 68
epistle on the cultivation of virtue he credits animals with the same self-seeking drives as human beings and casts the divine law as the antidote in the human case, again without telling the reader why animals could manage without it, or even whether they could:[13] there were people in his time, in fact pupils of his own teacher al-Naẓẓām, who held that animals did have prophets and religious laws just as humans did,[14] an idea that al-Jāḥiẓ derided.[15] This makes his own refusal to explain the difference all the more surprising.

The last point that al-Jāḥiẓ makes in this passage is that the Dahrī is given to criticizing the scriptures and finding fault with both them and the imams, presumably including the prophets. This is a sign of the Dahrī's perversity, for he does not expect to gain any reward for it in the next world, nor does he think that he would be punished for it after his death if he stopped.

---

11 Cf. Abū Ḥātim al-Rāzī (1977), *Aʿlām al-nubuwwa*, ed. Ṣ. al-Ṣāwī, Mu'assasa-yi Pizhūhishī-i Ḥikmat wa Falsafa-yi Īrān, Tehran, p. 183, 2 sq. (and, implicitly, 3, 11; 181, 7; 274, 2).

12 *Rasā'il Ikhwān al-Ṣafā wa-khullān al-wafā'*, 4 vols., Dār Bayrūt, Beirut 1957, vol. II, pp. 203–377, esp. pp. 324–329; L.E. Goodman (tr.) (1978), *The Case of the Animals versus Man before the King of the Jinn: A Tenth-Century Ecological Fable of the Pure Brethren of Basra*, Twayne, Boston, esp. pp. 156–165.

13 Al-Jāḥiẓ, "Al-Maʿāsh waʾl-maʿād", *Rasā'il*, ed. Hārūn, vol. I, p. 102, 12 sq.

14 The best known is Aḥmad b. Khābiṭ/Ḥā'iṭ, cf. Muṭahhar b. Ṭāhir al-Maqdisī (1899–1919), *Kitāb al-Bad' waʾl-taʾrīkh*, ed. C. Huart, 6 vols., Ernest Leroux, Paris, vol. III, pp. 8 sq.; ʿAlī b. Aḥmad Ibn Ḥazm (1317–1321H.), *Kitāb al-Faṣl fī ʾl-milal waʾl-ahwā' waʾl-niḥal*, 5 vols., Cairo, vol. I, pp. 78 sqq.; TG, vol. III, pp. 430 sqq.

15 Al-Jāḥiẓ, *K. al-Ḥayawān*, ed. Hārūn, vol. V, p. 424; tr. TG, vol. VI, p. 214, on Aḥmad b. Khābiṭ and prophets to the bees.

Rule-Bound Universe versus Divine Intervention

Elsewhere in his animal book al-Jāḥiẓ gives us concrete examples of Dahrī criticism of the scriptures. In one passage it is merely implicit. He tells us that some Dahrīs flatly denied the existence of metamorphosis (*maskh*), the process whereby God had turned some humans into monkeys and pigs (Q. 5:60; cf. 2:65; 7:166); other Dahrīs accepted its existence, but explained it as the outcome of environmental damage and its effect on the elementary qualities for which no supernatural intervention was required.[16] In another passage the Dahrīs attack the Qur'ān directly, finding fault with the story of Solomon and the Queen of Sheba. They object that on the one hand, this story presented Solomon as having asked for, and apparently been granted, kingship of a kind never granted to anyone else (Q. 38:35), that is to say power over not just humans, but also spirits (*jinn*) and the winds, and knowledge of the language of the birds. But on the other hand, the story claims that Solomon needed the *hudhud* bird to tell him about the existence of the Queen of Sheba, though she was hardly all that far away. Al-Jāḥiẓ quotes the Dahrīs as saying,

> 69 "Our kings today, who have less power than Solomon, are not unaware of the rulers of the Khazars, the Rūm, the Turks, or the Nubians, so how could Solomon be unaware of this queen, when their lands were so close and also contiguous, without any seas or rugged land in the way?" This and the like, they said, "is evidence of the corrupt nature of your historical tradition" (*dalīl ʿalā fasād akhbārikum*).[17]

Al-Jāḥiẓ replies by granting that if it were the case that God abstained from intervention in the world and governance of its affairs, letting them run in their normal way, then the Dahrīs would be right; but sometimes God diverted people's minds (*ṣarafa awhāmahum*), so that for example Jacob and Joseph did not recognize each other in Egypt even though both were prophets, and so that the Israelites wandered in the desert for forty years without finding their way to their destination, which would not normally have been so difficult either. His argument is that "they were diverted from the chance to learn the truth by divine providence", because it was not yet right for them to learn it, as Lactantius had put it some six hundred years earlier.[18] Al-Jāḥiẓ adduces several

---

16 Al-Jāḥiẓ, *K. al-Ḥayawān*, ed. Hārūn, vol. IV, pp. 70 sqq. (with the *ṭabāʾiʿ* at p. 73, 4); cf. M. Cook (1999), "Ibn Qutayba and the Monkeys", *Studia Islamica* 89, pp. 43–74 (p. 60).

17 Al-Jāḥiẓ, *K. al-Ḥayawān*, ed. Hārūn, vol. IV, pp. 85 sq.

18 Ibid., vol. IV, pp. 86 sqq; Lactantius, *Divine Institutes*, IV, 2:5, tr. by A. Bowen and P. Garnsey, Liverpool Univ. Press, Liverpool, 2003, p. 227; *cf.* TG, vol. III, pp. 411 sq.

other examples of *ṣarfa*, including the *jinn* who keep trying to eavesdrop on conversions in heaven, apparently never learning better; but he seems to be aware that this is an argument that only believers would accept, for he adds that the Dahrī cannot expect the same (sort of reasoning) "from people who accept worship and messengers as from the pure Dahrī (*al-dahrī al-ṣirf*), who does not acknowledge anything other than what he sees himself (*mā awjadahu ʾl-ʿiyān*) and that which works in the same way as seeing things for oneself (*mā yajrī majrā ʾl-ʿiyān*)".[19] Here as in the reference to the corrupt nature of the historical tradition we are being told something about Dahrī epistemology: a Dahrī is someone who deems information transmitted from others to be unacceptable if it does not conform to reason and to whom evidence consists in what he sees for himself and what is of the same nature as that (which is not further explained). Al-Jāḥiẓ continues:

> The Dahrī knows [that we believe][20] we have a lord who has brought the bodies into existence (*ikhtaraʿa al-ajsām*) and that He is alive, but not through life, knowing, but not through knowledge, that He is a thing, but cannot be divided, that He has no length, breadth, or depth, and that the prophets can revive the dead, all of which the Dahrī holds to be impossible (*mustankar*).[21]

Once again, the Dahrī, or rather the "pure Dahrī", is identified as somebody who 70
does not believe in God, not even God as defined by the Muʿtazilites. So he holds the bodies of which the world is made up to exist on their own and denies that prophets (or anyone, presumably) can bring people back to life.

Al-Jāḥiẓ makes several of the same points in another discussion of the *jinn* who try to eavesdrop on discussions in heaven.[22] The Qurʾān says that the *jinn* in question had balls of fire thrown at them when they tried to do so (Q. 72:8 sq.; cf. 15:17 sq.; 37:7 sq.). "Some people", later identified as Dahrīs, claimed that it was absurd to suppose that creatures endowed with superior intelligence should go on trying: they would have learnt from the Qurʾān (which they had heard) that God always does as He threatens; and that apart, they would have learnt from their long experience (*ṭūl al-tajriba*), from plain seeing for themselves (*al-ʿiyān*

19 Al-Jāḥiẓ, *K. al-Ḥayawān*, ed. Hārūn, vol. IV, pp. 89 sq.
20 Inserted by the editor, though it seems superfluous.
21 Al-Jāḥiẓ, *K. al-Ḥayawān*, ed. Hārūn, vol. IV, p. 90.
22 Ibid., vol. VI, pp. 265 sqq.; partial tr. in C. Pellat (1967), *The Life and Works of Jāḥiẓ*, translations of selected texts, tr. from the French by D.M. Hawke, Routledge, London, pp. 176 sqq.

al-ẓāhir), and from some telling each other about it (*ikhbār baʿḍihim li-baʿḍ*).[23] That the *jinn* should have learnt from the Qur'ān is an argument based on the opponents' premises. The rest tells us what counted as legitimate sources of knowledge to the Dahrī: experience, seeing for oneself, and information from others (*empeiria, autopsia*, and *historia* in the terminology of Greek empiricist doctors).[24]

Al-Jāḥiẓ once more seems to accept that the Dahrīs are right in terms of the normal rules of things, for he responds by invoking the *ṣarfa* theory again, once more adducing the Israelites in the desert and other examples, including Solomon and the Queen of Sheba, and explaining that God diverts the minds of people so as to expose them to trials (*al-miḥna*), for it is when people are tested that obedience and disobedience become manifest. Once more he is aware that his explanation will not be acceptable to Dahrīs, for he mentions that there are other examples "which go against the Dahrī method (*mimmā yukhālafu fīhi ṭarīq al-dahriyya*)", and explains that "the Dahrī does not acknowledge anything other than sense impressions and regularities (*al-maḥsūsāt wa'l-ʿādāt*), in contrast with this doctrine (of *ṣarfa*)".[25] Again, the Dahrīs are identified as empiricists. Earlier we were told that they only believed in what they saw for themselves or what was of the same nature, or in experience, seeing for themselves, and information from others (when it accorded with reason); here, the
71 basis on which one accumulates experience and acquires the | ability to reason about it is implicitly defined as sense impressions, including the observation of regularities.

Al-Jāḥiẓ adds that the Dahrī cannot use the *ṣarfa* argument

> as long as he persists in not believing in monotheism (*al-tawḥīd*) and continues not to recognise anything but the heavenly sphere (*al-falak*) and its doings, and continues to hold the dispatch of messengers (*irsāl al-rusul*) to be impossible, and to believe that the command and prohibition, as also the reward and punishment, are other than what we say, and that God cannot order by way of testing things, only by way of uniform/irreversible decree (*lā yajūzu an ya'mara min jihat al-ikhtibār illā min jihat al-ḥazm/jazm*).[26]

---

23 Al-Jāḥiẓ, *K. al-Ḥayawān*, ed. Hārūn, vol. VI, pp. 4sq.

24 Cf. R.J. Hankinson (1995), *The Sceptics*, Routledge, London, ch. 13, esp. pp. 227sq.

25 Al-Jāḥiẓ, *K. al-Ḥayawān*, ed. Hārūn, vol. VI, p. 269.

26 Ibid., vol. VI, pp. 269sq. The text has *al-ḥazm*; *al-jazm* was suggested to me by Joseph Witztum.

In other words, the regularities one observed did not admit of exceptions: God could not break His own laws in the Dahrī view. Once again the Dahrī replaces God with the celestial sphere, rejecting the reality of prophets, divine law and otherworldly retribution, but here he actually speaks of God, possibly because al-Jāḥiẓ has made him do so, but more probably because he would do so in actual fact, if only for purposes of the argument. The Dahrīs also argue on the basis of their opponents' premises in the discussion of the *jinn*, where they refer to the *jinn* as creatures endowed with superior intelligence even though they did not believe in *jinn* themselves, or for that matter in devils, angels, veridical dreams (*al-ruʾyā*), or charms, as al-Jāḥiẓ tells us elsewhere.[27] But the Dahrī was not a monotheist to al-Jāḥiẓ: he did not believe in *al-tawḥīd*. Elsewhere, al-Jāḥiẓ casually refers to "the difference between the *madhāhib al-dahriyya* and *madhāhib al-muwaḥḥidīn* (the doctrines of the Dahrīs and the doctrines of the monotheists)".[28] A Dahrī failed to count as a monotheist because he had no God, not because he had many: a *muwaḥḥid* is here the opposite of an atheist, not of a *mushrik*.

On the question of Dahrī cosmology al-Jāḥiẓ says more in a passage in which he is quoting from his teacher al-Naẓẓām. According to the latter, Dahrīs did not all have the same beliefs. "Some of them say that this world of ours is made of four principles (lit. pillars, *arkān*), heat, cold, dryness, and moisture, and that other things are outcomes, combination, and generation (*natāʾij wa-tarkīb wa-tawlīd*)". Others also claimed that the world is made of four principles, but identified them as "earth, air, water, and fire", i.e. the elements rather than the elementary qualities. The first group cast the elementary qualities as bodies (*ajsāman*), the latter cast the elements | as substances (*jawāhir*) and the 72
elementary qualities as accidents.[29] They, apparently all of them, gave priority to the sense of touch (by which the four elements and elementary qualities could be perceived) and held all smells, colours, and sounds to be composed of those four. Al-Jāḥiẓ devotes many pages to his teacher's refutations of their physics, but we may leave them aside here, except for his observation that some people held there to be a fifth pillar in the form of spirit (*rūḥ*).[30]

27 Ibid., vol. II, p. 139.

28 Ibid., vol. I, p. 217, 8 sq.

29 Ibid., vol. V, p. 40.

30 Ibid., vol. V, p. 47, 5.

Other Issues

So far, we have only considered al-Jāḥiẓ's book on animals, but he discusses Dahrīs in other works as well. In his *ʿUthmāniyya* he has a passage in which he accuses the Shīʿites of making the imamate unduly complicated: they made it more difficult than problems such as assessing the probity of transmitters (*taʿdīl* and *tajwīr*), distinguishing between things done on the basis of innate nature and those stemming from free choice (*al-faṣl bayna ʾl-ṭibāʿ waʾl-ikhtiyār*), the arguments for and against anthropomorphism (*al-tashbīh*), and the relative status of information handed down by the tradition versus rational arguments (*majīʾ al-akhbār wa-ḥujaj al-ʿuqūl*). He held this to be excessive because

> we have never seen anyone turning godless (*alḥada*) or dualist (*tazandaqa*) because of an error in the doctrine of the imamate or disagreement over it, whereas those who have apostatised as dualists and Dahrīs (*man irtadda zindīqan aw dahriyyan*) over these questions are uncountable.[31]

Two of the questions over which people would turn dualist or Dahrī are theological (anthropomorphism, the determination of our acts), and two are epistemological (the reliability of transmitters and the value of transmitted information versus rational arguments). To start with the former, the Dahrīs must have been among those who stripped God of His anthropomorphic features, in their case by reducing Him to mere nature in the form of the heavenly sphere or to nothing at all; and they must have held our acts to be determined by nature. On this second point al-Jāḥiẓ offers some corroborating evidence. He tells us that al-Naẓẓām had a brother-in-law called Abū ʾl-ʿAbbās who "believed in the stars (*kāna yadīnu biʾl-nujūm*) and did not believe anything to happen except in accordance with nature (*ṭibāʿ*)".[32] One takes it that he was a Dahrī, though al-
73 Jāḥiẓ politely avoids branding a member of his teacher's family as | such; and the *ṭibāʿ* which Abū ʾl-ʿAbbās saw as determining events was presumably the particular mixture of the four elementary qualities in things, including ourselves, in conjunction with the rotation of the heavenly sphere. Elsewhere al-Jāḥiẓ mentions the importance of distinguishing between the science of the natures (*ʿilm al-ṭabāʾiʿ*) and free will (*al-ikhtiyār*), implying that if one did not, belief in the four natures would lead to determinism.[33]

---

31 Al-Jāḥiẓ (1955), *Kitāb al-ʿUthmāniyya*, ed. ʿA.-S.M. Hārūn, Dār al-Kitāb al-ʿArabī, Cairo, pp. 270 sq.

32 Al-Jāḥiẓ, *K. al-Ḥayawān*, ed. Hārūn, vol. I, p. 148, 6 sqq.

33 Ibid., vol. I, p. 218, 5.

As regards the reliability of transmitters and the relative role of tradition (*akhbār*) and rational arguments (*ḥujaj al-ʿuqūl*), we have seen that Dahrīs took the implausible features of the story of Solomon and Sheba as evidence of the corrupt nature of the historical tradition (*fasād akhbārikum*). In line with this, they seem to have impugned the veracity of the Muslim transmitters, possibly taking up the science of *taʿdīl* and *tajwīr* in order to demonstrate its uselessness. They themselves clearly judged reports from others on the basis of their contents, rejecting them if they failed to conform to reason. They operated on the tacit assumption that divine intelligence would not be radically different from that of humans, so that information coming from a divine source would not clash with our own sense of true and false, or right and wrong, and they picked out what to them were absurd stories in the Qurʾān in order to prove that the book could not be of divine origin. To traditionalist believers, by contrast, there was no guarantee that information coming from a divine intelligence vastly superior to ours would conform to our limited reasoning. Since humans had no access to the metaphysical realm apart from the revelation that God had made available to them, they could not evaluate the authenticity of the information coming from that realm (in the form of Qurʾān and Ḥadīth) on the basis of its contents, only on the basis of the chains of transmission through which it had been passed down: if the material had been properly transmitted, the authoritative nature of the contents was guaranteed. Al-Jāḥiẓ occupies a position midway between the two, for as a Muʿtazilite he shared the Dahrī view that there was continuity between divine and human reason, without wanting to jettison either the Qurʾān or the tradition whenever they seemed to say something unreasonable: this is why he likes the *ṣarfa* doctrine, which offers a rational explanation for seemingly irrational claims in the Qurʾān.

Dahrism on the Ground 74

Al-Jāḥiẓ clearly thinks of Dahrīs and Zindīqs as closely related: it was as one or the other that people had been brought to apostasy by the difficult questions, and he links the two elsewhere as well.[34] The fact that he thinks of them as apostates shows they are people within the Muslim community who have come to subscribe to unacceptable ideas, not unbelievers from outside it. This is also

34 Cf. ibid., vol. IV, pp. 432–434, where he tells the Christians that they are neither Zindīqs nor Dahrīs, Muslims nor Jews; "Ḥujaj al-nubuwwa", in *Rasāʾil*, ed. Hārūn, vol. III, p. 281, where he notes that no hypocrite, Zindīq, or Dahrī can relate that Muḥammad ever held back or fled from a battle; and the references given below, nn. 37, 45, 48.

clear from the Dahrī familiarity with the Qurʾān, and from the general manner in which al-Jāḥiẓ refers to them: it is within his own community that they are dissenters. He intimates that they were numerous: uncountable numbers have apostatised as Zindīqs and Dahrīs, as he says. But he is clearly speaking hyperbolically. In his *Tarbīʿ* he tells us that they had never constituted a polity. "How come that we have never seen a nation of Dahrīs when we know that it is not possible for a Dahrī to claim prophethood?" "How come that no king has ever become a Dahrī?"[35] This seems to be meant as a teasing question: the obvious explanation is precisely that no Dahrī could claim prophethood, for nations were assumed to be formed on the basis of revealed laws; this is also why kings had no use for Dahrī doctrine. But if his reader had replied along these lines, al-Jāḥiẓ would probably have come up with a counter-example. In the next passage, in which he lets the reader try the obvious answer to the question why there had never been a nation of Manichaeans, namely that they did not allow fighting, he responds by adducing the Byzantines, whose religion did not endorse fighting either. Here he might have replied that actually there had been a nation of Dahrīs, for elsewhere he tells us that the ancient Greeks had been Dahrīs.[36] In any case, the crucial observation is the one that follows: "How come that we only find the doctrine of the Dahriyya among individuals, people here and there, and the occasional man (*fī ʾl-khāṣṣ waʾl-shādh waʾl-rajul al-nādir*)?" In other words, we should not envisage the Dahrīs as a sect or a school. Dahrism was an individual opinion, no doubt more commonly found in some circles than in others, like atheism today, but not a doctrine that could serve as the basis of community life. In so far as the Dahrīs had any collective existence, it will not have been as Dahrīs, but rather as devotees of sciences and
75 professions in which their opinions were widely encountered. It is | clear from what al-Jāḥiẓ has told us that the Dahrīs he knew were *aṣḥāb al-ṭabāʾiʿ*, people concerned with the four elementary qualities. Three sciences in particular are known to have been associated with the four elementary qualities, namely astrology, medicine, and alchemy. It seems to have been particularly in circles engaged in the study of the first two that Dahrism was common in al-Jāḥiẓ's time. At least we do not hear of any alchemists among them.

Al-Jāḥiẓ has already told us that the Dahrīs assigned God's role as governor of the universe to the heavenly sphere, suggesting that they were astrologers. In his refutation of Christianity he adds further evidence that they were often

35 Al-Jāḥiẓ (1955), *Kitāb al-Tarbīʿ waʾl-tadwīr*, ed. C. Pellat, Damascus, § 137 (drawn to my attention by Kevin van Bladel). Pellat suggests emending the passage to say that a Dahrī could claim prophethood, but this makes no sense.

36 Cf. below, n. 54.

envisaged as having studied astronomy/astrology and medicine, and also that they were associated with philosophy. He claims that the Jews did not approve of philosophical enquiry (*al-naẓar fī 'l-falsafa*) or rationalising theology (*al-kalām fī 'l-dīn*) on the grounds that such enquiries engendered all kinds of specious questions (*shubha*), that the only true knowledge is in the Torah and the books of the prophets, and that belief in medicine and the astrologers was among the things that caused people to become Zindīqs and Dahrīs (*wa-anna 'l-īmān bi'l-ṭibb wa-taṣdīq al-munajjimīn min asbāb al-zandaqa wa'l-khurūj ilā 'l-dahriyya*).[37] Medicine and astrology, then, had the same effect as difficult theological and epistemological questions.

It seems to be medicine and astrology that count as *al-naẓar fī 'l-falsafa* as opposed to *al-kalām fī 'l-dīn* in this passage. Elsewhere al-Jāḥiẓ speaks of *kalām al-falsafa* as opposed to *kalām al-dīn*,[38] here as there contrasting philosophy as pursued by *mutakallim*s (dialectitians) with theology as practised by them. *Kalām* was dialectics, a method of debating by questions and answers which was practised in disputations. Like so many other things in the Near East, it had a long history in the region, but all we need to note here is that disputation was the prime vehicle of intellectual enquiry in the Near East in al-Jāḥiẓ's time, both within religious communities and between them, and among friends no less than opponents. Eventually, *kalām* came to mean theological enquiry as pursued in books written in the style inherited from disputations, but this is not what it meant to al-Jāḥiẓ. To him, theological enquiry was just one branch of *kalām*; the other was philosophy, and it is clear from another passage in his book on animals that philosophy in this context meant enquiry into the physical universe, above all the elements or the elementary qualities of which it was widely assumed to be composed. A good *mutakallim* had to master the whole field, he said; he would not count as a leader

> unless he becomes equally good at the *kalām* of religion and the *kalām* 76
> of philosophy. The (true) scholar, in our opinion, is the one who combines the two, and the person who has got things right is the one who harmonises verification of monotheism (*taḥqīq al-tawḥīd*) with recognition of the essential characters (*ḥaqā'iq*) of the actions of the natures/elementary qualities (*al-ṭabā'i'*). He who claims that there can be no true monotheism without rejection of the essential characters of the elemen-

37 Al-Jāḥiẓ, "Al-Radd 'alā 'l-naṣārā", in *Rasā'il*, ed. Hārūn, vol. III, p. 314 (drawn to my attention by Krisztina Szilagyi).

38 Cf. below, n. 39.

> tary qualities (*anna ʾl-tawḥīd lā yaṣiḥḥu illā bi-ibṭāl ḥaqāʾiq al-ṭabāʾiʿ*) has carried over into monotheism his own weakness at *kalām*; and likewise, if he claims that there can be no true elementary qualities when they are linked with monotheism (*anna ʾl-ṭabāʾiʿ lā taṣiḥḥu idhā qarantahā biʾl-tawḥīd*): whoever says [that] has carried his own weakness at *kalām* into the elementary qualities. The godless person (*mulḥid*) will only despair of you when your respect for monotheism does *not* cause you to belittle the truth about the elementary qualities ... By my life, there is some difficulty (*shidda*) in their combination. I implore God that I will not tear down a pillar from my own doctrine every time my spear touches a gate of *kalām* that is difficult of entry! There is no benefit in anybody who is like that.[39]

There are two fields of *kalām* and there is tension between them. Some claim that one cannot be a true monotheist without rejecting everything said about the elementary qualities (*ṭabāʾiʿ*), evidently because the elementary qualities are what *mulḥid*s will discuss; and conversely there are people, whom one takes to be the *mulḥid*s, who say that one cannot be a good *mutakallim* without rejecting monotheism, i.e. belief in God. Al-Jāḥiẓ thinks that this is a mistake. In his view it is only by getting into the field and mastering it that one can make the *mulḥid* despair, undoubtedly because the *mulḥid* does not want the monotheists to colonise his science and take it over, hitching it to their world view at the cost of his own. Al-Jāḥiẓ is aware that taking over the field is a dangerous enterprise: he prays that he will not tear down any of his own doctrines whenever he comes to a difficult subject of *kalām*. But what he wants to do is precisely to make natural science compatible with monotheism and to expropriate it for the believers. The *mulḥid* whom al-Jāḥiẓ sees himself as confronting is presumably a Dahrī and/or Zindīq.

Here then we have a first-hand admission that getting into the science of the four natures was difficult for a believer, coupled with an assurance that it could be done. It is not surprising if some Jews held that it was best to stay away from medicine and astronomy, or that the jurist Abū Yūsuf held, or was reputed to have said, that "he who seeks the religion by means of *kalām* has become a Zindīq (*man ṭalaba ʾl-dīn biʾl-kalām tazandaqa*)".[40]

---

39 Al-Jāḥiẓ, *K. al-Ḥayawān*, ed. Hārūn, vol. II, pp. 134 sqq.

40 Cited in ʿAbd Allāh b. Muslim Ibn Qutayba (1966), *Taʾwīl mukhtalif al-ḥadīth*, ed. M.Z. al-Najjār, Maktabat al-Kulliyyāt al-Azhariyya, Cairo, p. 61, 6; cf. also *Kull al-kalām siwā ʾl-Qurʾān zandaqa*, attributed to an anonymous scholar from Shāsh in Abū Bakr Aḥmad b.

Among the tricky questions that al-Jāḥiẓ knew Dahrīs to ask was that "of 77
the anvil and the hammer, and the egg and the chicken", both clearly designed to prove that the world must always have existed: you cannot have an anvil without a hammer, but you cannot make the hammer without an anvil; you cannot have an egg without a chicken or a chicken without an egg.[41] It was such questions that caused people to tear down the pillars of their own doctrine when they came to difficult gates in *kalām*. But al-Jāḥiẓ practised what he preached: among his lost books there is one on the actions of the elementary qualities (*afʿāl al-ṭabāʾiʿ*).[42]

He was not the only one to be keen on science. All the Muʿtazilites were busy getting into physics at the time, writing books on atoms, bodies, natures, and more besides. They were appropriating the entire domain of ancient science as it had been transmitted to them in Iraq. At the same time, they were busy writing refutations of *mulḥid*s, Zindīqs, and the Dahriyya.[43] It is precisely because the Muʿtazilites were the scientific pioneers of the Muslims that they were the ones to confront the Dahrīs and so our chief sources of information about them. It is for the same reason that Muʿtazilites had a constant tendency to go off the rails, tearing down one pillar after another of their good monotheist beliefs as they got into the dangerous domain in which the Dahrīs specialised. Abū Saʿīd al-Ḥaḍrī, al-Ḥaddād, Abū ʿĪsā al-Warrāq, and Ibn al-Rāwandī are the best known examples.[44] But all that takes us away from al-Jāḥiẓ.

Al-Jāḥiẓ tells us more about the Dahrīs in his book in defence of prophethood, devoted to the criteria by which genuine reports from the past (*akhbār*) can be distinguished from false ones. Here he admits that many people can agree on an error: the Jews, Christians, Zoroastrians, Zindīqs, Dahrīs, and Buddhists (*aṣḥāb al-bidada*) all deny that the Prophet had wrought miracles and brought a revelation.[45] He insists that he is not writing his book because the criticisms of the godless (*ṭaʿn al-mulḥidīn*) were having any effect whatever

ʿAlī al-Khaṭīb al-Baghdādī (1971), *Sharaf aṣḥāb al-ḥadīth*, ed. M.S. Khaṭīboghlu, Dār Iḥyāʾ al-Sunna al-Nabawiyya, Ankara, p. 79, no. 170.

41 Al-Jāḥiẓ, *K. al-Tarbīʿ*, ed. Pellat, § 46.

42 *TG*, vol. VI, p. 314, no. 14.

43 Cf. above, n. 3. For refutations of unspecified *mulḥids*, *zindīqs*, and *aṣḥāb al-ṭābāʾiʿ* written about the same time, see Ibn al-Nadīm, *Fihrist*, ed. Tajaddud, pp. 204, 3, 11; 205, 8; 206, 13 sq.; 214, 15; 215, 2, 4, 7, 9.

44 *Cf. TG*, vol. IV, pp. 89 sqq., 289 sqq.

45 Al-Jāḥiẓ, "Ḥujaj al-nubuwwa", in *Rasāʾil*, ed. Hārūn, vol. III, p. 250. Cf. also the reference to some who *yatabaddadu* and some who *yatadahharu* at vol. III, p. 246, 9.

on the community.[46] For all that, he observes that if the pious ancestors who collected the Qurʾān had also collected the signs, miracles, and proofs of the prophet,

> 78 then it would not have been possible today for a denying Zindīq, a stubborn Dahrī, a libertine dandy, a misled person of feeble intelligence/education, or a duped young man (*lā zindīq jāḥid wa-lā dahrī muʿānid wa-lā mutaẓarrif*[47] *mājin wa-lā ḍaʿīf makhdūʿ wa-lā ḥadath maghrūr*) to deny the reality and truth of these events [...]. Nor would the godless person (*mulḥid*) have found an opportunity to win over the stupid person or deceive the young[48] [...]. If we didn't have so many people of weak intelligence/education (*ḍuʿafāʾ*) and so many intruders (*dukhalāʾ*) who speak our language and seek the help of our intellects against our stupid and foolish ones, then we would not take it upon ourselves to lay bare what is already clear.

The ancestors had omitted this task because it had not been necessary in their time, and what had caused the "ignorant, young, foolish, and reprobate people" to appear now was that they would "apply to their intellects more subtleties of *kalām* than they can master before having learnt the bulk of it", with the result that they "stray from the truth to the right and to the left".[49]

Here we have another indication of the social circles in which Dahrism, as also Zandaqa, flourished: the smart set. The questions over which people were in danger of apostatising appealed to the young and clever who liked to see themselves as sophisticated (*ẓarīf*) and who would adopt a nonchalant attitude to conventions, indulge in *mujūn* (playful inversion of norms), and generally madden their elders with their inappropriate behaviour. The Dahrīs and the Zindīqs are depicted as interlopers: they are non-Arabs using our language, that is to say people who have been brought into the community by the conquests and whose baleful influence is now all too widely felt. They seek the help of "our intellects" (*ʿuqūlinā*) against the foolish, presumably meaning that

46 Ibid., vol. III, pp. 224 sqq.

47 Thus the edition of Ḥ. al-Sandūbī (1933), *Rasāʾil al-Jāḥiẓ*, al-Maktaba al-Tijāriyya al-Kubrā, Cairo, p. 119, 7 (Hārūn has *mutaṭarrif*).

48 Reading *ghabī* for *ghanī* with al-Sandūbī, and *yastamīluhu* for *yastamlihu* with Hārūn.

49 Al-Jāḥiẓ, "Ḥujaj al-nubuwwa", in *Rasāʾil*, ed. Hārūn, vol. III, pp. 226 sq. (ed. al-Sandūbī, p. 119); for other translations, see C. Pellat (1953), *Le Milieu baṣrien et la formation de Ğāḥiẓ*, Librairie d'Amerique et d'Orient Adrien-Maisonneuve, Paris, p. 84; id., *Life and Works*, p. 40.

they seek to mobilise our rationality against our faith, succeeding among the young.[50] They are numerous and dangerous in that they seduce the young, and their means of seduction is *kalām*, which clever young people think they master without having any proper knowledge of it. "One misfortune is that every Muslim thinks that he is a *mutakallim* and that nobody is more entitled to argue with the *mulḥid*s than anyone else", as al-Jāḥiẓ remarks elsewhere, implicitly admitting that the encounters took place as much because the Muslims sought them out as because the godless were conspiring to undermine the faith of the believers.[51]

Kalām in this material is not simply a defensive tool, as later Muslims were 79
often to see it,[52] but on the contrary the all too enticing instrument of the very people who had to be combated, certainly the only means by which they could be combated, but also a lure and a snare, even in the eyes of someone like al-Jāḥiẓ, to whom *kalām* was the queen of the sciences. He depicts the half-studied people who thought they were masters of the craft as one of its banes in his epistle extolling the virtues of *kalām* as well.[53] As a professional, he wanted to keep control of his craft. But there can be no doubt that all those who were hostile to *kalām*, whether Jews or Muslims, had good reason to be worried by it; they were not simply being obscurantist.

Al-Jāḥiẓ also gives us some evidence on the cultural origins of Dahrism. "We all know that the intelligence of the ancient Greeks (*al-yūnāniyya*) was greater than suggested by their belief in Dahrism (*al-diyāna bi'l-dahriyya*) and their attentive worship of the signs of the zodiac and the stars", he casually remarks, noting that the intelligence of the Indians is likewise greater than suggested by their obedience to *al-budd* and worship of *al-bidada*, presumably meaning the Buddha and Buddha-idols.[54] Dahrism was pagan Greek thought to him; he did not associate it with India. In line with this, the Christians of al-Jāḥiẓ's time claimed that the Muslim philosophers were made on the model of the Christians (*iqtadaw ʿalā mithālihim*).[55] Christians did in fact speak of their theologians as philosophers, and they were prominent in medicine and astrology too,

---

50 Pellat has "s'aident de nos spéculations" (*Le Milieu*, p. 84), and "taking advantage our debates" (*Life and Works*, p. 40).

51 Al-Jāḥiẓ, "Al-Radd ʿalā 'l-naṣārā", in *Rasā'il*, ed. Hārūn, vol. III, p. 320.

52 Thus for example Ibn Khaldūn (n.d.), *Muqaddima*, Beirut, p. 507; F. Rosenthal (tr.) (1958), *The Muqaddimah: An Introduction to History*, 3 vols., Princeton Univ. Press, Princeton, vol. III, p. 34.

53 Al-Jāḥiẓ, "Ṣināʿat al-kalām", in *Rasā'il*, ed. Hārūn, vol. IV, p. 246.

54 Al-Jāḥiẓ, *K. al-Ḥayawān*, ed. Hārūn, vol. v, p. 327, 5.

55 Id., "Al-Radd ʿalā 'l-naṣārā", in *Rasā'il*, ed. Hārūn, vol. III, p. 315, 10.

as al-Jāḥiẓ himself noted with regret, stressing that the sciences which made them so prestigious were in fact taken over from the ancient Greeks.[56] The religion of the Christians resembled Zandaqa and Dahrism in some respects, he says, and the Christians were the source of all perplexity, being more strongly affected by Zandaqa, confusion, and perplexity than anyone else.[57] Indeed, it was thanks to their *mutakallims*, doctors, and astrologers that the Manichaean, Marcionite, Bardesanite, and other books had fallen into the hands of the elegant set, the frivolous and foolish young men whose desire to put on airs he bewails again. But here the complaint is entirely about Zandaqa without reference to Dahrism.[58]

80 Conclusion

Al-Jāḥiẓ's information may be summarised as follows. Dahrism was a conviction based on an empiricist epistemology to the effect that all genuine knowledge must be based on sense impressions, especially things one has seen for oneself, that is personal experience, and that information from others must be judged on the basis of reason, which in its turn must respect the rule-bound nature of the universe. Nothing in our experience or reason enables us to affirm the existence of God, angels, spirits, prophets, divine revelation, prophetic revival of the dead, or other divine violations of the natural order, nor does it allow for any belief in an afterlife. It does enable us to affirm that matter has always existed, that it has not been created, and that it is not regulated by a deity standing outside it, but on the contrary regulates itself. The regulatory mechanism is the heavenly sphere or (though this is only hinted at in al-Jāḥiẓ) a fifth entity called spirit. The irreducible components of the world are the four elementary qualities (heat, cold, dryness, and moisture) envisaged as bodies, or the four elements (fire, earth, air, and water) envisaged as substances, with the elementary qualities as accidents. Everything in the world is made of combinations of these four or, in the case of those who admitted the existence of spirit, these five.

Adherents of such views did not form a sect or a school. Dahrism was an individual opinion associated above all with the study of medicine and astrology, but like Zandaqa, with which it is often concatenated, it also appealed

56 Ibid., pp. 313 sq.

57 Ibid., p. 315.

58 Ibid., pp. 320 sq.

to those who saw themselves as sophisticated. It was pursued in disputations through the medium of *kalām*, both that of the type called *kalām al-falsafa* (medicine, astrology/astronomy, cosmology) and that called *kalām al-dīn* (theology, including epistemology). It was dangerous because it clashed with the monotheist world view and appealed to the young. In terms of cultural origin, it was seen as Greek, not Indian, and associated, again like Zandaqa, with the sciences of the Christians.

Dahrism (again like Zandaqa) was combated by the Muʿtazilites, but the two sides should not be envisaged as hostile camps in social terms. Like so many adherents of opposing views at the time, they moved in the same circles and were often personal friends, or even related by marriage. Al-Jāḥiẓ himself writes about them in a calm tone, though he disagrees sharply with their views and likes to think of them as immoral foreigners corrupting the good old Muslim ways.

The information in al-Jāḥiẓ tallies well with that given in other ninth-century sources, notably Ibn Qutayba, Muḥammad b. Shabīb, and Abū ʿĪsā, though this has not been demonstrated here. Needless to say, much information about the Dahriyya in the Islamic tradition is problematic and some of it is certainly useless, but the automatic assumption that hostile accounts of minorities credited
with views | completely unlike those of the majority must be dismissed as mere 81
constructions of the "other" is no better than the automatic belief that everything they say must be true. Not only were the Dahrīs real, they clearly played a major role in the formation of Muʿtazilite doctrine, some of which was formulated in opposition to them, and which occasionally came dangerously close to their views. In short, they were people of considerable importance.

Bibliography

Sources

Abdel Haleem, M.A.S. (tr.) (1995), *Chance or Creation? God's Design in the Universe*, attributed to al-Jāḥiẓ, Garnet, Reading.

Goodman, L.E. (tr.) (1978), *The Case of the Animals versus Man before the King of the Jinn: A Tenth-Century Ecological Fable of the Pure Brethren of Basra*, Twayne, Boston.

Ibn Ḥazm, ʿAlī b. Aḥmad (1317–1321H.), *Kitāb al-Faṣl fī ʾl-milal waʾl-ahwāʾ waʾl-niḥal*, 5 vols., Cairo.

Ibn al-Malāḥimī, Maḥmūd b. Muḥammad (1990), *Kitāb al-Muʿtamad fī uṣūl al-dīn*, ed. M. McDermott and W. Madelung, al-Hoda, London.

Ibn al-Nadīm, Muḥammad b. Isḥāq (1971), *Kitāb al-Fihrist*, ed. R. Tajaddud, Maktabat al-Asadī, Tehran.

Ibn Qutayba, ʿAbd Allāh b. Muslim (1966), *Taʾwīl mukhtalif al-ḥadīth*, ed. M.Z. al-Najjār, Maktabat al-Kulliyyāt al-Azhariyya, Cairo.

Ibn Khaldūn, see also Rosenthal.

Ibn Khaldūn (n.d.), *Muqaddima*, Beirut.

Ikhwān al-Ṣafā (1957), *Rasāʾil Ikhwān al-Ṣafā wa-khullān al-wafāʾ*, 4 vols., Dār Bayrūt, Beirut.

Al-Jāḥiẓ, see also Hārūn, Pellat, al-Sandūbī.

Al-Jāḥiẓ (attrib.) (1928), *Kitāb al-Dalāʾil waʾl-iʿtibār ʿalā ʾl-khalq waʾl-tadbīr*, ed. M.R. al-Ṭabbākh, al-Maṭbaʿa al-ʿIlmiyya, Aleppo.

Al-Jāḥiẓ (1938), *Kitāb al-Ḥayawān*, ed. ʿA.-S.M. Hārūn, 7 vols., Maktabat Muṣṭafā al-Bābī al-Ḥalabī, Cairo.

Al-Jāḥiẓ (1955), *Kitāb al-ʿUthmāniyya*, ed. ʿA.-S.M. Hārūn, Dār al-Kitāb al-ʿArabī, Cairo.

Al-Jāḥiẓ (1955), *Kitāb al-Tarbīʿ waʾl-tadwīr*, ed. C. Pellat, Damascus.

Al-Khaṭīb al-Baghdādī, Abū Bakr Ahmad b. ʿAlī (1971), *Sharaf aṣḥāb al-ḥadīth*, ed. M.S. Khaṭīboğlu, Dār Iḥyāʾ al-Sunna al-Nabawiyya, Ankara.

Lactantius (2003), *Divine Institutes*, tr. A. Bowen and P. Garnsey, Liverpool Univ. Press, Liverpool.

Al-Maqdisī, Muṭahhar b. Ṭāhir (1899–1919), *Kitāb al-Badʾ waʾl-taʾrīkh*, ed. C. Huart, 6 vols., Ernest Leroux, Paris.

Al-Māturīdī, Muḥammad b. Muḥammad (1970), *Kitāb al-Tawḥīd*, ed. F. Kholeif, Dar al-Mashreq, Beirut.

Pellat, C. (1967), *The Life and Works of Jāḥiẓ*, translations of selected texts, tr. from the French by D.M. Hawke, Routledge, London.

82 Al-Rāzī, Abū Ḥātim (1977), *Aʿlām al-nubuwwa*, ed. Ṣ. al-Ṣāwī, Muʾassasa-yi Pizhūhishī-yi Ḥikmat wa Falsafa-yi Īrān, Tehran.

Rosenthal, F. (tr.) (1958), *The Muqaddimah: An Introduction to History*, 3 vols., Princeton Univ. Press, Princeton.

Al-Sandūbī, Ḥ. (1933), *Rasāʾil al-Jāḥiẓ*, al-Maktaba al-Tijāriyya al-Kubrā, Cairo.

Studies

Cook, M. (1999), "Ibn Qutayba and the Monkeys", *Studia Islamica* 89, pp. 43–74.

Daiber, H. (1999), "Rebellion gegen Gott. Formen atheistischen Denkens im frühen Islam", in F. Niewöhner and O. Pluta (eds.), *Atheismus im Mittelalter und in der Renaissance*, Harrassowitz, Wiesbaden, pp. 23–44.

Goldziher, I., and Goichon, A.-M. (1965), "Dahriyya", *Encyclopaedia of Islam*, 2nd edition, Brill, Leiden, vol. II, pp. 95–97.

Hankinson, R.J. (1995), *The Sceptics*, Routledge, London.

Pellat, C. (1953), *Le milieu baṣrien et la formation de Ǧāḥiẓ*, Librairie d'Amérique et d'Orient Adrien-Maisonneuve, Paris.

Shaki, M., and Gimaret, D. (1993), "Dahrī", *Encyclopaedia Iranica*, http://www.iranicaonline.org.

Stern, S.M. (1960), "Abū ʿĪsā al-Warrāq", *Encyclopaedia of Islam*, 2nd edition, Brill, Leiden, vol. I, p. 130.

Van Ess, J. (1991–1997), *Theologie und Gesellschaft im 2. und 3. Jahrhundert Hidschra, eine Geschichte des religiösen Denkens im frühen Islam*, 6 vols., De Gruyter, Berlin/New York.

Walker, J.T. (2004), "Against the Eternity of the Stars: Disputation and Christian Philosophy in Late Sasanian Mesopotamia", in G. Gnoli and A. Panaino (eds.), *La Persia e Bisanzio* (Atti dei Convegni Lincei 2001), Accademia Nazionale dei Lincei, Rome, pp. 518–535.

Walker, J.T. (2006), *The Legend of Mar Qardagh: Narrative and Christian Heroism in Late Antique Iraq* (Transformation of the Classical Heritage, 40), University of California Press, Berkeley/Los Angeles/London.

CHAPTER 6

Ungodly Cosmologies[1]

The reader may wonder both what the title means and why a subject of this nature should be included in a volume on Islamic theology. The answer is that a number of cosmologies of late antique origin which left little or no room for God in the creation and management of the world played a major role in the development of Muslim *kalām*, a field normally translated as (dialectical) theology. In fact, *kalām* covered much the same range of topics as Greek physics, if in a very different way: the principles (in the sense of the ultimate constituents of the universe), the origin and end of the material world, the nature of man, God and his relationship with us. To Greek philososphers, physics was a key to the nature of the gods; to Muslim theologians, it was God who was a key to physics. This was a well-known source of tension between reason as the sole basis of the search for the truth and reason as the handmaid of revelation. Al-Jāḥiẓ (d. 255/869), who distinguished between *kalām al-falsafa*, dialectical philosophy (covering natural science), and *kalām al-dīn*, dialectical theology (covering God and his relationship with us), readily admitted that philosophy was dangerous, but nonetheless insisted that a good practitioner of *kalām* had to master both fields (Crone 2010–2011: 75f.).

When the curtain opens on Muslim *kalām* in the mid-second/eighth century, the field of *kalām al-falsafa* was dominated by thinkers whom Muslims called Zindīqs and Dahrīs and bracketed as *mulḥid*s, a term sometimes translated as 'atheists' but better rendered as 'godless' or 'ungodly people'. All *mulḥid*s denied that God had created the world from nothing, and some denied his creation, government, and ultimate judgement of the world altogether along with any form of afterlife. The Muslims had to develop their own cosmology to counter the ungodly systems, and they did so by assimilating and gradually transforming those of their rivals. The ungodly cosmologies thus show us a bridge between late antique and Islamic thought.

Cosmology had acquired great religious importance in late antiquity, for Zoroastrians, Gnostics, and Platonists (Christian, pagan, and other) had all come to share the convictions that the key to our troubled human condition was to be found in primordial events leading to the creation of this world, rather than in early human history. All offered detailed accounts of these events,

1 I am indebted to Michael Cook for reading and commenting on a draft of this article.

© KONINKLIJKE BRILL NV, LEIDEN, 2016 | DOI: 10.1163/9789004319318_007

and most drew on Greek philosophy for their formulation. Thinkers such as Basilides (fl. 120–140), Valentinus (d. *c.* 160), Marcion (d. *c.* 160), Bardesanes/Bar Dayṣān (d. 222), and Origen (d. *c.* 254), who had a huge impact on Near Eastern thought on both sides of the Euphrates, all drew their main philosophical inspiration from Middle Platonism and Stoicism. So too did the immensely influential physician Galen (d. *c.* 200). The Platonic-Stoic legacy is still discernible in the thought of the Zindīqs and Dahrīs, and in *kalām* influenced by them, along with occasional input from the rival Sceptical and Epicurean schools and intriguing suggestions of a strong interest in the Presocratics. Also discernible, however, is the magnetic pull exercised from perhaps the sixth century onwards by Aristotle's *Categories*, treated as a guide to ontology, not just to logic. But by the fourth/tenth century the irresistible force was Neoplatonism, carried by Ismailis and philosophers (*falāsifa*) of a new type who owed their ideas to Arabic translations of Plato, Aristotle, and the Neoplatonist commentators. Henceforth it was the emanatory scheme of the Neoplatonists that dominated cosmological debates; the old-style *mulḥid*s no longer played a major role in them, though they still attracted attention, especially for their denial of the creator and of the afterlife (Dhanani 1994: 4f., 182–187; *Encyclopaedia of Islam*², s.v. 'Dahriyya'; *Encyclopaedia Iranica*, s.v. 'Dahrī'; *Encyclopaedia of Islam*³, s.v. 'Dahrīs').

1 The Actors

The *mulḥid*s had complicated backgrounds. Some were Marcionites, Bardesanites, or Manichaeans by origin, that is to say they came from Christian communities of a type proscribed by the victorious Christian churches. (Even the Manichaeans counted themselves as Christians.) But by early Islamic times the Marcionites and Bardesanites had become so heavily Iranianized that they were barely recognizable as Christians, and the Muslims classified all three sects as dualist, deeming them ineligible for protected status. The communities nonetheless survived, but many of their members appear to have been forced to convert, or to have found it prudent to do so. It was nominal converts from these three religions and others attracted to their beliefs who were called Zindīqs. The term is derived from the Aramaic *ṣaddīq* by which the Manichaean 'elect' were known,[2] and the Muslims sometimes used it of real Manichaeans too. Just

2 Cf. *Encyclopaedia of Islam*², s.v. 'zindīḳ' (de Blois), decisively eliminating the derivation of the word from *zand*.

as the Zindīqs were not true Muslims, however, so they were not true adherents of the religions they had left behind. A Zindīq in the period *c.* 750–900 was usually a man who had lost faith in any positive religion, or even in any God.

The Dahrīs mostly seem to have their intellectual roots in the older belief systems dismissed by Christians as 'pagan'. When the emperor Justinian (r. 527–565) set out to eradicate paganism from the Roman empire, he took the precaution of also persecuting those pagans who had 'decided to espouse in word the name of Christians' (Procopius, *Anecdota*, 11: 32), and it was probably as nominal Christians that most of them survived. Those persecuted by the Sasanians, who imposed Zoroastrianism as understood in Pārs (Ar. Fārs) on their Iranian and occasionally also non-Iranian subjects, seem likewise to have included pagans in the sense of people who were not Zoroastrians, Jews, or Christians,[3] but mostly they were bearers of local, non-Persian forms of Zoroastrianism (cf. Crone 2012a: chs. 15–16). The *Baga Nask*, an Avestan book preserved only in a Pahlavi summary, tells of 'apostates' (*yašarmogān*) who had been defeated and kept their apostasy concealed, reluctantly calling themselves Zoroastrian priests and teaching the good religion despite their heretical inclinations (*Dēnkard*, book IX, 52: 3). These 'apostates' would hardly have been forced to officiate on behalf of official Zoroastrianism if they had not been priests of what the Sasanians took to be deviant forms of their own faith.

Whatever their origin, Dahrīs shared with Zindīqs the feature of having lost belief in their ancestral religion without having acquired belief in another. A dillusioned attitude is attested even among pagans who had not been forced into any religious community. In the Jewish-Christian Pseudo-Clementines, probably composed in Antioch or Edessa *c.* 300–360, one of the heroes is a well-born pagan who believes in astrology and denies the existence of both God and providence on the grounds that everything is governed by chance and fate, meaning the conjunctions under which one happens to have been born, and who resists conversion because he simply cannot believe that souls are immortal and subject to punishment for sins. Nemesius of Emesa (*c.* 390) also mentions deniers of providence and the afterlife (Nemesius, *Nature*, 213 f., 217). So too does Theodoret of Cyrrhus (d. *c.* 460), but now they were nominal Christians to whom it was still physics that provided a key to God rather than the other way round: it is by appeals to nature and the ancient Greeks that Theodoret tries to persuade them (Theodoret, *Providence*, 9: 23 f.). Saint Simeon

3 Cf. Theodore Bar Koni, *Liber*, mimrā I, 29 f.; Moses Bar Kepha, *Hexaemeronkommentar*, I.13.1–15; Muqammiṣ, *ʿIshrūn*, 7: 6, where they are *ṣābiʾa*, clearly in the sense of pagans, not Sabians of Harran; compare Yaʿqūbī, *Tārīkh*, 1: 166, 179 (Greek, Roman, and Iranian kings as Sabians); Balīnūs, *Sirr*, 1: 2.3.6, p. 35.

the Younger (d. 592) found Antioch to be teeming with impious mockers whose errors included denial of the resurrection, astrological beliefs to the effect that natural disasters and human misbehaviour were caused by the position of the stars, 'automatism' (presumably meaning the view that the world had arisen on its own), and the claim, here characterized as Manichaean, that the creation was due to fate or chance (van den Ven 1962: §§157, 161). On the Sasanian side there is evidence for denial of the resurrection already in the third century. The first attestations could concern belief in reincarnation, widespread in the Jibāl and elsewhere, but by the sixth century the denial is coupled with loss of faith in God/the gods, the creation, and afterlife of any kind. When the famous physician Burzoē, active under Khusraw I (r. 531–570), lost faith in his ancestral religion, he *tried* not to 'deny the awakening and resurrection, reward and punishment'. A Pahlavi advice work informs us that man becomes wicked on account of five things, one of which is lack of belief 'in the (imperishableness of) the soul', i.e denial of afterlife of any kind; and several other works stress that one should be free of doubts concerning the existence of the gods, paradise, hell, and the resurrection (Crone 2012a: 373 ff.). Burzoē remained an unhappy sceptic who held the truth to be beyond us, but others turned into assertive materialists, that is to say Dahrīs.

In short, the *mulḥid*s had their roots in proscribed communities whose members had been directly or indirectly forced into Christianity or Persian Zoroastrianism, and thereafter into Islam. Dahrīs were insincere Muslims who professed Islam out of fear of the sword, as al-Qummī remarks (*Tafsīr*, 2: 270, *ad* Q. 45: 24).[4] There can hardly be much doubt that the massive use of coercion on behalf of God in late antiquity and early Islam had played a role in eroding their faith in anything except their own reason, but other factors were also at work. One was the sheer diversity of rival religions. When religions compete in a free market situation, as in modern America, the competition can apparently increase religiosity (Stark and Finke 2000, and other works by the same authors; Kraus 1934: 15 ff.), but it certainly did not do so in the past, when religion was not a freely purchased commodity and when the competition between rival forms was often felt to undermine the truth of all of them. In the sixth century the sheer diversity of beliefs troubled Burzoē and Paul the Persian; by the tenth century it troubled Muslims too (Crone 2006: 21 f.). The only way to evaluate the competing claims was by use of reason.

One way in which reason came to sit in judgement over religious claims was by disputation, a competitive sport of enormous popularity on both sides of

4 For the Dahrīs as interlopers, see also Jāḥiẓ, *Ḥujaj*, 118.

the Euphrates both before and after the rise of Islam (Lim 1995; Cook 1980; Cook 2007). The rules required the disputers to base their arguments on shared premisses, meaning that appeals to scripture and tradition were only allowed in disputation with co-religionists, and even then it was reason which had to sit in judgement over the different interpretations. Debaters thus learnt to translate their beliefs into claims that could stand on their own and be defended by Aristotelian logic. The *Categories* was the disputer's Bible. Already the third-century Apelles, a deviant Marcionite, had used dialectical syllogisms to discredit the Pentateuch, and the Manichaeans soon learned to set aside their extravagant mythology to become fearsome disputers (Grant 1993: ch. 6; Lim 1995: ch. 3). There is no trace of mythology in the debate staged by Justinian at Constantinople between a (chained) Manichaean and a certain Paul the Persian representing the Christian side,[5] nor is there in the cosmologies of Manichaean, Marcionite, Bardesanite, and Zoroastrian origin that the Zindīqs and Dahrīs fielded in disputation with the Muslims. Inevitably, many disputers came to regard reason rather than scripture and tradition as the ultimate authority at all times, not just for purposes of disputation. Al-Jāḥiẓ complains that young men would foolishly rush into disputations with *mulḥid*s, convinced of their own dialectical skills, only to be seduced by them, and roundly declares that 'countless' people had apostatized as Zindīqs and Dahrīs over complicated questions of *kalām* (Crone 2010–2011: 72). It was in their relentless refusal of claims based on scripture and tradition that both the godlessness and the seductiveness of the Zindīqs and Dahrīs lay.

Zindīqs and Dahrīs are first mentioned in the 120s/740s and receive particular attention in the third/ninth century, though they continue to be attested down to the Mongol invasions. They formed loose clusters of individuals, not sects. Dahrīs seem mostly to have been doctors, astrologers, and others interested in the workings of nature; Zindīqs were predominantly secretaries, courtiers, poets, and other members of the elegant set. How far similar convictions flourished among uneducated urbanites and villagers is unknown.[6] In learned gatherings Zindīqs and Dahrīs would pick out inconsistencies in the Qur'ān and *ḥadīth*, scoff at accounts of claims running counter to normal experience, and sometimes mock Islamic ritual. But they lived like everyone else, observing the normal rules of propriety and formalities of the law (Masʿūdī, *Murūj*, 5: 84 [3, §1846]; Ṭabarī, *Tārīkh*, 3: 422 f.; Van Ess 1991–1997: ii. 17; al-Rāzī, *Tafsīr*, 23: 18, *ad*

5 Photinus, *Disputationes*. On the several persons called 'Paul the Persian', see Gutas 1982: 239 n.

6 For a suggestion that the *ʿāmmī* might be a Dahrī, see Maqdisī, *Badʾ*, 1: 121.2; cf. also Maimonides on the multitudes (below, n. 73 and the text thereto).

Q 22: 17 f.), and relations between them and Muʿtazilite *mutakallims* appear to have been friendly. Al-Naẓẓām (d. *c.* 220–230/835–45), who wrote against both Dahrīs and *mulḥids*, had a brother-in-law who attributed everything to natural causes and the stars (Jāḥiẓ, *Ḥayawān*, 1: 148). Zindīqs were particularly close to the Shīʿites. Shīʿite sources abhor them and invariably depict the imams as refuting them in Medina (Vajda 1938: esp. 222 f.; Chokr 1993: esp. 109, 111–113), but it is clear from the doctrines of the Shīʿite *mutakallim* Hishām b. al-Ḥakam (d. *c.* 179/795) that the interaction was in Iraq and involved Muslim appropriation and reshaping of the rival doctrines, not just refutation of them.

Dahrīs seem rarely to have been persecuted,[7] but Zindīqs came in for a purge under the caliph al-Mahdī (r. 775–785), to whom a Zindīq seems to have been anything from a genuine Manichaean to an irreverent courtier. There is no mention of Dahrīs in this connection, perhaps because the two terms were sometimes used synonymously, but more probably because the Zindīqs flourished at the court, where they sometimes inclined to Manichaeism in a religious sense and where the poets would shamelessly jockey for position by denouncing their rivals as Zindīqs. *Mutakallims*, by contrast, would close ranks against outsiders (Jāḥiẓ, *Ḥayawān*, 4: 450; 6: 37). Al-Mahdī is reported to have ordered the *mutakallims* to write refutations of the *mulḥids* (Masʿūdī, *Murūj*, 8: 293 [5, § 3447]; Yaʿqūbī, *Mushākala*, 24), and whatever he may have meant by that term (if he used it), the *mutakallims* did not limit their refutations to Zindīqs. Books against dualists, Manichaeans, Dahrīs, and *mulḥids* in general were composed by theologians active under and after al-Mahdī. But only their titles survive, and we have no statements by the Zindīqs or Dahrīs themselves. We do, however, have works presenting cosmologies closely related to theirs in the *Book of Treasures* by the Christian doctor Job of Edessa (writing *c.* 817), the *Sirr al-khalīqa* attributed to Apollonius of Tyana (Balīnūs, Balīnas) (*c.* 205/820?), and the mostly fourth/tenth-century alchemical corpus attributed to the Shīʿite Jābir (heavily Neoplatonized). We hear of books by Zindīqs, including a *Kitāb al-shukūk* by a Zindīq espousing Sceptical views, but not of books by Dahrīs (Ibn al-Nadīm, *Fihrist*, 204, 401; trans. Dodge, i. 387; ii. 804).[8] Whether they wrote or not, all *mulḥids* aired their views in disputations, the main vehicle of religious and philosophical discussion at the time.

7 For an exception, see Rashīd b. al-Zubayr, *Dhakhāʾir*, 140.

8 Cf. Van Ess 1991–1997: ii. 17 and n. 20. This Zindīq, Ṣāliḥ b. ʿAbd al-Quddūs, is also credited with dogmatist views.

II Epistemology

(a) *Scepticism*

The *mulḥid*s included both doubters and deniers (Jāḥiẓ, *Ḥayawān*, 6: 35f.). Some doubters were people suffering from religious uncertainty and loss of faith, like Burzoē, but those who fielded doubts in disputations were Sceptics in the technical sense of adherents of an epistemology to the effect that we can never know the true nature of things. Such Sceptics were known as *shākkūn*, *juhhāl*, *mutajāhilūn*, *ḥisbāniyya*, *muʿānida*, *lā adriyya*, and the like, and also, for reasons that remain obscure, as Sūfisṭāʾiyya, 'sophists' (Van Ess 1966: index s.v. 'Skepsis'; Van Ess 1968).

Scepticism is attested both as dogmatic assertion of our inability to know and as suspension of judgement. Al-Jāḥiẓ mentions a Sceptic who held that one could only know things by preponderance (*biʾl-aghlab*). This was the position of Academic Sceptics, and Galen had expounded both their views and those of their Pyrrhonic rivals in his *De optimo docendi*; perhaps al-Jāḥiẓ's Sceptic had found inspiration in this work (Jāḥiẓ, *Ḥayawān*, 6: 37; Floridi 2002: 17). More commonly, however, it is Pyrrhonic Scepticism with its suspension of judgement that is reflected in the sources. Pyrrhonic Scepticism had gone into empiricist medicine (Hankinson 1995: ch. 13), and also into disputation practice. As Gregory of Nazianzus (d. 389) remarked, Pyrrho, Sextus, and the practice of 'arguing to opposites' had infected the churches (Floridi 2002: 12); the sixth-century disputer Uranius is reported by Agathias to have been a Sceptic in Sextus' tradition, and Manichaean missionaries would apparently field Sceptical arguments in order to undermine the beliefs of potential proselytes and convert them (Agathias, *Histories*, 2: 29.1, 7; Pedersen 2004: 207).

According to Sceptical *mulḥid*s, all claims about reality had to be based on sense impressions, preferably or exclusively autopsy (*ʿiyān*, what one had seen for oneself) (Jāḥiẓ, *Ḥayawān*, 4: 449; *Ḥujaj*, 247; Muqammiṣ, *ʿIshrūn*, 14: 1; Ibn Qutayba, *Taʾwīl*, 133; trans. 149 [§170]). Bashshār b. Burd (d. 163/783), a poet variously classified as a Zindīq, Dahrī, and *mutaḥayyir* (somebody perplexed or sceptical),[9] is said to have believed only in what he had seen for himself and what was similar to it (*mā ʿāyantuhu aw ʿāyantu mithlahu*) (Abū ʾl-Faraj, *Aghānī*, 3: 227). The meaning of 'similar' is unclear. Perhaps he was referring to the principle of 'transition to the similar' current in empiricist medicine (if you had personal experience of a disease affecting the upper arm, you could apply it

9 Ibn Durayd, *Ishtiqāq*, 299; Abū ʾl-Faraj, *Aghānī*, 3: 147 (*mutaḥayyir mukhallaṭ*); Chokr 1993: 285.

to the upper leg);[10] but he could also have meant unanimous transmission from others. In any case, as this and other passages show, Scepticism was based on empiricist premisses.

The premisses were meant for rejection, however, for even sense impressions were unreliable, the Sceptics said. They would trot out the better-known tropes of their Greek predecessors (honey tastes bitter to a jaundiced patient; buildings appear small at a distance; poles appear bent under water, and so on); and as in antiquity their exasperated opponents would react by wanting to slap or beat them in order to demonstrate the reality of the sense impressions they were dismissing (Van Ess 1966: 172 f.; Van Ess 1968: 1 f.; Māturīdī, *Tawḥīd*, 153.18). As Sextus said, this rested on lack of familiarity with Sceptical doctrine: Sceptics did not reject the sense impressions that induced assent involuntarily, but merely refused to dogmatize about the reality behind them; they granted that honey *appeared* to be sweet, but whether it was sweet in *essence* only a dogmatist would claim to know (Sextus Empiricus, *Outlines*, 1.13.19 f.). This was the position of the Sūfisṭāʾīs too. Unlike their Greek predecessors, however, they are often presented as doubting the very existence of such a truth or essence (*ḥaqīqa*), not just its knowability (this could reflect Buddhist influence, cf. Crone 2012b: 31 f.).

A Sceptic who asserted that we cannot know the truth laid himself open to the charge of self-contradiction, since his assertion was a truth-claim. The prudent Sceptic would suspend judgement. Though both positions are reflected in the arguments against Sceptics in the Muslim material, there is no term for suspension of judgement there: the prudent Sceptic merely says, 'I don't know' (e.g. Baghdādī, *Uṣūl*, 319). Two terms for it turn up among the believers, however. One is *irjāʾ*, coined around 100/720 by Murjiʾites on the basis of Q 9: 107. The Murjiʾites subscribed to the Sceptical claim that one could only judge things on the basis of autopsy and unanimous information from others; since neither was available in the case of the caliph ʿUthmān (killed in 35/656), one had to suspend judgement on the divisive question whether he had been rightly guided or a sinner (Cook 1981: chs. 5, 7). The scope of their scepticism was narrow and the term *irjāʾ* remained tied to their doctrines. The other term is *wuqūf* or *tawaqquf*. Al-Jāḥiẓ, for example, observes that the common people are less prone to doubt than members of the elite because they do not 'hold back' (*yatawaqqafūna*), but rashly declare things to be true or false (Jāḥiẓ, *Ḥayawān*, 6: 36 f.). The term appears in later texts too, but it is less prominent

10 Hankinson 1995: 229. Ḥunayn was later to translate 'transition to the similar' as *al-intiqāl min al-shayʾ ilā nāẓirihi* (Strohmaier 1981: 188).

than *takāfuʾ al-adilla*, the expression for the equal weight (*isostheneia*) of competing proofs that made suspension of judgement necessary. We first hear of belief in the equipollence of proofs in the mid-third/ninth century; a century later the philosopher Abū Sulaymān al-Manṭiqī (d. *c.* 375/985) depicted it as a characteristic of *mutakallims* in general, including their leading men, saying that he would give their names if he did not prefer to leave them alive (Tawḥīdī, *Muqābasāt*, 227 [no. 54]).[11] The proofs that were so often found to be of equal weight, and thus to cancel each other out, were those tried and tested in disputations about *kalām al-dīn*. Some adherents of *takāfuʾ al-adilla* would suspend judgement on inner-Islamic disagreements alone, but others found it impossible to affirm anything apart from the existence of the creator; and still others would suspend judgement even on him (Ibn Ḥazm, *Faṣl*, 5: 119 f.).[12] There were also Sceptics who declared all religious tenets to be sound, the truth being relative to those who asserted it (Baghdādī, *Uṣūl*, 319.10; Ibn al-Jawzī, *Talbīs*, 41, citing Nawbakhtī); the judge al-ʿAnbarī (d. 168/784) upheld this principle in inner-Islamic disagreements (Goldziher 1920: 178 f.). Scepticism affected Christians and Jews no less than Muslims (Jāḥiẓ, *Radd*, 315; Saadia, *Amānāt*, 13, 65 ff.; trans. 17, 78 ff.), and it had its uses for believers too. The tropes against the reliability of sense impressions were apparently adduced in support of Ashʿarite atomism (Macdonald 1927: 336; Van Ess 1966: 178), and all arguments against the ability of humans to reach the truth could be used in a fideist vein.

(b) *Dogmatism*

Most *mulḥid*s were dogmatists. They agreed with the Sceptics that all claims about the realities of things had to be based on sense impressions, preferably or only on autopsy,[13] but unlike the Sceptics they deemed sense impressions to be reliable and admitted a modest amount of inference from them. One could make deductions (*istidlāl*) from perceptions to the reality of things, provided that they were perceptions of regularities (*al-ʿādāt*) (Jāḥiẓ, *Ḥayawān*, 6: 269). Anything regularly observed in large or common objects could be postulated for small or rare ones too, since quantity did not affect their epistemological status (*ḥukm qalīl al-shayʾ ka-ḥukm kathīrihi*). The nature of invisible or absent things could similarly be observed from those observed (*mā ghāba ʿanhum mithl alladhī shūhida*), but only as long as they were of the same type: 'they assign everything to its likes (*ashkāl*) and oblige it to follow the rules of the

11 Cf. Van Ess 1966: 221 ff.; Van Ess 1991–1997: index, s.v. 'takāfuʾ al-adilla'.

12 Typically, he does not name any Muslims, only two Jewish doctors.

13 E.g. Jāḥiẓ, *Ḥayawān*, 4: 89 f., 449.4; 6: 269.5; Ibn Qutayba, *Taʾwīl*, 133; trans. 149 (§ 170); Māturīdī, *Tawḥīd*, 111.–2; Saadia, *Amānāt*, 63; trans. 75; Ibn al-Jawzī, *Talbīs*, 41.

genus (*jins*)' (Abū 'Īsā al-Warrāq in Ibn al-Malāḥimī, *Mu'tamad*, 550 f./597 f.). They would reject all postulates about the invisible world (*al-ghā'ib 'anhum*) that ran counter to what they themselves could observe (*al-ḥāḍir 'indahum*); they applied 'criteria for corporeal things to spiritual entities', as Ibn Qutayba said in defence of *ḥadīth* that the *mulḥids* deemed ridiculous (Ibn Qutayba, *Ta'wīl*, 127.1; trans. 142 f. [§ 164 f.]). Information from others (*akhbār, sam'*) they admitted only if it conformed to these rules. Accordingly, they rejected the Qur'ānic account of sinners who were transformed into monkeys and pigs, or accepted it only in a naturalist interpretation. They scoffed at the Qur'ānic story of the *jinn* who tried to listen in to conversations in heaven only to have balls of fire thrown at them (Q 72: 8 f.; cf. 15: 17 f.; 37: 7 f.), objecting that creatures supposedly endowed with superior intelligence would have learnt better from the Qur'ān (which they had supposedly heard), from their long experience, from plain seeing for themselves, and from information passed around among themselves. They also found fault with the Qur'ānic story of Solomon and the Queen of Sheba, deeming it to be 'evidence of the corrupt nature of your historical tradition' (*dalīl 'alā fasād akhbārikum*) (Jāḥiẓ, *Ḥayawān*, 4: 70 ff., 85 f.; 6: 265 ff.; cf. Cook 1999: 60). That the *jinn* should have learnt from the Qur'ān is an argument based on the opponents' premisses; the rest tells us what counted as legitimate sources of knowledge to the *mulḥid*: experience, seeing for oneself, and information from others (*empeiria*, *autopsia*, and *historia* in the terminology of Greek empiricist doctors) (Hankinson 1995: 227 f.).

Both al-Aṣamm (d. *c*. 200/815) and al-Naẓẓām were empiricists in some respects (Ash'arī, *Maqālāt*, 331.7; 335.13; Van Ess 1991–1997: ii. 399; iii. 334 f.). For the rest the believers refuted the *mulḥids* on the latter's own premisses by means of the argument from design: one could see with one's own eyes that the world had been created by a wise and provident maker; it simply was not credible that so intricate and well-designed a construction should have come about on its own (Jāḥiẓ, *Ḥayawān*, 7: 12 f.; Eutychius, *Burhān*, § 4).[14] These points are developed at length in a work falsely attributed to al-Jāḥiẓ and in the Imāmī Shī'ite works *Kitāb al-Tawḥīd* and *Kitāb al-Iḥlīlija* (Jāḥiẓ, *Dalā'il*; Chokr 1993: 97 ff.).

14 Other arguments include the need for someone to hold the conflicting 'natures' (cf. below) together.

III Cosmology

All the godless people denied creation *ex nihilo*. Some believed God to have created the world out of pre-existing material, others held it to have originated on its own, and still others held that it had always existed. We may start with the Zindīqs.

(a) *Zindīqs*

Zindīqs believed the pre-eternal principles to be two, light and darkness, and explained the world as the outcome of their mixture. Those who retained belief in God typically held the highest God to have sent a figure, variously identified as Jesus, the holy spirit, or the apostle of light, to impose order on the chaos resulting from the mixture; the Marcionites diverged by crediting this task to the devil. Other Zindīqs explained the formation of the world in terms of natural processes that are not further identified. Both the creationists and the automatists often saw the mixture as having come about by accident.[15]

The synthesis of Middle Platonism and Stoicism was attractive to dualists because the Platonists shared their negative view of matter, sometimes deeming it positively evil (Dunderberg 2008: 125f.), while the Stoics also explained the world as a mixture of two pre-eternal principles, one active, that is God/*logos*/*pneuma*, and the other passive, that is matter or 'unqualified substance'. The concept of a divine *logos* (reason, word) or *pneuma* (spirit) that shapes and regulates pre-existing matter, now as a demiurge sent by the highest God and now as an impersonal principle, appears in several Platonizing and Gnosticizing systems in late antiquity, including that of Bardesanes. The latter is said also to have shared the Stoic view that everything which exists is a body (Syriac *gushmā*, Arabic *jism*) (Furlani 1937: 350), even a line or a sound (Ephrem, *Prose Refutations*, 2: 20, 29f.; trans. ix, xiii; cf. Ramelli 2009: 19). This implies that he also held that bodies could completely interpenetrate and blend with one another without losing their separate substance, a doctrine developed by the Stoics to explain how *pneuma* could be present throughout matter;[16]

15 Cf. *Encyclopaedia Iranica*, s.v. 'Bardesanes'; *Encyclopaedia of Islam*[3], s.v. 'Dayṣanīs'; Crone 2012a: ch. 10. The beginning was *bi-ihmāl lā ṣanʿa fīhi wa-lā taqdīr wa-lā ṣāniʿ wa-lā mudabbir*, as Ibn Abī 'l-ʿAwjāʾ says in Jaʿfar al-Ṣādiq (attrib.), *Tawḥīd*, 9.

16 Cf. Long and Sedley 1987: no. 48: the soul pervaded the whole body while preserving its own substance in mixture with it, as did fire and glowing iron, and a drop of wine in the ocean (contrary to what Aristotle said). Long and Sedley adopt 'blending' for complete

instead, however, Bardesanes is reported to have been an atomist. According to Ephrem, he held that the pure elements (light, air, water, and fire), suspended in the vacuum between God and darkness (inert matter), were composed of atoms (*perdē*, seeds) and that the same was true of darkness;[17] some Bardesanites held reason (*hawnā*), power (*ḥaylā*), and thought (*tarʿīthā*) likewise to be composed of atoms (Ephrem, *Prose Refutations*, 2: 220; trans. civ; Possekel 1999: 119 f.). Both the Stoic concept of interpenetration, based on the premiss that bodies are infinitely divisible, and the Epicurean concept of atoms, directed against infinite divisibility, allow two ingredients to blend completely without losing their identity, a crucial point to those who saw the world as composed of ultimately separable light and darkness. (The Zoroastrians, to whom the world was composed out of Ohrmazd's own substance, saw darkness as mixed in by juxtaposition.[18]) And whatever Bardesanes himself may have said, both doctrines seem to have been current in his and other schools. All things commingled were capable of being separated again, as third-century Sethians of apparently Mesopotamian origin declared, encouraging their disciples to study the doctrine of *krasis* and *mixis* (Hippolytus, *Refutatio*, 5: 21.1 f., 4 f.).[19] Interpenetration is reported under the name of *mudākhala* in Muslim sources on the Manichaeans (Ashʿarī, *Maqālāt*, 327.15),[20] and it appears without a name of its own in the Melkite Christian Eutychius (d. 940) in explanation of the mixture of the divine and human nature in Christ.[21] The idea that all things are bodies interpenetrating one another went into early Muslim cosmology

interpenetration without destruction of the bodies involved (fire and red-hot iron; a drop of wine in the ocean), and use 'fusion' for the mixture of the type in which the bodies are destroyed and another generated (as in drugs); but there seems to be no consistent terminology in the Greek material: the qualification *di' holou/holōn* is used in connection with both blending and fusion, and both are called *krasis* and *mixis* too.

17 Ephrem, *Refutations*, 1: 53 (vacuum); 2: 214 ff.; trans. lv; 11, ciff. (darkness at 215; trans. cii); *Encyclopaedia Iranica*, s.v. 'Bardesanes'; Possekel 1999: 116 ff. Ephrem is the only source for Bardesanite atomism.

18 Cf. de Ménasce 1973: no. 403: light and darkness do not mix absolutely, as proved by fire; light has merely adjoined smoke.

19 For these Sethians, cf. Crone 2012a: 200 f. Note also the Valentinian idea that Jesus, the Church, and Wisdom formed a complete blending of bodies (*di' holōn krasis tōn sōmatōn*) in Casey 1934: 17.1.

20 Cf. Ashʿarī, *Maqālāt*, 349.11 on the Dayṣānīs, where the term is *imtizāj*.

21 Eutychius, *Burhān*, nos. 122 f., with the soul and body, fire and glowing iron as examples. The use of Stoic mixture theory in this context goes back to Gregory of Nazianzus (cf. Stewart 1991: 182, 186).

in the physics of Hishām b. al-Ḥakam, al-Aṣamm (at least partially), and al-Naẓẓām.[22] Other *mutakallims* rejected infinite divisibility and interpenetration in favour of atomism.

Muslim sources report atomism for some Manichaeans/dualists, including one al-Nuʿmān al-Thanawī (executed by al-Mahdī), Isḥāq b. Ṭālūt, and Ibn Akhī Abī Shākir (al-Dayṣānī) (Ibn al-Malāḥimī, *Muʿtamad*, 566f., 590/611, 631; ʿAbd al-Jabbār, *Mughnī*, 5: 20; trans. 173). But more mainstream Christians also seem to have included atomists, for Epicurus, normally denounced by Christians as an atheist and hedonist, is praised as one of the great philosophers by the West-Syrian David Bar Paulos (Brock 1982: 25);[23] and the mid-third/ninth-century Muʿtazilite Ibn Mānūsh, a pupil of al-Naẓẓām of Origenist/Evagrian background, envisaged humans in pre-existence as atoms (Baghdādī, *Farq*, 258, trans. Van Ess 1991–1997: vi. 220; cf. Crone 2014). The idea of disembodied humans as atoms was probably due to Plato, who had defined the soul as 'uncompounded, indissoluble, and indivisible', according to Albinus' handbook, or, as Israel of Kashkar (d. 877) put it, as a *jawhar wāḥid ghayr munqasam ajsāman*, 'one substance/an atom, not divisible into bodies'.[24] The idea of man as an atom was also espoused by the Muʿtazilites Muʿammar (d. 215/830) and Hishām al-Fuwaṭī (d. 220s/840s?), both atomists in cosmological terms as well (Ashʿarī, *Maqālāt*, 331.13; ʿAbd al-Jabbār, *Mughnī*, 11: 311). In short, atomism probably reached the Muslims from both Christians and dualists.

Muslim *mutakallims* seem to have accepted the existence of atoms as a matter of course, reserving their ire for the infinite divisibility of bodies because there could not in their view be infinity in the created world. Atoms and accidents were all there was to it in their view. Some third/ninth-century *mutakallims* held atoms to have sides, explained as accidents, while others denied that they had either sides or magnitude (Ashʿarī, *Maqālāt*, 316.1, 10, cf. also 8; trans. with comments in Dhanani 1994: 99, nos. 1, 3, cf. also 2). Both groups seem to have conceived of the atom as an Epicurean minimal part: several such minimal parts (*elachista, minima*) made up an atom according to Epicurus, though it could not in practice be divided. To Epicurus, however, the minimal parts had magnitude. To the *mutakallims*, by contrast, magnitude was either added as accidents which could not in practice be separated from it, or else it was generated by the combination of several atoms. On their

---

22 Cf. Van Ess 1991–1997: i. 362, 365f.; ii. 398ff.; iii. 335ff.; Van Ess 1967: 250ff. The doctrine of *mudākhala* is not mentioned in the exiguous material on Ḍirār.

23 Democritus is also lauded, but he had come to stand for many things.

24 Albinus, *Didaskalikos*, 59 (cf. Plato, *Phaedo*, 80b); Israel of Kashkar, *Unity*, no. 49. The date of the work is not certain.

own, the minimal parts had lost their dimensions. The first known Muʿtazilite propounder of the atom without dimensions is Abū ʾl-Hudhayl (d. 226/841), according to whom bodies had length, breadth, and depth, whereas atoms did not.[25] It has long been suspected that he and others were indebted to dualists such as Bardesanites or Manichaeans for their atomism (Pretzl 1931: 127 ff.; Dhanani 1994: 4 f., 182 ff.), and he must be refuting dualists when he denies that atoms have life, power, or knowledge, the characteristics of light. He also denied that they possessed colour, taste, or smell, the properties possessed by Bar Dayṣān's elements and, presumably, the atoms of which they were composed (Ashʿarī, *Maqālāt*, 315.5). But only corporeal atoms are attested for the dualists. Bar Dayṣān's elements varied from light to heavy and fine to coarse;[26] and the atoms of al-Nuʿmān al-Thanawī, a Manichaean who disputed with Abū ʾl-Hudhayl (Van Ess 1991–1997: i. 443), certainly had three dimensions (Ibn al-Malāḥimī, *Muʿtamad*, 590/631; ʿAbd al-Jabbār, *Mughnī*, 5: 20; trans. 173). By contrast, humans in pre-existence are unlikely to have possessed corporeal dimensions, since they were with God; and some Christians or dualists do in fact seem to have envisaged the lightest atoms as mere points, for the sixth-century Barḥadbeshabbā envisages Epicurus and Democritus as believing in fine bodies which were 'incorporeal atoms' (*perdē delā geshūm*).[27]

It was probably from Christians of some kind that atoms passed to the author of the *Sirr al-khalīqa* (c. 210/825?). He operates with a prime substance (*al-jawhar al-awwal*) which is present in everything (*Sirr*, 1: 1.1.3, p. 3.9), which was clearly pre-eternal in the work he was adapting (*Sirr*, 2: 4.1, pp. 104 f.; 2: 5.1, pp. 109 ff.),[28] and which must be the source of the atoms (*ajzāʾ lā tatajazzaʾu*) of which he says that the world was built and the whole macrocosmos made (*Sirr*, 2: 18, p. 197.9; 2: 19.1, p. 203.ult.). As to how this happened, all we are told is that the substance was uniform until the accidents arose in it, whereupon its particles or atoms (*ajzāʾ*) diversified (*Sirr*, 1: 1.1.3, p. 3.10). Mostly the author writes as one of the *aṣḥāb al-ṭabāʾiʿ* (discussed in Section III[b]) to whom 'everything is from the four natures, which are heat, cold, moisture, and dryness' or 'which are fire, air, water, and earth' (*Sirr*, 1: 1.1.3, p. 3.4; 3: 20, p. 307.5), and the only atoms that interest him are those of light and subtle things such as fire, the subtlest of all bodies, composed of heat and atoms, or 'resting air', composed

25 Ashʿarī, *Maqālāt*, 307.10, where Muʿammar and al-Jubbāʾī agree. Abū ʾl-Hudhayl died after Muʿammar, but at the age of around a hundred.

26 Ephrem, *Refutations*, 1: 52 f.; trans. livf.; 2: 159; trans. lxxiv; cf. Ehlers 1970: 346 f.

27 Barḥadbeshabbā, *Cause*, 365. He locates them in Alexandria.

28 Cf. Weisser 1980: 174 f.

of warmth, moisture, and atoms, or the air between the spheres, which is full of atoms (*Sirr*, 2.18, p. 197.9, cf. 2: 17.2, p. 192; 2: 16.3, p. 190.1; 2: 19.1, p. 203.11). The different types of spiritual beings (*rūḥāniyyāt*) or angels were created out of the subtle (particles) of the prime substance (*laṭīf al-jawhar al-awwal*), more precisely from the heat of the wind, the light of fire, and the flow of water. Like the prime substance before the onset of accidents, they were *jawhar wāḥid* (lit. 'one substance'), here in the sense of uncompounded, and they were so subtle that they had no corporeal matter (*lā ajrāma lahā*) and did not take up space; 'everything which is not a body with six sides (*jirm musaddas*) does not take up space (*makān*)' (*Sirr*, 2: 15.1, p. 149; 2: 15.3, pp. 153 f.). In short, spiritual beings formed part of the created, material world, but not that of gross, tangible matter (*jirm, ajrām*). They had spiritual bodies, as one might say. Like everything else, they must have been made of atoms, but apparently these atoms lacked dimensions. Abū 'l-Hudhayl called an atom a *jawhar wāḥid* and he too distinguished them from bodies with six sides, meaning top, bottom, front, back, left, and right, an archaic definition of bodies which appears four times in the *Sirr* (Ashʿarī, *Maqālāt*, 302 f.; *Sirr*, 1: 3.5.2, p. 64; 1: 3.9.4, p. 94; 6: 28.7, p. 510), but which is replaced by the standard three dimensions in later summaries of Abū 'l-Hudhayl's doctrine.[29] The evidence of the *Sirr* suggests that it was the desire to identify the atomic structure of intelligibilia below the level of God himself (angels, humans in pre-existence and in spiritual afterlife, numbers, and ideal geometric figures) that had generated the concept of incorporeal atoms.[30]

It was clearly atoms of Greek rather than Indian origin that the dualists transmitted (Dhanani 1994: 97 ff.), though the Muslim recipients are unlikely to have been aware of their ultimate cultural origin. The *Mīzān al-ṣaghīr* attributed to Jābir, which expounds a cosmology related to that of the *Sirr*, tells us that the prime substance is dust which becomes visible when the sun shines on it (Haq 1994: 55). According to Lactantius (d. *c.* 325), who wrote against Epicureans, Leucippus had compared the atoms to 'little particles of dust in the sun when it has introduced its rays and light through a window'.[31] This comparison could

---

29 Thus already Ashʿarī, *Maqālāt*, 307.11, 314.14; two further examples in Van Ess 1991–1997: v. 37.

30 Cf. Dhanani 1994: 185, who points to the role of geometry. Sextus Empiricus' *Against the Mathematicians* and the late antique development of Aristotle's concept of noetic matter might repay a study from this point of view. Both Epicureans and Pyrrhonic Sceptics rejected Euclidean geometry (Dhanani 1994: 103). Cf. also Langermann 2009, suggesting that Galen played a role.

31 Lactantius, *De ira Dei*, 10: 9. Lactantius quotes him as calling the atoms seeds (*semina*, 10:

also have reached the Muslims via Platonist Christians and/or dualists, whose formative period lay in the second and third centuries; back then the Epicurean school tradition was still alive.

(b) *Dahrīs:* Aṣḥāb al-ṭabāʾiʿ

Dahrīs were either *aṣḥāb al-ṭabāʾiʿ* or *aṣḥāb al-hayūlā*. The former, whom I shall henceforth call physicists, owed their name to their belief that everything in this world is composed by four 'natures' (Greek *physeis*, Syriac *kyānē*, Arabic *ṭabāʾiʿ*), that is the four elementary qualities, hot, cold, dry, and wet, which combined to form the four elements, fire, water, air, and earth. Each element had two qualities according to Aristotelians (fire was hot and dry), but only one according to the Stoics (fire was hot). Since the Stoics identified both the elements and their qualities as bodies, they did not distinguish sharply between the two, as Plutarch (d. 120), Galen (d. *c.* 200), and Alexander of Aphrodisias (fl. *c* .200) complained (Lammert 1953: 489f.); and assisted by the medical humour theory, the qualities came to acquire ontological, as opposed to purely analytical, priority. When late antique authors speak of the elements, they often mean the qualities,[32] and the term 'natures' was used of both.[33] In Arabic the 'natures' are usually the qualities, but sometimes the elements, otherwise known as *usṭuqussāt*, *ʿanāṣir*, and *ummahāt* (mothers).[34]

Some physicists refused to affirm the existence of anything other than the four elementary qualities, whereas others added a fifth (Abū ʿĪsā in Ibn al-Malāḥimī, *Muʿtamad*, 547.13/594.17; Ashʿarī, *Maqālāt*, 348.5f.). Just as the diverse colours produced by dyers were all mixtures of white, red, black, and green, so all things in this world were really mixtures of hot, cold, moisture, and dryness, the former said, using a comparison strikingly similar to that of Empedocles, the ultimate author of the four-elements theory (Māturīdī, *Tawḥīd*, 112,

---

3), cf. Syriac *perdē*. For the dust as partless (*habāʾ lā juzʾ lahu*), see Kraus 1942: 154 n.; Fakhr al-Dīn al-Rāzī in Pines 1997: 157, on the atomic theories of the ancients (who could be Greeks or Muslims).

32 The elements are identified as the qualities in, for example, Philastrius, *Diversarum*, XIX: 5 (47, 5f.), citing the mid second-century Apelles; Athanasius, *Contra Gentes*, par. 27; Job of Edessa, *Treasures*, 1: 1 (p. 78; trans. 5).

33 Cf. Kraus 1942: 45, 165 n. 7; Ephrem, *Commentary*, 75 and n. 24, *ad* Gen. 1: 1; Jacob of Sarug, *Sermons*, 2: 177, cf. 4: 319f.; Jacob of Edessa in Teixidor 1997: 125.

34 For the mothers, see Yaʿqūbī, *Tārīkh*, 1: 170.11; *Sirr*, 2: 16.2, p. 187.ult.; 3: 20, p. 308.2; *mulḥaq* 1, pp. 532f.; Weisser 1980: 176, citing *K. Isṭamāṭīs*; Abū Ḥātim al-Rāzī, *Iṣlāḥ*, 166.15; Māturīdī, *Tawḥīd*, 60.17, where they are coupled with 'fathers', i.e. the spheres and the stars or the lords in charge of their motion, cf. Walker 1993: 103 (al-Sijistānī); Madelung 2005: 159.

141).[35] The fifth nature added by others was often identified as spirit (*rūḥ*), which pervaded and regulated everything and was also life: this was presumably another Stoic legacy (Abū ʿĪsā in Ibn al-Malāḥimī, *Muʿtamad*, 547/594; Ashʿarī, *Maqālāt*, 335.4, 11).[36] Others held the fifth nature to be a wind different from moving air, perhaps related to the breath or breeze (*nasīm*) that some held to be life (Baghdādī, *Uṣūl*, 53.10; cf. Abū ʿĪsā in Ibn al-Malāḥimī, *Muʿtamad*, 549.9/596.3), or else it was space (*al-faḍāʾ*), identified as the place of things (*makān al-ashyāʾ*) (Abū ʿĪsā in Ibn al-Malāḥimī, *Muʿtamad*, 549.2/596.10), or knowledge (Yaʿqūbī, *Tārīkh*, 1: 170.14, of Greek and Roman Dahrīs). Still others opted for the heavenly sphere (Maqdisī, *Badʾ*, 1: 132.–2; Baghdādī, *Uṣūl*, 320.12),[37] which acted on the four qualities and so caused generation and corruption, or which was the source of the four natures and everything else in the world.[38] Al-Māturīdī had heard an astronomer compare the universe to a giant weaving machine, with the heavenly bodies producing the variegated textile that is life down here (Māturīdī, *Tawḥīd*, 143). Those who identified the heavenly spheres as the source of everything else often credited their science to Hermes and associated figures,[39] but devotees of Hermes believed in spiritual realities and credited themselves with both inner and external senses,[40] whereas Dahrīs had no inner eye (Asadī, *Garshāspnāma*, 140.11; trans. 2: 31).

The Christian physician and philosopher Job of Edessa (writing *c.* 817) held God to have created the 'simple elements' (i.e. the qualities) and put them together as 'compound elements', meaning the fire, water, air, and earth of which everything was composed (Job of Edessa, *Treasures*, 1: 4; 1: 6). Several Muslim *mutakallim*s, al-Jāḥiẓ, Thumāma b. Ashras, and al-Māturīdī among them, also operated with 'natures' created by God, without being Dahrīs, as al-Juwaynī noted (disapproving of their view that the natures had causative power).[41] But the author of the *Sirr* is a creationist only in the sense that his

---

35 Cf. Empedocles, fr. 23, on painters who mix pigments to make pictures of everything.

36 Cf. al-Naẓẓām in Jāḥiẓ, *Ḥayawān*, 5: 47; Baghādī, *Uṣūl*, 53.12; Daiber 1999: 40.

37 This view is ascribed to Aristotle (e.g. Maqdisī, *Badʾ*, 2: 9) and to Hermes and Ptolemy (Israel of Kashkar, *Unity*, no. 34).

38 Jāḥiẓ, *Ḥayawān*, 7: 12 f.; Māturīdī, *Tawḥīd*, 60.16; Maqdisī, *Badʾ*, 1: 126.12; Asadī, *Garshāspnāma*, 139; trans. 2: 30; al-Rāzī, *Tafsīr*, 27: 269 f., *ad* Q. 45: 24. cf. Balīnūs, *Sirr*, 2: 19.8, p. 212, where their motion generates the *mawālīd*; cf. also Saadia, *Amānāt*, 58; trans. 70.

39 For a (perhaps) ninth-century summary of Hermetic doctrine, see Israel of Kashkar, *Unity*, nos. 28–35; cf. also van Bladel 2009.

40 Balīnūs, *Sirr*, 1: 1.1.1, p. 2 and index s.v. 'al-ḥawāss al-bāṭina/ẓāhira'.

41 Juwaynī, *Shāmil*, 237 f.; Frank 1974 (where the *ṭabāʾiʿ* are not properly distinguished from *ṭabʿ*); cf. Ashʿarī, *Maqālāt*, 517.2, where we hear of physicists with views on God's speech.

God sets the formation of the elements in motion with his creative command; for the rest the process unfolds on its own. Other Dahrīs agreed that the world had originated in time, but not that it had a creator: it had been born of the four eternal 'uncompounded simples' (*al-afrād al-sawādhij*), i.e. the elementary qualities, which made things grow on their own without intent, wish, or will.[42] Still other physicists held the natures to be pre-eternal, but put together by God; and one Ibn Qays apparently held God to have joined them since pre-eternity, so that the world was pre-eternal too (Baghdādī, *Uṣūl*, 70, 320). This aligned him with the common physicist view that the four or five natures had always existed in a state of combination or mixture (both mechanical and chemical terms are used), so that the world as we know it had always been and always would be.[43] The universe had neither beginning nor end, be it in terms of time or extent (*misāḥa*), and apparently not in terms of number (*kathra*) either;[44] the several worlds implied were presumably successive rather than concurrent, and separated by Stoic-type conflagrations, for at least some Dahrīs saw time as cyclical.[45]

In agreement with the Stoics the *aṣḥāb al-ṭabāʾiʿ* identified the four or five natures as bodies rather than incorporeal characteristics (al-Naẓẓām in Jāḥiẓ, *Ḥayawān*, 5: 40; Ashʿarī, *Maqālāt*, 348.4). Space (*al-faḍāʾ*), defined as the place of things (*makān al-ashyāʾ*), is explicitly said not to have been a body, suggesting that it is the Stoic *topos* or place, identified as 'that which is able to be occupied by what is' and counted as one of the four incorporeals (Abū ʿĪsā in Ibn al-Malāḥimī, *Muʿtamad*, 549.2/596.3; cf. Long and Sedley 1987: nos. 27, 49). According to the pneumatic physicists, the four bodies had always been in motion, either because movement was natural to them or because the spirit was moving them, and their movements caused them to come together.

42 Balīnūs, *Sirr*, 2: 3, p. 103; Yaʿqūbī, *Tārīkh*, 1: 170.7, of Greek and Roman Dahrīs (*sawādhij* is an Arabic plural of the Middle Persian form of Persian *sādha*, simple); compare Saadia, *Amānāt*, 61; trans. 73, where those who hold heaven and earth to have originated by chance explain the process along the same lines as the *Sirr*, without God's creative command to set the process going.

43 Abū ʿĪsā in Ibn al-Malāḥimī, *Muʿtamad*, 547.12, 549.18/594.18, 596.19; Māturīdī, *Tawḥīd*, 143.12. But Saadia, *Amanat*, 55; trans. 66, and Juwaynī, *Shāmil*, 239.5, present them as claiming that the four originally existed in isolation.

44 Abū ʿĪsā in Ibn al-Malāḥimī, *Muʿtamad*, 549.19, 552.9/596.20, 598.21; *Sirr*, 1: 3.9.3, p. 93.10.

45 Yaʿqūbī, *Tārīkh*, 1: 168.6 (*inna ʾl-dahr dāʾir*), of Greek and Roman Dahrīs; Maimonides, *Guide*, 2: 13 (28b); Ibn Kathīr, *Tafsīr*, 4: 150, *ad* Q. 45: 24 (cycles of 36,000 years); cf. the cycles in the thought of the communities from which Dahrīs seem often to have been drawn (Crone 2012a: 209f., 235f., 239, 245f., cf. also 481).

This sounds Epicurean, but they interpenetrated in the Stoic style (*yaghullu baʿḍuhā fī baʿḍin*) instead of simply combining. By mixing in different ways they became sounds, smells, minerals, plants, and so on (Abū ʿĪsā in Ibn al-Malāḥimī, *Muʿtamad*, 547.16; 548.4; 551.12/594.21,[46] 595.9, 598.4). The matter (*mādda*) formed by their mixture was composed of particles (*ajzāʾ*), presumably infinitely divisible, and things were strengthened and weakened by conjunction with similar and contrasting forms (*ashkāl* and *aḍdād*). When a living being died, the particles dispersed to join the concordant forms closest to it, and the same particles might accidentally come together to form a living being of the same kind, or of a different kind, or just a plant, or the particles might simply be dispersed in water or the earth.[47] In short, the physicists allowed for the possibility of what others called reincarnation, but explained it in materialist terms. If their roots went back to the third century, they could have picked up this explanation from the Epicurean school tradition (cf. Lucretius, *On the Nature of Things*, 3: 845–860). But whether they did so or not, it is not the only evidence to suggest that they hailed from communities in which belief in reincarnation was widespread. In fact, while some members of these communities were making godless science out of their ancestral beliefs, to be dismissed as Dahrīs, others were reformulating them as Muslim doctrine, to be dismissed as Khurramīs and Ghulāt (Crone 2012a: 248f.).

Neither the dualists nor the *aṣḥāb al-ṭabāʾiʿ* needed a material substratum to carry their corporeal qualities, for even qualities were bodies, so they did not accept the Aristotelian concept of prime matter,[48] nor the Aristotelian distinction between substance (*jawhar*) and accidents (*aʿrāḍ*). Some had come round to accepting one accident, however, namely motion, a key concept in that it was coterminous with action and change.[49] But there were also some who claimed that there was no such thing as motion or any other accident.[50] The Muʿtazilite al-Aṣamm shared this view (Ashʿarī, *Maqālāt*, 343.12; Baghdādī, *Uṣūl*, 7.14; cf. Van Ess 1991–1997: ii. 398f.; v. 194f.). Motion was a body, i.e. the

46 Wrongly *yuqillu* for *yaghullu* in the new edition.

47 Abū ʿĪsā in Ibn al-Malāḥimī, *Muʿtamad*, 548.1, 9/595.6, 13; cf. *Sirr*, 1: 1.1.3, p. 4.4; Ashʿarī, *Maqālāt*, 329.6; Maqdisī, *Badʾ*, 1: 127.11.

48 It is rejected as nonsense in Job of Edessa, *Treasures*, 1: 2. Jābir, who does operate with a substrate, mentions those who do not (Kraus 1942: 169f.).

49 Abū ʿĪsā in Ibn al-Malāḥimī, *Muʿtamad*, 548.17, 566.13/595.20, 611.8; Ashʿarī, *Maqālāt*, 348.7, 12; 349.12; Ibn Shabīb in Māturīdī, *Tawḥīd*, 141.15, 143.21.

50 Ibn al-Malāḥimī, *Muʿtamad*, 549.15/596; Muqammiṣ, *ʿIshrūn*, 3:11; Ashʿarī, *Maqālāt*, 348.11; 349.6, 15; Baghdādī, *Uṣūl*, 52.16.

body moving, as some put it, which is also what a Stoic would have said.[51] As a certain Plato the Copt from Ḥulwān is reported to have declared, we do not see motion or any other action, only the person or thing moving or acting.[52] The *Sirr* refutes him as if he were a Sceptic, assimilating him to a different set of people who denied the reality of change as an illusion, claiming that the created word was all one and the same, and who seem to have invoked Parmenides ('Munīs').[53] It is those who dismiss diversity (*ikhtilāf*) as an illusion generated by the senses who trot out Sceptical tropes in al-Yaʿqūbī's account of Greek and Roman Dahrīs (Yaʿqūbī, *Tārīkh*, 1: 168 f.).

Many Dahrīs had succumbed to the advancing tide of Aristotelianism, however. They defined the elements as substance and the elementary qualities as accidents (al-Naẓẓām in Jāḥiẓ, *Ḥayawān*, 5: 40), and postulated a substrate in the form of prime matter (*hayūlā, ṭīna*).

(c) Aṣḥāb al-hayūlā

Some people held the world to have been created from nothing while others held it to be drawn from matter (*hylē*), Paul the Persian observed (Land 1862–1875: 4, fo. 56r; trans. 2). Two centuries later the adherents of the latter view were known as *aṣḥāb al-hayūlā* and singled out for refutation by al-Naẓẓām (Van Ess 1991–1997: vi. 1 [no. 3]). Some *aṣḥāb al-hayūlā* were creationists who held God to have created the world out of pre-existing matter (Greek *hylē*) by means of movement and rest, which caused accidents to arise. The author of the *Sirr*, who tacitly operates with prime matter, is an example.[54] Al-Maqdisī, who deemed them guilty of dualism, informs us that they also held that the creator had always created (a Platonist view rooted in the *Timaeus*), so they were eternalists too.[55] Judging from the frequency with which the emergence of the world is described in impersonal terms, other *aṣḥāb al-hayūlā* were automatists. Their Platonism notwithstanding, the adherents of prime matter are mostly envisaged as Aristotelians,[56] with some justice in that their *hayūlā*

---

51 Ibn al-Malāḥimī, *Muʿtamad*, 566.–5/611.13 (Manichaean majority); Ashʿarī, *Maqālāt*, 349.2; cf. 346.6, on Jahm b. Ṣafwān (on different grounds); Sedley in Algra et al. 1999: 399.

52 *Sirr*, 1: 2.2.11, p. 28.

53 *Sirr*, 1: 2.2.10, pp. 26 f.; cf. Rudolph 1995: 133 f.

54 Theodore Bar Koni, *Liber*, mimrā I, 30; Maqdisī, *Badʾ*, 1: 92; compare the *Sirr*, 2: 3 ff., pp. 103 ff.

55 Maqdisī, *Badʾ*, 1: 92; Māturīdī, *Tawḥīd*, 86.13; Pines 1997: 41, 48, on the tenth-century Īrānshahrī, one of the *aṣḥāb al-hayūlā*; Goodman 1993: 148; Plato, *Timaeus*, 29e.

56 Job of Edessa, *Treasures*, 1: 2; Yaʿqūbī, *Tārīkh*, 1: 170.14 (*aṣḥāb al-jawhar*); Māturīdī, *Tawḥīd*, 147; cf. Bar Koni, *Liber*, mimrā XI, 9, and Zurqān in Maqdisī, *Badʾ*, 1: 140, on Aristotle himself.

(also called *ṭīna*) was clearly Aristotle's *protē hylē*, a material substrate devoid of extension, dimensions, or any other properties, endowed with the potential to be anything. (They do not seem to have known about Simplicius' and Philoponus' modifications of Aristotle on this point. Māturīdī, *Tawḥīd*, 147.5; Sorabji 1988: ch. 2.) *Hayūlā* was empty of accidents, as the sources will say (Maqdisī, *Bad'*, 1: 47.8; Baghdādī, *Uṣūl*, 57.5), thinking in terms of substance and accidents (as in the *Categories*) rather than matter and form.[57] Thanks to its potentiality (*quwwa*), which often seems to be envisaged as a separate entity, accidents arose in it, and the appearance of accidents transformed the *hayūlā* into substance (*jawhar*) (Māturīdī, *Tawḥīd*, 147; cf. also 30.17). Some called prime matter 'substance' or 'simple substance' or 'first substance' (*jawhar basīṭ/awwal*) from the start. The term *'unṣur* also came to be used. Some held every species of being to have its own prime matter (Baghdādī, *Uṣūl*, 53.5).

The *aṣḥāb al-hayūlā*, then, held that matter/substance was pre-eternal (*qadīm*), but accepted that accidents originated in time (*ḥadītha*), with or without divine intervention. They held that the bodies preceded the accidents, as al-Baghdādī puts it (*Uṣūl*, 55.8). He held this to distinguish the *aṣḥāb al-hayūlā* from other Dahrīs, for most of the Dahrīs who operated with accidents were eternalists in respect of them too, in three different ways. Some, labelled Azaliyya Dahrīs by al-Baghdādī, did agree that the accidents originated in time, but they added that before every origination there had always been another: the process had no beginning; the world had always existed as we see it now with its stars, animals, procreation, and so on.[58] Others held that the accidents had always existed in potentiality (*bi'l-quwwa*). According to them, and also to (some?) Manichaeans, the accidents or the world or the phenomena (? *ma'ānī*) were in the prime matter/substance in potentiality and emerged from there into actuality (*ẓaharat bi'l-fi'l*); in support of this they would adduce the presence of the man in the sperm, of the animal in the sperm or egg, of the tree in the kernel, and so on.[59] This doctrine was also known to the Zaydī al-Qāsim b. Ibrāhīm (d. 246/860), whose *mulḥid* opponent adduces the date palm

57 All things are either substance (*ousia*) or accident, as Job of Edessa remarks (*Treasures*, 1: 3, p. 81; trans. 10). The terminology was to be revised in the light of the translations, cf. matter versus form (*ṣūra*) and the elementary qualities as *kayfiyyāt* in Shahrastānī, *Nihāya*, 163 ff.; Shahrastānī, *Milal*, 257.ult.; trans. 2: 187.

58 Baghdādī, *Uṣūl*, 55, 59; Muqammiṣ, *'Ishrūn*, 5: 36, 42; Ibn al-Malāḥimī, *Mu'tamad*, 566.14/611.9 (of some dualists, apparently Manichaeans); Maqdisī, *Bad'*, 1: 123.4.

59 Māturīdī, *Tawḥīd*, 63.9, cf. 30.16; Muqammiṣ, *'Ishrūn*, 5: 8, 10, 14 (claiming to know nobody adhering to this view, but associating it with Dahrīs and Manichaeans); Guidi, *Lotta*, 46.9; trans. 107.

in the pit (Pines 1997: 165f.). Finally, some Dahrīs held that the accidents had always existed in the bodies, apparently in actuality. Colours, tastes, and smells were hiding in the earth, water, and fire and became manifest in fruit by transfer (*intiqāl*) and the conjunction of likes (*ashkāl*) (Ashʿarī, *Maqālāt*, 329.4; cf. Maqdisī, *Badʾ*, 1: 47, 134.6). The adherents of this view were the *aṣḥāb al-kumūn waʾl-ẓuhūr*, 'those who believed in latency and manifestation', and al-Baghdādī may have conflated them with the defenders of the second position (Baghdādī, *Uṣūl*, 55.12 [where the second position is omitted]; Maqdisī, *Badʾ*, 1: 47.4). They too seem to have adduced the chicken and the egg, the wheat in the grain, and so on by way of confounding those who believed the world to have a beginning and an end, or perhaps all Dahrīs did so.[60] At all events, they said that when one accident was manifest, its opposite disappeared from view and was hidden in the body until the roles were reversed, as for example in the case of motion and rest, and so it would go on forever.[61] There was no origination (*ḥudūth*).[62]

Wolfson thought that the Dahrīs were Aristotelians, with reference to their doctrines of potentiality and *kumūn* (Wolfson 1976: 504ff.); Horovitz related these views to the Stoic concept of 'seminal reasons' (*logoi spermatikoi*), according to which the creative fire or reason was 'like a seed' containing the causes of all things past, present, and future (Horovitz 1903: 186); and Nyberg thought that al-Naẓẓām's *kumūn* theory (cf. below) must be rooted in the concept of Plato's ideas as thought (and thus potentiality) in the mind of God.[63] But whatever philosophical language the Dahrīs may have used, what they, and sometimes also Zindīqs, really wished to express was a deep-seated Near Eastern conviction, namely that everything is endless recurrence. This is what shaped their understanding of Greek philosophy, and also what gave them an affinity with the Presocratics. Whether the chicken or the egg was originated or pre-eternal, hidden in the body, in Aristotelian potentiality, in Stoic 'seminal reasons', or in the mind of God, the point was that there was nothing new under the sun. The chicken produced eggs which produced chickens which produced eggs; so it had always been and so it always would be. Denial of origination and destruc-

60 Jāḥiẓ, *Tarbīʿ*, no. 46; Kraus 1935: 299f. (where the doctrine is primarily Manichaean); Maqdisī, *Badʾ*, 1: 118f., 133; 2: 134; Baghdādī, *Uṣūl*, 319.14; Juwaynī, *Shāmil*, 224.1; Ibn al-Malāḥimī, *Muʿtamad*, 160/152.

61 Muqammiṣ, *ʿIshrūn*, 5:12; Baghdādī, *Uṣūl*, 55; Baghdādī, *Farq*, 139.

62 Yaʿqūbī, *Tārīkh*, 1: 168.3; Guidi, *Lotta*, 45.6; trans. 105.

63 Nyberg 1919: 52, adding that al-Naẓẓām linked it with Anaxagoras' homoiomery theory, which must be a slip for Anaxagoras' opposite theory that 'there is a portion of everything in everything'.

tion coupled with belief in eternal recurrence and pantheism also appears in the Hermetic corpus (Copenhaver 1992: xii. 15–17). Simon Magus is credited with the view that fire, the principle of all things, possessed hidden and manifest parts corresponding to the potentiality and actuality of Aristotle, the intelligible and sensible of Plato (Hippolytus, *Refutatio*, 6.9.5 f., adduced by Wolfson 1976: 510). The Gnostic Basilides, who believed in a 'not-being God' (*ouk ōn theos*) utterly beyond us, held this deity to have caused a seed to exist in which all things were contained just as the entire plant is contained in the mustard seed and the multicoloured peacock and other birds in the egg (Hippolytus, *Refutatio*, 7:21).[64] Basilides' system, or something similar to it, was known to al-Yaʿqūbī, according to whom one of the Dahrite groups among the pagan Greeks and Romans believed the origin (*aṣl*) of things in pre-eternity (*al-azaliyya*) to be a seed (*ḥabba*) which split open, whereupon the world with all the diversity of colours and other sense impressions appeared from it (Yaʿqūbī, *Tārīkh*, 1: 168.16): here as elsewhere, al-Yaʿqūbī's ancient Dahrīs are actually late antique and/or Islamic. Al-Maqdisī also knew them.[65]

Al-Naẓẓām, who shared the view of everything as interpenetrating bodies, also held that motion was the only accident and subscribed to the theory of *kumūn*: God created everything in one go, hiding future things in the bodies; and fire was not originated, but hidden in the stone.[66] His view that God created the world all at once aligns him with Origen, but almost all his other views on physics align him with the Dahrīs. His affinities were with the physicists, as al-Shahrastānī said.[67] The same was true of other early Muʿtazilites.[68] The *aṣḥāb al-hayūlā* also had an afterlife as *falāsifa*, represented by Īrānshahrī and Abū Bakr al-Rāzī (the latter an atomist) (Pines 1997: 41 f., 47, 48).

---

64 Hippolytus saw him as a follower of Aristotle.

65 Maqdisī, *Badʾ*, 1: 141.11, on *aṣḥāb al-juththa* (read *aṣḥāb al-ḥabba*? For *inqalaʿat*, read *infalaqat*).

66 Cf. Van Ess 1991–1997: iii. 339 ff., 360 ff., 367 ff. (where it is noted that he is also credited with the opposite doctrine that God creates everything new in every moment).

67 Shahrastānī, *Milal*, 1: 39; trans. 208; cf. Baghdādī, *Farq*, 113 f., 127, 139; Baghdādī, *Uṣūl*, 48 (with much polemical exaggeration); cf. Van Ess 1991–1997: iii. 307, 332.

68 Shahrastānī, *Milal*, 1: 44, 52, 53; trans. 228, 257, 260, on Bishr b. al-Muʿtamir and Jāḥiẓ; Baghdādī, *Uṣūl*, 36.ult., on al-Aṣamm; cf. also Van Ess 1991–1997: iii. 333.

IV Godless Religion

Dahrīs are often said not to have believed in God,[69] and some must indeed have denied his existence. But others clearly believed in him,[70] and in any case the key issue between Dahrīs and 'monotheists' (*muwaḥḥidūn*) was not whether God existed or not, but rather what significance he had for humans. To monotheists he had created the world and administered it, sent prophets to mankind to make his wishes known, and would eventually call everyone to account. To 'pure Dahrīs' all this was nonsense: whether there was a deity or not, there was no creator, providential ruler (*mudabbir*), or lord (*rabb*) of the world, nor any angels, spirits, prophets, religious laws, veridical dreams, or afterlife of any kind.[71] The alleged miracles of prophets could be explained rationally, and demons (*shayāṭīn*), spirits (*jinn*), paradise, and hell had been invented to deceive people and make them obey.[72] Like the Zindīqs, the Dahrīs saw the world as simply too full of inequality, injustice, illness, violence, hostility, pain, and death to have a creator or providential overseer.[73] Some, however, accepted that the world had a creator (*muḥdith*), but held that he had ceased to exist. 'We see people fall into water without being able to swim, or into fire, and call upon the provident maker (*al-ṣāniʿ al-mudabbir*), but he does not rescue them, so we know the creator is non-existent (*maʿdūm*)', unidentified philosophers observed. After completing the world and finding it good the creator had destroyed himself so as not to add or detract from his handiwork, leaving behind the laws (*aḥkām*) current among the living beings and things he had made. Alternatively his particles had dispersed in the world so that every force in it was of the divine essence. Or a defect (? *tawalwul*) had appeared in the essence of the creator so that all his power and light had been

69 E.g. Abū 'l-Faraj, *Aghānī*, 13: 280; al-Māturīdī, *Taʾwīlāt*, 4: 94, *ad* Q. 4: 150; cf. Kulaynī, *Kāfī*, 1: 76.9, on a Zindīq.

70 Cf. Ibn Qays and his likes (above, note 43 and the text thereto).

71 Jāḥiẓ, *Hayawān*, 7: 12 ff.; Abū ʿĪsā in Ibn al-Malāḥimī, *Muʿtamad*, 587.13; Khushaysh in al-Malaṭī, *Tanbīh*, 72; Yaʿqūbī, *Tārīkh*, 1: 168.1; Maqdisī, *Badʾ*, 1: 119.3. For the 'pure Dahrī', see Jāḥiẓ, *Ḥayawān*, 4: 90.1. For *tadbīr* (and *siyāsa*) as a translation of Syriac *purnāsā*, rendering Greek *pronoia*, see Daiber 1980: 12.

72 Jāḥiẓ, *Ḥujaj*, 3: 263 f. (cf. also 278, 281); Māturīdī, *Taʾwīlāt*, 17: 400.ult., *ad* Q. 114: 4–6; Maqdisī, *Badʾ*, 5: 25; Asadī, *Garshāspnāma*, 139; trans. 30 (ch. 44); Pretzl 1933: *23; trans. 46.

73 Kaʿbī on Dahrīs in Maqdisī, *Badʾ*, 1: 116; Ṣāliḥ b. ʿAbd al-Quddūs in Van Ess 1991–1997: ii. 18; another Zindīq (Ibn al-Muqaffaʿ?) in Guidi, *Lotta*, 22.23, 24.3; trans. 52, 54; cf. Maimonides, *Guide*, 3: 2 (18a) on Abū Bakr al-Rāzī, noting that the multitudes often shared this view. Sextus had also shared it, showing us yet another affinity between Sceptics and Manichaeans (cf. Hankinson 1995: 238).

sucked out of him and into this world; all that remained of him was a cat (! *sinnawr*), which would suck the light out of this world again so that eventually he would be restored; meanwhile he was too weak to attend to his created beings; their affairs were left unattended with the result that injustice had spread.[74] The *sinnawr* could be a misreading for something to do with *nūr*, but the members of the Hāshimite movement in Khurāsān were accused of worshipping cats, so maybe we should take it as it stands; al-Māturīdī confirms that there were *mulḥid*s who held God to suffer defects and illnesses (*āfāt*) (*Akhbār*, 282; Māturīdī, *Taʾwīlāt*, 15: 283, *ad* Q. 67: 1). All these explanations accounted for the orderly design of the world, the key argument against Dahrism, while also explaining its unjust nature. There was nobody up there to look after us anymore. The heavens were no longer inhabited, as Zindīqs reportedly said (Kulaynī, *Kāfī*, 1: 75 [*kharāb laysa fīhā aḥad*]; cf. Māturīdī, *Taʾwīlāt*, 16: 309, *ad* Q. 75: 36).

Opponents occasionally accused Dahrīs of making the elements or the heavenly sphere divine, but rarely of actually worshipping them. Though natural scientists often had a strong occult side to them, as they do in the *Sirr al-khalīqa* and the Jābir corpus, the 'pure Dahrīs' and their Zindīq counterparts come across as reductionists singularly lacking in religious feelings. Their ethics were rationalist. People were obliged to know and avoid naturally evil things such as anger, killing, and theft, nothing else, as Bashshār al-Burd said (Ibn al-Malāḥimī, *Muʿtamad*, 590/631 f.; ʿAbd al-Jabbār, *Mughnī*, 5: 20; trans. 173); Dahrīs determined right and wrong (*ḥasan*, *qabīḥ*) on the basis of their own fancy, as al-Jāḥiẓ caricatured them (Jāḥiẓ, *Ḥayawān*, 7: 13). Like atheists everywhere, they were often envisaged as utterly immoral and depraved.

V The Persistence of Godlessness

Muʿtazilite and Shīʿite *mutakallim*s who interacted with Zindīqs and Dahrīs sometimes became unhinged (*khulliṭa*), as their colleagues said. They include the third/ninth-century Abū Saʿīd al-Ḥaḍrī/Ḥuṣrī, the fourth/tenth-century Abū Isḥāq al-Naṣībī,[75] and Abū Ḥafṣ al-Ḥaddād (Van Ess 1991–1997: iv. 89–91), as well as the notorious Ibn al-Rāwandī (d. mid or late fourth/tenth century).[76]

74 Yaḥyā b. Bishr b. ʿUmayr al-Nihāwandī (writing before 377/987 f.) in Ibn al-Jawzī, *Talbīs*, 46 (ch. against the *falāsifa*).

75 Tawḥīdī, *Imtāʿ*, 1: 141; cf. id., *Akhlāq al-wazīrayn*, 202, 211 f., 297.

76 Cf. *Encyclopaedia of Islam*², s.v. 'Ibn al-Rāwandī'; Stroumsa 1999: ch. 2; Van Ess 1991–1997: iv. 295 ff.

The latter is said to have written a book on the eternity of the world and another on its evil, but he is more famous for his view that prophets were tricksters whose alleged miracles were open to rational explanation. This was a theme of considerable prominence in fourth/tenth- and fifth/eleventh-century theology and philosophy (another famous exponent was Abū Bakr al-Rāzī); so too was the denial of the afterlife, but covering these developments would require another chapter. Dahrī cosmology, on the other hand, went into a phase of *kumūn*,[77] to make a *ẓuhūr* in post-Mongol Iran. It was now Sufis who said that 'there is nobody here except us', that the world has always existed, that God does not look after it, that he does not send messengers to it, that there is no afterlife, and that time is endless recurrence, while Dahrī materialism reappeared in the Nuqṭawī heresy of Maḥmūd Pasīkhānī (d. 831/1427 f.). But the tone was no longer scoffing, nor was the materialism irreligious. Maḥmūd claimed that the four elements were all that existed, but what he meant was that God was those elements, not that he did not exist, and though his explanation of reincarnation was materialist (humans had no soul), it was merit which determined how one was reborn.[78] Such cosmologies were still heterodox, but they were no longer ungodly.

References

'Abd al-Jabbār (*Mughnī*). *al-Mughnī*. Vol. 5. Ed. M.M. al-Khuḍayrī. Cairo: Wizārat al-Thaqāfa wa'l-Irshād al-Qawmī, 1965 [partially trans. G. Monnot, *Penseurs musulmans et religions iraniennes*. Paris: J. Vrin, 1974]. Vol. 9. Ed. M.'A. al-Najjār and 'A.-Ḥ. al-Najjār. Cairo: Wizārat al-Thaqāfa wa'l-Irshād al-Qawmī, 1965.

Abū Ḥātim al-Rāzī (*Iṣlāḥ*). *Kitāb al-Iṣlāḥ*. Ed. Ḥ. Mīnūchihr and M. Muḥaqqiq. Tehran: Mu'assasa-yi Muṭāla'āt-i Islāmī, Dānishgāh-i Tihrān, McGill University, 1998.

Agathias (*Histories*). *The Histories* [= *De imperio et rebus gestis Iustiniani*]. Trans. J.D. Frendo. Berlin: de Gruyter, 1975.

Abū 'l-Faraj al-Iṣfahānī (*Aghānī*). *Kitāb al-Aghānī*. Cairo: Dār al-Kutub al-Miṣriyya/al-Hay'a al-Miṣriyya al-'Āmma lil-Kitāb, 1927–1974.

Akhbār al-dawla al-'Abbāsiyya wa-fīhi akhbār al-'Abbās wa-waladuhu li-mu'allif min al-qarn al-thālith al-Hijrī. Ed. 'A.-'A. al-Dūrī and 'A.-J. al-Muṭṭalibī, Beirut: Dār al-Ṭalī'a lil-Ṭibā'a wa'l-Nashr, 1971.

77 The last presentation in which it is alive, as opposed to an object of routinized refutation, is Asadī's *Garshāspnāma* (ch. 44), completed in 458/1065 f.

78 See the eighth/fourteenth- or ninth/fifteenth-century heresiography *Haftād u sih millat*, nos. 5, 19, 26, 33–35, 71; Crone 2012a: 481 ff.

Albinus (*Didaskalikos*). *The Platonic Doctrines of Albinus* [= *Didaskalikos*]. Trans. J. Reedy. Grand Rapids, MI: Phanes Press, 1991.

Algra, K., et al. (eds.) (1999). *The Cambridge History of Hellenistic Philosophy*. Cambridge: Cambridge University Press.

Asadī Ṭūsī, Aḥmad b. ʿAlī (*Garshāspnāma*). *Garshāspnāma*. Ed. Ḥ. Yaghmāʾī. Tehran: Būrūkhīm, 1317/1938 [trans. C. Huart and H. Massé, *Le Livre de Gerchasp: Poème persan*. 2 vols. Paris: P. Geuthner, 1926].

al-Ashʿarī (*Maqālāt*). *Die dogmatischen Lehren der Anhänger des Islam* [= *Maqālāt al-islāmiyyīn wa-ikhtilāf al-muṣallīn*]. 2 vols. Ed. H. Ritter. Istanbul: Devlet Matbaasi, 1929–1933.

Athanasius (*Contra Gentes*). *Contra Gentes*. Ed. and trans. R.W. Thomson. Oxford: Clarendon Press, 1971.

al-Baghdādī, ʿAbd al-Qāhir (*Farq*). *al-Farq bayna ʾl-firaq*. Ed. M. Badr. Cairo: Maṭbaʿat al-Maʿārif, 1328/1910.

al-Baghdādī, ʿAbd al-Qāhir (*Uṣūl*). *Uṣūl al-dīn*. Istanbul: Devlet Matbaasi, 1928.

Balīnūs al-Ḥakīm (attrib.) (*Sirr*). *Buch über das Geheimnis der Schöpfung und die Darstellung der Natur*, [*oder*], *Buch der Ursachen* = *Sirr al-khalīqa wa-ṣanʿat al-ṭabīʿa*, [*aw*], *Kitāb al-ʿilal*. Ed. U. Weisser. Aleppo: Maʿhad al-Turāth al-ʿIlmī al-ʿArabī, Jāmiʿat Ḥalab, 1979.

Barḥadbeshabbā (*Cause*). *Cause de la fondation des écoles*. Texte syriaque publié et traduit par A. Scher. Paris: Firmin-Didot, 1908.

Brock, S. (1982). 'From Antagonism to Assimilation: Syriac Attitudes to Greek Learning'. In N. Garsoian et al. (eds.), *East of Byzantium: Syria and Armenia in the Formative Period*. Washington, DC: Dumbarton Oaks, Center for Byzantine Studies, Trustees for Harvard University, 17–34.

Casey, R.P. (ed. and trans.) (1934). *The Excerpta ex Theodoto of Clement of Alexandria*. London: Christophers.

Chokr, M. (1993). *Zandaqa et zindīqs en Islam au second siècle de l'hégire*. Damascus: Institut français de Damas.

Cook, M. (1980). 'The Origins of Kalām'. *Bulletin of the School of Oriental and African Studies* 43: 32–43.

Cook, M. (1981). *Early Muslim Dogma*. Cambridge: Cambridge University Press.

Cook, M. (1999). 'Ibn Qutayba and the Monkeys'. *Studia Islamica* 89: 43–74.

Cook, M. (2007). 'Ibn Saʿdī on Truth-Blindness'. *Jerusalem Studies in Arabic and Islam* 33: 169–178.

Copenhaver, B.P. (1992). *Hermetica: The Greek Corpus Hermeticum and the Latin Asclepius in a New English Translation, with Notes and Introduction*. Cambridge: Cambridge University Press.

Crone, P. (2006). 'Post-colonialism in Tenth-Century Islam'. *Der Islam* 83: 2–38 [Ed.: included as article 7 in the present volume].

Crone, P. (2010–2011). 'The Dahrīs According to al-Jāḥiz'. *Mélanges de l'Université Saint-Joseph* 63: 63–82 [Ed.: included as article 5 in the present volume].

Crone, P. (2012a). *The Nativist Prophets of Early Islamic Iran: Rural Revolt and Local Zoroastrianism*. Cambridge: Cambridge University Press.

Crone, P. (2012b). 'Al-Jāḥiẓ on *aṣḥāb al-jahālāt* and the Jahmiyya'. In R. Hansberger et al. (eds.), *Medieval Arabic Thought: Essays in Honour of Fritz Zimmermann*. London: Warburg Institute, 27–40 [Ed.: reprinted in P. Crone, *The Iranian Reception of Islam: The Non-Traditionalist Strands*, vol. 2 of *Collected Studies in Three Volumes*, ed. H. Siurua, Leiden: Brill, 2016, art. 8].

Crone, P. (2014). 'Pre-existence in Iran: Zoroastrians, Ex-Christian Muʿtazilites, and Jews on the Human Acquisition of Bodies'. *Aram* 26: 1–27 [Ed.: reprinted in P. Crone, *The Iranian Reception of Islam: The Non-Traditionalist Strands*, vol. 2 of *Collected Studies in Three Volumes*, ed. H. Siurua, Leiden: Brill, 2016, art. 13].

Daiber, H. (ed. and trans.) (1980). *Aetius Arabus: Vorsokratiker in arabischer Überlieferung*. Wiesbaden: Steiner.

Daiber, H. (1999). 'Rebellion gegen Gott: Formen atheistischen Denkens im frühen Islam'. In F. Niewöhner and O. Pluta (eds.), *Atheismus im Mittelalter und in der Renaissance*. Wiesbaden: Harrassowitz, 23–44.

Dēnkard. *The Dinkard: The Original Péhlwi Text*, the same transliterated in Zend characters, translations of the text in the Gujrati and English languages, a commentary and a glossary of select terms by P.D.B. Sanjana. 19 vols. Bombay: Duftur Ashkara Press, 1874–1928.

Dhanani, A. (1994). *The Physical Theory of Kalām: Atoms, Space, and Void in Basrian Muʿtazilī Cosmology*. Leiden: Brill.

Dunderberg, I. (2008). *Beyond Gnosticism: Myth, Lifestyle, and Society in the School of Valentinus*. New York: Columbia University Press.

Ehlers, B. (1970). 'Bardesanes von Edessa, ein syrischer Gnostiker'. *Zeitschrift für Kirchengeschichte* 81: 334–351.

Ephrem (*Commentary*). 'Commentary on Genesis'. In E.G. Matthews and J.P. Amar (trans.), *St Ephrem the Syrian: Selected Prose Works*. Washington, DC: Catholic University of America Press, 1994, 59–213.

Ephrem (*Refutations*). *Ephraim's Prose Refutations of Mani, Marcion, and Bardaisan: Transcribed from the palimpsest* BM *Add. 14623*. 2 vols. Ed. and trans. C.W. Mitchell. London: Williams and Norgate, 1912 [repr. Piscataway, NJ: Gorgias Press, 2008].

Eutychius (Saʿīd b. Biṭrīq) (*Burhān*). *Kitāb al-Burhān*. Ed. and trans. P. Cachia and W.M. Watt. Louvain: Secrétariat du Corpus Scriptorum Christianorum Orientalium, 1960–1961.

Floridi, L. (2002). *Sextus Empiricus: The Transmission and Recovery of Pyrrhonism*. Oxford: Oxford University Press.

Frank, R.M. (1974). 'Notes and Remarks on the *ṭabāʾiʿ* in the Teaching of al-Māturīdī'. In

P. Salmon (ed.), *Mélanges d'islamologie: volume dédié à la mémoire de Armand Abel par ses collègues, ses élèves et ses amis*. Leiden: Brill, 137–149.

Furlani, G. (1937). 'Sur le Stoicisme de Bardesane d'Édesse'. *Archiv Orientální* 9: 347–352.

Goldziher, I. (1920). *Die Richtungen der islamischen Koranauslegung*. Leiden: Brill.

Goodman, L.E. (1993). 'Time in Islam'. In A.N. Balslev and J.N. Mohanty, *Religion and Time*. Leiden: Brill, 138–162.

Grant, R.M. (1993). *Heresy and Criticism: The Search for Authenticity in Early Christian Literature*. Louisville, KY: Westminster/J. Knox Press.

Guidi, M. (ed. and trans.) (1927). *La lotta tra l'Islam e il manicheismo: un libro di Ibn al-Muqaffa' contro il Corano confutato da al-Qāsim b. Ibrāhīm*. Rome: R. Accademia Nazionale dei Lincei.

Gutas, D. (1982). 'Paul the Persian on the Classification of the Parts of Aristotle's Philosophy'. *Der Islam* 59: 231–267.

Haftād u sih millat, yā iʿtiqādāt-i madhāhib, risāla-yi dar farq-i Islām az āthār-i qarn-i hashtum-i Hijrī. Ed. M.J. Mashkūr. Tehran: Mu'assasa-yi Maṭbūʿātī-yi ʿAṭā'ī, 1341/1962.

Hankinson, R.J. (1995). *The Sceptics*. London: Routledge.

Haq, S.N. (1994). *Names, Natures and Things: The Alchemist Jābir ibn Ḥayyān and His Kitāb al-Aḥjār (Book of Stones)*. Dordrecht: Kluwer.

Hippolytus (*Refutatio*). *Refutatio omnium haeresium*. Ed. M. Marcovich. Berlin: de Gruyter, 1986 [trans. J.H. MacMahon, *The Refutation of all Heresies*. Edinburgh: T. & T. Clark, 1868 (the chapter divisions are those of the edition)].

Horovitz, S. (1903). 'Über den Einfluss des Stoicismus auf die Entwickelung der Philosophie bei den Arabern'. *Zeitschrift der Deutschen Morgenländischen Gesellschaft* 57: 177–196.

Ibn Durayd (*Ishtiqāq*). *al-Ishtiqāq*. Ed. ʿA.-S.M. Hārūn. Cairo: Maṭbaʿa al-Sunniyya al-Muḥammadiyya, 1958 [references are to the marginal pagination].

Ibn Ḥazm (*Faṣl*). *al-Faṣl fī 'l-milal wa'l-ahwā' wa'l-niḥal*. Cairo: n.p., 1899–1903.

Ibn al-Jawzī (*Talbīs*). *Talbīs Iblīs*. Ed. M.M. al-Dimashqī. Cairo: Idārat al-Ṭibāʿa al-Munīriyya, 1928.

Ibn Kathīr (*Tafsīr*). *Tafsīr*. Cairo, n.d., n.p.

Ibn al-Malāḥimī (*Muʿtamad*). *al-Muʿtamad fī uṣūl al-dīn*. Ed. M. McDermott and W. Madelung. London: Al-Hoda, 1991 [revised and enlarged edition by W. Madelung, Tehran: Institute of Philosophy, 2012 (cited in that order, separated by a slash)].

Ibn al-Nadīm (*Fihrist*). *al-Fihrist*. Ed. R. Tajaddud. Tehran: Ibn-i Sīnā, 1971 [trans. B. Dodge, *The Fihrist of al-Nadīm: A Tenth-Century Survey of Muslim Culture*. 2 vols. New York: Columbia University Press, 1970].

Ibn Qutayba (*Ta'wīl*). *Ta'wīl mukhtalif al-ḥadīth*. Ed. M.Z. al-Najjār. Cairo: Maktabat al-Kulliyyāt al-Azhariyya, 1966 [trans. G. Lecomte, *Le Traité des divergences du hadīṯ d'Ibn Qutayba (mort en 276/889)*. Damascus: Institut français de Damas, 1962].

Ibn al-Zubayr, Aḥmad b. al-Rashīd (*Dhakhā'ir*). *Kitāb al-Dhakhā'ir wa'l-tuḥaf*. Kuwait: Dā'irat al-Maṭbū'āt wa'l-Nashr, 1959.

Israel of Kashkar (*Unity*). *A Treatise on the Unity and Trinity of God by Israel of Kashkar (d. 872)*: Introduction, edition, and word index by B. Holmberg. Lund: Plus Ultra, 1989.

Jacob of Sarug (*Sermons*). *Quatre homélies métriques sur la creation*. Ed. and trans. K. Alwan. Louvain: Peeters, 1989.

Ja'far al-Ṣādiq (attrib.) (*Tawḥīd*). *Kitāb al-Tawḥīd*. Ed. M.'A.-R. Ḥamza. N.p.: Dār al-Salām, 1329/1911.

al-Jāḥiẓ (*Ḥayawān*). *Kitāb al-Ḥayawān*. Ed. 'A.-S.M. Hārūn. Cairo: Maktabat Muṣṭafā al-Bābī al-Ḥalabī, 1938–1958.

al-Jāḥiẓ (*Ḥujaj*). *Ḥujaj al-nubuwwa*, in al-Jāḥiẓ, *Rasā'il*. Ed. 'A.-S.M. Hārūn. Cairo: Maktabat al-Khānjī bi-Miṣr, 1979, 3: 222–281.

al-Jāḥiẓ (*Radd*). *al-Radd 'alā 'l-naṣārā*, in al-Jāḥiẓ, *Rasā'il*. Ed. 'A.-S.M. Hārūn. Cairo: Maktabat al-Khānjī bi-Miṣr, 1979, 3: 302–351.

al-Jāḥiẓ (*Tarbī'*). *Kitāb al-Tarbī' wa'l-tadwīr*. Ed. C. Pellat. Damascus: Institut français de Damas, 1955.

al-Jāḥiẓ (attrib.) (*Dalā'il*). *Kitāb al-Dalā'il wa'l-i'tibār 'alā 'l-khalq wa'l-tadbīr*. Cairo: Maktabat al-Kulliyyāt al-Azhariyya, 1987 [trans. M.A.S. Abdel Haleem, *Chance or Creation? God's Design in the Universe*, Reading: Garnet, 1995].

Job of Edessa (*Treasures*). *Encyclopædia of Philosophical and Natural Sciences as Taught in Baghdad about* A.D. *817, or, Book of Treasures, by Job of Edessa*. Ed. and trans. A. Mingana. Cambridge: W. Heffer, 1935.

al-Juwaynī (*Shāmil*). *al-Shāmil fī uṣūl al-dīn*. Ed. 'A.S. al-Nashshār et al. Alexandria: Munsha'āt al-Ma'ārif, 1969.

al-Khayyāṭ (*Intiṣār*). *Kitāb al-Intiṣār wa'l-radd 'alā Ibn al-Rāwandī al-mulḥid*. Ed. A.N. Nader. Beirut: al-Maṭba'a al-Kāthūlīkiyya, 1957.

Kraus, P. (1934). 'Zu Ibn al-Muqaffa''. *Rivista degli Studi Orientali* 14: 1–20.

Kraus, P. (ed.) (1935). *Mukhtār Rasā'il Jābir b. Ḥayyān*. Cairo: Maktabat al-Khānjī wa-Maṭba'atihā.

Kraus, P. (1942). *Jābir b. Ḥayyān. Contribution à l'histoire des idées scientifiques dans l'Islam*. Vol. ii: *Jābir et la science grecque*. Cairo: Impr. de l'Institut français d'archéologie orientale.

al-Kulaynī (*al-Kāfī*). *Al-Uṣūl min al-Kāfī*. 8 vols. Ed. 'A.A. al-Ghaffārī. Tehran: Dār al-Kutub al-Islāmiyya, 1377–1381/1957–61.

Lactantius (*De ira Dei*). *De ira dei. Vom Zorne Gottes*. Ed. and trans. H. Kraft and A. Wlosok. Darmstadt: Gentner, 1971.

Lammert, H. (1953). 'Zur Lehre von Grundeigenschaften bei Nemesios'. *Hermes* 81: 488–491.

Land, J.P.N. (1862–1875). *Anecdota syriaca*. Collegit, edidit, explicavit. 4 vols. Leiden: Brill.

Langermann, Y.T. (2009). 'Atomism and the Galenic Tradition'. *History of Science* 47: 277–295.

Lim, E. (1995). *Public Disputation, Power and Social Order in Late Antiquity*. Berkeley: University of California Press.

Long, A.A., and D.N. Sedley (1987). *The Hellenistic Philosophers*. 2 vols. Cambridge: Cambridge University Press.

Lucretius (*De rerum natura*). *De rerum natura = On the Nature of Things*. Ed. and trans. W.H.D. Rouse, rev. M. Ferguson Smith. Cambridge, MA: Harvard University Press, 1982.

Macdonald, D.B. (1927). 'Continuous Re-creation and Atomic Time in Muslim Scholastic Theology'. *Isis* 9: 326–344.

Madelung, W. (2005). 'An Ismaili Interpretation of Ibn Sīnā's *Qaṣīdat al-Nafs*'. In T. Lawson (ed.), *Reason and Inspiration in Islam: Theology, Philosophy and Mysticism in Muslim Thought. Essays in Honour of Hermann Landolt*. London: I.B. Tauris, 157–168.

Maimonides (*Guide*). *The Guide of the Perplexed*. Trans. S. Pines. Chicago: University of Chicago Press, 1963.

al-Malaṭī (*Tanbīh*). *Kitāb al-Tanbīh wa'l-radd ʿalā ahl al-ahwāʾ wa'l-bidaʿ*. Ed. S. Dedering. Istanbul: Maṭbaʿat al-Dawla, 1936.

al-Maqdisī (*Badʾ*). *Kitāb al-Badʾ wa'l-tārīkh = Livre de la création et de l'histoire*. Ed. and trans. C. Huart, Paris 1899–1919 [references are to the Arabic text].

al-Masʿūdī (*Murūj*). *Murūj al-dhahab*. 7 vols. Paris, 1861–1917 [ed. C. Pellat, Beirut: al-Jāmiʿa al-Lubnāniyya, 1966–1979 (cited in that order, by page and paragraph respectively; the volumes are identical)].

al-Māturīdī (*Tawḥīd*). *Kitāb al-Tawḥīd*. Ed. F. Kholeif. Beirut: Dar el-Machreq, 1970.

al-Māturīdī (*Taʾwīlāt*). *Taʾwīlāt al-Qurʾān*. Ed. B. Topaloğlu et al. Istanbul: Dār al-Mīzān, 2005–2010.

de Ménasce, J. (trans.) (1973). *Le Troisième Livre du Dēnkart*. Paris: C. Klincksieck.

Moses Bar Kepha (*Hexaemeronkommentar*). *Der Hexaemeronkommentar des Moses bar Kepha*. Einleitung, Übersetzung und Untersuchungen von L. Schlimme. Wiesbaden: Harrassowitz, 1977.

al-Muqammiṣ (*ʿIshrūn*). *Dāwūd ibn Marwān al-Muqammiṣ's Twenty Chapters (ʿIshrūn Maqāla)*. Ed. and trans. S. Stroumsa. Leiden: Brill, 1989.

Nemesius of Emesa (*Nature*). *On the Nature of Man*. Trans. R.W. Sharpless and P.J. van der Eijk. Liverpool: Liverpool University Press, 2008.

Nyberg, H.S. (1919). *Kleinere Schriften des Ibn al-ʿArabī*. Leiden: Brill.

Pedersen, N.A. (2004). *Demonstrative Proof in Defence of God: A Study of Titus of Bostra's Contra Manichaeos. The Work's Sources, Aims, and Relation to its Contemporary Theology*. Leiden: Brill.

Philastrius (*Diversarum*). *Diversarum Hereseon Liber*. Ed. F. Marx. Vienna: F. Tempsky, 1898.

Photinus (*Disputationes*). 'Disputationes Photini Manichaei cum Paulo Christiano'. *Patrologia Graeca* 88 (1864): 529–578.

Pines, S. (1997). *Studies in Islamic Atomism*. Trans. M. Schwarz. Jerusalem: Magnes Press, 1997.

Possekel, U. (1999). *Evidence of Greek Philosophical Concepts in the Writings of Ephrem the Syrian*. Louvain: Peeters.

Pretzl, O. (1931). 'Die frühislamische Atomenlehre'. *Der Islam* 19: 117–130.

Pretzl, O. (1933). *Die Streitschrift des Ġazālī gegen die Ibāḥīja, im persischen Text hrsg. und übersetzt*. Munich: Verlag der Bayerischen Akademie der Wissenschaften, 1933.

Procopius (*Anecdota*). *Anecdota*. Trans. H.B. Dewing. London/Cambridge, MA, 1969.

al-Qummī (*Tafsīr*). *Tafsīr*. 2 vols. Ed. Ṭ. al-Mūsawī al-Jazā'irī. Beirut: Dār al-Surūr, 1991.

Ramelli, I. (2009). *Bardaisan of Edessa: A Reassessment of the Evidence and a New Interpretation*. Piscataway, NJ: Gorgias Press.

al-Rāzī, Fakhr al-Dīn (*Tafsīr*). *al-Tafsīr al-kabīr* [*Mafātīḥ al-ghayb*]. Tehran: Intishārāt-i Asāṭīr, 1413/1992–1993.

Rudolph, U. (1995). 'Kalām im antiken Gewand: Das theologische Konzept des *Kitāb Sirr al-Ḫalīqa*'. In A. Fodor (ed.), *Proceedings of the 14th Congress of the Union Européenne des Arabisants et Islamisants. Budapest ... 1988. Part 1*. Budapest: Eötvös Loránd University Chair for Arabic Studies & Csoma de Kőrös Society, Section of Islamic Studies, 123–136.

Saadia Gaon (*Amānāt*). *Kitāb al-Amānāt wa'l-i'tiqādāt*. Ed. S. Landauer. Leiden: Brill, 1880 [trans. S. Rosenblatt, *The Book of Beliefs and Opinions*. New Haven, CT: Yale University Press, 1948].

Sextus Empiricus (*Outlines*). *Outlines of Pyrrhonism*. Ed. and trans. R.G. Bury. Cambridge, MA: Harvard University Press, 1933.

al-Shahrastānī (*Milal*). *Kitāb al-Milal wa'l-niḥal*. Ed. W. Cureton. London: Printed for the Society for the Publication of Oriental Texts, 1842–1846 [trans. D. Gimaret and G. Monnot, *Livre des religions et des sectes*. Paris: Peeters, 1986 (which preserves the paginations of both Badrān's and Cureton's editions)].

al-Shahrastānī (*Nihāya*). *The summa philosophiae of al-Shahrastānī = Nihāyat al-aqdām fī 'ilm al-kalām*. Ed. with a summary translation A. Guillaume. Oxford: Oxford University Press, 1934.

Sorabji, R. (1988). *Matter, Space, and Motion: Theories in Antiquity and their Sequel*. Ithaca, NY: Cornell University Press.

Stark, R., and R. Finke (2000). *Acts of Faith: Explaining the Human Side of Religion*. Berkeley: University of California Press.

Stewart, C. (1991). *'Working the Earth of the Heart': The Messalian Controversy in History, Texts, and Language to AD 431*. Oxford: Oxford University Press.

Strohmaier, G. (1981). 'Galen in Arabic'. In V. Nutton (ed.), *Galen: Problems and Prospects*. London: Wellcome Institute for the History of Medicine, 197–212.

Stroumsa, S. (1999). *Freethinkers of Medieval Islam: Ibn al-Rāwandī, Abū Bakr al-Rāzī and their Impact on Islamic Thought*. Leiden: Brill.

al-Ṭabarī (*Tārīkh*). *Tārīkh al-rusul wa'l-mulūk*. Ed. M.J. de Goeje et al. Leiden: Brill, 1879–1901.

al-Tawḥīdī (*Akhlāq*). *Akhlāq al-wazīrayn*. Ed. M. al-Ṭanjī. Beirut: Dār Ṣādir, 1992.

al-Tawḥīdī (*Imtāʾ*). *Kitāb al-Imtāʾ wa'l-muʾānasa*. Ed. A. Amīn and A. al-Zayn. Cairo: Lajnat al-Ta'līf wa'l-Tarjama wa'l-Nashr, 1939–1944.

al-Tawḥīdī (*Muqābasāt*). *al-Muqābasāt*. Ed. M.T. Ḥusayn. Baghdad: Maktabat al-Irshād, 1970.

Teixidor, J. (1997). 'Les Textes syriaques de logique de Paul le Perse'. *Semitica* 47: 117–137.

Theodore Bar Koni (*Liber*). *Liber scholiorum* (*Seert version*). Ed. A. Scher. Paris: E Typographeo Reipublicae, 1910, 1912 [trans. R. Hespel and R. Draguet. Louvain: Peeters, 1981–1982].

Theodoret (*Providentia*). *On Divine Providence* [= *De providentia*]. Trans. T. Halton. New York: Newman Press, 1988.

Vajda, G. (1938). 'Les Zindīqs en pays d'Islam au début de la période abbaside'. *Rivista degli Studi Orientali* 17: 173–229.

van Bladel, K. (2009). *The Arabic Hermes: From Pagan Sage to Prophet of Science*. Oxford: Oxford University Press.

van den Ven, P. (ed. and trans.) (1962). *La Vie ancienne de S. Syméon Stylite le Jeune* (*521–592*). 2 vols. Brussels: Société des bollandistes.

Van Ess, J. (1966). *Die Erkenntnislehre des Aḍudaddīn al-Īcī: Übersetzung und Kommentar des 1. Buches seiner Mawāqif*. Wiesbaden: Steiner.

Van Ess, J. (1967). 'Ḍirār b. ʿAmr und die "Cahmiya", I'. *Der Islam* 43: 241–279.

Van Ess, J. (1968). 'Skepticism in Islamic Religious Thought'. *al-Abḥāth* 21: 1–18.

Van Ess, J. (1991–1997). *Theologie und Gesellschaft im 2. und 3. Jahrhundert Hidschra: Eine Geschichte des religiösen Denkens im frühen Islam*. Berlin: de Gruyter.

Walker, P.E. (1993). *Early Philosophical Shiism: The Ismaili Neoplatonism of Abū Yaʿqūb al-Sijistānī*. Cambridge: Cambridge University Press.

Weisser, U. (1980). *Das 'Buch über das Geheimnis der Schöpfung' von Pseudo-Apollonios von Tyana*. Berlin: de Gruyter.

Wolfson, H.A. (1976). *The Philosophy of the Kalam*. Cambridge, MA: Harvard University Press.

al-Yaʿqūbī (*Mushākala*). *Mushākalat al-nās li-zamānihim wa-mā yaghlibu ʿalayhim fī kull ʿaṣr*. Beirut: Dār al-Kitāb al-Jadīd, 1962.

al-Yaʿqūbī (*Tārīkh*). *Tārīkh*. 2 vols. Ed. M.T. Houtsma. Leiden: Brill, 1883.

CHAPTER 7

Post-Colonialism in Tenth-Century Islam* 2

Carl-Heinrich Becker, the scholar who is commemorated in these lectures, wrote about the Arabs as colonisers, comparing them with modern colonial powers such as the British, and he would probably have been interested in post-colonialism, too, if he had he lived to see it.[1] In a way you could say that he did live to see it, for the term "post-colonialism" is often taken to refer to the culture of peoples affected by colonial government from the very moment they were conquered, not simply from their recovery of independence.[2] But it was only after the collapse of the colonial empires, in the wake of the Second World War, that the concept of post-colonialism acquired prominence, and Becker died in 1935. Even if he had been familiar with the concept, moreover, the fact that he saw the parallel between the Arab and the modern European empires does not necessarily mean that he would have deemed it appropriate to analyse the result in terms of post-colonialism. The wisdom of applying a concept referring to a modern experience to the tenth-century Muslim world may well strike many readers of this paper as questionable, too.

The Two Rāzīs 3

For the moment I shall leave such readers to their scepticism, for I should like to start by discussing something completely different, namely a public disputation which took place around 920 or 930 in Rayy, the medieval precursor

* I should like to thank Prof. Lawrence Conrad for inviting me to deliver the Becker lecture. I am also indebted to audiences in Cambridge, Napoli, Berkeley, Paris and above all Hamburg for their responses to different versions of that lecture, and to Sarah Savant for most helpful comments on the penultimate draft. [Ed.: This article is reproduced in the form in which it originally appeared in *Der Islam*, with the exception of silent correction of minor typographical or editorial errors and a few bracketed editorial interventions.]

1 C.H. Becker, "Die Araber als Koloniatoren", in his *Islamstudien*, II (Leipzig, 1932), esp. 2f. For a more recent invocation of the similarity between the Arab and the European conquests, see A. Hannoum, *Colonial Histories, Post-Colonial Memories: the Legend of the Kahina* (Portsmouth, 2001), ch. 1, esp. 5, 9. Cf. also below, n. 31.

2 Thus for example B. Ashcroft, G. Griffiths and H. Tiffin, *The Empire Writes Back*[2] (London, 2002), 2.

© KONINKLIJKE BRILL NV, LEIDEN, 2016 | DOI: 10.1163/9789004319318_008

of modern Tehran.[3] The two participants in the debate were both called Rāzī. One was Abū Bakr al-Rāzī (d. 313/925 or 323/935), the famous physician and philosopher who was known in medieval Europe as Rhazes. The other was Abū Ḥātim al-Rāzī (d. 322/934), a missionary on behalf of Ismāʿīlism, the radical Shīʿī movement which had begun some 50 years before the disputation took place. We know about the disputation because the Ismāʿīlī missionary wrote a book refuting the philosopher's claims, both as presented on that occasion[4] and as recorded in a lost book (or books) of his.[5]

The disputation was about revealed religion—religion in the sense of a message sent down by God to mankind through a specially selected human being, a
4 prophet. Was there any such thing? The philosopher de|nied it. More precisely, he said that there was no such thing as prophets. The idea was not compatible with divine wisdom and mercy in his view. If God wanted to communicate the truth to mankind, why should He only tell one single person? Why should He favour one man over all others?[6] It was a well-known source of conflict and warfare, he said, stressing the role of religion as a provoker of bloodshed.[7] Besides,

---

3 The debate is said by al-Kirmānī (see the following note) to have taken place in Rayy in the presence of the *amīr* Mardāwīj. Since Mardāwīj only occupied Rayy in 318/930, this clashes with al-Bīrūnī's information that Abū Bakr al-Rāzī died in 313/925. Maybe al-Rāzī only died in 323/935, as other authorities say, or maybe the *amīr* was Aḥmad b. ʿAlī (d. 311/923 f.) rather than Mardāwīj, as suggested by S.M. Stern, "The Early Ismāʿīlī Missionaries in North-West Persia and in Khurāsān and Transoxania", in his *Studies in Early Ismāʿīlism* (Jerusalem and Leiden, 1983), 202, cf. also 196, 198.

4 Abū Ḥātim al-Rāzī, *Aʿlām al-nubuwwa*, ed. Ṣ. al-Ṣāwī (Tehran, 1977), 3–28; I refer to the pages because the absence of the chapter, section, and paragraph numbers from the running heads makes it difficult to locate passages by means of them. The parts relating to Abū Bakr al-Rāzī were first edited by P. Kraus in "Raziana II", *Orientalia* 5 (1936), 35–56, 358–378; it was re-edited, this time including al-Kirmānī's account of the debate, by P. Kraus, *al-Rasāʾil al-falsafiyya li-Abī Bakr ... al-Rāzī*, I (no sequel published) (Cairo, 1939). For an English translation of the first chapter of the *Aʿlām*, which contains the disputation, see L.E. Goodman, "Rāzī vs Rāzī—Philosophy in the *Majlis*", in H. Lazarus-Yafeh, M.R. Cohen, S. Somekh and S.H. Griffith (ed.), *The Majlis: Interreligious Encounters in Medieval Islam* (Wiesbaden, 1999) (based on the text as given in Kraus, *Rasāʾil*), 84–107.

5 The title of the book (cf. *Aʿlām*, 28.1) is not given. Kraus and Pines identify it as *Fī ʾl-nubuwwāt*, also known as *Naqḍ al-adyān*; *EI*[1], s.v. "al-Rāzī"; cf. al-Bīrūnī, *Risāla fī fihrist kutub Muḥammad b. Zakariyyāʾ al-Rāzī*, ed. P. Kraus (Paris, 1936), no. 173. For another possibility, see below, n. 14.

6 Abū Ḥātim, *Aʿlām*, 3 (Goodman, 85). As noted by S. Stroumsa, *Freethinkers of Medieval Islam* (Leiden, 1999), 95n, he uses *qawm* to mean "certain individuals" rather than "some people" (cf. Abū Ḥātim's response at 8.9).

7 Abū Ḥātim, *Aʿlām*, 3 f. (Goodman, 85 f.), 181 ff., 186; Nāṣir-i Khusraw citing Rāzī's *Theology* in Kraus, *Rasāʾil*, 177; in Stroumsa, *Freethinkers*, 106.

it was not easy for a single man to persuade the rest of mankind that he, and he alone, possessed the truth. Why should God use so cumbersome a method?[8] It struck the philosopher Rāzī as much more plausible that God in His wisdom and mercy should have given all humans equal access to the truth, by endowing them with innate knowledge of what was good and bad for them, in respect of this world and the next alike, just as he had given animals innate knowledge of what *they* needed to know.[9] All humans should engage in critical investigation to the best of their ability, for it was only by philosophical study that one could reach salvation—which he envisaged as release from this world.[10] His own philosophy was certainly a religion, but it was a religion based entirely on reason. As he saw it, the revealed variety only gave you lies and fairy tales (*al-akādhīb wa-l-khurāfāt*).[11] All the different revelations claimed to be true with reference to the same arguments, and they all contradicted one another, and indeed themselves as well, as he demonstrated with merciless criticism of the scriptures.[12] People only accepted them as true because they took things on trust from their leaders, from whom they had heard them for so long that these things had become second nature to them.[13] The miracles supposedly performed by the would-be prophets were mere juggleries and sleights of hand, in so far as people had actually seen them.[14] The so-called prophets were people | 5
who caused discord and bloodshed because demons had appeared to them in the guise of angels and persuaded them that God had chosen them, he said,[15] presumably adopting mythological language for didactic purposes, but showing that he saw the prophets as deluded people rather than swindlers. As for the religious scholars, they were mere "goatbeards"—men who impressed uneducated people with their long beards and white clothes and who transmitted inconsistent material from past authorities, prohibiting critical investigation, and branding every opponent as an unbeliever who could be freely killed.[16]

8 *Aʿlām*, 181.

9 Ibid., 3 f. (Goodman, 86), 181, 183; cf. also 274.2.

10 *Aʿlām*, 12 f. (Goodman, 91).

11 *Aʿlām*, 13.5 (Goodman, 92, on the *sharāʾiʿ* of the prophets), 32.7 (on the doctrines of religious scholars).

12 *Aʿlām*, 69 ff., 171.

13 Ibid., 31 f., 171.

14 Ibid., 192. He wrote a book on this subject (*Fī ḥiyal al-mutanabbiyyīn*, also known as *Makhāriq al-anbiyāʾ*, in Bīrūnī, *Fihrist*, no. 174), and Abū Ḥātim could be drawing on it here. Conceivably, he had it as part of the book referred to above, n. 5.

15 Nāṣir-i Khusraw citing Rāzī's *Theology* in Kraus, *Rasāʾil falsafiyya*, 177; Stroumsa, *Freethinkers*, 106.

16 Abū Ḥātim, *Aʿlām*, 31 f.

The Ismāʿīlī Rāzī was horrified by all this. Prophets were real to him, and he vehemently refutes the philosopher's assertions. But one soon notices that there is something peculiar about his view of prophets, too. He sees them first and foremost as communal leaders. Moses and Jesus were the men best endowed in their time with the qualities that an imam needs to govern people in this world and the next, he says; of course this was even truer of Muḥammad, whose power and extensive conquests he vaunts.[17] Even those who deny their prophetic status and their miracles ought to accept that they were men of superior intelligence and ability, he says, sounding rather like a modern historian.[18] Prophets discipline people and keep them in order with their wondrous governance (*siyāsa ʿajība*).[19] They are needed because people are equal only in respect of the nutritional and reproductive needs they share with other animals, not in respect of the knowledge they require for moral and civilized lives in this world and salvation in the next.[20] Their different endowments in this regard are plain for everyone to see: this is why some have to act as teachers and leaders to others. Abū Ḥātim clearly sees himself as having refuted his opponent with this statement, but the philosopher did not of course dis-
6 agree: all he denied was that such teachers had superhuman knowl|edge.[21] Like so many heirs to the ancient Near Eastern tradition, however, the Ismāʿīlī Rāzī found it impossible to think of religion, morality and culture as something that humans had evolved on their own: even medicine and other sciences owed their existence to revelation in his view, not to human use of innate gifts, as the philosopher claimed. Once the human need for teachers and leaders had been established, the need for prophets thus followed automatically as he saw it.[22] He also argues on the basis of his own premises when he tacitly

17 Ibid., 89.

18 Ibid., 89.17, 90.10. A century later another missionary (al-Mu'ayyad) said much the same in response to Ibn al-Rāwandī's *K. al-zumurrud*: even if the deniers of prophethood were right, they ought to speak of the prophets with respect, given the latter's ability to govern people and keep order. See P. Kraus, "Beiträge zur islamischen Ketzergeschichte", *Rivista degli Studi Orientali* 14 (1933), 109; Stroumsa, *Freethinkers*, 139.

19 Abū Ḥātim, *Aʿlām*, 8f. (Goodman, 89f.).

20 Abū Ḥātim, *Aʿlām*, 6f. (Goodman, 88), 183ff.

21 Abū Bakr al-Rāzī does come across as an "epistemological democrat", as Goodman puts it ("Philosophy in the *Majlis*", 104), but when he says that humans are equal, he means that they all have the same generic abilities, not that these abilities are evenly distributed among them or that humans do not learn from one another. Abū Ḥātim's presentation does not allow for subtle distinctions, however.

22 For the Ismāʿīlī Rāzī's vehement denial that the philosophers have developed the sciences on their own, see *Aʿlām*, 273ff.

assumes leadership to rest on knowledge, so that the political and social hierarchy of a particular community reflects (or ought to reflect) the distribution among its members of knowledge originating from above.[23] What prophets did in his view was to establish such a hierarchy. God was very wise to send the truth to just one man, so that people had to defer to others in order to get access to it: hierarchy and subordination were what the religious law was all about.

Religion and Political Organization

What is so striking about the debate is that both the Rāzīs associated prophets with power and war. Up to a point, of course, this is as might be expected, for Islam owed its existence to the fact that Muḥammad had established a polity in Medina. He had brought a law and united the Arabs in obedience to it, and this had indeed involved warfare, which had continued when the Arabs proceeded to conquer the world outside Arabia. Tenth-century Muslims generally assumed their own case to be paradigmatic: all prophets were founders of polities in their view, or rather this was true of all the prophets who brought laws. In explanation of this idea they said that human beings were social (*madanī*) animals who depended on one another for their many needs, meaning that they had to live together, but that they were also anti-social animals given to ruthless competition and fighting, meaning that they would perish if they were left | alone: they needed a higher authority, a neutral outsider, to set the rules 7
of the game for them, and to enforce them. God in His mercy set the rules for them in the form of a law; a prophet would transmit the law to human beings and found a polity in which it could be enforced; and after the death of the prophet, other rulers would take over the task of maintaining the polity and ensuring that the law was maintained. What God revealed, in short, was first and foremost a moral order, shaped as a law, and what the prophet created was a polity within which people could live together in safety and trust, by adhering to the shared rules.[24]

This view of prophets was particularly popular with rationalizing theologians (*mutakallims*), philosophers, and Shīʿīs, but practically all educated Muslims knew that revealed religion was first and foremost a blueprint for commu-

23 Cf. Goodman, "Philosophy in the *Majlis*", 103.

24 Cf. P. Crone, *Medieval Islamic Political Thought* (Edinburgh, 2004; American title *God's Rule: Government and Islam: Six Centuries of Medieval Islamic Political Thought*), ch. 17.

nal organization and that man would go to rack and ruin without it, in this world and the next alike. It enabled them to think about the socio-political functions of religion in very sophisticated terms. What modern sociologists call the "latent functions" of religion was mostly perfectly manifest to them. Religion existed for the organization of collective affairs, they said; it created communities by enjoining obedience to higher powers, it enabled humans to internalize moral codes and thus to counteract the destructive effects of individual desire (*hawā*), keeping them on the straight and narrow by a combination of carrot and stick—the promise of Paradise and the threat of Hell. It stabilized government by legitimating rulers, increasing people's respect for them, and so on.[25] In short, revealed religion and societal organization were two sides of the same coin.

The two Rāzīs took this view of prophethood for granted. But they went further than that, for they thought that the law brought by a prophet was *only* about communal order. This was where they took off into heresy. To the philosopher Rāzī, the so-called revelation was simply politics in disguise: the so-called prophets *claimed* that their warfare and (by implication) the political activities leading to it were ordered by God, but God had nothing to do with mundane affairs. As he saw it, the truth was elevated above such affairs, and accessible through the intellect which all humans shared, not through membership of this or that community, and it was not a prescription for order in this world at all, but on the contrary something that purified your soul of
8 worldly concerns and | caused you to be released from this world. Genuine religion was spiritual. Had the philosopher Rāzī lived today, he would have been a secularist—an adherent of the view that religion is an individual matter and must be kept out of public affairs.

To the Ismāʿīlī Rāzī, on the other hand, revealed religion was genuine enough, not a mere mask for political interests: organizing people was exactly what God meant His prophets to do.[26] The law they brought just was not the *highest* form of religion. There was a spiritual realm above it. For religion had two levels, a higher and a lower or, as the Ismāʿīlīs preferred to say, an inner and an external one. It was only the external, overt and literal meaning of the revelation that concerned communal order. At the level of the literal meaning of the revelation (or law: *sharʿ*), religion was indeed mundane, and also changeable: every scriptural prophet brought a new religion/law abrogating that of his predecessor, reflecting the new circumstances of his time. But the

25 Ibid., 265 f., 285, 393.

26 Abū Ḥātim, *Aʿlām*, e.g. 108.15.

apparent contradictions between their messages to which this gave rise did not affect the inner meaning (*al-bāṭin*) of the revelation, which was eternal, unchanging, the same for all human beings anywhere. At this level the revelation had nothing to do with communal organization. On the contrary, it was totally divorced from the particulars in which we live in the here and now, totally unmired by matter, wholly spiritual, just as the philosopher said. The philosopher's mistake lay in his failure to understand that there were two sides to religion. If the revealed laws were not from God and the *ẓāhir* were all there was to them, then he would be right, Abū Ḥātim says, but they were indeed from God, and there were spiritual meanings behind their literal wording.[27] One found these meanings by treating the literal meaning of the revelation as parables, symbols and allegories pointing to higher things, relying for guidance here not on the prophets, but rather on the imams who followed them. You could not live properly in this world without the law and its socio-political prescriptions, but otherwordly salvation lay entirely in the inner spiritual message.[28]

There was a further twist to Ismāʿīlī doctrine. The Ismāʿīlīs were awaiting a 9
mahdī, a messiah. He was due to come any moment, and he would be the last prophet. Like the earlier prophets, he would abrogate the law of his predecessor, but unlike them, he would not bring a new one. Mankind would live by the inner spiritual meaning alone, without all the limitations imposed on us by our incarceration in gross bodies. The sociopolitical and legal apparatus associated with the law would wither way. There would be no more organized religion, no more hierarchy, and also no more division of mankind into different polities. The inner spiritual meaning would be directly accessible to all of us. *Then* we would indeed have equal access to the truth. And *then* there would be no more

---

27 Ibid., 114.11; similarly 104.7, 113.12, 115.3.

28 Modern Ismāʿīlīs find it difficult to accept that their distant forebears denied the saving role of the law, but Abū Ḥātim makes a clear distinction between the *ẓāhir*, which people must be forced to accept for reasons of social and political order, and the inner meanings which they are free to seek for themselves and in which their salvation lies (*mā fīhi najātuhum min al-maʿānī allatī taḥta sharāʾiʿihim al-ẓāhira*) (*Aʿlām*, 111 f.; similarly 110.13). Compare also the account of the Ismāʿīlīs in al-Nawbakhtī and Qummī, composed in the 280s/890s, in which the Ismāʿīlīs claim that "the whole of the Book and the *Sunna*, which outwardly contain obligations imposed by God on men, are parables expressing inner meanings: it is these inner meanings which must one act upon in order to be saved. If one follows the outward meaning, which consists of prohibitions, one perishes" (W. Madelung, "The Account of the Ismāʿīlīs in *Firaq al-Shīʿa*", in Stern, *Studies*, 52).

communal divisions and war. Mankind would be united in what would amount to a return to Adam's Paradise. But the philosopher was mistaken in thinking that humans had been made that way.[29]

In other words, *both* Rāzīs denied that salvation lay in the revealed law: it lay in reason according to the one, in the inner allegorical meaning of the law according to the other. One Rāzī said that prophets could not save you, meaning that you had to seek the truth yourself; the other said that prophets could not save you on their own, meaning that you had to turn to the imams, the religious leaders from the Prophet's family, for elucidation of the inner meaning. One Rāzī said that prophets did not actually exist, the other said that they did, but that the era of prophets was about to come to an end: either way, they saw the highest truth as lying beyond prophethood. And the two Rāzīs were not alone. Doubts about the existence of prophethood (and other aspects of revealed religion) are common in the tenth-century literature, and Ismāʿīlism was spreading like wildfire.

Post-Colonialism

Why did people have such strange ideas? What was going on? This, at last, is where I get to the subject announced in the title: post-colonialism.

Like the author and the reader of this article, the two Rāzīs were living in a society dominated by the cultural after-effects of a great imperial expansion. In their case as in ours, the after-effects owed their character to a combination of three basic facts. First, the conquerors had passed on their key beliefs and values to the conquered peoples: just as the elites that took over government from the French and the British were westernized, so the elites that took over from the Arabs were islamized, and in both cases these new elites presided over further westernization/islamization of the people below them. Secondly, the conquered peoples nonetheless retained their own identity, invariably in the case of the European expansion, and sometimes in that of the Arabs: just as the Indians under British rule did not become Englishmen even when they were fully anglicized, so the Iranians under Arab rule did not become Arabs even when they were fully islamized (whereas converts in Egypt and the Fertile Crescent eventually did). Thirdly, the empire broke up without putting an end to the close relationship between the former rulers and subjects. Just as

29 For a concise account of Ismāʿīlī doctrine, see for example H. Halm, *Die Schia* (Darmstadt, 1987; tr. J. Watson, *Shīʿism*, Edinburgh, 1991), ch. 4.

the West and its former colonies could not simply forget about each other when the Western powers withdrew, so the Arabs and the peoples they had conquered could not simply revert to the pre-conquest situation when the caliphate collapsed. In both cases there was a political divorce, but (for very different reasons) not a cultural one. In both cases the parties continued to live together, on new terms, with much recrimination and uncertainty and much effort to find new standards acceptable to both sides. It is this tense relationship that I like to call post-colonialism. The term seems more commonly to be used with reference to the culture and outlook of the conquered peoples during and after their political subjection,[30] but the empire evidently affects both sides, and nobody would talk about post-colonialism today if it were not for the continuing relationship: the term was coined to articulate a grievance against the former bearers of empire by people writing in the latter's language and sharing their conceptual world. In short, post-colonialism as I see it refers to a situation in which the conquered peoples have adopted the key beliefs and values of their conquerors without having been being absorbed by them in ethnic terms, and also without being able to ignore the former conquerors when they cease to be ruled by them.

Now let me give you a bird's-eye view of how the Muslims got themselves 11
into the post-colonial relationship.

The Arabs began their expansion in the 630s and had a major empire a mere 30 years later. This was a colonial empire of the classic type, with a separate metropole (Arabia) and periphery (Syria, Egypt, Iraq and Iran). But for all the well-known similarities between the ports of the British and the garrison cities of the Arabs,[31] the Arab empire was terrestrial rather than maritime, so the distinction between metropole and periphery did not remain sharp for long; and since the metropole was also considerably less well developed than the conquered lands, it soon lost its politically dominant role. In 41/661 "Muʿāwiya placed his throne in Damascus and refused to go to the

30 Usage varies enormously. Sometimes, colonialism and post-colonialism seem to mean little more than domination and exploitation of a capitalist type, making them terms of abuse rather than analytical tools (a fate suffered by all terms of great contemporary political relevance).

31 Both were located on the edge of the lands they controlled to facilitate easy retreat, via the desert in the case of the Arabs, via the sea in the case of the British, and both accommodated a population that had no desire to mix with the natives. The comparison is so old that I do not know who first came up with it. See also N. AlSayyad, "The Islamic City as a Colonial Enterprise", in N. AlSayyad (ed.), *Forms of Dominance: on the Architecture and Urbanism of the Colonial Enterprise* (Aldershot, 1992).

seat of Muḥammad", as a Christian observer put it.[32] It was a fateful step—somewhat as if the capital of the British empire had been moved from London to Cairo.[33]

The capital remained in Syria down to 132/750, when the Umayyad caliphate was toppled by revolutionaries from eastern Iran. Contrary to what many people expected, the revolutionaries did not chase out the Arabs or restore the Persian empire.[34] On the contrary, they enthroned another Arab dynasty. But they moved the capital to Iraq, where the Persian emperors had also had their centre, so now it was somewhat as if the capital of the British empire was being moved to Delhi, where the Mughal emperors had resided (though Iraq was of course less alien to the Arabs than India to the British). The bureaucrats recruited in Iraq were all natives, usually from families who had served under
12 the Persians;[35] and | the revolutionaries themselves were a mixed bunch of Arabs and Iranians,[36] so the ruling elite was losing its Arab ethnicity. And Spain seceded in 756, so the empire was also beginning to break up. Most of it was kept together for another hundred years. But by the 860s it was fast disintegrating.[37] There still was an Arab caliph. In fact, there continued to be one all the way down to 1258, but he was becoming ceremonial. Real power had passed to others, both at the centre and in the provinces. By the time of the disputation in Rayy the whole of Iran was ruled by Iranians again.

In short, the ninth century was a period of decolonization, and by the tenth century the process was complete. It has to be stressed that unlike the British and the French, or for that matter the Mongols in China, the Arabs were never forced to withdraw physically. On the contrary, they stayed on for long enough to arabize the indigenous peoples of Syria, Egypt and Iraq. This is important, for this was one way in which the relationship between the two parties continued: not by economic ties, globalization, or immigration by the conquered peoples to the old metropole, but rather by the conquerors' bequeathing their identity

---

32 Maronite chronicler in R.G. Hoyland, *Seeing Islam as Others Saw it* (Princeton, 1997), 136.

33 No Muslim comment comparable to that of the Maronite chronicler seems to survive, but the change of capital is clearly one factor behind the conviction that Muʿāwiya's accession marked the end of the rightly guided caliphate.

34 For these expectations, see the references in P. Crone, "The ʿAbbāsid Abnāʾ and Sāsānid Cavalrymen", *Journal of the Royal Asiatic Society*, Third Series, 8 (1998), 12, n. 101.

35 The closest to a prosopography is D. Sourdel, *Le Vizirat ʿabbāside* (Damascus, 1959–1960).

36 S.S. Agha, *The Revolution which Toppled the Umayyads: Neither Arab nor ʿAbbāsid* (Leiden, 2003), part iii; cf. also Crone, "ʿAbbāsid Abnāʾ", 11f.

37 On which, see H. Kennedy, "The Decline and Fall of the First Muslim Empire", *Der Islam* 81 (2004) (the first Becker lecture).

to a substantial segment of the conquered population. As rulers the Arabs lost out, but as colonists they not only stayed on but hugely expanded their originally tiny ranks.

The other way in which the relationship continued was by the converts having adopted an Arab prophet and scripture, so that their relationship with their own ancestral tradition had permanently changed. This was the crucial factor. They could not get the conquerors out of their cultural system even when they resumed political control of themselves.[38] Their inability to do so would probably have sufficed to produce a reaction among them even if the Arabs had reverted to their pre-conquest insignificance when the caliphate broke up. Perhaps it would have done so even if the Arabs had disappeared altogether, as the Romans so kindly did | after the collapse of their empire in the West. But 13
disappearance was not on the cards, since the Arabs retained their homeland intact and stayed on for long enough outside the Arabian peninsula to generate a substantial population of neo-Arabs. It was the converts who had not (or not yet) been arabized, and above all the Iranians, who found themselves in a situation resembling that of the post-colonial world today.

The reader may object that it is absurd to speak about decolonization and post-colonialism in a situation in which the colonists stayed on, and so in a sense it is. In fact, there is something inept about the entire modern terminology. A colony properly speaking is a settlement on foreign soil of people who remain culturally or politically connected with their homeland, like the Greeks in Anatolia, the Romans in their newly conquered lands, the Arabs in their garrison cities or the British in Rhodesia.[39] Decolonization thus ought to mean the removal of the foreign settlers. There was no decolonization in that sense in the Muslim case, except much later, in the Iberian peninsula, where the Arabs had lived for so long by the time they were expelled that one can hardly call them colonists anymore. Nor was there any decolonization in that sense in British India, since there were hardly any colonists there.

38 Unlike Jesus, who lost his Jewish identity when he was adopted by the gentiles, Muḥammad remained an Arab, just as the Qurʾān remained in Arabic and the sanctuary remained in Arabia. The fact that the Arabs had arrived as conquerors had given them a control over their own religion vis-à-vis the non-Arab converts that the Jews who disseminated the Jesus-movement among the gentiles had not enjoyed over theirs.

39 For a narrower definition, see M.I. Finley, "Colonies—an Attempt at a Typology", *Transactions of the Royal Historical Society* 26 (1976), according to whom the settlement is only a colony if the continuing relationship is political, and then only if it is one of dependence. This eliminates most of what is normally called colonies, including the Greek ones (stressed at 173 f.).

But nowadays a colony has come to mean a foreign dependency, with or without colonisation. A colony is distinguished from a protectorate or a sphere of influence: the words are about degrees of control, not about settlement, and the entity they designate is no longer the community planted on foreign soil but rather the much larger area it controls as the representative of an imperial power. So decolonization has come to mean the *end of empire*, and post-colonialism is a word for the cultural state of the indigenous peoples *affected by this empire* or, as I prefer to use the term, for the cultural relationship between the two parties *brought together* by an empire. It is in that sense there was both decolonisation and post-colonialism in the Muslim case.

The reader may also object that if the modern terminology is inept, there is no point in using it, and that on the contrary it might be better to apply terminology derived from the Arab caliphate (or some other imperial experience in
14 the past) to our modern situation. So indeed it might. | But the modern terminology has the advantage of being known to everyone and conjuring up a familiar world complete with a sense of the main actors, their ways of interaction, the feelings they voice and the sheer variety and complexity of the relationships, all of which tends to get lost when the fullness of experience possessed by the living is reduced to a couple of pages in a handful of ancient sources. The world encountered in the Muslim sources is not our own, but it has strong similarities with ours because in some crucial respects it was shaped by similar developments, and historians have a habit of focusing on what they recognize best in the past. In retrospect, it may look as if each generation is rewriting history in its own image, but what is actually happening is that the past and the present are allowed to illuminate each other, often in ways that permanently change our perceptions of the historical events in question even when the next generation deems the recognition to have been exaggerated or debatable. It is in the hope of providing such illumination that the comparison of the Arab past and our own present is offered here.

Shuʿūbiyya

With this apologia let me return to the Arabs. The cultural effects of the development sketched above manifested themselves soon enough, in two separate stages, the Shuʿūbī movement before the break-up of the empire and what we may call the tenth-century crisis after it.

The Shuʿūbī movement was a literary attack on the Arabs and their heritage by assimilated natives who were heard with increasing frequency after the rev-

olution of 750.[40] The natives in question were mostly Iranian Muslims who had risen high in the conquerors' society. Typically, they occupied high bureaucratic or academic positions in the capital, where, like many articulate descendants of the victims of colonialism today, they were active participants in what is nowadays called the production of hegemonic culture. They always wrote in Arabic, addressing themselves to the bearers of empire and assimilated natives, never to natives back in their original homes; and what they wrote often reflected the prejudice to which their fathers and grandfathers had been exposed under Arab rule: sheer anger is prominent in their statements, as are horror stories of the | ways in which the Arabs had maltreated converts to their faith.[41] For 15
the Arab conquerors had regarded themselves as ethnically superior, much as did the Europeans. A native who adopted the culture of the British, including the scientific and other "progressive" beliefs which the British saw as their distinguishing feature and in terms of which they explained their own success, did not thereby become a full member of British society (nor did a native convert to Christianity, whatever his degree of assimilation).[42] Rather, he would be seen as a "westernized Oriental gentleman" (or "wog" for short). Similarly, a native who adopted the culture of the Arabs, including the monotheistic religion which the Arabs saw as their distinguishing feature and in terms of which they explained their own success, did not thereby become a full member of Arab society. Rather, he became a *mawlā*, "client", a legal term which came to be widely used in the broad sense of "assimilated native". To be a *mawlā* was to be someone who had lost his position in his native society without being fully accepted into the new one; it was to have one's career circumscribed and to endure regular humiliation by people less able and intelligent than oneself, because of prejudice, not a legitimate hierarchy: this is what had made it unbearable.[43]

---

40 In general, see I. Goldziher, *Muhammedanische Studien*, I (Halle, 1889), chs. 3–5; S. Enderwitz, *Gesellschaftlicher Rang und ethnische Legitimation* (Freiburg, 1979).

41 See for example Rāghib al-Iṣbahānī, *Muḥāḍarāt al-udabāʾ* (Beirut, 1961), I, 347; Ibn ʿAbd Rabbih, *al-ʿIqd al-farīd*, ed. A. Amīn, A. al-Zayn and I. al-Abyārī (Cairo, 1950–1953), III, 413 f. = B. Lewis (tr.), *Islam from the Prophet Muhammad to the Capture of Constantinople* (Oxford, 1987), II, 204 f.

42 The British expansion was not legitimated in religious terms, and it was only where the missionaries dominated that conversion to Christianity was seen as the key that unlocked the door to the conquest society.

43 Cf. P. Crone, "*Mawālī* and the Prophet's Family: a Shīʿite View", in M. Bernards and J. Nawas (eds.), *Patronate and Patronage in Early and Classical Islam* (Leiden, 2005), 184–185, where I first made this point.

By the ninth century, however, all this was in the past. All Muslims now said that prejudiced behaviour was wrong; Arab and non-Arab Muslims were all the same, or almost the same (the sense that the Arabs were a chosen people never entirely disappeared), and in terms of careers, non-Arab ethnicity was not the slightest impediment any more; on the contrary, non-Arabs now dominated at elite level. Yet Shuʿūbism continued, or indeed intensified. For what was at stake was not just career prospects, but also self-respect and, above all, the character of the culture that converts were now sharing with the conquerors.

Converts to Islam were in the disagreeable position of owing their innermost
16 convictions to people they disliked. The Arabs had dragged them | to paradise in chains, as a famous saying had it.[44] How were they supposed to react? By being grateful? Yes, many people said, on the grounds that the Arabs had brought the truth, whatever else they had done. All religious scholars seem to have taken this view regardless of their ethnic origins. In the caliphal army, too, allegiance to the Arabs was widely seen as essential even though the soldiers were more often than not assimilated Iranians: without the original bearers of the religion, they feared, Islam might drown in the sea of unconverted and/or unassimilated natives.[45] But there were also people who, whatever gratitude they might feel to God for being Muslims, found it impossible to feel grateful to the Arabs for having conquered them. Typically, they were Iranians working in and around the court, as bureaucrats, translators, copyists and other purveyors of professional knowledge and skills.

What do you do if you owe your beliefs and values to people who have defeated your ancestors and treated them badly thereafter? If you cannot, or do not want to, become one of them, the only solution is to dissociate the beliefs that you want to retain from the carriers that you want to discard. Just as modern science and other aspects of secular modernity are coming to be seen not as something specifically Western, but rather as a human development which simply happens to have played out its most recent phase in the West, so Islam had to be seen as part of a divine process which simply happened to have culminated in Arabia. Both interpretations are eminently defensible in historical terms, yet neither made its appearance before the respective bearers of empire had lost their monopoly on power: it was the desire to have the belief

---

44 Al-Bukhārī, *al-Jāmiʿ al-ṣaḥīḥ*, ed. L. Krehl (Leiden, 1862–1908), II, 250; al-Haythamī, *Majmaʿ al-zawāʾid*, third printing (Beirut, 1982), V, 333; cited in Ibn ʿAbd Rabbih, *ʿIqd*, III, 412; tr. Lewis, II, 203.

45 Cf. Crone, "ʿAbbāsid Abnāʾ", 14 f.

system without indebtedness to the bearers of empire that caused people to rethink history, and it was the new distribution of power that caused the result to be heard on both sides.

The spirit in which the Shuʿūbīs presented their rethinking was usually polemical rather than academic. They argued, quite correctly, that all the prophets before the rise of Islam had been non-Arabs, some minor exceptions apart, and inferred that it was really the non-Arabs who had discovered the truth, or most of it (the equivalent claims nowadays mostly refer to science); they added that various early converts to Islam had been non-Arabs, too, so that Islam could be said (with some exaggeration) to have been half non-Arab from the start. Besides, the Shuʿūbīs intimated, the Arabs had shown themselves to be bad Muslims by their ter|rible treatment of non-Arab converts, whereas the 17
latter had taken Islam to heart: assimilated natives were now *better* bearers of the belief system than the conquerors. Moreover, they said, with the partial exception of the belief system, the non-Arabs owed *nothing* to the Arabs, for all the kings before the rise of Islam had been non-Arab, as had all science, technology, art and literature, with the partial exception of poetry.[46] Their tone was as shrill as that of their modern counterparts: we had civilization while you Arabs were still eating lizards in the desert, as they put it (while you Westerners were still swinging in the trees, as their modern counterparts say today). And just as their modern counterparts talk more about prejudice and colonial attitudes today than they did in the past when they were truly exposed to them, so the Shuʿūbīs harped on the prejudiced behaviour of the Arabs at the very time when it had ceased to affect them much. By constantly pouring abuse on the Arabs while stressing their own contribution to religion, government and culture before (and indeed after) the rise of Islam, the Shuʿūbīs informed the world that the Arabs did not deserve a special place in Islam, let alone in the high culture with which the belief system was associated.

Though the Shuʿūbīs disliked the Arabs, it was not their ambition to destroy the caliphate, in which they were doing very well, and with one famous exception, they expressed no hope for the return of the Persian empire.[47] Rather, they took it for granted that all Muslims were now sharing the same political house: what they were debating was their own status within this house, and the character of the culture it was to accommodate.[48] They did not resent using Arabic

46 Ibn ʿAbd Rabbih, *ʿIqd*, III, 404 ff.; partial tr. Lewis, *Islam*, II, 201 ff.

47 S.M. Stern, "Yaʿqūb the Coppersmith and Persian National Sentiment", in C.E. Bosworth (ed.), *Iran and Islam* (Edinburgh, 1971).

48 Thus H.A.R. Gibb, "The Social Significance of the Shuubiya", in his *Studies on the Civilization of Islam*, ed. S.J. Shaw and W.R. Polk (Princeton, 1962).

as the shared imperial language, either. But they did not want to think of the beliefs they had internalized as something they owed to conquerors, and what they wanted to read in Arabic, apart from the Qur'ān, were islamized versions of their own cultural traditions, not traditions relating to Arabia. It is no accident that debates over the literary canon were raging at the same time as the Shu'ūbī controversy, though it is unclear how far the poets pioneering
18 "modern" (*muḥdath*) poetry were Shuʿūbīs themselves.[49] People were | tired of reading the output of dead tribal males. They wanted poetry, Persian culture, Greek philosophy, Indian statecraft and anything else available in the Near East. In short, their outlook could be summarized as "Hey ho, Arab civ. has gotta go", except that they denied that there was any such thing as Arab civilization.[50]

The Tenth-Century Crisis

The "tenth-century crisis" is a shorthand for developments over the next three centuries, roughly 850–1150, for which no name seems to exist. Fazlur Rahman spoke of them as a crisis,[51] and it peaked in the tenth and early eleventh centuries: hence the nomenclature adopted here.

There were still Shuʿūbīs in the tenth century, but the intellectual climate had changed and they no longer held the centre stage, for by now the caliphate had broken up and the differences between the conquerors and the conquered peoples had been even further effaced. In political terms, both Muslims and non-Muslims were now living under secular kings, usually of non-Arab origin: it was an upstart Iranian ruler who presided over the disputation between the two Rāzīs at Rayy.[52] The new rulers were secular (or profane) in the sense of "not prescribed by the Sharīʿa", not in the sense that they kept religion out of the public sphere; on the contrary, they saw themselves as servants of Islam, or at least they were supposed to, so Islam retained its political dominance. But the

---

49 For the question whether Abū Nuwās was actually a Shuʿūbī, see E. Wagner, *Abū Nuwās* (Wiesbaden, 1965), 136 ff.

50 The Berkeley students who shouted this slogan in 1968 (in its original version, "hey ho, Western civ. has gotta go") were mostly members of the empire-bearing people, however, or rather of their American successors, whereas Arabs never seem to have been Shuʿūbīs (Ḍirār b. ʿAmr, sometimes adduced as an exception, is not really one). The post-imperial bad conscience displayed by Westerners should presumably be related to the weakness of secularism as an imperial creed.

51 F. Rahman, *Prophecy in Islam: Philosophy and Orthodoxy* (London, 1958), 63.

52 See above, n. 3.

sacred polity distinguishing Muslims from all others had disappeared, or rather turned into a purely notional religious community. Moreover, as the Iranians were returning to power inside the Muslim community, so the Byzantines were returning outside it, conquering northern Syria and broadcasting wild visions of reconquering Jerusalem, Egypt, and more besides.[53]

Culturally, too, the pre-conquest Near East was resurfacing in a recognizable 19
way. We are now in the period that some call the Iranian intermezzo and others the Renaissance of Islam, with reference to the return of the above-mentioned Iranian rulers plus Persian culture and the Persian language on the one hand and that of Greek science and philosophy (without the rulers) on the other. The debate between the two Rāzīs is symptomatic in that respect, too, for both men were Iranians and most of what they said had long roots in Near Eastern culture. In cultural terms, Muslims and *dhimmī*s, too, were converging, especially at the level of the elite. Educated Muslims and non-Muslims were now speaking and writing the same language (if not usually in the same scripts) and participating in the same high culture. As secretaries, astrologers and doctors, *dhimmī*s often moved in courtly circles, enjoyed great wealth, and were hard to distinguish from the Muslims. At elite level, in other words, the natives had been largely assimilated now even though they had not all converted.

In short, the Muslims were no longer clearly marked off from their non-Muslim subjects by ethnicity, culture or worldly success. Of course, Islam was still politically dominant, but things did not look good on the ground. When Daylamite mercenaries established a protectorate over the caliph in Baghdad, adopting the Persian imperial title of *shāhanshāh* ("King of Kings") and ordering their protegé to treat them with proper honours, it was somewhat as if a Gurkha mercenary had taken power in London after the dissolution of the British empire, calling himself Maharaja and telling members of Parliament to get down on their knees before him.[54] Symbolically, the conquerors *had* been forced to withdraw. As the poet al-Maʿarrī put it, if al-Manṣūr had risen from the grave, his reaction would have been to regret having killed Abū Muslim on the grounds that "the sons of Hāshim dwell in the desert, and their empire has passed to the Daylamites".[55] Moreover, the transfer of power from

53 A.A. Vasiliev, *History of the Byzantine Empire* (Madison and Milwaukee, 1964), I, 306–311; G. von Grunebaum, "Eine poetische Polemik zwischen Byzanz und Bagdad im X. Jahrhundert", in *Analecta Orientalia* 14 (*Studia Arabica* I, Rome 1937).

54 Cf. ʿAḍud al-Dawla's message to the caliph in 370/980 in H. Busse, "The Revival of Persian Kingship under the Būyids", in D.S. Richards (ed.), *Islamic Civilisation 950–1150* (Oxford, 1973), 62.

55 R.A. Nicholson (ed. and tr.), "The Meditations of al-Maʿarrī", in his *Studies in Islamic Poetry*

20 the conquerors | to the conquered peoples had involved extreme political fragmentation: there no longer was a unitary Muslim state to counter the Byzantine empire, and the political control of the new rulers was limited. Al-Masʿūdī shuddered at the thought of invasions by Turks, Allans, Khazars and others "with the weakness and evanescence of Islam at this time, the victory of the Byzantines over the Muslims, the ruination of the pilgrimage, the absence of *jihād*, the unsafe and dangerous nature of the roads, and what with people setting themselves up as independent rulers in any locality they inhabit after the fashion of the 'party kings' after the death of Alexander up to the reign of Ardashīr".[56] Above all, the cultural fusion, though deeply exciting to a modern scholar, was painful to live through. It is no secret that multi-culturalism and the incipient fusion of traditions observable in the West today looks to many as the beginning of the end of Western civilization even though Western science and technology, political models, gender roles, clothing, eating patterns, and many other things are spreading throughout the world (where they are perceived as threats to the prevailing cultures in their turn). In the same way, the resurfacing of pre-conquest culture in the Near East struck many Muslims as heralding the end of what they took to be Islam, even though the religion was constantly recruiting new adherents both within and beyond its political borders while at the same time Arabic and New Persian, as well as the high culture associated with them, were spreading among the Jews, Christians, and Zoroastrians (generating fears for the survival of their traditions in turn). As far back as the eighth century there were Arabs who grumpily blamed all ills on non-Arab Muslims, whom they saw as an unwelcome presence in their society, much as many people in Britain see Asian immigrants today;[57] and Ismāʿīlism was commonly identified as a conspiracy by the conquered peoples to subvert Islam

---

(Cambridge, 1921), 237 = 100f. (no. 106). Compare the poem put into the mouth of the Byzantine emperor: "You have accepted the Daylamite as caliph and become slaves of the Daylamite slaves. Return in ignominy to the land of the Ḥijāz and leave the land of the Byzantines, noble men" (von Grunebaum, "Poetische Polemik", verses 38f.).

56 al-Masʿūdī, *Murūj al-dhahab*, ed. C. Pellat (Beirut, 1966–1979), i, § 504.

57 ʿUthmān supposedly predicted that things would go wrong with the coming of prosperity, the achievement of adulthood by the children of captive women, and both Arabs and non-Arabs reciting the Qurʾān (al-Ṭabarī, *Taʾrīkh al-rusul wa-l-mulūk*, ed. M.J. de Goeje et al. (Leiden, 1879–1901), I, 2803f.); ʿUmar predicted that the Arabs would perish when the children of Persian women grew up and said that the Israelites had done well until the *muwalladūn abnāʾ al-sabāyā* led them astray. See Ibn Abī Shayba, *al-Muṣannaf*, ed. M.A. al-Nadwī (Bombay, 1979–1983), XII, no. 12516; Sayf b. ʿUmar al-Tamīmī, *Kitāb al-ridda wa-l-futūḥ*, ed. Q. Al-Samarrai (Leiden, 1995), 18, no. 21. Abū Ḥanīfa and others said the same of the Muslims; Abū Zurʿa, *Taʾrīkh*, ed. Sh. Al-Qawjānī (Damascus, 1980), no. 1339.

from within by | means of a fatal mixture of Zoroastrian, Manichaean and Greek 21
philosophical ideas.[58] Then as now, too, the fusion generated the phenomenon of *trahison des clercs*: Western intellectuals denouncing their forebears for their colonial sins and attacking their own cultural tradition; Muslim intellectuals embracing Greek and/or Iranian ideas in order, as it seemed, to subvert their own religion. To ʿAbd al-Jabbār there were enemies of Islam everywhere, but above all in the Muslim community itself: translators of Greek, Persian and Indian books into Arabic, physicians, philosophers, crypto-Manichaeans, Ismāʿīlīs and other Shīʿīs, all came across to him as so many auto-immune diseases.[59]

The fact was that at elite level all the confessional communities of the Middle East were coming together in a single cultural world, all of them were finding that their cherished beliefs were being transformed and relativized by the encounter. Back in the seventh and eighth centuries, the absolute truth of Islam had seemed self-evident to its adherents: nothing else in the world was the source of so much dazzling power and success; God was clearly siding with the Arabs. Even those who refused to convert found it impossible to resist the pull of the new religion, borrowing this or that key idea in the hope of defeating its bearers with their own arms, and imitating them in other ways, too, because the ways of the powerful are attractive. (These factors are conspicuous in the spread of Western ideas, too.) But the very power which makes a belief system seem self-evidently true while its bearers are on top of the world has a way of placing a question mark over its validity when they lose their dominant position. Just as the collapse of the European empires has been followed by doubt about the validity of Western institutions (even as they are spreading), so the collapse of the Arab caliphate was followed by doubts about the beliefs it left behind (even as they were spreading, too). Now that Islam had lost its epistemological privilege, it was no longer self-evident what it had over other systems of belief.

In the Muslim case, 300 years of Islamic dominance had endowed all the competing systems (Zoroastrianism included) with the same basic structure:
all operated with a single (good) God, saw Him as having com|municated with 22
mankind through prophets, preserved the communication in a scripture, and authenticated the scripture with reference to a tradition which was deeply

58 Thus, among many others, Ibn al-Nadīm, *Kitāb al-fihrist*, ed. R. Tajaddud (Tehran, 1971), 239 f.; tr. B. Dodge (New York, 1970), I, 469; al-Ghazālī, *Faḍāʾiḥ al-bāṭiniyya* (Amman, 1993), 24 (ch. 3, ii).

59 ʿAbd al-Jabbār, *Tathbīt dalāʾil al-nubuwwa*, ed. ʿA.-K. ʿUthmān (Beirut, 1966), 70 ff. (translators), 51, 128 f. (Abū ʿĪsā, Ibn al-Rāwandī and other *mulḥids and zindīqs*), 129 f. (Baḥrayn affair), 623 ff. (Rāzī), 626 ff. (physicians), 631 (Kindī), etc.

meaningful to insiders but had no probative value to outsiders. Which one of them was true? The only way of judging between them was by reason, but reason proved incapable of delivering a verdict, for rational arguments in favour of one tenet could always be countered by others of equal weight against it, as the *mutakallims* soon found out thanks to disputations in which the rival religions or sects were defended on the basis of rational arguments alone. The superiority of Islam could not be proved, except to the converted; nor could that of any other religion, or of any subdivisions within them. To those in search of proof, the increasingly even positioning of the various systems in the socio-political hierarchy made all of them look much the same in epistemological terms as well, generating the feelings of relativism and doubt that so often appear where rival belief systems compete on an equal footing, and causing Muslims and *dhimmīs* alike to go on real or imagined journeys in quest of wisdom. By the later ninth century, religious scepticism with reference to the equipollence of proofs (*takāfuʾ al-adilla*) is well-attested.[60] There were also philosophers who denied that humans could know anything for certain at all, claiming that all truth was relative so that everything was both true and false at the same time, or even that life itself was an illusion.[61] And then as today, the suspicion arose that all that the privileged system had ever had over the others was power, or at the very least that it was badly contaminated by power.

In the Muslim case the problem posed by power owed its formulation to the fact that back in the days when the natives were Christians, Zoroastrians, and Gnostics, they had often claimed that Islam was false because it was spread by the sword (debiting its invincibility to their own sins rather than to God's agreement with it). Initially they said it in Greek, Syriac and other local languages, then they said it in Arabic, and from the tenth century onwards one finds it in Muslim writings as an embarrassing charge that had to be refuted.[62] By then, the charge was also being made by Muslims. There were Shīʿīs, for example, who used it to discredit the Companions, claiming that they had only followed Muḥammad for the sake of plunder and power, not because they knew
23 him to be a true | prophet (which ʿAbd al-Jabbār took to mean that the Shīʿīs in question denied Muḥammad's prophethood as well);[63] and the issue also came

60 J. van Ess, "Skepticism in Islamic Religious Thought", *al-Abḥāth* 21 (1968), 7.

61 Van Ess, "Skepticism", 1f.; P. Crone, "al-Fārābī's Imperfect Constitutions", *Mélanges de l'Université Saint-Joseph* 57 (2004) [Ed.: reprinted in P. Crone, *The Iranian Reception of Islam: The Non-Traditionalist Strands*, vol. 2 of *Collected Studies in Three Volumes*, ed. H. Siurua (Leiden, 2016), art. 12], notes 79–87.

62 Crone, *Medieval Islamic Political Thought*, 375f.

63 ʿAbd al-Jabbār, *Tathbīt*, 35.

up between the two Rāzīs, for it was above all with warfare that the philosopher associated prophets, requiring the Ismāʿīlī Rāzī to explain why the fact that Muḥammad used the sword did not invalidate his message.[64] In sum, what worried people now was not the role of Arabs in the rise and spread of Islam, but rather that of power.

Accordingly, the tenth and eleventh centuries are dominated by attempts to dissociate the ultimate truth from the political and military concerns with which the Prophet had fused it. People were looking for a single absolute truth which had nothing to do with power, which all humans could accept regardless of the perspective from which they saw it, and which spoke to them as individuals rather than members of this or that confessional community. Unlike the philosopher Rāzī, who simply discarded the confessional boundaries as the creations of deluded men, most people wished to combine belief in this absolute truth with continued membership of the communities into which they had been born, remaining loyal to their prophet and the tradition of which he was seen as the founder. But one way or the other, the universalism that the Shuʿūbīs had fought for within Islam now had to embrace all human beings. It was a disturbing development to the religious scholars, whether *mutakallim*s or traditionalists, Sunnīs or Imāmīs, given that it threatened to reduce the truths they worked with to parochial formulations of something higher shared by all mankind. But though they wrote against the new trends, they do not seem to have had any answers to the questions they posed. It was the philosophers and the Ismāʿīlīs who embraced the new developments and who knew how to handle them.

The New Leaders

Post-colonialism was not the only factor at work: another was the rise to prominence of educated laymen. Secretaries, administrators, doctors, astrologers, copyists, and other professionals (and to some extent also poets) all owed their wealth and status to secular know-how rather than mastery of the religious tradition (though they were usually well schooled in that tradition too). Highly educated and trained to think on the basis of human rather than revealed information, they were often disinclined to | defer to religious scholars, whom they 24
frequently rivalled in terms of wealth and influence as well. They rose to prominence after the revolution in 132/750, when they benefitted from the ʿAbbāsid

64 Abū Ḥātim, *Aʿlām*, 3 f., 181 ff., 186 ff.

expansion of the bureaucracy, and they benefitted again from the political break-up of the caliphate from the ninth century onwards because the new rulers usually modelled their courts on that of Baghdad and so felt obliged to patronize whole bevies of such men. In the ninth century the professionals tended to be rationalizing theologians (*mutakallim*s) rather than traditionalists, and it was also from their ranks that the Shuʿūbīs were recruited; but in the tenth century they tended to be philosophers. As philosophers, they were rivals of the *mutakallim*s (and had no time for traditionalists at all), so there is sometimes an element of anti-clericalism in their thinking, most obviously in that of Abū Bakr al-Rāzī. This gives them a similarity with the *philosophes* of enlightenment in Europe, with whom they have much in common in terms of their actual ideas as well. But unlike the *philosophes*, they were also heirs to an empire that had united different ethnic and religious communities, and anti-clericalism is less pronounced in their thinking than a desire simply to rise above the clerics. Jewish, Christian and Muslim members of the professional elite often had more in common with each other than with their own coreligionists: in such circles the idea of single truth above the many had strong appeal.

Ismāʿīlīs were sometimes secretaries, too, but their first leaders seem to have been villagers and petty townsmen engaged in local transport, trade or crafts, in keeping with the humble milieux in which Gnosticism appears to have flourished in the first centuries of Islam. At least some of them were literate and wrote books, but they were not truly educated, and they had no links with the political and cultural establishments. Why such people should have felt the need to project themselves onto the public scene is hard to say, though the fact that the agrarian economy seems to have undergone a fair degree of commercialization in (or by) the tenth century may come into it.[65] The Ismāʿīlīs moved closer to elite level in both social and intellectual terms in the course of the tenth century, when they overlaid their Gnosticism with Neoplatonist philosophy (especially in Iran) and rose to political power in Fāṭimid North Africa and Egypt. But their leaders (known as missionaries,
25 though they soon became the | equivalent of bishops) were primarily suppliers of pastoral care to local communities, and they were less willing and/or able to transcend their own familiar world than the philosophers. All prophets, according to Abū Ḥātim, had preached the same inner message which was

65 Cf. A. Mez, *Die Renaissance des Islams* (Heidelberg, 1922), ch. 24 (still useful); A.L. Udovitch, "International Commerce and Rural Society in Egypt of the 11th Century", in A.K. Bowman and E. Rogan (eds.), *Agriculture in Egypt from Pharaonic to Modern Times* (London, 1999).

soon to become the creed for all mankind, but when he set out to explain this thesis, the inner message he discerned in all the revelations was in effect Islam.[66]

The Symptoms

It was among the rationalizing theologians (*mutakallims*) of the ninth century that the doubts about the absolute truth of traditional religion began. Its earliest manifestation was scepticism (*ḥayra*, also translated "perplexity") about the truth of any one religion. Asked why he followed his particular religion, one such sceptic in Sīstān replied that he did not know it to be truer than any other (he accepted the principle of *takāfuʾ al-adilla*), that he had simply been brought into it by his parents, but that long familiarity had made it dear to him: he was like a traveller in a caravanserai, he said; the manager had showed him into a room without consulting him, and when it began to rain, the ceiling proved to be leaking; so he had wondered whether to get himself another room, but then he saw that the courtyard was muddy and that the ceiling was leaking in the other rooms too, so he decided to stay where he was.[67]

Rationalizing theologians were also the first to have doubts about the existence of prophethood. Such doubts were not in fact the only way in which the dwindling of confidence in conventional religion displayed itself: loss of faith in bodily resurrection, or in any kind of afterlife at all, was also prominent, as was the problem of reconciling a single omnipotent God with the existence
of evil.[68] But prophets were at the centre of | the debate because it was in 26
them that the confessional communities originated: remove them and you had what the European Enlightenment thinkers called natural religion; that is, a religion in which the relationship between God and the individual was based directly on human nature, without the intermediary of institutions posited by

---

66 When other religions differ from Islam, their tenets are declared not to come from the prophets, but rather from later innovators who corrupted their faith in a bid for power (Abū Ḥātim, *Aʿlām*, 160, 171 ff.). The once common view that the Ismāʿīlīs were particularly inclined to supra-confessionalism rests on the *K. al-balāgh*, a forgery in which the (grossly distorted) ideas often seem to be rooted in philosophy rather than Ismāʿīlism. See Stern, *Studies*, ch. 4; cf. Crone, "Fārābī's Imperfect Constitutions", note 69, on grades of initiation; below, notes 93–94, on the prophets as impostors.

67 al-Tawḥīdī, *K. al-Imtāʿ wa-l-muʾānasa*, ed. A. Amīn and A. al-Zayn (Cairo, 1939–1944), III, 193 f.; cited in Van Ess, "Skepticism", 6 f.

68 I hope to deal with this in a longer work on the subject.

prophets and maintained by others claiming to have special knowledge about God, such as priests, imams or religious scholars. Medieval Muslims did not use the expression natural religion, though they came close at times; rather, they spoke about rational religion. But what they meant was the same: a religion which freed the thinking individual from dependence on the institutions and conventions of the community in his relationship with God, allowing him instead to approach God directly, as a single soul on his own.

Among the *mutakallims* the first to attack communal religion were Abū ʿĪsā al-Warrāq (d. 247/861 or later) and Ibn al-Rāwandī (d. between 240s/860s and 298/912). One or the other, or both, famously declared that either the prophets said things in conformity with reason, in which case they were superfluous, or else they said things contrary to reason, in which case they were wrong; and Ibn al-Rāwandī apparently added that prophets were magicians and tricksters.[69] We also hear of a tenth-century *mutakallim*, Abū Isḥāq al-Naṣībī (fl. around 370/980), who had his doubts about prophetic missions.[70] But by his time the initiative had passed to the philosophers. Thus al-Sarakhsī (d. 286/899) is credited with a book dismissing the prophets as tricksters;[71] the tenth-century philosopher Abū l-ʿAbbās al-Īrānshahrī is said not to have believed in any existing religion, only in one which he had devised for himself.[72] Abū Bakr
27 al-Rāzī allegedly plagiarized his scientific ideas.[73] After al-Rāzī we find | al-Fārābī (d. 339/950) writing against people who dismissed the prophets (or "lawgivers", as he called them) as jugglers and tricksters, al-Rāzī presumably among them.[74] But there were others of the same kind. According to the Brethren of Purity (wrote 360s/970s?), there were intelligent people who would engage in philosophy and reject the stories of Adam, Eve, the angels and the like because they took them literally instead of following their spiritual meaning, so

---

69 Stroumsa, *Freethinkers*, ch. 2.

70 Tawḥīdī, *Imtāʿ*, I, 141 (*yashukku fī l-nubuwwāt kullihā*); cf. id., *Akhlāq al-wazīrayn*, ed. M. al-Ṭanjī (Beirut, 1991), 202, 211 f., 297.

71 Bīrūnī in F. Rosenthal, *Aḥmad b. aṭ-Ṭayyib al-Saraḫsī* (New Haven, 1943), 51.

72 Al-Bīrūnī, *Taḥqīq mā li-l-Hind*, ed. E. Sachau (London, 1887), 4. According to Abū l-Maʿālī, *Bayān al-adyān*, ed. H. Raḍī (Tehran, 1342), 67, Īrānshahrī claimed to be a prophet sent to the *ʿajam* and wrote a book in Persian which he claimed to have from an angel; i.e. he is here a nativist prophet rather than a rationalist freethinker. But his scientific views as recorded by Bīrūnī in a variety of works rule out this interpretation, cf. S. Pines, *Studies in Islamic Atomism* (Jerusalem, 1997), 41 f., 48, 54, 65–67.

73 Nāṣir-i Khusraw, *Zād al-musāfirīn*, in Kraus, *Rasāʾil*, 255 f., 259.

74 Al-Fārabī, *K. ārāʾ ahl al-madīna al-fāḍila*, ed. and tr. R. Walzer (Oxford, 1985), 17, § 6; cf. Crone, "Fārābī's Imperfect Constitutions".

that they would fall into scepticism and doubt, though they might hide it for fear of the sword, and that sometimes they would reject the prophetic books on the grounds that reason made revelation unnecessary.[75] According to al-ʿĀmirī (d. 381/996) there were "pretentious people" (*mutaẓarrifa*), probably in Iran, who dismissed all religions as conventional institutions designed to facilitate social life, arguing that they would not have been based on revelation (*tawqīf*) rather than reason if there had been any truth to them, and that there would not have been so many of them either.[76] Rāghib al-Iṣfahānī (fl. early 5th/11th c) also knew of people who rejected positive religion, some of them on the grounds that there were too many rival forms of it,[77] while a friend of Ibn Sīnā (d. 428/1037) had trouble believing in prophethood, causing Ibn Sīnā to write an epistle affirming it.[78] The poet al-Maʿarrī (d. 449/1058) repeatedly voiced views strikingly similar to al-Rāzī's: prophets were tricksters in search of a livelihood, all positive religion was instituted by humans, he said (or presented others as claiming); "They all err, Muslims, Christians, Jews and Zoroastrians; two make humanity's universal sect: one man intelligent without religion, and one religious without intellect", as he put it in what must be his most famous line on the subject.[79] Both al-Māwardī (d. 450/1058) and al-Ghazālī (d. 505/1111) wrote against the belief that reason made revelation unnecessary, that prophetic miracles were mere sleights of hand, and that the prophets were liars whose untruths were meant to deceive the world | according to some, to benefit it 28
according to others;[80] and al-Ghazālī reported that loss of faith in prophethood was widespread.[81] The real or pseudonymous ʿUmar Khayyām (d. c. 517/1123) provides us with yet another example: "Will no one ever tell us truthfully whence we have come and whither we go?", as one of the quatrains circulating under his name exclaims.[82] This takes us into the twelfth century but thereafter the attestations peter out.

---

75 *Rasāʾil Ikhwān al-Ṣafā* (Beirut, 1957), IV, 10, 100.

76 al-ʿĀmirī, *K. al-iʿlām fī manāqib al-Islām*, ed. A.ʿA.-Ḥ. Ghurāb (Cairo, 1967), 101. [Ed.: The originally published text read, erroneously, "based on reason rather than revelation."]

77 Rāghib al-Iṣfahānī, *al-Iʿtiqādāt*, ed. Sh. al-ʿIjlī (Beirut, 1988), 109 f.

78 Ibn Sīnā, "Fī ithbāt al-nubuwwāt", in his *Tisʿa rasāʾil*, ed. H. ʿĀsī ([Beirut], 1986), 95.

79 Nicholson, "Meditations of al-Maʿarrī", no. 239, with discussion at pp. 164 ff.

80 al-Māwardī, *Aʿlām al-nubuwwa*, ed. M.M. al-Baghdādī (Beirut, 1987), 50 f.; al-Ghazālī, *Tahāfut al-falāsifa*, ed. and tr. M.E. Marmura (Utah, 1997), muqad. 4; id., *Fayṣal al-tafriqa*, ed. S. Dunyā (Cairo, 1961), 184; tr. S.A. Jackson (Oxford, 2002), 101; tr. F. Griffel (Zürich, 1998), 67.

81 al-Ghazālī, *al-Munqidh min al-ḍalāl*, ed. and tr. F. Jabre (Beirut 1959), 46 = 110.

82 A. Dashti, *In Search of Omar Khayyam* (London, 1971), 117.

The Remedies

What kind of truth *did* reason supply? To al-Maʿarrī and others, the answer seems to have been, not much of one, in the sense that he and others lived with uncertainty about the metaphysical realm and based their moral decisions on rational considerations as best they could. Al-ʿĀmirī's "pretentious people" recommended following the injunctions shared by all religions and leaving off the rest; Rāghib's sceptics held it best to stop thinking about religious divisions and to work in fields known to be good for mankind, such as medicine and agriculture, a solution also recommended (as Rāghib notes) by Burzoē in his introduction to *Kalīla wa-Dimna*.[83] It is about as far as many people get today. But to others, reason meant philosophy in the technical sense, and that in its turn meant a two-tiered concept of religion similar to that adopted by the Ismāʿīlīs. The upper level was occupied by Aristotelian and/or Neoplatonist philosophy, which gave you eternal verities for all mankind; the lower level was occupied by positive religion, which gave you approximations of the highest truth expressed in mythical and allegorical form for the many who could not understand philosophy. The revealed religions differed from one community to the next, but there was no need to be worried by this, for the differences were required for socio-political functions they served, and the eternal verities they reflected were the same. Unlike the Ismāʿīlīs, however, the philosophers
29 had no intention of ever abolishing the lower | level. They mostly accepted it in its Sunnī form, and though they did not usually display enough of an interest in this level to be associated with a particular legal school (Ibn Rushd is the great exception), they held communal life to be impossible without the law. They did not believe in the spiritual perfectibility of man and had no hopes for a world without religious or political divisions. At the most they held that individual philosophers could perfect themselves to the point of dispensing with the Prophet's injunctions, but this was not something they would broadcast. The Ismāʿīlīs had higher hopes because they expected the final unification of mankind to be effected by God, that is they awaited a new revelation. They were not alone in this; and unlike the philosophers and others who placed their faith in reason, those who expected Muḥammad's law to be abrogated often seem to have expressed themselves in anti-Arab terms reminiscent of Persian restorationism. Back in the ninth century, for example, a certain ʿAbdallāh al-ʿĀdī or ʿAbdī had written an astrological work predicting the coming of a man who would unite all of mankind in a single community

83 Above, nn. 77 f., 79.

and put an end to evil: he would do this by restoring Zoroastrianism and eliminating the power of the Arabs (*mulk al-ʿarab*).[84] An Ibāḍī by the name of Yazīd b. Unaysa, perhaps also active about this time, predicted that God would raise up a non-Arab/Iranian prophet who would bring a new book and follow the religion of the Sabians mentioned in the Qurʾān, i.e. he would bring a religion foretold in the scripture which would both fulfil and abrogate that scripture as a more universal form of its predecessor.[85] In a more violent vein a number of apocalyptic traditions preserved in a tenth-century Imāmī Shīʿī book predict the coming of a messiah who would conquer the Chinese, the Turks, the Indians and others, bring a new law, and slaughter the Arabs.[86] When the tenth-century Ismāʿīlīs took political action in the belief that the coming of this messiah was imminent, they found him in an Iranian captive of whom it was said that he descended from the kings of Persia and hailed from | Isfahan, 30
a city from which astrologers other than (or perhaps including) ʿAbdallāh al-ʿĀdī had predicted the rise of a new religion;[87] and there was an obvious Zoroastrian element in some of the outrageous measures with which this messiah, inaugurated in Baḥrayn in 319/931, tried to show that Muḥammad's law had been abrogated.[88]

At first sight, this anti-Arab streak is surprising, especially in Shīʿism, for neither Imāmism nor Ismāʿīlism was a movement to restore the Persian empire or rehabilitate the Iranians at the cost of the Arabs. On the contrary, Ismāʿīlism was a movement to overcome all such earthly divisions so as to unite mankind in a single spiritual religion. But Islam was still felt to be too closely tied to the Arabs to allow for ethnic divisions to be completely transcended within it, just

84 al-Bīrūnī, *al-Āthār al-bāqiya ʿan al-qurūn al-khāliya*, ed. C.E. Sachau (Leipzig, 1923), 213 = *The Chronology of Ancient Nations*, tr. C.E. Sachau (London, 1879), 196f. His *nisba* is given as al-ʿAdī.

85 J. van Ess, *Theologie und Gesellschaft* (Berlin 1991–1997), II, 614–618, summarizing id., "Yazīd b. Unaisa und ʿĪsā al-Iṣfahānī", in *Studi in onore di Francesco Gabrieli* (Rome, 1984), places him in the first/seventh century. Unfortunately, there is no real evidence either way.

86 Ibn Abī Zaynab al-Nuʿmānī, *al-Ghayba* (Beirut, 1983), 154f.; cf. S.A. Arjomand, "Islamic Apocalypticism in the Classic Period", in *The Encyclopaedia of Apocalypticism*, ed. B. McGinn, II (New York, 1999), 264.

87 al-Masʿūdī, *K. al-tanbīh wa-l-ishrāf*, ed. M.J. de Goeje (Leiden, 1894), 391f.; id., *Murūj*, v, § 3600; Bīrūnī, *Āthār*, 132 = 129; W. Madelung, "The Assumption of the Title Shāhānshāh by the Būyids and 'the Reign of the Daylam' (*Dawlat al-Daylam*)", *Journal of Near Eastern Studies* 28 (1969), 87n.

88 Bīrūnī, *Āthār*, 213 = 196f. For an account of the entire episode, see H. Halm, *Das Reich des Mahdi* (Munich 1991), 222–236; tr. M. Bonner (Leiden, 1996), 247–264.

as its law was felt to be too externalist to allow for the religious unification of mankind. Complete universalism could only be achieved at the cost of both. Ismāʿīlī (or more precisely Qarmaṭī) missionaries in Baḥrayn expressed this by preaching that it was the Arabs who had killed Ḥusayn.[89] What they were articulating was the Shīʿī equivalent of the Christian charge that the Jews had killed Christ: just as one could not be both a Jew (a Christ-killer) and true Israel (i.e. a Christian), so one could not be both an Arab (a Ḥusayn-killer) and a true Muslim (i.e. an Ismāʿīlī Shīʿī). Most Ismāʿīlīs in Baḥrayn were ethnic Arabs, just as most early Christians were ethnic Jews, but the issue was not ethnicity on its own. Just as a "Jew" was an ethnic Jew who clung to the old dispensation instead of following Christ, so an "Arab" was an ethnic Arab who clung to the externalist features that the Ismāʿīlīs were abolishing instead of following the Mahdī: all those who adopted the right belief were *ipso facto* gentiles. In both, ethnicity rested on a combination of descent and belief.[90] By refusing to be
31 Jews, the Christians broke with | the community in which they originated to form a separate religion of their own.[91] By rejecting Arab ethnicity the Qarāmiṭa did the same.

The fact that the Qarāmiṭa chose a Persian prophet to preside over their break with old Islam does not mean that they had a particular attachment to things Persian, but rather that they envisaged their messiah as everything that Muḥammad was not: the man who abrogated the old community was simply an inversion of the man who had founded it. His various Persian qualifications served to identify him as anti-matter to Islam, so to speak, not to mark him out as the representative of a highly valued political, religious or cultural past. The Qarāmiṭa would not of course have needed such anti-matter if they had broken with old Islam gradually rather than in one single radical operation, but unlike the Christians, they were political no less than religious revolutionaries; the severance had to be total, public, and enacted with dramatic, preferably deeply

---

89 Goldziher, *Muhammedanische Studien*, I, 175. Compare *Akhbār al-dawla al-ʿabbāsiyya wa-fīhi akhbār al-ʿabbās*, ed. ʿA. ʿA. al-Dūrī and ʿA.-J. al-Muṭṭalibī (Beirut, 1971), 198.8.

90 Compare the participants in the ʿAbbāsid revolution, who also saw Arab identity as resting on a combination of descent (or naturalisation) and a belief they rejected: they too saw themselves as gentiles whether they were Arab by ancestry or not. See P. Crone, "The Significance of Wooden Weapons in al-Mukhtār's Revolt and the ʿAbbāsid Revolution", in I.R. Netton (ed.), *Studies in Honour of Clifford Edmund Bosworth*, I (Leiden 2000), 179 f.; cf. also ead., "*Mawālī* and the Prophet's Family", 184 ff.

91 More precisely, that is how they talked, but reality was a good deal more complicated, cf. A.H. Becker and A.Y. Reed (eds.), *The Ways that Never Parted: Jews and Christians in Late Antiquity and the Early Middle Ages* (Tübingen, 2003).

shocking, rituals which brought it home to the participants that the old world had been destroyed, that they were on the threshold to a new world, and that they were on their own.

Among the deeply shocking rituals that served this purpose was ceremonial cursing of the prophets, including the founder of Islam. Unlike the Christians, the Qarāmiṭa could not retain the founder of the parent religion among their sacred figures. It had not in fact been easy for the Christians to do so either: Marcion had rejected Moses as representing the God of law overcome by Christianity, Gnostics of various kinds had rejected the Old Testament God as downright evil, deriding his law as shackles that had to be cast off for the sake of spiritual perfection. Since the Qarāmiṭa were Gnostics by origin and moreover revolutionaries, they too saw the law as shackles and their messiah now told them to cast it off, instituting ritual cursing of the lawgiver prophets, Moses, Jesus and Muḥammad, or perhaps of all prophets, as mere tricksters in search of power.[92] *Das war also des Pudels Kern*, his enemies responded. But the thesis of the three impostors (which the Sunnīs also credit to the Ismāʿīlīs | in other 32
contexts)[93] actually reflects the sentiments of Ibn al-Rāwandī, al-Sarakhsī, Abū Bakr al-Rāzī, and other radical philosophers better than those of the Ismāʿīlīs, who must have borrowed it from such philosophers, wittingly or unwittingly,[94] not because they hated the prophets, but on the contrary because they loved them too much: they had to vilify and throw dirt at them in order to enable themselves to part with them for the sake of the new world, and what the radical philosophers offered was a ready-made language with which to do it. (One wonders whether it was really via the Ismāʿīlīs rather than the philosophers

92 Ibn Rizām citing Abū Ṭāhir's physician, cf. Halm, *Reich*, 231f.; tr. Bonner, 258ff.; Niẓām al-Mulk, *Siyāsatnāme*^{2}, ed. H. Darke (Tehran, 1985), 309; tr. H. Darke (London, 1960), 236 (ch. 46, §36), probably reflecting the same source.

93 *K. al-balāgh* in al-Baghdādī, *al-Farq bayna l-firaq*, ed. M. Badr (Cairo, 1910), 278ff.; cf. L. Massignon, "La legende 'De tribus impostoribus' et ses origines islamiques", in his *Opera Minora*, ed. Y. Moubarac (Beirut, 1963), I, 83f. See also Maḥmūd of Ghazna to the caliph in 420/1029 in Ibn al-Jawzī, *al-Muntaẓam*, VIII (Hyderabad, AH 1359), 39, where the Ismāʿīlīs are said to regard all religions as made up by sages; Ghazālī, *Bāṭiniyya*, 24 (ch. 3, ii), where godless philosophers, dualists and sceptics concoct such beliefs for Shīʿī consumption. Both Abū Ḥātim al-Rāzī and Abū Yaʿqūb al-Sijistānī wrote books affirming their belief in prophethood in no uncertain terms, but to no avail.

94 Cf. *EI*^{1}, s.v. "al-Rāzī" (Kraus and Pines), where it is suggested that the Qarāmiṭa studied Abū Bakr al-Rāzī's books, on the basis of questionable evidence. It seems more likely that the Qarāmiṭa had simply picked up this language, which was widely diffused at the time.

themselves that the theme of the three impostors passed to Europe, where it was to serve as dynamite against established religion in the Enlightenment.)[95]

As it turned out, the Persian messiah did not prove equal to the task, but rather lost control of his community, to be killed by his own adherents. The transition to the new post-prophetic order had failed. The coming of a new religion continued to be predicted,[96] and the Baḥrayn Ismāʿīlīs did eventually succeed in abolishing the law in circumstances unknown, but by then they were too peripheral to count. Meanwhile, another branch of Ismāʿīlīs had decided to postpone the coming of utopia. This second and, as it turned out, much more important branch consisted of the followers of the Fāṭimids, who estab-
33 lished themselves in North | Africa in 297/909, moving on from there to Egypt in 358/969; and having acquired real power, the Fāṭimids unsurprisingly did their best to suppress messianic expectations. The prophets were not cursed, but on the contrary venerated as indispensable for salvation in North Africa and Cairo. Individual Ismāʿīlīs seem to have thought, much like the philosophers, that they could rise above the rules laid down by the Prophet, but the era of collective liberation from externality ceased to be just around the corner. Ismāʿīlism thus lost the ability to conjure up a new world on which its early magnetism had rested. When it reappeared as a major attraction in the sixth/twelfth century, it was as a very different creed.[97]

The Seljuqs

A new era did none the less come, just not as people had imagined it. In 431/1040 the eastern frontier broke, and Turkish tribes poured into Iran, Iraq and Syria. They reached Baghdad in 447/1055 under the leadership of the Seljuq family. More Turks were to follow a century later, and still more in the 650s/1250s, when they came as participants in the Mongol invasions. It was the end of both Arab *and* Iranian power: from 1055 down to 1918 practically all rulers in the Muslim Middle East were Turks.

---

95 It is first attested in Frederick II's Sicily around 1239 and reappears in Lisbon in the 1340s; M. Esposito, "Les hérésies de Thomas Scotus", *Revue d'Histoire Ecclésiastique* 33 (1937), 59, 65, 69. See further F. Niewöhner, *Veritas sive Varietas* (Heidelberg, 1988); S. Berti, F. Charles-Daubert and R.H. Popkin (eds.), *Heterodoxy, Spinozism, and Free Thought in Early-Eighteenth-Century Europe: Studies on the Traité des Trois Imposteurs* (Dordrecht, 1996).

96 Nicholson, "Meditations of Maʿarrī", no. 263:4 (*wa-qīla yajīʾu dīnun ghayru hādhā*).

97 Cf. Crone, *Medieval Islamic Political Thought*, 205–208, 325 f.

Here the parallel with our own post-colonial world comes to a drastic end. Nothing comparable has happened to us and nothing comparable probably will, given that there are no outsiders left to play the Turks any more. It was also the beginning of the end of the post-colonial malaise in the Muslim world itself. After the Turkish invasions, the religious scholars return to the driving seat, the confessional borders reassert themselves, and by the twelfth century the evidence for scepticism, relativism, and unbelief begin to peter out along with that for Shuʿūbism. Exactly how all this happened remains unknown. The question has traditionally been discussed under the name of "the Sunnī revival", an unfortunate label which is now so heavily associated with the religious activities of the last caliphs of pre-Seljuq Baghdad on the one hand[98] and with conscious policies rather than the inadvertent effects of a barbarian in|vasion 34
on the other,[99] that it seems best to do without it. But pursuing the question is in any case impossible here. I shall confine myself to some comments on the solution that won the day.

Sufism and al-Ghazālī

Tenth-century Sufism could not be said to provide a two-tiered religion. In its pietist form of renunciation, asceticism and observance of the law for love of God rather than fear of Him, it represented an interiorized form of conventional religion rather than an upper-level form shorn of ties with this world. As a spiritual search for direct experience of God, it left the status of conventional religion undefined. Its attractions were limited, too, or so at least to the educated elite in Iraq: Sufis were there seen as people who moved in humble circles, mixed with low life, had questionable morals, knew how to milk people for money, and spoke nonsense in grandiloquent and abstract terms.[100] A friend of al-Tanūkhī even tried the equivalent of a Sokal spoof on them.[101] One would not have guessed that it was with them that the future lay.

---

98 Cf. G. Makdisi, *Ibn ʿAqīl et la résurgence de l'Islam traditionaliste au XIe siècle* (Damascus, 1963); id., "The Sunnī Revival", in D.S. Richards (ed.), *Islamic Civilisation 950–1150* (Oxford, 1973).

99 Cf. for example G. Leiser's introduction to his edition and translation of I. Kafesoglu, *A History of the Seljuqs* (Carbondale and Edwardsville, 1988), 4.

100 F. Sobieroj, "The Muʿtazila and Sufism", in F. de Jong and B. Radtke (eds.), *Islamic Mysticism Contested* (Leiden, 1999); P. Crone and S. Moreh, *The Book of Strangers* (Princeton, 2000), 175 f.; Crone, "Fārābī's Imperfect Constitutions", notes 61–68.

101 Al-Tanūkhī, *Nishwār al-muḥāḍara*, ed. ʿA. Shāljī (Beirut, 1971–1972), I, 99; tr. D.S. Margo-

As spiritually centred on direct experience of God, Sufism shared with Ismāʿīlism and philosophy the feature of addressing the believer as a naked soul, shorn of worldly attachments, and of handing the key to salvation to the individual rather than his community: one could not be born as a Sufi, a philosopher or an initiate into the *bāṭin* that constituted the upper level in Ismāʿīlism; one had to choose one's own path, to take one's salvation into one's own hands. In all three cases this involved relativization of the law and society into which one was born, but Sufism was by far the most otherworldly persuasion of the three: all institutions in this world were deemed to be impediments to the quest for God; all had to be abandoned in the course of the journey to Him. At best,
35 this reduced | the law and the society based on it to secondary importance; at worst, it completely drained them of religious significance, or even deprived them of regulatory force, given the tendency for antinomian behaviour to blend into immoral or criminal behaviour of the normal type. This has to be borne in mind when it comes to explaining why there was so much hostility to Sufism of the type centred on direct experience of God in the early days. The fact that most Sufis probably lived by the law did not answer the question how they expected their coreligionists to accommodate a spirituality that placed a question mark over the value of marriage, homes, gainful employment, wealth, power, book-learning, cleanliness or even clothes. When al-Ghazālī became a Sufi, he resigned from his job and abandoned his wife and small children to save his soul.[102] As it happens, the outcome was books that seemed to save the soul of the Muslims at large, so that in retrospect his behaviour looks noble; but this may not have been how his family and pupils saw it, and in any case one could not maintain a society by indiscriminate encouragement of this kind of behaviour, as al-Ghazālī himself was well aware. It was up to the Sufis, then, to demonstrate not only that they accepted both levels of religion, but also that they knew how to fit the two together. Al-Qushayrī (d. 465/1072) made a contribution to this with his *Risāla*, in which he denounced antinomianism (*ibāḥa*) as a corruption of the original movement, but it was al-Ghazālī himself who answered the question by providing a complete guide to observance of the law as part of a spiritual life. He too wrote against antinomianism (in Persian, sug-

liouth, *The Table-talk of a Mesopotamian Judge* (London, 1922), 58f. (like the editors of *Social Texts*, the members of the circle accepted it, but the shaykh saw through it).

102 Ghazālī, *Munqidh*, 38 = 99. That his children were small is clear from the fact that he had still been unmarried when he arrived in Baghdad four years earlier; D. Krawulsky (tr.), *Briefe und Reden des Abū Ḥāmid Muḥammad al-Ġazzālī* (Freiburg, 1971), 135.

gestive of where he saw it as prevalent),[103] but his key contribution was his *Iḥyāʾ*, in which to be a Muslim is to be a Sufi.

It should be noted that al-Ghazālī was fighting on two fronts, for he also had to argue against those who held the law to be so important that the whole of Muslim society was vitiated by its failure to live in accordance with it. *Both* attitudes led people to reject normal society; *both* resulted in a view of Muslim society as standing in the way of salvation. The obverse of *ibāḥa* was refusal to handle money, earn a living or live in the Muslim community in anything but a geographical sense, claiming | that it had no caliph and that 36
the whole *umma* had merged with the abode of *kufr*. Al-Ghazālī did his best to get both groups back into the community, assuring them that it was still a legitimate version of the community founded by the Prophet, that it still had a legitimate caliph, and that it was with God's blessing that power had passed to the Turks; and he wrote in great detail on precisely what kind of dealings one could and could not have with rulers without violating the law, what kind of money one could take from them and what not.[104] Throughout, his aim is to impress on people that the Muslim community was still the saving vehicle, that it had not been corrupted to the point of disappearing, and that people should concentrate on getting their social life onto a moral footing again.

In the fourth/tenth century, all the greatest minds had been trying to *transcend* the Muslim community, to seek some unification of thinking men above it. This is what is reversed with al-Ghazālī in the fifth/eleventh. Like his predecessors, he had a strong sense of the difference between the conventional religion and the natural (God-given) capacity of the human mind to know the ultimate truth,[105] and he seems to have been more of a Neoplatonist philosopher in private than one would guess from his pastoral works.[106] But at the same time he had a genuine sympathy and respect for traditional believers and common people, and also an intense sense of the importance of keeping the Muslim community together. Accordingly, he refused to cast positive religion as mere parables or fairy tales for the masses designed to keep them in order while the elite pursued the highest truth. He insisted that the Prophet's

---

103 O. Pretzl, "Die Streitschrift des Ġazālī gegen die Ibāḥīja", *Sitzungsberichte der Bayerischen Akademie der Wissenschaften*, Phil.-hist. Abt., 1933; cf. also Krawulsky, *Briefe*, 210 ff.

104 Al-Ghazālī, *Fātiḥat al-ʿulūm* (Damascus, n.d.), 139 ff.; id., *Iḥyāʾ ʿulūm al-dīn* (Cairo, AH 1282), II, 110 ff. (*K. al-ḥalāl wa-l-ḥarām*, ch. 5); Crone, *Medieval Islamic Political Thought*, 237 ff., 305, 348.

105 H. Landolt, "Ghazālī and '*Religionswissenschaft*'", *Asiatische Studien* 45 (1991), 19.

106 Cf. Landolt on his *Mishkāt al-anwār* (in the article in the preceding note).

revelation, the law on which Muslim society was based, was meant for *all* members of this society: the revelation was the starting point for the exploration of higher spirituality, not a substitute for it. Conversely, *all* members of Muslim society were free to participate in the pursuit of the highest truth, that is to say as Sufis: spiritual gifts were randomly distributed, did not require expensive education, and did not have to be licensed by an imam. But however high the Sufis soared, they had to respect the confessional boundaries on the ground.
37 In effect, al-Ghazālī was herding his coreligionists | back into the community and providing them with their lower and higher forms of religion alike within it.

From Scepticism to Sufism

It was as a person who had experienced the post-colonial malaise in person that al-Ghazālī found Sufism to be the remedy, and set about pairing it with conventional religion: he had suffered deeply from scepticism in his youth. Where Sufism came to the rescue was in its epistemology. Like so many others, al-Ghazālī had reasoned his way to the limits of reason: where was he to go from there? One option was to live with uncertainty: many clearly did. But this he found impossible. The only alternative was to postulate that some humans in the here and now possessed a faculty higher than reason through which such knowledge could be obtained. This he fully accepted. The question was what humans? According to the Ismāʿīlīs, the higher faculty was possessed by the Imām, in whose instruction (*taʿlīm*) the believer could find the escape from perplexity: it was *taʿlīm*, not messianism, that was the great attraction of Ismāʿīlism when it reappeared as a major challenge. But to al-Ghazālī, the only bearer of instruction so authoritative was the Prophet, who was dead and gone. What he accepted instead was that there were ordinary people in the present who had similar gifts in the form of *dhawq*, the lived, intuitive and entirely subjective experience of divine realities by direct vision (*mushāhada*) and "unveiling" (*mukāshafa*) that the Sufis cultivated.[107] It was by seeking such subjective experience, or by recognizing that others had it, that one prevented reason from running wild in scepticism and kept it working instead for the belief system that one knew to be true.

---

107 Cf. Ghazālī, *Munqidh*, 15 = 67 f., on the four groups in which the truth had to be found, each representing an epistemological route to the ultimate truth.

Many were to opt for the same way out. It was in Sufism that ʿUmar Khayyām tried to find certainty, inspired by al-Ghazālī,[108] but apparently with considerably less success: he was deemed to have remained in perplexity on the basis of his quatrains.[109] It was on "unveiling" and direct experience (*al-kashf wa-l-dhawq*) that Yaḥyā al-Suhrawardī, a former Peripa|tetic, based his philosophy of 38
illumination. One had to start by observing the spiritual realities, he said, then build up to the divine sciences: whoever did it differently would remain a prey to doubt.[110] Reason produced a thousand explanations but ultimately it just produced doubt, ʿAṭṭār agreed: knowledge of God was better reached through the heart and the soul.[111] In short, as a two-level religion, Sufism was increasingly to supplant and absorb the systems developed by the philosophers and the Ismāʿīlīs.

---

108 He reproduces Ghazālī's four groups in his *Risālat al-wujūd*; see the translation in S.H. Nasr, *Islamic Cosmological Doctrines*, second ed. (Albany, 1993), 20, and the preceding note.

109 Najm al-Dīn Rāzī Dāya, *The Path of God's Bondsmen*, tr. H. Algar (New York, 1982), 54 and n. 10.

110 Al-Suhrawardī, *Ḥikmat al-ishrāq*, ed. and tr. J. Walbridge and H. Ziai (Provo, 1999), XVII, 4.

111 H. Ritter, *Das Meer der Seele* (Leiden, 1978), 79 f.

CHAPTER 8

What Are Prophets For? The Social Utility of Religion in Medieval Islamic Thought*

Why do humans have religion? Many years ago I was surprised to discover that there were people in both antiquity and the Islamic world who thought they knew why. That is what I shall talk about here, or rather I shall talk about the Muslim case, with occasional reminders of the Greek precedent.

So let me start with al-Jāḥiẓ, a famous litterateur and theologian who died in 868. He tells us that human beings need a God-given law in order to survive. He notes that there is a big difference between what he calls "original nature" (*al-ṭabʿ al-awwal*) and acquired habit which, as he says, becomes second nature (*ṭabʿan thāniyan*).[1] As regards our original nature, he explains that God has given all living beings a strong desire to secure benefits for themselves and to avoid harm. That is built into all of them, humans and animals alike, he says,[2] but he only discusses the case of humans. It is in the nature of the self to crave wealth and ease, power, influence, high status and so on, and if God left people alone to follow their own natural habits,[3] the result would be disastrous, for there would be nothing but rivalry. There would be no mutual affection or kindness (*al-tabārr*), and without that, there could be no society: people would stop reproducing, and mankind would die out.[4] But God *knew* that mankind would not be able to have any social life without discipline (*taʾdīb*), so he issued commands and prohibitions—meaning a revealed law. He also knew that his commands and prohibitions would not

* A version of this essay was presented at the University of California at Davis on March 31, 2011.

1 Jāḥiẓ, 'Al-Maʿād wa'l-maʿāsh', in his *Rasāʾil*, ed. in ʿA.-S.M. Hārūn, *Rasāʾil al-Jāḥiẓ*, Cairo 1964–1979, i, 91–133, at 97. Habit was identified as second nature by Hippokrates (M. Ullmann, *Islamic Medicine*, Edinburgh 1978, 57), but the saying was better known from Aristotle.

2 Jāḥiẓ, 'Al-Maʿād', i, 102: *hādhā fīhim ṭabʿun murakkab wa-jibilla maftūra, lā khilāf bayna 'l-khalq fīhi, mawjūdun fī 'l-ins wa'l-ḥayawān.*

3 *Law tarakahum wa-aṣl al-ṭabīʿa* (ibid., i, 103; cf. 104: *law tarakahum wa'l-ṭibāʿ al-awwal wa-jarū ʿalā sunan al-fiṭra wa-ʿādat al-shīma*). He has a remarkably large vocabulary for "nature", but it is always the nature of things, never nature in the sense of the cosmos.

4 Ibid., i, 103.

© KONINKLIJKE BRILL NV, LEIDEN, 2016 | DOI: 10.1163/9789004319318_009

have any effect without reward and punishment, so he instituted hell to restrain people from following their own desires and paradise as a compensation for all the many things they have to renounce in this world in order to obey him.[5] In short, Jāḥiẓ is saying that God made civic life possible by giving people laws to suppress their anti-social tendencies and by instituting paradise and hell as the carrot and the stick to ensure that His law would be obeyed.

So here we have a ninth-century author wondering what a revealed law is for. In effect, he is asking why human beings need *religion*, or more precisely religion of the type variously called positive or conventional, for revealed law (*sharʿ*) and positive religion (*dīn*) were practically synonymous concepts in medieval Islam. What's more, Jāḥiẓ formulates his answer in terms of functional sociology: a religious law has certain *social functions* that enable human groups to survive; it serves to curb human selfishness; it makes people sacrifice their own individual interests for the sake of the common good. In effect, that is also the explanation that the sociologist Durkheim offered in 1912. The reason that Jāḥiẓ could think like a sociologist is that he shared two fundamental presuppositions with his contemporaries.

The first is that prophets are lawgivers, not spiritual figures. (Prophets are not actually mentioned in the epistle, but they are presupposed, as they are the intermediaries though whom God's law is transmitted to mankind.) Their role is to get people together in a single community and subject them to the same law, so that they can escape from moral, social and political anarchy. Religion means unity and order. It brings people together in the same vehicle of salvation and makes them obey rules that enable them to travel together in peace and quiet to their destination in this world and the next. This is modelled on Muḥammad, who united the Arabs in a polity. It also fits Moses, who organised his people for the exodus from Egypt. But it does not fit Jesus, and modern Westerners do not usually think of religion as a synonym for law and order either. To them, religion is first and foremost an individual relationship with God, a source of spiritual sustenance, direction and support, and its social functions are what the sociologist Merton called latent functions, that is to say side-effects that people do not notice, though they may be exceedingly important in practice. But these functions were not latent at all to Muslims of al-Jāḥiẓ's time, for to them, religion was first and foremost about community formation. As a tenth-century work tells us, no religion was ever instituted for the benefit of the individual, or as another says, religion is collective obe-

5 Ibid., i, 104 f.

dience to a single authority.[6] All the so-called pillars of Islam were (and are) collective acts: the daily ritual prayers, the weekly congregational service, the annual fast, the pilgrimage once in a lifetime, and the charity that should be practised at all times. These were all public, external acts that people performed together or at least at the same time, in obedience to the ruler of the polity, God.[7]

In other words, as medieval Muslims saw it, revealed religion was first and foremost a civic religion—a religion that regulates your life as a member of a *polity* and marks it out from others. God stood for the community. In worshipping God a society is worshipping itself, as Durkheim famously declared. He should know. He came from a strictly observant Jewish family: God and the community were two sides of the same coin in that tradition too.

So that was one of al-Jāḥiẓ's presuppositions: revealed religion is civic religion. Al-Jāḥiẓ's second presupposition was that human nature is highly antisocial. Left on their own, people would engage in ruthless competition, nobody would defer to anyone else, and they would destroy one another. God made them that way: they need their strong drives in order to survive. But God also made them incapable of living alone. They need to come together and take up different occupations to satisfy their many needs, as many observed, including al-Jāḥiẓ himself in another work.[8] So humans are both social and deeply antisocial animals, and they could not resolve that contradiction on their own. If God had left them alone in what Westerners call a state of nature, they would have perished. In short, al-Jāḥiẓ tells us that revealed religion exists because it is eminently useful, indeed indispensable for social life. Brought by prophets, it made civilisation possible.[9]

The Muslim view of things has often been compared with Hobbes' contract theory. Hobbes famously said that humans in a state of nature would fight: their lives would be nasty, brutish and short. A contract with a sovereign solved the problem. In Hobbes' view, the sovereign was a human king. In the Muslim vision, he was God.

---

6 P. Crone, *Medieval Islamic Political Thought* (American title *God's Rule*), Edinburgh and New York 2004, 393, citing al-ʿĀmirī and *Rasāʾil Ikhwān al-Ṣafā*.

7 "Wherever there is a *general* need, there the obligation is to *God*", as Ibn Taymiyya put it (cited by Crone, *Medieval Islamic Political Thought*, 394).

8 Cf. Crone, *Medieval Islamic Political Thought*, 260, 341f., citing both al-Jāḥiẓ and many other authors.

9 The Muslims also inherited Aristotle's contrary view that humans are social/political animals by nature, and they often combined them. But even those who stressed the social nature of mankind tended to agree that without prophets there would be no law or government.

In fact, the two contract theories probably share a remote ancestor in Democritus. According to Democritus, followed by Epicurus, humans originated without language, love, altruism, group solidarity and so on; they had painfully and gradually worked their way to civilisation, but it all rested on convention and institutions, not on their inbuilt nature, and it could collapse at any time. As a third-century Epicurean said:

> Those who have established the laws, customs, kings and magistrates in cities have placed our life in the greatest security and peace and done away with trouble. But *if* one did away with all that, we would live the life of beasts, and everyone would eat anyone if they could.[10]

That's exactly what al-Jāḥiẓ is saying, except that he did not think that humans had done it on their own: without divine intervention, it would never have happened.

Or take Critias, Plato's uncle. According to him, human beings originally lived like beasts, ruled by force, without any reward for good men or punishment for the wicked. That's the Democritan view we have just met. According to Critias, humans eventually established laws so that they would be ruled by justice; but people would still commit crimes when they were alone, so a wise man hit on the idea of fear of the gods: he told people about immortal divinities who see and hear everything we do, even when we are alone. In short, Critias held that an ancient lawgiver had invented the gods to curb people's anti-social behaviour.[11] Critias' gods punished people by means of natural phenomena such as thunderbolts, not requital in the hereafter, but that was soon added. Polybius, for example, said that the common people were fickle, full of lawless desires and violent passions, so the only way to keep them in check was by religion; if all men could be philosophers, it might not be necessary, but they couldn't, so the ancients were very wise when they introduced beliefs about the gods and *punishments in Hades*.[12] This argument

10 Plutarch, 'Reply to Colotes', 30, 1124D.

11 Sextus Empiricus, *Against the Physicists*, I, 54. Compare Aristotle, *Metaphysics Lambda*, 1074b, on how some myths had been added "with a view to the persuasion of the multitude and to its legal and utilitarian expediency".

12 Polybius, 6.56 (cf. P.A. Brunt, 'Laus imperii', in *Imperialism in the Ancient World*, ed. P.D.A. Garnsey and C.R. Whittaker, Cambridge 1978, 166). According to Polybius, it was scrupulous fear of the gods that kept the Roman commonwealth together. By this he meant that fear of the gods had an extraordinary effect on Roman behaviour, not that the gods were rewarding the Romans for their observance; but nor is he lending support to the view

was extremely widespread, in both Greek and Latin, and it lived on in new forms in Islam, though one can only speculate as to how it had been transmitted.[13]

In al-Jāḥiẓ's rendition the argument has changed in two important ways. First, the ancient sages and lawgivers have turned into prophets: they no longer invent myths *about* the gods and Hades, but rather bring messages *from* God about paradise and hell. What they say is true. Secondly, we *all* need to be restrained by laws, we all need reward and punishment, not just the ignorant masses. That's also true of the Democritan tradition, but not usually otherwise. In al-Jāḥiẓ, however, monotheism has done away with the sharp distinction between a philosophically trained elite and common people;[14] and it is this monotheist reworking that transforms the old argument into good sociology, for now it has become an explanation of how a whole *society* works—not just an elitist argument about the management of the masses.

So the lawgivers now bring true messages from God, but for all that al-Jāḥiẓ has not the slightest compunction about explaining religion in utilitarian terms. To him, it merely goes to demonstrate God's providence: everything God does for us is for the best; God gave us competitive natures *and* God gave us the religion to keep our competitive natures under control. One encounters this view elsewhere as well. The theologian al-Māwardī (d. 1058), for example, tells us that revealed religion keeps people in order by getting to dominate people's inner lives, so that they feel ruled by it even when they are alone.[15] That's what Critias said, but al-Māwardī doesn't doubt that the revelation is

---

that "all elite Romans were complete sceptics who were in a conspiracy to deceive other sections of the population" (pace J.A. North, *Roman Religion*, Oxford 2000, 30, cf. 77). What impresses him is the cohesion that fear of the gods induces and the sacrifices that everybody will make for the sake of the common good, not the manipulation of the masses. In fact, it is not only the masses that the Roman gods affect: it is everybody, including unphilosophical members of the elite. All had to be virtuous, only the means differed. Polybius wishes that the unphilosophical common people would fear religion as much back home in Greece, where those who do not cultivate philosophy have no virtue at all.

13 You can follow it down to the third century AD, then it disappears. The Christians derided it as an example of how the nasty pagans had deliberately lied to the masses so as to exploit them. The Christians did not think of their own religion in utilitarian terms. How the Muslims came to do so is unknown.

14 God is so infinitely greater than human beings that the differences among us cease to matter: we all turn into the same tiny, fallible specks. And God's revelation is so infinitely above anything that human reason can work out that philosophy is neither here nor there.

15 Al-Māwardī, *Adab al-dunyā wa'l-dīn*, ed. M. al-Saqqā, Cairo 1973, 136 (ed. Beirut 1987, 133).

true. By contrast, when Durkheim discovered the social functions of religion he felt that he had unmasked positive religion as a purely human creation. But then metaphysical truth and social utility had grown up in different compartments in the West and were not compatible. They still aren't, as one can see in the interminable debates whether this or that is *really* religious or *just* political.

But it has to be admitted that al-Jāḥiẓ's argument is not entirely watertight. What about animals and infidels? al-Jāḥiẓ explicitly says that God has endowed animals and humans with the same inbuilt nature. So why do animals have social lives without religion of any kind? Why have *they* not gone extinct for lack of cooperation? You might have expected him to consider that problem. He wrote a whole book about animals, frequently adduces animal parallels to human features and had a colleague who said that animals *did* have religion. According to this colleague, Ibn Khābiṭ, all animals received prophets from their own species and were punished and rewarded by reincarnation in animal or, eventually, human form in accordance with their deeds until they reached salvation. But al-Jāḥiẓ just ridicules him.[16] That didn't make the problem go away. Less than a century later you have the famous Iranian philosopher al-Rāzī—Rhazes to the Latin Christians. He did not think that animals had prophets, but he argued that since animals managed without them, humans could do so too: they had no genuine need of prophets; wittingly or unwittingly, the prophets were actually frauds.[17] This view takes us from one extreme to the other. There was a third variant, represented by a tenth-century Shiite group. They accepted both that animals don't have prophets *and* that we humans do, but they hankered for the day when we humans wouldn't need positive religion any more. They wanted natural religion, like the animals as they imagined them. They told a fable in which the animals praise God and do

---

16 J. van Ess, *Theologie und Gesellschaft im 2. und 3. Jahrhundert Hidschra*, Berlin and New York 1991–1997, iii, 430 ff.; cf. P. Crone, 'Al-Jāḥiẓ on *aṣḥāb al-jahālāt* and the Jahmiyya', in *Medieval Arabic Thought: Essays in Honour of Fritz Zimmermann*, ed. R. Hansberger, M. Afifi al-Akiti and C. Burnett, London and Turin 2012 [Ed.: reprinted in P. Crone, *The Iranian Reception of Islam: The Non-Traditionalist Strands*, vol. 2 of *Collected Studies in Three Volumes*, ed. H. Siurua, Leiden 2016, art. 8], 27–40, at 34 ff., here in connection with the claim that everything, even animals and stones, was rational, though he does mention Ibn Khābiṭ for his views on animal prophets too.

17 For his views in brief, see P. Crone, 'Post-colonialism in tenth-century Islam', *Der Islam* 83, 2006, 2–38 [Ed.: included as article 7 in the present volume], at 4–6 (with references); for a longer treatment, see S. Stroumsa, *Freethinkers of Medieval Islam*, Leiden 1999, ch. 2.

the right things of their own accord, without law, scriptures, mosques, religious scholars, prayers, fasting or any of the paraphernalia we need to achieve some kind of decency.[18] These Shiites were suffering from the discontent of civilisation. But al-Jāḥiẓ doesn't seem to have devoted any thought to the contrasting cases of animals and humans.

What about infidels, then? Many infidels managed to live social lives without a revealed law or belief in reward and punishment after death. Al-Jāḥiẓ did actually take some note of that, for in another epistle he has a Turkish chief in Central Asia and a Muslim general compare the relative merits of manmade and revealed law. Here he simply has the general say that you Turks have manmade law, law based on reason; we Muslims prefer a revealed law. He doesn't say there could be no community without it. So he is being inconsistent. But the Turks were tribesmen, a bit like the Arabs before the rise of Islam: good fighters, but not *civilised*. al-Jāḥiẓ did not know of any *civilised* people who lived without a religious law. And he certainly didn't know of whole societies without belief in reward and punishment after death. So the counter-examples didn't weigh on his mind. It was not until the fourteenth century that it was pointed out by two quite different thinkers, Ibn Taymiyya and Ibn Khaldūn, that it was perfectly possible to form a polity without a revealed law, and that many peoples had done so. Eventually, this was to become all too well known, for the peoples in question included the Europeans, and it was when they rose to world dominance that the idea of a purely manmade law and political order acquired major importance.

So far, so good, but not everybody held that positive religion was both true and useful. Some said that it was *neither* true *nor* useful—that was the old Epicurean view—and still others said it was useful all right, but not true—the same view as in Critias.

Neither True nor Useful

Of those who dismissed positive religion as neither true nor useful, the earliest were the so-called Dahrīs, who seem to have existed in Iraq well before the conquests, but who were at their height in al-Jāḥiẓ's time, the ninth century. There was a bewildering variety of them.[19] All denied the creation ex nihilo; many

18 *Rasā'il Ikhwān al-Ṣafā*, Beirut 1957, epistle 22; ed. and tr. L.E. Goodman and R. McGregor, Oxford 2009.

19 See P. Crone, 'Ungodly cosmologies', in *The Oxford Handbook of Islamic Theology*,

denied that there was a creator at all or at least explained the creation without recourse to such a figure; the most extreme of them dismissed the entire metaphysical realm along with the creator: there were no angels, demons, prophets, revelation, holy law or scriptures, and no afterlife of any kind either. All this is fascinating, but what did they say about *why* we have religion? We don't know, though there are suggestions that some of them regarded the prophets as tricksters: they credited them with knowledge of the astrological and medical sciences.[20]

They are quoted as speaking about positive religion in the same dismissive tone as Richard Dawkins or Daniel Dennett, and they may not have given any more thought to the question why something so stupid (in their view) should have won close to universal acceptance than the latter do. There was also an interesting set of people about whom, unfortunately, we only have a couple of lines. They were creationists all right, but they didn't think the universe had a ruler any more. "We see people fall into water without being able to swim, or into fire, and call upon the provident maker (*al-ṣāniʿ al-mudabbir*), but he does not rescue them, so we know the creator is non-existent (*maʿdūm*)". One group explained that after completing the world and finding it good the creator had destroyed himself so as not to ruin his handiwork, leaving behind the laws (*aḥkām*) current among the created things and living beings. Another group held that, rather, a *tawalwul* had appeared in the essence of the creator and it had sucked all his power and light out of him and into itself: that *tawalwul* was the world, and all that remained of the creator was a cat (*sinnawr*), which would suck the light out of this world again so that eventually he would be restored; meanwhile he was too weak to attend to his created beings; their affairs were left unattended with the result that injustice had spread.[21] A third group agreed that all the divine power had gone into the world, but envisaged the process as a dispersal of particles rather than light. Or he had run out of energy in some other way and was now too feeble to do anything. I don't know what *tawalwul* means, but it is clearly some kind of defect, and I suspect it is a medical term: the world was some kind of parasitic growth on the creator and had reduced

ed. S. Schmidtke, Oxford 2016 [Ed.: included as article 6 in the present volume]. P. Crone, 'The Dahrīs according to al-Jāḥiẓ', *Mélanges de l'Université Saint-Joseph* 63, 2010–2011, 63–82 [Ed.: article 5 in the present volume], does not cover all of them.

20 Cf. al-Jāḥiẓ, 'Ḥujaj al-nubuwwa', in his *Rasāʾil*, ed. ʿA.-S.M. Hārūn, iii, 263f., on why Muḥammad cannot be dismissed as an astrologer; Māturīdī, *Taʾwīlāt*, xvii, ed. A. Vanlioğlu and B. Topaloğlu, Istanbul 2010, 400.ult. (*ad* Q. 114:4–6).

21 Yaḥyā b. Bashīr b. ʿUmayr al-Nihāwandī (wr. before 377/987f.) in Ibn al-Jawzī, *Talbīs Iblīs*, ed. M.M. al-Dimashqī, Cairo 1928, 46 (ch. against the *falāsifa*).

him to such a feeble state that he might as well not exist. So why did these people think that people accepted positive religion? We don't know.

There were also people who believed in God all right, just not in prophets. We know several of them by name, but we only have details about two of them. The first is Ibn al-Rāwandī, who flourished in Baghdad a bit after al-Jāḥiẓ. He began as a theologian of the same theological school as al-Jāḥiẓ, and there is general agreement that he was brilliant. He was too clever for his own good, they said. I suspect he had also had too many disputations with the Dahrīs, for a fair number of those who argued with them ended up by going off the rails one way or the other. In any case, at some point Ibn al-Rāwandī started writing highly offensive books attacking the prophets, especially Muḥammad, and the Quran. The extant fragments have the scoffing tone of the Dahrīs. Then he wrote more books refuting all his outrageous works, though he died before he had finished the task. Maybe he was a sceptic trying to prove that for every argument in favour of something there was another against it; in short, you could not know anything. We don't know.

In any case, in his outrageous books he said that there was no need for revelation, for either it was in conformity with reason, in which case it was superfluous, or else it was contrary to reason, in which case it was false. So why did people believe in prophets? Because they were duped. The so-called prophets were frauds who used trickery and sorcery to produce their alleged miracles. They knew about the powers of magnets, for example; their predictions were of the kind that any half-decent astrologer could come up with; some of the alleged miracles could be dismissed because of the small number of witnesses, and others simply did not make sense: for example, if angels assisted the believers in the battle at Badr, where the believers won, where were they at Uḥud, where the believers lost?

What motivated the men who claimed to be prophets? Ibn al-Rāwandī does not say, but others did: the so-called prophets were after power, money or both. That was a very old explanation of other people's false prophets. What was unusual about Ibn al-Rāwandī is that he applied it to all the prophets, including his own. He and his likes denied the whole category. There was not and could not be any such thing as a genuine prophet.

The other person we have some details about you know already: the Iranian philosopher and medical doctor al-Rāzī. Unlike the brash, offensive Ibn al-Rāwandī, he was by all accounts a very affable and likable man, and he was not a scoffer. But he didn't like revealed religion, and in his case we know why. He didn't want civic religion to come between himself and God. True religion in his view spoke directly to the individual, it was above communal divisions, it was universally true for all men, and it had nothing to do with mundane polities, law or war. He said that you reached God through philosophy, through your own reason, and that all humans had the same ability to reach him. If God wanted to reveal himself to mankind, why should do so to just one man? It struck al-Rāzī as an absurd idea. God must have revealed himself to everyone, by implanting the ability to reach him—by means of reason—in every human being, just has he had implanted knowledge of what animals need to know in every animal. It followed that prophets were impostors. Their miracles were mere magic and sleights of hand, their books contradicted each other and themselves. The would-be prophets had been seduced by evil spirits who appeared to them in the form of angels: in other words, in Rāzī's view they were deluded, and later generations only believed them because they had been reared on such beliefs since childhood. We don't know how he explained why the prophets' contemporaries had followed them, but others said that they, too, were after power and money.

It was a widespread view at the time, in part because there were so many competing politico-religious leaders, all with their own religious messages and preachers who would wheedle money out of people with their stirring sermons. Al-Maʿarrī, an eleventh-century Syrian who also held that true religion rested on reason, gives us this example:

> For his own sordid ends
> The pulpit he ascends,
> And though he disbelieves in resurrection,
> Makes all his hearers quail
> Whilst he unfolds a tale
> Of Last Day scenes that stun the recollection

And here is his most famous verse:

> They all err—Muslims, Christians, Jews and Magians [i.e. Zoroastrians].
> Two make humanity's universal sect:
> One man intelligent without religion, and one religious without intellect.[22]

You hear more about such cynical views of prophetic religion from the famous theologian al-Ghazālī (d. 1111). He wrote, among other things, against those

22 Al-Maʿarrī, ed. and tr. in R.A. Nicholson, 'The meditations of Muʿarrī', in his *Studies in Islamic Poetry*, Cambridge 1921, nos. 128, 239.

who said that hell was invented to scare people and that everything said about paradise was just blandishment, to make people behave.[23] So we are back with Critias and Polybius, except that we don't know whether al-Ghazālī's opponents held religion to be useful.

In short, a fair number of people held that the entire religious institution was a giant fraud, created by scheming tricksters who were after power and money.

Useful but Not True

Finally, we have those who held that religion was useful, but not true. Most or all of them seem to have been Iranians. Round about 900 we hear this about an obscure sect in eastern Iran:

> They claim that it is impossible (*muḥāl*) that God should send a messenger to mankind from among themselves; rather, Muḥammad was a sage (*ḥakīm*) who copied this book about [*sic*; from?] the remains of the ancients to be of use for people's lives/livelihoods.[24]

In other words, Muḥammad made up a book to provide the shared norms which enable people to have peaceful dealings with each other—get married, inherit, engage in commercial transactions and so forth. Muḥammad was a wise man who had instituted the law, just like the ancient lawgivers that Critias and Polybius talked about. Apparently, these sectarians were Sufis of some kind, so they probably saw true religion as spirituality.

In a related vein the philosopher al-ʿĀmirī (d. 381/996) tells us that there were people, clearly in Iran, who dismissed all religions as consisting of nothing but legal rules from which everyone picked what enabled them to provide for their material needs. If these religions were true, they said, they would not resort to revelation (*tawqīf*).[25] And in 1066, the year in which the Normans conquered England, an Iranian called Asadī wrote an epic which mentions the Dahrīs. He said that there were two kinds of them, and he credited one kind with a softer view of revealed religion than they had had in the past. Their view was that

---

23 Al-Ghazālī, *Kimiyā-yi saʿādat*, ed. Ḥ. Khadīvjam, Tehran 1380, i, 113; cf. id., 'Die Streitschrift des Ġazālī gegen die Ibāḥīja', ed. and tr. O. Pretzl, *Sitzungsberichte der Bayerischen Akademie der Wissenschaften*, Phil.-hist. Abt., 7, 1933, 23 = 46.

24 Abū Muṭīʿ Makḥūl al-Nasafī, 'Kitāb al-radd ʿalā 'l-bidaʿ', ed. M. Bernand, *Annales Islamologiques* 16, 1980, 111.

25 Al-ʿĀmirī, *K. al-Iʿlām bi-manāqib al-islām*, ed. A.ʿA.-Ḥ. Ghurāb, Cairo 1967, 101.

> every now and again a wise man appears and shows another religion and road. "I am sent by God", he says, "from the creator: all the things he says I bring to you". He puts in front of people a hell and a paradise, so that everyone may think about his work.[26]

There's no scoffing here. The prophet is a wise man who deceives people for altruistic reasons. The same view reappears in a Persian heresiography written in the fourteenth or fifteenth century, probably in Tabriz. Here some people say that

> the prophets and messengers were intelligent and learned men ... and philosophers (*ḥakīmān*) who ... used wisdom out of mercy for people. They made a law and rules (for use) among people, called it Sharīʿa and said it was God's decisions, and they formulated wisdom, saying it was God's speech, to make it more effective.

Again, the prophets are actually human lawmakers, but they credit their law to God to lend authority to it; their motives are entirely altruistic. How do we know that they were not sent by God? Because

> the people of the earth are much too puny for a messenger to come to them from heaven. As has been proved in the science of astronomy, the body of the sun and the width of its disc are 7 times 7,000 by 7,000 parasangs. ... As has been said:
>
> > The earth from the view of this coloured glass ceiling (the sky)
> > is like a poppy seed on the surface of the sea.[27]

It is astronomy which has bred unbelief again. Astronomy shows you that we humans are nothing on the scale of the universe. These people did not doubt the existence of God, but they saw him as far, far removed from us and our affairs. Religious law was just a human institution for the regulation of worldly affairs; but they clearly regarded it as useful.

---

26 Asadī, *Garshāspnāma*, ed. Ḥ. Yaghmaʿī, Tehran 1938, 139; tr. H. Massé, Paris 1951, ii, 40.

27 Anon., *Haftād u sih millat*, ed. M.J. Mashkour, 2nd printing, Tehran 1962, sect no. 35. The opening lines (in Arabic) are taken from Abū Muṭīʿ Makḥūl al-Nasafī, cited above, note 24.

Taqiyya

How did people who held such negative views of positive religion manage to coexist with ordinary believers? Well, in the same way that they had in antiquity, by participating in the public religious cult and keeping discreet about their real beliefs—practicing *taqiyya*, as the Muslims called it. Even the Epicureans, who believed that the gods had done nothing whatever to this world, would participate in the public cult. As Plutarch said:

> Out of fear of public opinion he goes through a mummery of prayers and obediences that he has no use for and pronounces words that run counter to his philosophy.

Dahrīs, al-Rāzī and their likes also practiced *taqiyya*. Civic religion was the price of citizenship; you had to conform in public: if you didn't, you would be persecuted. You were not allowed to rock the boat that everybody was sailing in, or you would be a traitor to your own people. But as an individual you could pursue any truth you liked, more or less, as long as you were discreet. You could discuss your views with likeminded individuals, in private scholarly gatherings, to some extent even in books, because in the good old days the masses were illiterate. There was no confession, no inquisition, no prying into your innermost heart; what you concealed in your innermost conscience was between you and God. In short, you could have your private convictions as long as you behaved *as if* you believed in the established religion.

If you really *could not* keep quiet in public, you should air your views in poetry, as al-Maʿarrī did, and/or use ambiguity. By al-Maʿarrī's time you could also become a Sufi holy fool and say the most outrageous things about God, or even to him: the fool could get away with it because he had stepped out of normality. In effect he was playing the role of court jester: he'd tell God all the nasty truths about the way he treated mankind that ordinary people would not dare to say. Some of Ibn al-Rāwandī's outrageous statements lived on as the sayings of holy fools, but usually in an affectionate tone quite different from Ibn al-Rāwandī's own. Some people, though, were extremely rude. The Bektashis were among them. You could find everything among them, from the highest mysticism to the purest atheism, with the whole range of beliefs in between.[28]

Alas, all this has completely changed. Practising *taqiyya* or expressing yourself in poetry will not protect you any more, nor is it accepted that you have a

---

28 Cf. J.K. Birge, *The Bektashi Order of Dervishes*, London and Hartford, Conn., 1937, 87.

private space in your interior where you are alone with God and where other humans cannot interfere. That is one respect in which modernity has made the Muslim world a less agreeable place than it was before.

CHAPTER 9

Oral Transmission of Subversive Ideas from the Islamic World to Europe: The Case of the Three Impostors*

In 1239 the good Christians of Europe were shocked by a bulletin from Pope Gregory IX announcing that the most powerful man in Latin Christendom, the emperor Frederick II, had made a terrible claim, namely that Jesus, Moses and Muḥammad were tricksters, or in other words that all the religions he knew were false.[1] This is the first mention in Europe of what European historians call "the three impostors thesis" (one allegedly earlier attestation notwithstanding),[2] but it was not the last. It crops up elsewhere in the Mediterranean thereafter, and by the sixteenth century it was everywhere. Rumours of an actual book called *De Tribus Impostoribus* generated intense interest in freethinking

---

* This article was originally drafted in connection with a series of workshops on the transmission of radical ideas from the Islamic world to Europe at the Institute for Advanced Study. I should like to thank Jonathan Israel for co-organizing the first of them together with Martin Mulsow and myself, and Martin Mulsow for co-organizing the second with me as well. The third unfortunately had to be cancelled and no publication was produced, except in the form of individual articles, of which this is one. I must also thank several of the participants in the workshops, not least Thomas Gruber, who introduced me to the three impostors in Europe; Robert Lerner, who provided important information on the same subject; and Kevin van Bladel, who opened my eyes to Near Eastern beliefs in pre-Adamites. I am also indebted to Michael Cook and Stefania Pastore for reading earlier drafts. [Ed.: In acknowledging Thomas Gruber's role in introducing her to the theme of the three impostors, the author is referring to the fact that he had covered several of the sources and ideas in this article in his contribution to the 2008 Princeton workshop, based on his doctoral project on the three impostors in Europe in the Middle Ages at the University of Oxford. Since then he has published some of his preliminary findings in Th. Gruber, 'A tribus barattatoribus deceptus: The Formula of the Three Impostors Travelling the Medieval Mediterranean', in A. Musco and G. Musotto (eds.), Coexistence and Cooperation in the Middle Ages. IV European Congress of Medieval Studies F.I.D.E.M. (Federation Internationale des Instituts d'Études Medievales), Palermo 23–27 June 2009, Palermo 2013.]

1 The classic account is by M. Esposito, 'Una manifestazione d' incredulità religiosa nel medioevo: il detto dei "Tre Impostori" e la sua trasmissione da Federico II a Pomponazzi', *Archivio Storico Italiano*, serie vii, 16, 1931, 3–48.

2 Simon of Tournai (1190s?) was accused of having voiced the impostor thesis by Thomas Cantimpré, who wrote between 1256 and 1263 (cf. Esposito, 'Manifestazione', 33 ff.). But since the charge was made after Gregory's publication of his bull against Frederick, when Simon had been dead for many years, it is not usually taken seriously.

© KONINKLIJKE BRILL NV, LEIDEN, 2016 | DOI: 10.1163/9789004319318_010

circles and much speculation about its authorship, without anyone succeeding in finding a copy.[3] But at the end of the 1680s a Latin work of this title materialised,[4] and it was soon followed by a French treatise entitled *Traité des Trois Imposteurs* or *L'Esprit de Spinoza*, which counts as "one of the most significant irreligious clandestine writings available in the Enlightenment".[5]

It has long been suspected that the idea, which worked so powerfully on the European imagination, originated in the Islamic world. Medieval authors sometimes attributed it to Averroes,[6] if only because "Averroism" was the standard rubric to which heresies suspected of Islamic origins were assigned, and early modern authors also thought it might be a Muslim theme.[7] In fact, Averroes had nothing to do with it, nor was there a book on the subject before European freethinkers took it upon themselves to produce one; but it was indeed Muslims who had developed the subversive idea. In what follows I briefly survey the history of this idea up to the time of its transmission to the West and examine the channels of transmission, arguing that more than one was involved.[8]

3 The suspected authors included Boccaccio, Pomponazzi, Pietro Aretino, Guillaume Postel, Campanella and many others, cf. G. Ernst, 'Campanella e il *De Tribus Impostoribus*', *Nouvelles de la Republique des Lettres* 2, 1986, 143–170. See also the highly informative entry 'Trattato dei tre impostori' in the Italian *Wikipedia*.

4 The date (late 1680s) and the author (Joachim Müller, professor of law at Hamburg) were established by W. Schröder in his introduction to his edition of *De impostoris religionum* (*De tribus impostoribus*), Stuttgart 1999.

5 For all this, see S. Berti, F. Charles-Daubert and R.H. Popkin (eds.), *Heterodoxy, Spinozism, and Free Thought in Early Eighteenth-Century Europe: Studies on the Traité des Trois Imposteurs*, Dordrecht and Boston 1996. The French work circulated in manuscript form from probably around 1678 onwards and was clandestinely printed for the first time in 1718 in The Hague by the Huguenot Spinozist Charles Levier (I believe I owe this information to Jonathan Israel). By then, the impostor idea was also encountered in many other works.

6 M. Esposito, 'Manifestazione', 29, 31, citing the *De Erroribus Philosophorum* of Aegidius Romanus (Giles of Rome, d. 1316), written between 1260 and 1274 (but without explicit mention of the impostor theme), and Benvenuto da Imola (d. 1388), *Commento latino sulla Divina Commedia di Dante Alighieri*, 1855, 138.

7 Cf. S. Åkerman in Berti, Chales-Daubert and Popkin, *Heterodoxy*, 403.

8 For literature on the question, see L. Massignon, 'La légende "de tribus impostoribus" et ses origines islamiques', in his *Opera Minora*, ed. Y. Moubarac, 1, Beirut 1963, 82–85; F. Niewöhner, *Veritas sive Varietas: Lessings Toleranzparabel und das Buch Von den drei Betrügern*, Heidelberg 1988; D. de Smet, 'La théorie des trois imposteurs et ses prétendues origins islamiques', in C. Cannuyer and J. Grand'Henry (eds.), *Incroyance et dissidences religieuses dans les civilisations orientales*, Bussels and Louvain-la-Neuve 2007, 81–93 (drawn to my attention by S. Traboulsi). His title notwithstanding, de Smet does not dispute the Muslim origin of the idea. See also F. Gunny, 'Le traité des trois imposteurs et ses origins arabes', *Dix-huitième Siècle* 28, 1996, 169–174, dealing with a motif attested in the French treatise, but not in earlier reports (drawn to my attention by G. Paganini).

Antiquity

The ultimate roots of the impostor idea lie in classical antiquity. A prophet in the ancient Greek world was a soothsayer or oracle, a person inspired by the divine who had the ability to predict the future, heal and work other wonders—in short, what the pre-Islamic Arabs called a *kāhin*. The Greeks, including Hellenised non-Greeks, often suspected such prophets of being swindlers who faked their apparent contact with the divine and had no genuine religious knowledge.[9] When, for example, a Syrian slave by the name of Eunus raised a major slave revolt in Sicily (135–131 BC), working miracles and making predictions, he was assumed to be a charlatan who had "deceived many" with his magic.[10] Eunus was unusual in that he used his divine inspiration to establish himself as a political leader. Most prophets in the Greek Mediterranean served private needs and acquired political importance only when rulers consulted them on the outcome of the acts they were planning, as Croesus did at Delphi. Accordingly, they were usually associated with money grubbing rather than political ambitions. There is a memorable portrait of the prophet as a swindler who milks the superstitious masses for money by the Syrian Lucian of Samosata (d. after 180) in his satirical account of the prophet Alexander, a contemporary of his.[11] Another Syrian, the Cynic Oenomaus of Gadara (d. c. 120) composed a withering critique of oracular practice combining satire, ridicule and invective under the title *Goētōn phōra*, "Exposé of Charlatans" or "Detection of Impostors".[12] The oracles, he said, did not proceed from a *daimon* or god, but were rather "frauds and tricks of human impostors cunningly contrived to deceive the multitude".[13]

The relevance of this to the present theme begins when Greek-speaking people unsympathetic to the Jews began to dismiss Moses as a swindler of this type. Moses was not, of course, a diviner or soothsayer, but rather a man whose contact with the divine had resulted in the liberation of his followers from bondage and the revelation of a divine law—in effect the role to which Eunus had aspired in Sicily. In Greek terms, Moses was a lawgiver (*nomothetēs*)

9 For early examples, see W.H.C. Guthrie, *The Sophists* (*A History of Greek Philosophy*, III), Cambridge 1971, 246 f.

10 Diodorus Siculus, *Bibliotheca Historica*, XXXIV, 2, 5–9, possibly from Posidonius.

11 Lucian of Samosata, *Alexander, the False Prophet*.

12 The fragments are preserved in Eusebius, *Praeparatio Evangelica*, starting at V, 18, 6. For a commentary (drawn to my attention by Yannis Papadoyannakis), see J. Hammerstaedt, *Die Orakelkritik des Kynikers Oenomaus*, Frankfurt am Main 1988.

13 Eusebius, *Praeparatio*, V, 21, 6.

and the founder of a colony. But it was as *prophētēs* that Hebrew *nabī'* had been translated into Greek, and Moses had also worked miracles, so he fell into the category of oracular soothsayer too. Josephus (1st century CE) reports that a number of Greeks "have maligned our lawgiver Moses as a magician (*goēs*) and impostor (*apateōn*)";[14] and there were probably Hellenised Jews who played around with the same idea, for Philo (d. c. 50 CE) envisages the Jews themselves as maligning Moses as a trickster during their sojourn in the desert.[15] Jesus too could be seen as a *nomothetēs* (in a less political sense) as well as an oracular soothsayer; and Lucian, who refers to him as the "first lawgiver" of the Christians, implicitly places the "crucified sophist" in the same company as the pseudo-prophet Alexander.[16] The second-century Celsus (wr. c. 180) dismissed both Moses and Jesus as magicians in his famous attack on Christianity, claiming that both of them had learnt magic in Egypt, and he tells the story of Jesus' life along lines known from the Jewish polemical work *Toledoth Ieshu*, in which Jesus is also a magician.[17] Dismissing Jesus as a magician became a standard Jewish[18] and pagan ploy;[19] and the pagans would also dismiss other Christian figures such as Paul and Peter as disseminators of deceit who owed their successes to sorcery or other trickery.[20] The

---

14 Josephus, *Against Apion*, II, 145.

15 Philo, *Hypothetica*, 356 (in Eusebius, *Praeparatio*, VIII, 6, 2).

16 Lucian, *The Death of Peregrinus*, 5, in S. Benko, 'Pagan Criticism of Christianity', in H. Temporini and W. Haase (eds.), *Aufstieg und Niedergang der römischen Welt* (hereafter ANRW), II, xxiii.2, 1095.

17 Cf. Benko, 'Pagan Criticism of Christianity', 1102; cf. S. Krauss, *Das Leben Jesu nach jüdischen Quellen*, Berlin 1902.

18 Cf. P. Schäfer, *Jesus in the Talmud*, Princeton 2007, 64, 102 ff., 137. For the earliest suspicions, see Mark 3:22. In the *Acts of Pilate* (*Gospel of Nicodemus*), I, 1; II, 1 (in W. Schneemelcher (ed.), *New Testament Apocrypha*, I, Louisville, Ky., 1991, 506 f.), the Jews are envisaged as calling Jesus a sorcerer on the basis of this passage. The Jews of third/ninth-century Iraq, on the other hand, would sometimes laugh at Jesus' miracles and sometimes get angry and dismiss him as a magician (*ṣāḥib ruqan wa-nīranjāt*), according to al-Jāḥiẓ, 'al-Radd 'alā 'l-naṣārā', in his *Rasā'il*, ed. 'A.-S.M. Hārūn, Cairo 1964–1979, III, 325.ult.

19 P. Courcelle, 'Anti-Christian Arguments and Christian Platonism: from Arnobius to St. Ambrose', in A. Momigliano (ed.), *The Conflict between Paganism and Christianity in the Fourth Century*, Oxford 1963, 153.

20 Origen, *Contra Celsum*, *passim* (Celsus on the Christians in general); Jerome, *Tract on Psalm 81* (some said Paul did it all for money; Porphyry said that they (the disciples?) worked miracles with magic because they were poor); Julian, *Against the Christians*, ed. and tr. W.C. Wright, Cambridge, Mass., and London 1923, 340 f. (100 A: Paul surpassed all magicians and charlatans); A. Meredith, 'Porphyry and Julian against the Christians', in ANRW, XXIII/2, 1120 f. (Hierocles on Paul, Peter and others).

target in these attacks was not prophecy as such, but rather the authoritative status of the particular figures in question.

The Islamic World

Casting other people's prophets as mere magicians was a convenient way of protecting one's own religious institutions, and the practice continued in the non-Greek Near East. Thus the Qurʾānic pagans dismissed Muḥammad as a magician (though they also found fault with his miracle-making abilities),[21] and they seem to have suspected him of using religion for political ends.[22] When claimants to prophethood appeared thereafter, the Muslims themselves dismissed them as magicians;[23] and when holy men and Sufis emerged serving much the same needs as the oracular prophets of the past, many regarded them too as tricksters who cleverly milked people for money.[24] But it is clear that something had changed. For one thing, the hegemonic polity of the Near East now owed its existence to a prophet of the Mosaic type, that is a lawgiver who had brought a law and founded a polity, and whose status was vindicated by miracles and oracular predictions. When the Greek philosophical tradition was translated into Arabic, the Muslims duly called Muḥammad a *wāḍiʿ al-nāmūs*/*al-sharīʿa*, a translation of "lawgiver" (*nomothetēs*). That the founder of a religion was a political figure now came to be taken for granted. Indeed, thanks to Muḥammad's paradigmatic status, Muslims commonly assumed that all polities were based on a revealed law, at least in so far as they were monotheist (a term with much the same connotations as "civilised"). Left on their own, it was argued, people would pursue their own selfish interests and engage in constant rivalry and strife: God had to give them rules in order for social life to be possible, and he told them about Paradise and Hell in order to

---

21 Q. 6:7; 34:43; 37:15; 38:4 f.; 43:30; 46:7; 74:24. Moses and Jesus are envisaged as having been rejected in the same way; see for example 5:110; 28:36; 40:24; 61:6.

22 "Have you come to turn us away from what we found our fathers following, so that you two may become great in the land?" (10:78), as the Egyptians say to Moses and Aaron, typifying the pagans that Muḥammad was up against.

23 Thus for example al-Muqannaʿ (cf. *Encyclopaedia Iranica*, s.v. 'Moqannaʿ').

24 Cf. al-Tanūkhī, *Nishwār al-muḥāḍara*, ed. ʿA. al-Shāljī, Beirut 1971–1972, I, 165 ff. (no. 84, al-Ḥallāj); II, 324 ff. (no. 170, street astrologer), 351 ff. (no. 187, holy man), 359 (no. 190, Sufi preacher); III, 119 (no. 75, Junayd), 120 (no. 77, Sufi); tr. D.S. Margoliouth, *The Table-Talk of a Mesopotamian Judge*, part I, London 1922, 86 ff., 277 ff., 289–292, 294; parts II and VIII, Hyderabad n.d., 180 f.

make them obey.[25] Seen as indispensable to civilised life, prophets came to occupy a much more central role in high-cultural thought than they had in the Greek Near East even after the victory of Christianity. Dismissing such figures as impostors was far more subversive than it had been in the Greek world.

For another thing, the Muslims operated with an abstract concept of prophethood (*nubuwwa*). *Nubuwwa* is usually translated as prophecy, and maybe this is what it means in the Qurʾān.[26] In classical Arabic, however, it stands for the status occupied by a prophet and the mission with which he is charged, not for the revelations (let alone predictions) that he utters; and what came to be discussed in Arabic was the very idea that there could be such a thing as a prophet, or in other words the proposition that God communicated with humans by means of revelation. The Muslims developed a new literary genre called "the proofs of prophethood" (*dalāʾil al-nubuwwa*), devoted to the defence of Muḥammad's prophetic status.[27] Most works of this genre concern themselves with his case alone, but some begin by vindicating the concept of prophethood as such,[28] for already by the second/eighth century, and probably before, there were some who rejected it. The target in these attacks was not just the authoritative status of the particular figures in question, but the very concept of a prophet.

The Deniers of Prophethood, c. 750–900

(a) Dahrīs and Zindīqs

That the entire idea of prophets was false was first maintained by thinkers within the Muslim community who went by the name of Dahrīs. They are attested from the mid-second/eighth century onwards, with the best evidence falling in the third/ninth, and they are presented as likeminded individuals who occupied themselves with medicine and astronomy/astrology, above all in Iraq.[29] According to ʿAbd al-Jabbār (d. 415/1025), a Sunnī theologian with

25 Cf. P. Crone, *Medieval Islamic Political Thought* (American title *God's Rule*), Edinburgh 2004, 261 ff.

26 Q. 3:79; 6:89; 29:27; 45:16; 57:26.

27 Cf. S. Stroumsa, 'The Signs of Prophecy: the Emergence and Early Development of a Theme in Arabic Theological Literature', *Harvard Theological Review* 78, 1985, 101–114.

28 The best known example is al-Māwardī (d. 450/1058), *Aʿlām al-nubuwwa*, ed. M.M.-A. al-Baghdādī, Beirut 1987, ch. 4 (pp. 49 ff.).

29 Cf. *Encyclopaedia of Islam*, 2nd ed., Leiden 1960–2004 (hereafter *EI*²), s.v. 'Dahriyya' (Goldziher and Goichon); *Encyclopaedia Iranica*, ed. E. Yarshater, London and Boston 1982–, s.v. 'Dahrī' (Shaki and Gimaret); P. Crone, 'The Dahrīs according to al-Jāḥiẓ', *Mélanges de*

a hyperbolic bent, most doctors rejected the idea of prophethood, deemed Muslims and other believers in revealed religion to be ignorant, and denied both God (*al-rubūbiyya*) and the resurrection.[30] Doctors and astrologers are singled out for their Dahrī views down to at least the seventh/thirteenth century.[31] Dahrīs are described as empiricists who held that all knowledge must be based on sense impressions and some limited forms of reasoning to the exclusion of revelation. In terms of physics, they were materialists who held the universe to be eternal, rule-bound, and explicable in terms of the mixture of the four elementary qualities (hot, cold, dry, wet) or the four elements, or in terms of accidents arising in prime matter. They came in many varieties. Some assigned God a role in the creation, but most denied that the world had a creator, let alone a providential ruler or judge, and some denied the very existence of God, along with that of prophets, angels, spirits, revealed scriptures and veridical dreams. All were adamant that there was no such thing as life after death. Dahrīs are strongly associated with other radicals called Zindīqs, who had slightly different views and who were drawn from different religious communities too. Whereas Dahrīs seem to have been drawn from Zoroastrian and pagan groups, Zindīqs were Manichaeans, Bardesanites and Marcionites by origin, and whereas Dahrīs were typically doctors and astrologers, Zindīqs were mostly bureaucrats, courtiers and poets. All, however, had lost their ancestral faith.[32]

---

l'Université Saint-Joseph 63, 2010–2011, 63–82 [Ed.: included as article 5 in the present volume]. For more on the scientific views involved, see P. Crone, 'Ungodly Cosmologies', in S. Schmidtke (ed.), *The Oxford Handbook of Islamic Theology*, Oxford 2016 [Ed.: article 6 in the present volume].

30 'Abd al-Jabbār, *Tathbīt dalāʾil al-nubuwwa*, ed. A.-K. 'Uthmān, Beirut 1966, I, 62.

31 Al-Mas'ūdī, *Murūj al-dhahab*, ed. C. Pellat, Beirut 1966–1979, III, §1846; al-Jāḥiẓ, *Kitāb al-ḥayawān*, VI, 269f.; VII, 12f.; cf. al-Jāḥiẓ, 'al-Radd 'alā 'l-naṣārā', in his *Rasāʾil*, III, 313f., 320f.; al-Ma'arrī, *Luzūmiyyāt*, ed. Ḥ. 'Abd al-Majīd and others, Cairo 1992–1994, III, no. 1074; al-Ghazālī, *Kimiyā-yi sa'ādat*, ed. Ḥ. Khadīvjam, Tehran 1380, I, 57, 65; Gaon Shmuel ben Eli (d. 1195), *Treatise on the Resurrection of the Dead*, Hebrew tr., quoted in S. Stroumsa, 'Twelfth-Century Concepts of Soul and Body: the Maimonidean Controversy in Baghdad', in A.I. Baumgarten, J. Assmann and G.G. Stroumsa (eds.), *Self, Soul and Body in Religious Experience*, Leiden 1998, 317; Maimonides in S. Stroumsa, '"Ravings": Maimonides' Concept of Pseudo-Science', *Aleph* 1, 2001, 146. Note also the claim that Abū Ma'shar studied astronomy until he 'turned godless' (*ḥattā alḥada*, Tanūkhī, *Nishwār*, IV, 66).

32 Cf. M. Chokr, *Zandaqa et zindīqs en Islam au second siècle de l'hégire*, Damascus 1993; Crone, 'Ungodly Cosmologies'; cf. also ead., *The Nativist Prophets of Early Islamic Iran*, Cambridge 2012, index, s.v. 'Dahrīs'.

Both Dahrīs and Zindīqs aired their views in disputations, the dominant vehicle of intellectual pursuit at the time, and we know about them only from their opponents, above all the Muʿtazilite theologians who shared their interest in cosmology while trying to refute their views on metaphysics. Their opponents' responses centred on the evidence for design in nature, from which one could infer the existence of a creator God and providence, not on the existence of prophethood, since it went without saying that without belief in God one could not believe in prophethood either. Prophethood must have been discussed as well, however, for we know that Dahrīs and Zindīqs had rational explanations for the alleged miracles of the prophets: they credited them with knowledge of the astrological and medical sciences.[33]

(b) "Brahmans"

There were also ninth-century thinkers who believed in God while rejecting the idea of prophets. In the terminology of the Enlightenment they were deists. The theologians called them "Brahmans" and presented them as good monotheists who denied the existence of revelation on the grounds that one could reason one's way to God and proper behaviour alike.[34] There are also reports in which the Barāhima accept one prophet, Adam, or two, Adam and Abraham. No genuine knowledge of the Brahmans of India is reflected in the information about them, and there can be little doubt that the label was used as a cover for views which originated in the Islamic world itself. Of one thinker, Ibn al-Rāwandī (d. mid-ninth century or later) we are explicitly told that he used the Brahmans as his mouthpieces.[35]

Ibn al-Rāwandī was one of a fair number of the Muʿtazilites who were sufficiently affected by the arguments of their Dahrī and Zindīq opponents for their own faith to be shaken.[36] He seems to have become a Skeptic, in the technical sense of a believer in the principle of the equipollence of proofs (*isostheneia/takāfuʾ al-adilla*), according to which every argument in favour of one view could always be balanced by another against it.[37] In the Greek world, this

33 Cf. al-Jāḥiẓ, 'Ḥujaj al-nubuwwa', in his *Rasāʾil*, III, 263f., on why Muḥammad cannot be dismissed as an astrologer; al-Māturīdī, *Taʾwīlāt al-Qurʾān*, XVII, ed. A. Vanlioğlu and B. Topaloğlu, Istanbul 2010, 400.ult. (*ad* 114:4–6).

34 Cf. *Encyclopaedia of Islam*, 3rd ed., Leiden 2008– (hereafter EI^3), s.v. 'Barāhima' (Crone).

35 Cf. S. Stroumsa, *Freethinkers of Medieval Islam*, Leiden 1999, 48.

36 Cf. EI^2, s.v. 'Ibn al-Rāwandī' (Kraus and Vajda); Stroumsa, *Freethinkers*, ch. 2; J. van Ess, *Theologie und Gesellschaft im 2. und 3. Jahrhundert Hidschra*, Berlin and New York, 1991–1997 (hereafter TG), IV, 295ff.

37 Cf. R.J. Hankinson, *The Sceptics*, London and New York 1995, 27. On the principle in

principle had applied to all knowledge claims about things which are not open to immediate perceptual inspection, not specifically to metaphysics; but in the Muslim world it was always in connection with claims rooted in revelation that the principle was used.[38] How far Ibn al-Rāwandī's Skepticism went we do not know, but like Protagoras of old and other Skeptics, he would write for and against the same position. Unlike his predecessors, however, he wrote his attack and defence in separate books. In his *Zumurrud* ("Emerald"), attributed to the Brahmans, he argued that there was no need for prophets, since their message would be either in conformity with reason, in which case it was superfluous, or contrary to it, in which case it had to be rejected. All prophets were imposters and their miracles were mere trickery (*makhāriq*) and sorcery:[39] for example, they knew about the powers of magnets;[40] their predictions were of the kind that any half-decent astrologer could come up with;[41] some of the alleged miracles could be dismissed because of the small number of witnesses,[42] and others simply did not make sense—for example, if angels assisted the believers in the battle at Badr, where the believers won, where were they at Uḥud, where the believers lost?[43] He also wrote a book in criticism of Muḥammad called *al-Farīd* ("The Unique") and yet another book, entitled *al-Dāmigh* ("The Brainbasher"), in which he discussed the inconsistencies in the Qur'ān which proved it not to

Islamic thought, see J. van Ess, *Die Erkenntnislehre des ʿAḍudaddīn al-Īcī*, Wiesbaden 1966, 221 ff., with Ibn al-Rāwandī at p. 223; cf. also index, s.v. 'Skepsis'; id., 'Skepticism in Islamic Religious Thought', *al-Abḥāth* 21, 1968, 1–18, with Ibn al-Rāwandī at p. 7.

38 Cf. Ibn Ḥazm, *al-Faṣl fī 'l-milal wa'l-ahwā' wa'l-niḥal*, Cairo 1317, V, 119 f. For a relatively mild case, see P. Crone, 'Abū Saʿīd al-Ḥaḍrī and the Punishment of Unbelievers', *Jerusalem Studies in Arabic and Islam* 31, 2006, 92–106 [Ed.: included as article 4 in the present volume].

39 Stroumsa, *Freethinkers*, 76–86; cf. the texts in *TG*, VI, 457 ff.

40 Ibn al-Jawzī, *al-Muntaẓam*, Hyderabad 1357–1359, VI, 100 f. (year 298); also in H. Ritter (ed. and tr.), 'Philologika. VI: Ibn al-Ǵauzīs Bericht über Ibn ar-Rēwendī', *Der Islam* 19, 1930, 4 = 12; cf. al-Māturīdī, *Kitāb al-tawḥīd*, ed. F. Kholeif, Beirut 1970, 186, where the argument is credited to Abū ʿĪsā al-Warrāq; *TG*, VI, 474 f., with discussion.

41 Ibn al-Jawzī, *Muntaẓam*, VI, 101; Ritter, 'Philologika', 4 = 12 (regarding a prediction by Muḥammad); cf. al-Warrāq in Māturīdī, *Tawḥīd*, 195.17 (corrupt); ʿAbd al-Jabbār, *Tathbīt*, II, 413.11; tr. Stroumsa, *Freethinkers*, 63 and note 104 (regarding Moses' and Jesus' prediction of Muḥammad).

42 Al-Mu'ayyad in P. Kraus, 'Beiträge zur islamischen Ketzergeschichte', *Rivista degli Studi Orientali* 14, 1933, 101 = 113 (no. 7). Even many people could agree on a falsehood, such as that Jesus had been crucified (Mu'ayyad in Kraus, 'Ketzergeschichte', 104 = 115 (no. 12); cf. al-Warrāq in *TG*, VI, 479–481).

43 Cf. Kraus, 'Ketzergeschichte', 105 f. = 115 f. (no. 13); attrib. al-Warrāq in Māturīdī, *Tawḥīd*, 199; tr. *TG*, VI, 477 f.

be divine,[44] picking out verses also used by Zindīqs and Dahrīs.[45] He then wrote a book against the *Zumurrud*, as well as a book in proof of prophethood, and a *Naqḍ al-Dāmigh* ("Refutation of the Brainbasher"), which he did not complete, presumably because he died.[46]

That Ibn al-Rāwandī was a Skeptic, or even a heretic, has recently been denied with reference to the fact that the tenth-century theologian al-Māturīdī (d. 333/944) quotes him as defending Islam against the very views he had voiced in the *Zumurrud*. In al-Māturīdī's work he does not acknowledge the subversive views as his own, but rather attributes them to Abū ʿĪsā al-Warrāq, a slightly earlier Muʿtazilite of dubious repute with whom he had been personally associated.[47] To Van Ess, this shows that Ibn al-Rāwandī was the victim of a black legend.[48] Van Ess does not dispute that Ibn al-Rāwandī wrote books containing outrageous views, but he thinks that he always credited these views to their real authors (such as Abū ʿĪsā al-Warrāq) and presented them simply to demonstrate the impossibility of proving anything: his aim was to cast doubt. Yet he was not a Skeptic: according to Van Ess, the fact that he eventually wrote refutations of these views shows that he knew where the solution lay.

It is difficult to agree. For one thing, the black legend hardly amounts to more than a normal reaction: a man who devoted whole books to the presentation of outrageous propositions in a strikingly impudent tone without refuting them

---

44 As Van Ess (*Erkenntnislehre*, 223) notes, the title of this book is curiously reminiscent of Protagoras' *Kataballontes*, "The Knocker-down". There is another Skeptical work of a similar title in the *Tattvopaplavasimha*, "The lion destroying all principles", written c. 800 (drawn to my attention by Michael Cook; cf. B.-A. Scharfstein, *Comparative History of World Philosophy*, Albany 1998, 252 f.).

45 Compare the questions in Ibn Ḥanbal (d. 241/855), *al-Radd ʿalā ʾl-Zanādiqa waʾl-Jahmiyya*, Cairo 1393, 8 ff., and Ibn al-Rāwandī's *Kitāb al-dāmigh* in Ibn al-Jawzī, *Muntaẓam*, VI, 99 ff.; H. Ritter, 'Philologika', 2 ff. Unfortunately, it is not clear that the *Radd* is actually by Ibn Ḥanbal, so some of the objections attributed to the Zindīqs could in principle be Ibn al-Rāwandī's (e.g. *Radd*, 8; *Muntaẓam*, VI, 103; Ritter, 'Philologika', 7 = 15, on 4:56).

46 Ibn al-Nadīm, *al-Fihrist*, ed. R. Tajaddud, Tehran 1971, 216 f.; cf. *TG*, VI, 434 ff., nos. 20, 34, 36, 38, 40, 42.

47 On him, see *EI*², s.v. (Stern); Van Ess, *TG*, IV, 289–294; Stroumsa, *Freethinkers*, 40 ff. The idea, present in some sources, that Abū ʿĪsā had written or contributed to the *Zumurrud*, is presumably a result of this ploy, cf. Stroumsa, *Freethinkers*, 75 (with a different explanation). Ibn al-Nadīm does not credit Abū ʿĪsā with any works against prophethood, nor does anyone say that he used the Brahmans as his cover.

48 J. van Ess, 'Ibn ar-Rēwandī, or the Making of an Image', *al-Abḥāth* 27, 1979, 5–26; shorter version under the title 'Al-Fārābī and Ibn al-Rēwandī', *Hamdard Islamicus* 3, 1980, 3–15.

there and then was bound to be understood as an adherent of the propositions in question, as Ibn al-Rāwandī must have known very well. For another thing, if his heart was not in the outrageous arguments, what reason do we have to believe that it was in the counter-arguments? He is simply switching sides in al-Māturīdī, casting doubt in the opposite direction, as one would expect him to do in his anti-works.[49] Of course he may have repented (as some said he did),[50] but that presupposes that he meant what he said when he was being outrageous. And if he was not a Skeptic, why was it so important to him to cast doubt?

Whatever his motives, Ibn al-Rāwandī was not the only theologian to air subversive views of this kind at the time. Of another lapsed Muʿtazilite, Abū Ḥafṣ al-Ḥaddād, we are told that he wrote a book on the equipollence of proofs (*takāfuʾ al-adilla*) and held the Prophet (Muḥammad) to have used tricks to convert his followers.[51] Maybe he too was simply trying to demonstrate that refuting the idea of prophethood was just as easy as defending it. Of yet another theologian, Abū Isḥāq al-Naṣībī (d. c. 370/980), it was said that he had doubts about all prophetic missions, but whether he suspected trickery we are not told.[52] Nor are we told how any of them explained the motives of the alleged impostors, but Ibn al-Rāwandī's tone certainly suggests that he saw them as self-seeking. We also hear of unnamed deniers of the prophets who would dismiss demons and *jinn* as invented by the would-be prophets in order to scare people into following them.[53]

---

49 Van Ess' interpretation originally rested on the assumption that al-Māturīdī was quoting from the *Zumurrud* (an assumption shared by Stroumsa in her argument against Van Ess): he inferred that all the outrageous views in that book had been willfully understood as Ibn al-Rāwandī's own, though the latter had clearly identified them as Abū ʿĪsā's. That Māturīdī was quoting from one of Ibn al-Rāwandī's works refuting his own position was first suggested by Madelung (cf. his review in *Zeitschrift der Deutschen Morgenländischen Gesellschaft* 124, 1974, 150, proposing the *Ithbāt al-rusul* in which he affirmed the reality of prophets). Van Ess himself has now suggested that al-Māturīdī could be quoting the anti-*Zumurrud*, yet he has not changed his position (*TG*, IV, 343).

50 Ibn al-Nadīm, *Fihrist*, 216.19. This, incidentally, shows that he had his defenders in Iraq as well. Van Ess' idea that Ibn al-Rāwandī was maligned in Iraq and remembered as a good theologian in Khurāsān also suffers from the fact that the quotation from al-Balkhī's *Maḥāsin Khurāsān* in Ibn al-Nadīm, *Fihrist*, 216.14, must include the statement that Ibn al-Rāwandī turned heretical: it is not formulated in the phrase that Ibn al-Nadīm himself uses of Muʿtazilites who went astray (cf. *Fihrist*, 215.–2; 216.5, 7).

51 For him, see Ibn al-Nadīm, *Fihrist*, 216; *TG*, IV, 89 f.

52 Al-Tawḥīdī, *Kitāb al-imtāʿ waʾl-muʾānasa*, ed. A. Amīn and A. al-Zayn, Cairo 1939–1944, I, 141; cf. id., *Akhlāq al-wazīrayn*, ed. M. al-Ṭanjī, Beirut 1992, 202, 211 f., 297.

53 Māturīdī, *Taʾwīlāt*, XVII, 400 f. (*ad* Q. 114:4–6).

There were others, however, who held the prophets, or at least Muḥammad, to have practised deceit in an altruistic vein. According to the theologian Abū Muṭīʿ al-Nasafī (d. 318/930), a certain sect, probably in Iran, regarded Muḥammad as a wise man who had composed the Qurʾān himself in order to make it easier for people to pursue their livelihoods, namely by giving them shared norms and thus allowing them to live together in peace.[54] This was a new version of the idea, widespread in pagan antiquity, that the ancient lawgivers had invented the gods and/or the punishments of afterlife in order to curb people's anti-social behaviour;[55] and it was generally accepted in the medieval Islamic world that religion had this effect.[56] The Greeks and the Romans had generally seen religion (or in other words positive religion as opposed to philosophy) as either true and necessary for political order, or else as false but still necessary.[57] The vast majority of Muslims adhered to the first view, but as al-Nasafī shows us, there were also some who adhered to the second. In the classical world, only the Epicureans held positive religion to be both false and unnecessary: this is the view of which Ibn al-Rāwandī's "Brahmans" give us a new version.

The Tenth and Eleventh Centuries

By the tenth century it was philosophers rather than theologians who were the pioneers in thoughts about prophethood, usually as defenders of the concept, but sometimes as its critics. Al-Sarakhsī (d. 286/890), a pupil of al-Kindī, wrote a book called *Takshīf asrār al-mumawwihīn*, "Revelation of the Secrets of Tricksters", in which he ridiculed the prophets.[58] Of another philosopher, the famous medical doctor Abū Bakr al-Rāzī (d. 313/925 or later), we know a little more.[59]

---

54 M. Bernand (ed.), 'Le *Kitāb al-radd ʿalā ʾl-bidaʿ* d'Abū Muṭīʿ Makḥūl al-Nasafī', *Annales Islamologiques* 16, 1980, 111 (109w). Their reasoning was that God would not have sent a fellow-human to mankind. Compare Ibn Dāʿī, *Tabsirat al-ʿawāmm*, ed. I. ʿAbbās, Tehran 1313, 65, where a judge who died in 463/1071 credits Ibn Karrām, perhaps by way of parody, with the question why God had not sent an angel rather than a human prophet, so that everyone would have believed (cf. A. Zysow, 'Two Unrecognized Karrāmī Texts', *Journal of the American Oriental Society* 108, 1988, 582 f. and note 44 on the judge).

55 Some of the best known passages are conveniently assembled in T.R. Glover, *The Conflict of Religions in the Early Roman Empire*, 11th ed., London 1927, 3 ff.

56 Cf. Crone, *Medieval Islamic Political Thought*, 187 f., 261 ff., 265 f.

57 Cf. A. Wardman, *Religion and Statecraft among the Romans*, Baltimore 1982, 53 f., 56.

58 J. Fück (ed.), 'Sechs Ergänzungen zu Sachaus Ausgabe von al-Bīrūnīs "Chronologie orientalischer Völker"', in his *Documenta Islamica Inedita*, Berlin 1952, 78; F. Rosenthal, *Aḥmad b. aṭ-Ṭayyib al-Saraḫsī*, New Haven 1943, 51.

59 On him, see *EI*[1], s.v. 'al-Rāzī, Abū Bakr' (Kraus and Pines); also *EI*[2], s.v. (Goodman);

Al-Rāzī rejected the idea of prophethood on the grounds that all humans had the same ability to reach God. It struck him as absurd that God should choose to reveal himself to mankind by informing just one person. In his view, God must have implanted the requisite knowledge in all human beings, just as he had given all animals the knowledge they needed to flourish. It followed that prophets were impostors. They had been seduced by evil spirits who appeared to them in the form of angels, and their miracles were mere magic and sleights of hand.[60]

Al-Rāzī engaged in scriptural criticism with a view to showing that the prophets contradicted one another, and sometimes themselves as well.[61] He seems to have known more about contradictions in the Old Testament than in the New, presumably because he was indebted to Marcionite and Manichaean criticism of the Old Testament (devoted to proving that the Old Testament deity was not the highest God). Many critics of monotheism of the Biblical type drew on Marcionite and Manichaean arguments, not just al-Rāzī. A ninth-century Zoroastrian also made heavy use them in his polemics against Judaism, as earlier Zoroastrians may have done already in Sasanian times;[62] and a ninth-century Jew, Ḥīwī of Balkh (wr. c. 870 CE), drew on them for his critique of his Judaism too.[63] Ḥīwī rejected prophetic miracles, explaining them rationally,[64] and found fault with his own scripture in the tradition of the scoffers with whom Philo had contended in Alexandria many centuries earlier.[65] Zindīqs came from a Marcionite and Manichaean (and Bardesanite) background, and

---

L.E. Goodman, 'Muḥammad ibn Zakariyyā' al-Rāzī', in S.H. Nasr and O. Leaman (eds.), *History of Islamic Philosophy*, I, London and New York 1996, ch. 13; M.M. Bar Asher, 'Abū Bakr al-Rāzī', in F. Niewöhner (ed.), *Klassiker der Religionsphilosophie: von Platon bis Kierkegaard*, Munich 1995.

60 Cf. Stroumsa, *Freethinkers*, ch. 3; P. Crone, 'Post-colonalism in Tenth-Century Islam', *Der Islam* 83, 2006 [Ed.: included as article 7 in the present volume], 3–5.

61 Abū Ḥātim al-Rāzī, *Aʿlām al-nubuwwa*, ed. Ṣ. al-Ṣāwī, Tehran 1977, 69 ff.

62 See P.J. de Menasce (ed. and tr.), *Škand-Gumānīk Vičār: une apologétique mazdéenne du IXe siècle*, Fribourg en Suisse 1945, ch. 13, and the introduction, pp. 179 f.

63 On him, see I. Davidson, *Saadia's Polemic against Ḥiwi al-Balkhi*, New York 1915; J. Rosenthal, 'Ḥiwi al-Balkhi', *Jewish Quarterly Review* 38, 1947–1948, 317–342, 419–430 (with his date at 319, n. 15); 39, 1948, 79–94. The pagan, Marcionite and Manichaean antecedents of his questions are fully documented in Rosenthal's 'Ḥiwi'. The view, voiced from time to time, that Ḥiwi was himself a Marcionite or Manichaean is both unnecessary and unpersuasive.

64 Cf. Rosenthal, 'Ḥiwi', 334 f.

65 Cf. Philo, *Questions and Answers in Genesis*, III, 43; *De mutatione nominum*, 61; *De confusione linguarum*, 2; *De ebrietate*, 65 ff.; *Quis rerum divinarum heres*, 81; *De somnis*, 93 f.

it was presumably from disputations with them that Ḥīwī,[66] Ibn al-Rāwandī[67] and al-Rāzī had learned how to pick holes in a scripture.[68]

Unlike Ibn al-Rāwandī, al-Rāzī was not a Skeptic (nor was he a scoffer). Philosophy to him was an avenue to God, and what he attacked was not religion as such, only positive or conventional (*waḍʿī*) religion, that is to say religion embodied in a set of institutions that come between the individual and God and that are credited with the right to lay down what others should believe and do to reach salvation. Al-Rāzī did not want the panoply of religious scholars and theologians (the "goatbeards", as he called them) to dictate to him. What he wanted was natural (Arabic *ʿaqlī*, rational) religion, that is the truth about God reached by the individual himself on the basis of his own inner resources, which had been implanted in him by nature/God and which were shared by all human beings; such religion, it was widely thought, would be the same for all mankind, unlike conventional religion, which sanctified one confessional community against another and divided mankind instead of uniting it. It was this desire for natural/rational religion and the corresponding hostility to the conventional institutions erected by all confessional communities that made Abū Bakr al-Rāzī and his likes freethinkers. (The word stands for a specific type of religious radical, not for any kind of them.) In early modern Europe al-Rāzī would have formed part of the radical Enlightenment; in later modern Europe, he would have been a secularist, in the proper sense of someone who wishes religion to be a private matter for the individual to decide on his own, not in the debased sense of an anti-religious person in which the word is often used today.

Al-Rāzī lived in a period that some have duly dubbed the "Muslim Enlightenment" (c. 300–500/900–1100). It was a period of political fragmentation in which Islam was competing on almost equal terms with other religions and in which educated laymen of Muslim, Christian and Jewish background mixed freely at the courts, where they were enjoying unusual prominence at the expense of the religious scholars.[69] Al-Rāzī was not the only Muslim to think in terms of a universal, rational truth versus the conventional religion represented by diverse

66 Cf. G. Vajda, 'Judeo-Arabica', *Revue des Études Juives* 99, 1935, 81–91, comparing Ḥīwī's questions with those asked by Zindīqs and rightly suggesting that he was a "radical freethinker" like Ibn al-Rāwandī rather than a Manichaean, a Christian Gnostic or the like, as proposed by earlier authors.

67 Cf. above, note 45.

68 Compare Abū Bakr al-Rāzī in Rāzī, *Aʿlām*, 69 f., on the burnt offering, and Ḥīwī in Rosenthal, 'Ḥiwi', 332.

69 For the wider context, see Crone, 'Post-colonialism', 18 ff.

confessional communities. There were many ways of coping with the diversity, however. One could postulate that all the prophets had really preached the same truth and envisage all confessional communities other than one's own as the outcome of some kind of corruption: only one form of positive religion was true (though they might all be useful). This was probably the most common view. Or one could see all the confessional communities as true in a more relative sense by casting them as local, time-bound and socially determined reflections of the universal truth. This was how most philosophers coped. Philosophy, they said, conveyed the absolute and universal truth to the few who could understand it wherever and whenever they were; revelation conveyed the same insights in a more metaphorical form accessible to the masses, adjusted to both their intellectual level and the particular time in which their communities flourished. This was also what the Ismaili Shīʿites said, with the difference that in their view the need for such time-bound metaphorical forms would disappear in the great spiritual resurrection with which they expected their Mahdī (messiah) to bring the world as we know it to an end. Finally, one could dismiss all revealed religion as devoid of truth value, but nonetheless indispensable for political order: this view continued to have adherents in (apparently) Iran, now among philosophically inclined people who held all revealed religions to be mere legal institutions used by the nations for the maintenance of their livelihoods.[70] But like Ibn al-Rāwandī, al-Rāzī took the even more extreme view once associated with the Epicureans, denying not only that positive religion was true, but also that it was useful. He held that all human beings, not just the elite, were capable of living without conventional religion here and now, not just when the messiah came: all could be saved through philosophy in his view. Accordingly, the prophets had to be impostors. Others only followed them because they had grown up with all these "superstitions" (*khurāfāt*), which had been dinned into them since childhood by the religious scholars (tacitly accused of imposture too).[71]

Al-Rāzī's views seem to have influenced the poet Abū ʾl-ʿAlāʾ al-Maʿarrī (d. 449/1058), whose verses abound in statements directed against positive religion: "Awake, awake, you dupes! All these religions (*diyānāt*) are mere trickery (*makr*) on the part of the ancients who wished to secure worldly goods for themselves". "In every nation falsehoods are taken as religion".[72] "They all err—Muslims, Christians, Jews and Magians; two make humanity's universal sect:

---

70 Al-ʿĀmirī, *K. al-iʿlām bi-manāqib al-islām*, ed. A.-ʿA.-Ḥ. Ghurāb, Cairo 1967, 101.

71 For the references, see Crone, 'Post-colonialism', 5 f.

72 R.A. Nicholson (ed. and tr.), 'The Meditations of Maʿarrī', in his *Studies in Islamic Poetry*, Cambridge 1921, nos. 249, 252 (with more poetic translations).

one man intelligent without religion, and one religious without intellect".[73] But unlike al-Rāzī's, al-Maʿarrī's tone is sarcastic, sceptic and deeply pessimistic.

In principle, the thought of all these men was politically explosive. Positive religion meant law, political obedience and social order; and the adherents of the impostor theory would now openly explain the prophets as motivated by a desire for political leadership, not simply for money, though the desire for wealth continued to be well represented too. To the philosopher al-Fārābī (d. 339/950), for example, those who dismissed revelation as downright false (which he did not) would cast its recipient as a mere "swindler seeking rulership and other things".[74] In practice, however, only the Ismailis were politically active. Whether they were Dahrīs or Zindīqs, theologians or philosophers, recluses or courtiers, the freethinkers convey no impression of wishing the political house that Muḥammad had built to come tumbling down, or even to purge it of its theologians and religious scholars, though they certainly resented the latter's encouragement of what they saw as uncritical attitudes and their tendency to brand anyone who disagreed with them as an infidel who could be lawfully killed.[75] The freethinkers come across first and foremost as educated laymen who wanted to make sense of the world for themselves, without regard for the custodians of the established order. They disliked the pairing of the highest truth with mundane social and political arrangements, and some of them, al-Rāzī included, were also offended by the concomitant linkage of the highest truth with war and bloodshed.[76] But it is not clear that they thought it could be changed.

To their opponents, freethinkers often came across as intellectual snobs. No doubt they often were, for then as now, it was chic to flirt with radical positions. Dahrism appealed to the smart set, as al-Jāḥiẓ (d. 255/869) informs us;[77] it was those who wanted to look clever who would take up positions against

---

73 Nicholson, 'Meditations', no. 239 (his translation).

74 Al-Fārābī, *Mabādiʾ ārāʾ ahl al-madīna al-fāḍila*, ed. and tr. R. Walzer, *Al-Farabi on the Perfect State*, Oxford 1985, ch. 17, 6 (283 = 284). Compare ch. 18, 12, 13 (304= 305): among the ancients [whose pernicious views have followers today] there were people who would dismiss the ideas of a provident deity, prayer, abstinence, and reward and punishment in the afterlife as mere tricks and ruses used by those who lacked the military strength to take the good things of life by force.

75 Abū Bakr al-Rāzī in Abū Ḥātim al-Rāzī, *Aʿlām al-nubuwwa*, 30f.

76 Cf. Crone, 'Post-colonialism', 4f., 22f.

77 Jāḥiẓ, 'Ḥujaj al-nubuwwa', in his *Rasāʾil*, III, 226f. (quoted in C. Pellat, *Le milieu baṣrien et la formation de Ǧāḥiẓ*, Paris 1953, 84); id., 'Radd ʿalā 'l-naṣārā', in his *Rasāʾil*, III, 320f.; id., 'Ṣināʿat al-kalām', in his *Rasāʾil*, IV, 246; Crone, 'The Dahrīs according to al-Jāḥiẓ'.

established religion, as many later authors observed, both Muslims[78] and Jews among them.[79] Precisely how deeply committed people were to the radical views they played with is often unclear, not least because it was unwise to reveal it. But some were certainly battling with loss of faith. According to Ibn Sīnā (d. 428/1037), Satan has followers who secretly whisper to the innermost hearts of man "that there is no resurrection, no requital for good and bad acts, and no being existing eternally on its own, reigning eternally over the kingdom (*wa-lā qayyūm ʿalā ʾl-malakūt*)".[80] He knew what he was talking about, for he had a friend who lost belief in the reality of prophethood and wrote a philosophical letter to persuade him of its truth.[81]

By medieval standards, the freethinkers did however enjoy considerable freedom to air their views, as long as they did so in private discussions, in the salons of the elite, and at the courts of tolerant rulers. One could debate radical propositions as if for the sake of argument alone. One could also voice them as part of *mujūn*, risqué statements or behaviour which bordered on the blasphemous, the scurrilous or the pornographic, and which were an accepted part of high culture as long as one expressed oneself with literary elegance and wit, and/or in poetry, and coupled one's daring with a good sense of precisely where to stop.[82] As regards literary expression, the fifth/eleventh-century ʿAbd al-Jabbār claims that many of the godless people (*mulḥida*, here probably Dahrīs), Zindīqs, and errant Muʿtazilites who had written against the prophets back in the days when the caliphate was strong had composed their books in secret, without even their wives and children knowing about them, and shown them only to individuals engaged in similar practices, though the books had eventually acquired such diffusion that one could now buy them in the Muslim

---

78 Cf. al-ʿĀmirī (above, note 70); al-Ghazālī, *Tahāfut al-falāsifa* (*The Incoherence of the Philosophers*), ed. and tr. M.E. Marmura, Provo, Utah, 1997, 1ff. (first *muqaddima*, 2–5).

79 They would flaunt their erroneous views and look down on the followers of truth, as Saʿadya Gaon (d. 942) observes with reference to such people among his own coreligionists in his *Kitāb al-amānāt waʾl-iʿtiqādāt*, ed. S. Landauer, Leiden 1880, 4; tr. S. Rosenblatt, *The Book of Beliefs and Opinions*, New Haven 1948, 7; they would ridicule the *midrashim*, casting themselves as cultivated men, physicians and philosophers who were wiser than the sages (Maimonides (d. 1204) in Stroumsa, '"Ravings": Maimonides' Concept of Pseudo-Science', 146).

80 Ibn Sīnā, *Ḥayy b. Yaqẓān*, ed. A. Amīn, 1947, 51; tr. A.-M. Goichon, Paris 1959, 174f.

81 Ibn Sīnā, 'Fī ithbāt al-nubuwwāt', in his *Tisʿa rasāʾil*, Cairo 1989, risāla no. 6.

82 See now Z. Szombathy, *Mujūn: Libertinism in Medieval Muslim Society and Literature*, E.J.W. Gibb Memorial Trust 2013; more briefly, see *EI*², s.v. 'Mu<u>dj</u>ūn' (Pellat); also P. Crone and S. Moreh (trs.), *The Book of Strangers*, Princeton 2000, 174f., 178f., for brief characterisations and some examples.

markets and everybody was talking about them.[83] This may be broadly true: we should perhaps envisage the medieval Islamic world as having a clandestine literature. But one could say many things in published books as well as long as one hid behind dead or otherwise absent dissenters and took care to counter them with some appropriate objections. (Oddly, we do not hear of anonymous publications.) In public, the opponents of conventional religion would conform to prevailing norms and practise *taqiyya* (precautionary dissimulation), as Abū Bakr al-Rāzī openly admitted.[84]

Very few freethinkers of the early Muslim world seem to have been penalised for their views. Some Zindīqs were executed in a purge of people broadly classified as Manichaeans in the later second/eighth century, but the subject is highly obscure.[85] Al-Sarakhsī was also executed, but not for his religious views. He was a polished courtier who would say daring things as witticisms, and though at least one of his fellow-courtiers professed not to be amused,[86] nobody knew why he suddenly fell from grace;[87] it was only later that his impiety seemed to be the obvious explanation.[88] Abū ʿAlī al-Jubbāʾī (d. 303/915 f.), a Muʿtazilite theologian, claims that both Abū ʿĪsā al-Warrāq and Ibn al-Rāwandī were pursued by the authorities and that Abū ʿĪsā died in jail while Ibn al-Rāwandī was forced to flee to a Jewish home, where he composed the *Dāmigh* and soon after died.[89] But it sounds like wishful thinking; it was certainly by wishful misreading of al-Jubbāʾī that the Ḥanbalite scholar Ibn ʿAqīl (d. 513/1119) declared Ibn al-Rāwandī to have been crucified.[90] That Abū Bakr al-Rāzī had died in his bed after a distinguished career as a doctor at diverse courts in Iran was never denied, but then his thought barely seems to have reached the religious scholars.

---

83 ʿAbd al-Jabbār, *Tathbīt*, I, 129.

84 He tells us that he had been blamed for not living like Socrates, an ascetic who did not consort with kings or "practise *taqiyya* vis-à-vis the masses or the ruler" (P. Kraus (ed. and tr.), 'La conduite du philosophe: Traité d'éthique d'Abū Muḥammad b. Zakariyyā al-Rāzī', *Orientalia* 4, 1935, 309 = 322; also tr. C. Butterworth, 'The Book of the Philosophic Life', *Interpretation* 20, 1993, 227).

85 Cf. Chokr, *Zandaqa et zindīqs*.

86 "Your unbelief will never be considered nice and witty", as Ibn al-Munajjim (d. 300/912) said in a poem dismissing al-Sarakhsī's religious observance as mere hypocrisy (F. Rosenthal, *Aḥmad b. aṭ-Ṭayyib al-Saraḫsī*, New Haven 1943, 32).

87 Many different explanations were offered, cf. Rosenthal, *Saraḫsī*, 32, 35 f.

88 Cf. Ibn al-Jawzī (d. 597/1200) and al-Ṣafadī (d. 764/1363) in Rosenthal, *Saraḫsī*, 29, 31. Rosenthal tends to agree with them (p. 34).

89 Ibn al-Jawzī, *Muntaẓam*, VI, 102.3; in Ritter, 'Philologika', 5 = 13.

90 Ibn al-Jawzī, *Muntaẓam*, VI, 105.4; in Ritter, 'Philologika', 9 = 17 (he read *ṣuliba* for *ṭuliba*).

The Twelfth to Fourteenth Centuries

Al-Ghazālī (d. 505/1111), a towering Sunnī theologian, devoted considerable attention to the enfeeblement of people's belief in the very idea (*aṣl*) and reality (*ḥaqīqa*) of prophethood, which he had found to be widespread.[91] In his view, it was people who mouthed philosophical views, thinking themselves ever so clever, who would dismiss the revealed law as manmade and explain its provisions as "embellished tricks" (*ḥiyal muzakhrafa*).[92] Some said that Hell was invented to scare people and that everything said about Paradise was just blandishment to make them behave.[93] Some of them were Dahrīs, of whom we are now explicitly told that they held the prophets to be tricksters.[94] According to the Persian epic poet Asadī (d. 465/1072 f.), there were also Dahrīs who regarded the prophets as learned (*farzāna*), men who had established new religions in what they appear to have regarded as a benevolent vein even though their claim to have been sent by God was false:[95] it is curious that the adherents of the theory of benevolent deceit always seem to be Iranians. It was known to the Andalusian Ibn Ḥazm, too, however: the laws of Islam were either given by God or else posited (*mawḍūʿa*) by agreement among the most virtuous sages (*afāḍil ḥukamāʾ*) for the governance of people and restraint from mutual oppression and vile things, as he says in polemics against unidentified philosophers who took the second view.[96] To al-Ghazālī it did not matter whether the Lawgiver was held to have aimed at deception (*talbīs*) or the welfare of the world (*maṣlaḥat al-dunyā*): either way, such views were incompatible with membership of the Muslim community.[97] Those who claimed to believe in prophecy but equated the prescriptions of the revealed law with philosophical wisdom did not believe in genuine prophecy either in his view,[98]

---

91 Al-Ghazālī, *al-Munqidh min al-ḍalāl*, ed. and tr. F. Jabre, Beirut 1959, 46; tr. W.M. Watt, *The Faith and Practice of al-Ghazálí*, Edinburgh 1953, 76.

92 Ghazālī, *Tahāfut*, 1 ff. (first *muqaddima* 2–5).

93 Ghazālī, *Kimiyā-yi saʿādat*, I, 113.

94 Al-Ghazālī, *Fayṣal al-tafriqa bayna ʾl-islām waʾl-zandaqa*, ed. S. Dunyā, Cairo 1961, 194; tr. F. Griffel, *Über Rechtgläubigkeit und religiöse Toleranz*, Zürich 1998, 75; tr. S.A. Jackson, *On the Boundaries of Theological Tolerance in Islam*, Oxford 2002, 111, without use of the word Dahrī (they deny the creator, deem the world always to have existed, deny prophethood and afterlife, and hold death to be pure nothing).

95 Asadī Ṭūṣī, *Garshāspnāma*, ch. 44, ed. Ḥ. Yaghmāʾī, Tehran 1317, 139; tr. H. Massé, Paris 1926–1951, II, 30.

96 Ibn Ḥazm, *Faṣl*, I, 95.

97 Ghazālī, *Tafriqa*, 184; tr. Jackson, 101; tr. Griffel, 67.

98 Ghazālī, *Munqidh*, 50 f.; tr. Watt, 84.

and he resented the ostentatious piety that such men would display in public. If one asked them why they would join the prayer when they did not hold prophethood to be genuine (*ṣaḥīḥa*), they would affirm that they did believe prophethood to be true and accepted the revealed law as genuine, or they would come up with explanations such as that praying was good exercise, or that it was local custom, or that they wanted to keep their wealth and children.[99]

Al-Ghazālī's efforts notwithstanding, the prophets continued to have their critics. Abū Shāma (d. 665/1266 f.) mentions the death, in 656/1258, of a Zindīq (here in the general sense of heretic) by the name of Shihāb al-Naqqāsh, who would speak in the manner of the philosophers (*ḥukamāʾ*) and deny the prophetic missions; this man lived in the Nūriyya Madrasa in Damascus, where a number of Zindīqs of his kind would gather around him.[100] Abū Shāma also records the death, in 657/1259, of another real or alleged Zindīq by the name of al-Fakhr (i.e. Fakhr al-Dīn) b. al-Badīʿ al-Bandahī, who had occupied himself with philosophy and ancient sciences; he lived in the "madrasas of the jurists" and would corrupt the creed of the young men who studied with him there by openly belittling the prophets.[101] How he belittled them we are not told. Some works on logic by this man are extant, without furnishing evidence of heretical views, and he may simply have cast the prophets as philosophers.[102] But it is at least clear from all this that philosophers and religious scholars were no longer distinct social groups, as they had been in the old days: they now lived and worked in the same institutions. Another philosopher, the Jew Ibn Kammūna (d. 683/1284 f.), still found it necessary to refute the arguments of those who denied the prophetic missions (*al-nubuwwāt*);[103] and by then philosophical ideas about the prophets had penetrated Sufi circles, too. Ibn al-Jawzī (d. 597/1200) knew of Sufis who did not believe in God and other Sufis

---

99 Ghazālī, *Munqidh*, 47 f.; tr. Watt, 78 f. There is no mention of keeping their lives.

100 Abū Shāma, *Tarājim al-rijāl al-qarnayn al-sādis waʾl-sābiʿ*, ed. M.Z. al-Kawtharī, Cairo 1366/1947, 200.–2. I owe this reference to Denis McAuley.

101 Abū Shāma, *Tarājim*, 202.10. This man's father claimed that he (the father?) had been a pupil of Fakhr al-Dīn al-Rāzī.

102 He is listed as the author of a commentary on al-Khūnajī's *Kashf al-asrār* in Ḥājjī Khalīfa, *Kashf al-ẓunūn*, Istanbul 1941–1947, II, 1486. I owe my knowledge of his identity, his works, and their apparent orthodoxy to Khaled El-Rouayheb, who is editing al-Khūnajī's work.

103 Ibn Kammūna, *Tanqīh al-abḥāth lil-milal al-thalāth*, ed. M. Perlmann, 18 ff.; tr. M. Perlmann, *Ibn Kammūna's Examination of the Three Faiths*, Berkeley, Los Angeles and London 1967 and 1971, 33 ff. Niewöhner, *Veritas*, 227–231, saw this work as a response to the three impostors idea as supposedly formulated by the Ismailis three centuries earlier (cf. below).

who denied prophethood.[104] The mystic Ibn ʿArabī (d. 638/1240) encountered a philosopher who denied prophethood and miracles in 586/1190 f., possibly in al-Andalus;[105] and Shams-i Tabrīzī, beloved of the mystic poet Rūmī (d. 672/1273), mentions philosophers who rejected the probative value of prophetic miracles, claiming that proof had to rest on the intellect and that the prophets had been deceived by the angels: this was why they had been orientated towards this world, busying themselves with people and taking wives; they had been "ambushed in the road by love for position and prophethood". One of the philosophers would say things of this kind with a wink.[106] But Rūmī himself was familiar with people who would cast the prophets as ordinary humans and compare their miracles with magic: such people, he said, were hypocrites who would join the ritual prayer "for quarrelling's sake, not for supplication".[107] A Persian heresiography probably composed in Tabrīz in the eighth/fourteenth or ninth/fifteenth century, which takes issue with numerous radical Sufi ideas, includes among its targets the claim that the prophets were intelligent men who used their wisdom in a benevolent vein to make rules for mankind, crediting them to God to make them sound impressive. The adherents of this view, an old one in Iran by now, held that humans were much too puny for a message to come to them from heaven: the earth was a mere poppy seed in relation to the sun, they said, specifying the size of the sun as calculated by the astronomers.[108]

In sum, there is ample evidence in the Islamic Near East for the view of the prophets as impostors from the third/ninth century to beyond the time by which the theme had appeared in Latin Christendom. It was aired in several books and was known in a wide variety of different formulations, some more radical than others, and was combated from Syria to Iran.

---

104 Ibn al-Jawzī, *Talbīs Iblīs*, ed. M.M. al-Dimashqī, Cairo 1928, 352; cf. Kraus, 'Ketzergeschichte', 348.

105 Ibn ʿArabī, *al-Futūḥāt al-makkiyya*, Būlāq n.d., II, 490.5 (ed. of bāb 185). I owe this reference to Denis McAuley.

106 W.C. Chittick (tr.), *Me & Rumi: the Autobiography of Shams-i Tabrīzī*, Louisville, Ky., 2004, 26 f., cf. also 62. The man who said it with a wink was Shihāb Hariwa (*sic*, Harawī?), perhaps a student of Fakhr al-Dīn al-Rāzī (d. 607/1209), a major theologian well versed in philosophy who was active in Iran.

107 Rūmī, *Mathnawī*, ed. and tr. R.A. Nicholson, London 1925–1940, verses 263 ff.

108 M.J. Mashkūr (ed.), *Haftād u sih millat*, Tehran 1341, 45 f. (This work was drawn to my attention by Masoud Jafari Jazi.)

The Focus on Three and the Ismailis

What is missing in the material reviewed so far is a focus on *three* prophets. Ibn al-Rāwandī dismissed Abraham along with Moses, Jesus and Muḥammad in his *Zumurrud*;[109] and Abū Bakr al-Rāzī discussed Zoroaster and Mani along with the three.[110] Naturally, Moses, Jesus and Muḥammad were the three most relevant prophets to the Muslims, and we do sometimes find them enumerated together on their own,[111] for example in the poetry of al-Maʿarrī:[112]

> The astrologer of the peoples is like a blind man
> who has scrolls with him that he reads by touch.
> He has been labouring for a long time, and how much he has struggled
> with lines that their writer has effaced.
> Moses preached, then Jesus stood up,
> and Muḥammad came with the five prayers.
> It is said that a religion other than this one will come
> while people are perishing between tomorrow and yesterday.
> Who assures me that the religion will become fresh again
> and quench the thirst of the one who has engaged in devotional exercises
> after going without water for a long time?

In other words, the astrologer has long been trying to figure out the truth on the basis of the stars, but is doing no better than a blind man trying to read by touch;[113] while he has been doing this, Moses, Jesus and Muḥammad have appeared and now a new religion is predicted (the Ismailis were among those who held their own belief system to be the religion in question), but will it be any better than its predecessors? The answer is clearly no.

For prose formulations of the view that the impostors were three, however, we need to turn to the Ismailis, adduced by Massignon in his note on the impos-

109 Al-Khayyāṭ, *al-Intiṣār*, ed. A.N. Nader, Beirut 1957, 12.8.

110 In Abū Ḥātim al-Rāzī, *Aʿlām*, 70.

111 E.g. Abū Ḥātim al-Rāzī, *Aʿlām*, 73.12, 91.15.

112 Maʿarrī, *Meditations*, ed. and tr. Nicholson, no. 263 (I have replaced Nicholson's beautiful translation with a more literal version); cf. no. 252 on the Furqān (i.e. Qurʾān), the Torah and the Gospel. See also the examples in the Ismaili Abū Ḥātim al-Rāzī, *Aʿlām*, 73.12, 91.15.

113 This could be taken to imply that some kind of Braille had been devised in al-Maʿarrī's time, but more probably it simply means that just as the blind cannot read books by touch, so astrologers cannot read the stars by sight.

tor theme many years ago. The Ismailis differed from the men considered so far in that they were not hostile to the prophets, but on the contrary devoted to them.[114] They did, however, form part of a wider phenomenon labelled "Bāṭinism", roughly translatable as a preference for religion as spirituality rather than law. How far a single attitude to the law prevailed among them before the establishment of the Fāṭimid caliphate is unclear, but all agreed that however indispensable it might be in our current, imperfect state, the law would be abolished when the Mahdī (messiah) came: he would preside over the political and spiritual regeneration of the world that they called the resurrection (*qiyāma*); positive religion would wither away, and unmediated access to the truth would prevail as it had done (according to some) in the time of Adam.[115] Since one cannot show that a religious law has been abrogated without acting contrary to its precepts, the Ismailis were in principle committed to a great act of ritual violation of the external aspect (*ẓāhir*) of Islam.

In practice, most of them ducked out of it. The movement split in 286/899, in the course of preparations for the coming of the Mahdī, and one branch (the one in which all modern Ismailis have their roots) proceeded to establish the Fāṭimid caliphate in North Africa and Egypt, where it affirmed its allegiance to the law and postponed the spiritual resurrection to a distant future. Another branch, usually known as Qarmaṭī, remained committed to the abolition of the external institutions of Islam, however. In 310/922f. the Qarmaṭīs in Baḥrayn began to launch regular attacks on Iraq, hoping to unseat the caliph; in 317/929 they attacked Mecca, slaughtered pilgrims, and carried away the black stone of the Kaʿba, reputedly desecrating it further back home, in order to demonstrate that Islam as everyone knew it was finished; and in 319/931 they proclaimed an Iranian captive of theirs to be the Mahdī and proceeded to engage in a number of outrageous acts under his direction. In the course of all this they are said to have declared the true religion to have come, namely the religion of Adam, and to have cursed the prophets as impostors.[116] This is not impossible. It is certainly hard to see how they could have parted with their beloved prophets without persuading themselves that they hated them. But the account is both sensationalist and polemical, and exactly what the Qarmaṭīs said we shall never know. Their acts deeply shocked other

---

114 For an account of their beliefs, aims and history in this period, see H. Halm, *Das Reich des Mahdi*, Munich 1991; tr. M. Bonner, *The Empire of the Mahdi*, Leiden 1996.

115 Whether there had or had not been (religious) law in the time of Adam was hotly debated by two fourth/tenth-century Ismailis, al-Nasafī and Abū Ḥātim al-Rāzī (see W. Madelung, 'Das Imamat in der frühen ismailitischen Lehre', *Der Islam* 37, 1961, 102ff.).

116 For all this, see Halm, *Reich*, 225ff./*Empire*, 250ff.

Muslims, however, and gave the Ismailis a scandalous reputation that has made them reluctant to discuss the episode to this day.

Their enemies responded by casting Ismailism as a conspiracy by the conquered peoples who lacked the military strength to recover their lands and who therefore planned to destroy Islam from within, namely by seducing Muslims into a doctrine which, though disguised as Shīʿism, would eventually be revealed to them as pure atheism. This theory was set out in a pamphlet known as "The Book of the Highest Initiation" (*Kitāb al-balāgh*) or "The Book of Policy" (*Kitāb al-siyāsa*), which survives only in quotations. Supposedly an Ismaili work, it is in fact a forgery not unlike the Protocols of the Elders of Zion in that it purports to be a record of the planning of the cynical masterminds believed to be behind the movement.[117] Formulated as instructions by the leader of the movement to the missionaries, it informs the reader that the highest law of the prophets was to deceive this perverted world, that the missionaries had to familiarise themselves with their impostures and contradictions, of which some illustrations relating to Jesus, Moses and Muḥammad are given, and that the missionaries also had to learn juggling and conjuring tricks so that they could secure the world and everything in it for themselves.[118] Thanks to this pamphlet, all good Muslims "knew" that the Ismailis were really enemies of the prophets, however many works in proof of prophethood they might compose.[119] After his conquest of Rayy (the precursor of modern Tehran) in 420/1029, for example, the Sunnī ruler of eastern Iran, Maḥmūd, reported to the caliph that he had uprooted heretics there, including Bāṭiniyya (i.e. Ismailis) who did not believe in God or his angels, or (revealed) books, messengers or the last day, but rather regarded all religion as trickery by the philosophers (*makhāriq al-ḥukamāʾ*); Maḥmūd or his secretaries had probably read all this in the "Book of Highest Initiation".[120] Al-Ghazālī, who must actually have known better, also credits the Ismailis with the idea that all the prophets were impos-

---

117 Cf. W. Madelung, 'Fatimiden und Baḥrainqarmaṭen', *Der Islam* 34, 1959, 69 ff.; S.M. Stern, 'The "Book of the Highest Initiation" and Other Anti-Ismāʿīlī Travesties', in his *Studies in Early Ismailism*, Jerusalem and Leiden 1983, 56–83. (The comparison with the Protocols is also made by de Smet, 'La théorie', 89.) For Ismailism as a conspiracy of the conquered peoples, see for example Stern, 'Abū ʾl-Qāsim al-Bustī and His Refutation of Ismāʿīlism', in the same work, 305 f.; al-Ghazālī, *Faḍāʾiḥ al-Bāṭiniyya*, ch. ii.2 (ed. Amman 1993, pp. 13 f.).

118 Stern, 'Book of Highest Initiation', 66 ff.

119 Abū Ḥātim al-Rāzī (d. 322/934) wrote one against Abū Bakr al-Rāzī (thereby preserving the latter's views for us, cf. above, note 61). Abū Yaʿqūb al-Sijistānī (d. after 361/971) wrote another, entitled *Ithbāt al-nubuwwāt* (ed. ʿA. Tāmir, Beirut 1966).

120 Ibn al-Jawzī, *Muntaẓam*, VIII, 39.

tors and depicts their missionaries as deceivers spreading false ideas in order to gain wealth and power, probably drawing on the same work.[121] A fourteenth-century author familiar with the pamphlet similarly assures us that the Ismailis denied the prophetic missions and miracles and claimed that the Prophet wrote the Qur'ān himself.[122]

Massignon, who wrote at a time when the history of Ismailism was still highly obscure, took the forgery to be a genuine Ismaili work and quoted the snippet to do with the imposture of Moses, Jesus and Muḥammad in his famous note on the Islamic origin of the three impostors theme.[123] He also adduced a passage from the *Siyāsatnāma* of Niẓām al-Mulk (d. 485/1092) along with an anti-Ismaili passage from al-Maʿarrī. According to Niẓām al-Mulk, the man who presided over the abduction of the black stone and the abolition of externalist Islam in Baḥrayn, Abū Ṭāhir, wrote to the first Fāṭimid caliph, informing him that "three persons have ruined mankind, a shepherd [Moses] and a doctor [Jesus] and a camel-driver [Muḥammad], and the camel-driver was more of a conjurer and juggler than the others".[124] A different version of Abū Ṭāhir's statement is found in an eighth/fourteenth-century Arabic source, where Abū Ṭāhir says that "it was a shepherd, a physician and a camel-driver that led this nation astray (*mā aḍalla hādhihi 'l-umma illā rā'in wa-ṭabīb wa-jammāl*)".[125] Thus is undoubtedly also based on the "Book of Highest Initiation", which Abū Ṭāhir had studied according to Niẓām al-Mulk.[126]

Whatever the Qarmaṭī leaders may or may not have said when they abolished exoteric Islam in Baḥrayn, all we have is a Sunnī formulation of what the Sunnīs believed them to have said. It could have been in this formulation

121 Ghazālī, *Faḍā'iḥ al-Bāṭiniyya*, ch. ii.3 (ed. Amman 1993, pp. 15 ff.).

122 Muḥammad b. al-Ḥasan al-Daylamī al-Yamānī (wrote 707/1307), *Qawāʿid ʿaqā'id al-bāṭiniyya*, ed. M.Z. al-Kawtharī, Cairo 1950, 90; cf. also Abū ʿUthmān b. ʿAbdallāh b. al-Ḥasan al-Ḥanafī al-ʿIrāqī (6th/12th century?), *al-Firaq al-muftariqa bayna 'l-zaygh wa'l-zandaqa*, ed. Ankara 1961, 100, where they dismiss Muḥammad as an impostor who deceived the rude Arabs thanks to their ignorance of philosophy and astronomy, without reference to the other prophets (my thanks to Masoud Jafari Jazi for drawing this work to my attention). The Assassins themselves are never credited with dismissing the prophets as impostors, nor is al-Ḥākim, to whom the legend of the Old Man of the Mountain was transferred (*pace* de Smet, 'La théorie', 92, who claims so with reference to F. Daftary, *The Assassin Legends*, London 1994, 118–120).

123 Massignon, 'La légende', 83 f.

124 Niẓām al-Mulk, *Siyāsatnāma*, ed. H. Darke, *Siyar al-mulūk*, 2nd ed., Tehran 1985 = *The Book of Government or Rules for Kings*, tr. H. Darke, London 1960, ch. 46, § 36 (p. 309 = 236).

125 Yamānī, *Qawāʿid*, 90.

126 Niẓām al-Mulk, *Siyāsatnāma*, ch. 46, § 32 (p. 306 = 234).

that the idea of the prophets as impostors reached Frederick II's court. It does not have to be, however. Poetry such as al-Maʿarrī's could have had the same effect.

Europe: Frederick II

In his bull of 1239, directed to all of Latin Christianity, Pope Gregory IX charged the emperor Frederick II with saying that "the whole world had been deceived by three deceivers (*barattatoribus*), to use his words, namely Christ Jesus, Moses and Muhammad".[127] The three impostors are enumerated in the order of importance to Christians, but no motive is imputed to them, nor are we told where Frederick had picked up the idea.[128] A fuller account is found in *Vita Gregorii IX*, and this work, composed in 1240, is of particular importance in that it was written for papal in-house use and so cannot be dismissed as a mere propaganda tool.[129] Here we are told that Frederick owed his bad ideas to conversation with Greeks and Arabs, who,

> mendaciously affirming that all things relative to government derive from the stars, instilled in him the pagan error that a man rejected by God appears to himself to be a God in human form; and he publicly affirmed that Moses, Christ and Muhammad were three tricksters (*truffatores*) who had come to deceive people, that Moses, after having been saved from the water, nourished himself with the bread of others, that Muhammad was a camel-driver of servile birth, that both of them by means of their cunning completed their lives supported by public favour; Christ was actually the son of an artisan and an impoverished woman who, deceived by a false belief, was justly recompensed by condemnation to the torments of the cross; he then accuses him with various arguments of not being God, affirming that the union of the creator and the created is impossible.

---

127 Esposito, 'Manifestazione' (above, note 1), 6.

128 *Pace* de Smet, 'La théorie', 91, neither the bull nor the *Cronica S. Petri Erfordensis Moderna* says that he had picked it up from the Assassins, though the bull implies and the Cronica says that he had obtained hired assassins from them.

129 *Vita Gregorii IX* in *Le liber censuum de l'église romaine* (written 1240), ed. P. Fabre, II, Paris 1905, 32 f.; cf. P. Fabre, 'Les vies de papes dans les manuscrits du *Liber Censuum*,' *Mélanges d'Archéologie et d'Histoire* 6, 1886, 147–161, at 154, 155n; P. Montaubin, 'Bastard Nepotism', in Frances Andrews (ed.), *Pope, Church, and City*, Leiden 2004, 129–176, at 154. I owe these references to Robert Lerner.

Here it is from Greek and Arab astrologers that Frederick learns that one can believe oneself to be divine even while being rejected by God. They are not explicitly identified as the source of the impostor thesis, but the text can certainly be read to imply it. Moses, Christ and Muḥammad, now in chronological order, are declared to be tricksters; Moses, a mere foundling, "nourished himself with the bread of others", while Muḥammad was "a camel-driver of servile birth" who used his cunning to complete his life "supported by public favour". Christ too had humble origins, but he suffered the punishment that the other two avoided. It is notable that here as in the statement imputed to the Qarmaṭī Abū Ṭāhir, Muḥammad is identified as a camel-driver, but the professions of Moses and Jesus are missing, so this is perhaps less important than it seems. As regards imposture for the purpose of living off public funds, this may be what al-Maʿarrī is speaking of when he says:

> Some parties declared that your God did not send Jesus and Moses (as prophets)
> to mankind,
> but they only provided a means of livelihood (*maʾkala*) for their followers
> and made a net/a law/a deceit to catch them all (*wa-ṣayyarū li-jamīʿi ʾl-nāsi nāmūsan*).[130]

But the reference could be to altruistic deceit: by providing a law, however fraudulent, Jesus and Moses enabled their followers to live and make transactions together. Muḥammad is not mentioned for obvious reasons, but nobody will have been fooled.

As many have surmised, Frederick II's heresy must have originated in the Islamic world. It is of course perfectly possible that the idea of religious leaders as tricksters in search of worldly wealth and power has suggested itself independently several times in history, but what we have here is not a case of the wheel being invented twice. In the first place, Moses, Jesus and Muḥammad were profoundly different figures to the Christians of Europe, who could hardly have cast them as tricksters of the same type on their own. By contrast, the Muslims venerated all three as prophets and so would naturally reject all three as embodiments of the same error if they turned against them.[131] In the second place, Christ is the figure of central concern to Frederick II, yet he does not

130 Maʿarrī, *Meditations*, tr. Nicholson, no. 248.

131 Noted by D. Weltecke, *"Der Narr Spricht: Es ist kein Gott". Atheismus, Unglauben und Glaubenszweifel vom 12. Jahrhundert bis zur Neuzeit*, Frankfurt am Main 2010, 143.

really fit the impostor pattern. Moses and Muḥammad successfully deceive others into granting them positions of wealth and honour, but Jesus does not seem to deceive anyone apart from himself: what he is punished for is his belief in his own divinity, though it is not clear that it got him anywhere. Finally, the theme appears suddenly on the Latin Christian side and remains rare for centuries, whereas it has a continuous history from antiquity onwards on the Islamic side, where we find it with a profusion of variations.

If we accept that the theme is of Islamic origin, by what channels was it transmitted to Europe? First, was it to Frederick II's court that it was transmitted? Some scholars deny it, if not on good grounds.[132] An alternative hypothesis would be that it was the Pope himself who had picked up the three impostors idea from Muslim informants and fathered it on Frederick II. This is not so ridiculous a thesis as it may sound, for the papal curia spearheaded the same type of culture as Frederick's court: Michael Scotus had been patronised by the popes Honorius III and Gregory IX before passing into the service of Frederick II, for example.[133] In addition, there was much traffic between the Roman curia and the Holy Land. But Gregory IX claims to be quoting Frederick II's own words in his bull ("the whole world had been deceived by three deceivers, *to use his words*"), and his word for deceivers (*barattatoribus*) is an unusual one, which he would hardly have imputed to Frederick if it had not figured in the reports he had received about him.[134] As we have seen, the account in the *Life of Gregory IX* also makes it difficult to dismiss the charge as a mere propaganda ploy. More probably, the idea of Moses, Jesus and Muḥammad as impostors was brought to Frederick II's court by people to whom it was a well-known view, which they did not necessarily share, but which they would air along with other explanations of prophethood in discussions of precisely what the prophets had been: philosophers who had achieved such perfection that they had come to be in receipt of revelation (from the First Intellect)? Philosophers who had not in fact received any revelation, but who had claimed to have their message from God for the sake of the good of mankind? Or just men (philosophers or otherwise)

132 Cf. D. Abulafia, *Frederick II: a Medieval Emperor*, London 1988, 254, claiming that the charge was "a stock accusation against disbelievers in the west well before he was born". In fact, only one possibly earlier case is known, that of Simon of Tournai (above, note 2), and it is normally rejected in favour of Frederick as the first case.

133 Cf. A. Paravicini Bagliani, 'Federico II e la corte dei papi: scambi culturali e scientifici', in his *Medicina e scienze della natura alla corte dei papi nel Duecento*, Spoleto 1991, 53–84; S.J. Williams, 'The Early Circulation of the Pseudo-Aristotelian *Secret of Secrets* in the West: the Papal and Imperial Courts', *Micrologus* 2, 1994, 132, 140, 142.

134 I owe this point to Thomas Gruber. [Ed.: see also Gruber, 'A tribus barattatoribus deceptus', 678 f.]

who had claimed to receive revelations in order to accumulate worldly power and wealth? Discussions of this kind are likely to have been conducted in philosophical circles all over the Muslim world, spiced with quotations of poetry by al-Maʿarrī and his likes; and since the statement about the shepherd, the physician and the camel-driver was witty, and probably also well known,[135] it may have formed part of such discussions as well, as a succinct formulation of the most extreme view.

Such discussions are likely also to have been conducted at Frederick's court in southern Italy (he did not return to Sicily after his youth). Among his courtiers were an otherwise unknown astronomer sent to him by al-Kāmil, the ruler of Egypt; a Christian doctor by the name of Theodore of Antioch, who had studied philosophy and science at Antioch, Mosul and Baghdad and who perplexed several Dominicans with philosophical arguments that they were unable to refute during Frederick II's siege of Brescia in 1238;[136] the astronomer/astrologer Michael Scotus, a Scot who had worked in Toledo, where he learned Arabic and translated al-Biṭrūjī's astronomical work *Kitāb fī 'l-hay'a* into Latin; and Jacob Anatoly, an in-law of the famous Ibn Tibbon family of translators in Provence (refugees from the Iberian peninsula), who worked as a translator of Aristotle and Averroes from Arabic to Hebrew at Frederick's court.[137] These are precisely the sort of men who would have felt free to discuss the nature of revelation. Theodore of Antioch, for example, will have thought of the founders of the great religions, including his own, as lawgiver prophets of the same type; and since from a Christian point of view, Muḥammad fell into the category of impostors motivated by a desire for worldly power, it raised the question how once could be sure that the same was not true of the other founders, meaning Jesus and Moses (since Zoroaster and Mani were not relevant in Italy). Theodore may have been genuinely worried by that question or he may just have liked to perplex other people with it. It was a nicely radical view for an intellectual to play with. The presence of just one scandalised observer from another part of Latin Christendom, where discussions of this risqué kind were not part of the high

135 According to de Smet, 'La théorie', 90, it is cited by innumerable Sunnī and Zaydī authors up to the Mamluk period. But he does not give any examples apart from Niẓām al-Mulk.

136 B.Z. Kedar and E. Kohlberg, 'The Intercultural Career of Theodore of Antioch', *Mediterranean Historical Review* 10, 1995, 165ff., 171; C. Burnett, 'Master Theodore, Frederick II's Philosopher', in *Federico II e le nuove culture*, Spoleto 1995, 225–285 (reprinted in his *Arabic into Latin in the Middle Ages*, Farnham 2009, no. IX), 225f., 228, 255f. [Ed.: see also Gruber, 'A tribus barattatoribus deceptus', 683.]

137 Abulafia, *Frederick II*, ch. 8; cf. T. Hockey and others (eds.), *The Biographical Encyclopedia of Astronomers*, New York 2007, s.v. 'al-Biṭrūjī'; Williams, 'Early Circulation', 138.

culture, would have been all that was required for Gregory IX to receive the horrendous news that Frederick II held the whole world to have been deceived by three impostors, namely Jesus, Moses and Muḥammad.[138] A Franciscan writing in 1261 claims that the person who heard Frederick utter this blasphemy was Heinrich Raspe, the landgrave of Thuringia who was elected Holy Roman emperor with papal backing when Frederick II was excommunicated in 1246. But the landgrave, contemptuously known as the *Pfaffenkönig*, had too strong an interest in supporting the pope against Frederick for this to carry much weight.[139]

There is of course no way to prove precisely how it happened. Maybe the idea had been brought to Italy in some other way. The main point is that we need not assume that Frederick II actually meant what he said, if indeed it was he who said it, or that anyone else at this court was convinced of it. They may have been or they may not, but the presence of the idea at Frederick's court does not depend on it. However it happened, the transmission must have been oral, for no Arabic book translated into Latin, whether at Frederick's court or elsewhere, contained the idea. It arrived by virtue of people from two different sides of the civilisational fence talking to each other, as they did in Sicily, southern Italy, the Iberian peninsula and elsewhere in the Mediterranean.

Later Attestations

After Frederick II the impostor thesis disappears from sight for a hundred years, then it turns in the Iberian peninsula. Here Thomas Scotus (no relation of Michael Scotus) declared in the 1340s that "There were three impostors in the world, sc. Moses who deceived the Jews, Christ who deceived the Christians and Muḥammad who deceived the Saracens ..."[140] This Thomas Scotus has been plausibly identified as Thomas of Braunceston, a Franciscan necromancer, alchemist and heretic who had been patronised by Pope John XXII and enrolled, on the latter's order, as a Dominican at Carcassonne in 1328. In 1333 "Thomas the Englishman", probably the same person, was appointed lec-

138 Compare the Andalusian scandalised by disputations in Baghdad in which Muslims and non-Muslims, even Dahrīs and Zindīqs, would debate on an even footing (M. Cook, 'Ibn Saʿdī on Truth-Blindness', *Jerusalem Studies in Arabic and Islam* 33, 2007, 169–178).

139 *Cronica S. Petri Erfordensis Moderna* in MPL 30, 398, cited in Niewöhner, *Veritas sive Varietas*, 149.

140 M. Esposito, 'Les hérésies de Thomas Scotus d'après le "Collyrium Fidei" d'Alvare Pélage', *Revue d'Histoire Ecclésiastique* 33, 1937, 59.

turer in natural philosophy for the convent at Rieux at the foot of the Pyrenees; and between 1341 and 1344 Alvarus Pelagius (d. 1352), bishop of Silves in Portugal, tells us of Thomas Scotus, an apostate of both the Franciscan and the Dominican orders whose heresies were known "in various parts of Spain and elsewhere".[141] Apart from dismissing the founders of Judaism, Christianity and Islam as liars, this Thomas denied the virgin birth and the divinity of Christ (as did Frederick II), as well as Christ's miracles (dismissed as magic), the angels, the afterlife and papal power. In positive terms he affirmed the eternity of the world, the superiority of philosophy over positive religion (Aristotle was better than Christ, a bad man hanged for his sins) and, most strikingly, the existence of human beings before Adam.[142] Thomas' impostor thesis seems to be identical with Frederick II's, but the pre-Adamites are new. The bishop of Silves linked Thomas' belief in pre-Adamites with his Aristotelian affirmation of the eternity of the world, and there can of course be little doubt that Thomas, a natural philosopher, was an Aristotelian. But a great many Aristotelians believed the world to be eternal without affirming that there were humans before Adam. Like the three impostors thesis, it was a view at home in the Islamic world which is sporadically reported in late medieval Europe and shoots to great popularity in the sixteenth and seventeenth centuries.[143] By then it was well known that pre-Adamites were an idea of Persian, Arabic or Jewish origin.[144]

141 P. Nold, 'Thomas of Braunceston O.M./O.P.', in T. Prügl and M. Schlosser (eds.), *Kirchenbild und Spiritualität: Festschrift für Ulrich Horst OP*, Paderborn 2007, 179–195. I owe my knowledge of this study to Robert Lerner.

142 Latin text in Esposito, 'Hérésies de Thomas Scotus', 59–62; summary English tr. in Nold, 'Thomas of Braunceston', 192–195.

143 M. Mulsow, 'Pre-Adamites and Astrology of History between the Middle East and Europe: Longue-Durée-Transfer or Entanglement?', unpublished paper (2013), partly published as 'Vor Adam. Ideengeschichte jenseits der Eurozentrik', *Zeitschrift für Ideengeschichte* 9, 2015, 47–66; R.H. Popkin, 'The Pre-Adamite Theory in the Renaissance', in E.P. Mahoney (ed.), *Philosophy and Humanism: Renaissance Essays in Honor of Paul Oskar Kristeller*, New York 1976, 59f., cf. 61 (Thomas Nash declared in 1592 and 1593 that "I hear say there be mathematicians abroad that will prove men before Adam"); A. Hamilton, *The Family of Love*, Cambridge 1981, 118, on the Surrey sectarians, confession of 1561; Paul Kocher, *Christopher Marlowe*, Chapel Hill 1946, 34, 43f.; cf. the Diggers, Ranters and others in P.C. Almond, *Adam and Eve in Seventeenth-Century Thought*, Cambridge 1999, 51; W. Poole, 'Seventeenth-Century Preadamism, and an Anonymous English Preadamist', *Seventeenth Century* 19, 2004, 2, 7f.; and Isaac de La Peyrère, *Prae-Adamitae*, published in 1655 (English tr. *Men before Adam*, 1656; he had aired the ideas from the 1640s onwards).

144 Popkin, 'Pre-Adamite Theory', 53, where this is explained to La Peyrère by the Biblical scholar Father Richard Simon.

Like the three impostors thesis, the idea of pre-Adamites may be rooted in antiquity. According to Photius (d. c. 893), Clement of Alexandria (d. c. 215) talked marvels about transmigrations of souls and about "many worlds having existed before Adam".[145] If this is correct, Clement, a Christian moulded by Platonism, was presumably trying to accommodate the Stoic-Platonic doctrine of many successive worlds in a Christian scheme in which the world containing Adam was the last. But it is only from Photius that we learn this, and Photius was not known in fourteenth-century Europe. Augustine (d. 430), who was very well known, was also aware of people who believed in many successive worlds, but he infers that they must believe in spontaneous generation of humans out of the elements, not that they must believe in humans before Adam.[146] The idea of successive worlds is also surprisingly well attested in rabbinic sources. Here we are told that God created worlds and destroyed them before creating this one, or that there were 974 generations before the creation of this world, all destroyed because of their wickedness, or that the 974 generations wanted to be created, but were not, though they were distributed as evil ones in every generation, and the like.[147] That there were humans before Adam is never explicitly stated, however.

In the Islamic world we hear both of many Adams and of humans before Adam from the mid-ninth century onwards. Some heretics said that God had created seven Adams, each of whom would preside over an era lasting 50,000 years.[148] Others merely insisted that Adam himself had ancestors.[149] The idea

145 Photius, *Bibl.*, 109.

146 Augustine, *City of God*, XII, 11.

147 *Bereshit Rabba* III, 7 (*ad* Gen. 1:5); IX, 2 (*ad* Gen. 1:31), XXVIII, 4 (*ad* Gen. 6:7); *Babylonian Talmud*, Hagiga, 13b–14a; cf. E.E. Urbach, *The Sages*, tr. I. Abrahams, Jerusalem 1975, ch. 9, 210f., citing these and other sources. (I owe my knowledge of the rabbinic material to Reimund Leicht and Oded Zinger.)

148 Cf. P. Crone, *The Nativist Prophets of Early Islamic Iran: Rural Revolt and Local Zoroastrianism*, Cambridge 2012, 209f., citing al-Nāshi' (attrib.), *K. uṣūl al-niḥal*, ed. J. van Ess, *Frühe mu'tazilitische Häresiographie*, Beirut and Wiesbaden 1971, § 58, probably composed in the first half of the ninth century; each era has a different population, without any carry-over from one to the other. Compare *Pirqe de Rabbi Eliezer* (c. 800?), tr. G. Friedlander, New York 1970, 141 (on the Sabbath): God created seven aeons, six "for the going in and coming out" and the seventh entirely Sabbath. Similar ideas appear in the Ḥurūfī *Maḥramnāma*, composed in the late fourteenth/early fifteenth century (cf. O. Mir-Kasimov, 'Notes sur deux textes *ḥurūfī*', *Studia Iranica* 35, 2006, 219f.), among the modern Yazīdīs (cf. P. Kreyenbroek, *Yezidism*, London 1995, 37: the Christians only know history from the last Adam onwards); and in an impeccably Imāmī Shī'ite village in the Zagros mountains in the 1970s (R. Loeffler, *Islam in Practice: Religious Beliefs in a Persian Village*, Albany 1988, 37, 39).

149 Cf. Khushaysh b. Aṣram (d. 253/867) in al-Malaṭī, *K. al-tanbīh wa'l-radd 'alā ahl al-ahwā*

of several Adams inaugurating successive eras was widely accepted by the Ismailis,[150] and it also turns up in Sufism: the Andalusian mystic Ibn ʿArabī (d. 638/1240) recollected a saying of the Prophet to the effect that "God has created a hundred thousand Adams".[151] The idea of humans before Adam was current in historical astrology, the study of the conjunctions determining the rise and fall of kings, dynasties, prophets, religions and other major events on earth and the predictions which can be made on that basis. The main Muslim authority on this subject was Abū Maʿshar (d. 272/886), whose *Book of Religion and Dynasties* was translated into Latin in the mid-twelfth century; but contrary to expectation, it does not mention pre-Adamites. Back in Iraq, however, an astrologer who flourished around 900 held that before Adam there had been "many nations, created beings, monuments, habitations, civilisations, religions, (forms of) kingship and kings", all quite different from ours, and that "Hermes lived a long time before Adam". He also wrote a book about conjunctions and predicted the coming of a man who would restore Zoroastrian sovereignty, unite the whole world and do away with the rule of the Arabs and others.[152] The self-proclaimed Chaldaean Ibn Waḥshiyya (fl. c. 320/930) similarly held that a sage called Dawanay lived before Adam, and that Adam was called the Father of Mankind only because of his contributions to science.[153]

---

wa'l-bidaʿ, ed. S. Dedering, Istanbul 1936, 72 ("They do not acknowledge Adam [as the first], but say that Adam also had ancestors"); similarly an old trader in Loeffler, *Islam in Practice*, 37, 39.

150 Cf. P.E. Walker, *Early Philosophical Shiism*, Cambridge 1993, 112, on Abū Yaʿqūb al-Sijistānī (d. c. 975); al-Baghdādī, *al-Farq bayna 'l-firaq*, ed. M. Badr, Cairo 1910, 280; al-Ḥusayn b. ʿAlī (Yemeni Ismaili, d. 667/1268) in B. Lewis, 'An Ismaili Interpretation of the "Fall of Adam"', *Bulletin of the School of Oriental and African Studies* 9, 1937–1939, 694, 697, cf. 697n on the modern Ismailis; H. Corbin, *Cyclical Time and Ismaili Gnosis*, London 1983, 42 ff., 78 ff. Kevin van Bladel, who has drafted a provisional article on pre-Adamism in the Islamic world, has many more Ismaili references.

151 Ibn ʿArabī, *al-Futūḥāt al-makkiyya*, Dār Ṣādir reprint, Beirut 1968, III, 549, line 13.

152 Al-Maqdisī, *Kitāb al-bad' wa'l-ta'rīkh*, ed. and tr. C. Huart, Paris 1899–1919, II, 97 f., 147 f.; cf. Baghdādī, *Farq*, 271 (where he is a Bāṭinī, i.e. Ismaili); al-Bīrūnī, *al-Āthār al-bāqiya ʿan al-qurūn al-khāliya*, ed. C.E. Sachau, Leipzig 1878 (repr. 1923), 213; tr. C.E. Sachau, *The Chronology of Ancient Nations*, London 1879 (repr. 1984), with the same pagination in the margin. Most of the material on this man (whose name appears in different forms) was presented by Kevin van Bladel at the first workshop on the transmission of radical ideas from the Islamic world to Europe.

153 Ibn Waḥshiyya in J. Hämeen-Anttila, *The Last Pagans of Iraq: Ibn Waḥshiyya and His Nabatean Agriculture*, Leiden 2006, 298, text 44. The works in this and the next note were also covered by van Bladel.

Ibn Waḥshiyya's views on pre-Adamites were reported by Judah ha-Levi (fl. c. 1130) in al-Andalus and by Maimonides in his *Guide*, written in Egypt, and so were known to Jews well before the *Guide* was translated into Latin (at Frederick II's court).[154] It was presumably from Jewish and/or Muslim astrologers in the Iberian peninsula that Thomas Scotus had picked up the idea.

Then there is silence for another hundred years.[155] In 1459, however, the impostor theme turns up again, this time among the heresies of Zaninus, a canon of Solcia in Lombardy.[156] Zaninus repented of a fair number of errors, including that God had created a world other than this one and that in its time many other men and women had existed, so that Adam was not the first man; that Jesus Christ, Moses and Muḥammad had ruled the world by the pleasure of their wills; that Jesus Christ suffered and died by the law of the stars, not to redeem the human race; that Christian law would come to an end through the succession of another law, just as the law of Moses has been terminated by the law of Christ; and that the world would be destroyed naturally rather than by divine fiat, by the heat of the sun consuming the humidity of the land and air and setting the elements on fire. Zaninus had clearly been studying historical astrology, and he too combined the impostor thesis with belief in pre-Adamites.

In Zaninus' case there cannot be much doubt that we have to do with independent transmission of the impostor theme, for he envisages all three founders of religion as rulers: they ruled the world by the pleasure of their wills, he says, i.e. as they saw fit, not on the basis of divine instructions. The political dimension of the impostor theory had surfaced in Europe well before Zaninus, for Matthew Paris (whose chronicle stops in 1258) credits Frederick II with the view that three conjurers (*prestigiatores*) cleverly seduced the world in order to *dominate* it (rather than to live off public funds, as the *Life of Gregory IX* has it).[157] How Matthew Paris had picked up this idea is unknown, but it can hardly be a Christian development, given that Jesus had not ruled anything at all. Casting him as a wielder of political power made sense because of the dominant role that the church had acquired, but it violated the historical record, and it does so in a particularly drastic form in Zaninus' formulation, since Jesus had asked for his death to be taken away from him. Further, the concept of a succession

---

154 Judah ha-Levi, *al-Kuzari*, I, 61; Maimonides, *Guide*, III, ch. 29, tr. C. Rabin, Indianapolis 1995, 177, 179; tr. S. Pines, Chicago 1963, II, 515f.

155 According to R.W. Southern, *Western Views of Islam*, Cambridge, Mass., 1962, 75, the impostor idea turned up again in Aragon in the 1380s, but his only reference is to Esposito on Thomas Scotus and I do not know what he has in mind.

156 Esposito, 'Manifestazione', 41ff.

157 Esposito, 'Manifestazione', 8.

of religious laws, each one abrogating its predecessor, is Islamic. It is particularly well developed in Ismailism, but historical astrologers were into the same game. Once again, the intermediaries could be Jews, for Zaninus also held that Jesus was illegitimate, presumably because he had been exposed to the *Toledoth Ieshu*, and the cyclical concept of time had gone into the Kabbalah by then. In addition, however, Zaninus subscribed to two views which are strikingly reminiscent of Muslim heresy, namely that "wantonness outside of matrimony is not a sin, except by the prohibition of positive laws"—only ecclesiastical prohibition stopped people from following the opinion of Epicurus—and that the taking of other people's property is not a mortal sin even when it is against the will of the owner.[158] The idea that women and property were free for all, once associated with the sectarians of western Iran known as Khurramīs, was current in Sufi circles, including those condemned by the heresiographer writing (probably) in fourteenth-century Tabrīz.[159] They were well known in Latin Europe too, where they were associated with the so-called Free Spirits. But the Free Spirits had no interest in astrology, science or pre-Adamites. Given that Zaninus' heresies form a coherent cluster of ideas, all well attested in the Islamic world, the chances are that all of them had travelled from Tabrīz to Europe, either via the Balkans, carried by Bektashis and other Sufis, or else via Constantinople, the route by which Maraghan astronomy made its way from Azerbaijan to Italy and, in ways still not precisely known, to Copernicus.[160]

The political dimension of the impostor theory is absent from the report of 1468 on the members of the Roman academy who dismissed Moses, Christ and Muḥammad as deceivers and seducers.[161] In some of these reports, the founders of religion are at least identified as lawgivers,[162] but it is not until the sixteenth century that positive religion is routinely cast as "but a device of policy", as Marlowe (d. 1593) reputedly described it when he dismissed Jesus and Moses as deceivers and the Bible as idle stories.[163]

---

158 Cf. Esposite, 'Manifestazione', 42 f.

159 Cf. M. Mashkūr (ed.), *Haftād u sih millat*, nos. 27, 37, 76; Crone, *Nativist Prophets*, 261 ff., 440, 448 ff., 482; cf. also 137, 257, 261 ff.

160 Cf. G. Saliba, *Islamic Science and the Making of the European Renaissance*, Cambridge, Mass., and London 2007, ch. 6, esp. 194 f.

161 E. Garin, *History of Italian Philosophy*, ed. and tr. G.A. Pinton, Amsterdam and New York 2008, 199.

162 Thus the versions attributed to Averroes, the report of 1468, and Matteo da Acquasparta (d. c. 1302) on Frederick II (Esposito, 'Manifestazione', 15).

163 J. Hotson, *The Death of Christopher Marlowe*, London and Cambridge, Mass., 1925, 11 f. ("a device of pollicie").

By then we also encounter a related idea, namely that religion, whether true or false, was a useful institution in that it allowed us to live together. In fact, we encounter this notion already in the *Policraticus* of John of Salisbury (d. 1180), who tells us that King Numa had civilised the barbarous Romans by means of (false) religious institutions.[164] In John's time this was a radically new idea: to Augustine and his many readers, Numa was a cynical manipulator exemplifying the deceit that pagan rulers would practise in order to consolidate their own power.[165] But as John had learnt from Pope Adrian IV (d. 1195), one should consider "the utility of all" instead of focusing on the harshness used by the church or secular princes, such as for example when they extracted money from all and sundry.[166] Are Islamic ideas lurking behind this as well? It is certainly striking that John speaks of "external worship" (*cultus exteriores*) for what the Ismailis called the *ẓāhir*, meaning external, manifest or plain religion (public worship to John), as opposed to the inner, esoteric (*bāṭin*) meaning pursued by initiates.[167] However this may be, there were soon Christians who denied that the law had anything *but* utilitarian value. Thus it was said of Pope Boniface VIII (r. 1294–1304) that already back in his days as a cardinal he had considered religious laws, including those of Muḥammad and of Christianity, to have been "invented by men in order to take people away from evil by means of the fear of punishment". There was no eternal punishment in his opinion: "thus, in religious laws the truth is nothing but the condition for men to live together civilly and quietly (*civiliter et quiete*) because of fear of spiritual punishment".[168] Thereafter

164 John of Salisbury, *Policraticus*, tr. J. Dickinson, New York 1927, V, 3 (68f.).

165 Thus Augustine, *City of God*, III, 4, 9; IV, 31, 32; VII, 34; VIII, 5, on Numa and Varro. John's most important source seems to be the *Epitome* of Florus (d. c. 130), based on Livy, still incompletely known in John's time. (John did not use Plutarch's *Numa*, for all that he freely invokes Plutarch's name.) Florus, a pagan, is favourable to Numa, but lacks the idea that the divine support was a sham: to him the "immortal gods" are real. John is the first to have the view that Numa's institutions were good *even though* they were what Augustine saw as devilish inventions.

166 John had naively assumed that the Church and the Pope should not take bribes, an idea to which Pope Adrian responded by laughing and telling him the story of the ancient Roman Menenius Agrippa, who taught his soldiers that all parts of the human body contributed to the body's welfare, even the stomach, which seemingly did nothing: if it was starved, the whole body would die (*Policraticus*, VI, 24).

167 John of Salisbury, *Policraticus*, III, 68.

168 In P. Dinzelbacher, *Unglaube im "Zeitalter des Glaubens"*, 2nd ed., Badenweiler 2009, 23; Ruggero di Simone in *Boniface VIII en procés*, ed. J. Coste, Rome 1995, 504. Many other witnesses made similar statements, also reproduced in Coste's book (of which I owe my knowledge to Gianluca Briguglia).

the idea of religion as socially useful surfaces in different forms in the works of Albert the Great (d. 1280),[169] the Paduan judge Geremia da Montagnone (d. 1321),[170] Marsilio of Padua (d. 1342)[171] and later figures; and by the sixteenth century we hear of Spanish and Italian Christians who held that religion was "a human invention for living well (*al ben vivere*)"[172] and that religion existed "so that we may live in peace (*para que viviéramos en paz, ut viverimus in pace*)".[173] In a related vein the miller Menocchio (Domenico Scandella) held the function of the eucharist to be to control people, in a civilising sense: it had been instituted so that men would not be like beasts.[174] But was religion really useful for everyone or just for kings and/or churchmen? Augustine's view that pagan

169 Albert, Commentary on *De Anima* of Aristotle, 407b19 ff., cited in M. Silk, 'Numa Pompilius and the Idea of Civil Religion in the West', *Journal of the American Academy of Religion* 72, 2004, 875: Albert held that it was because Pythagoras wanted "to make citizens cultivate piety and justice" that he made up the story that the souls of bad citizens would depart from one body into another of worse condition, e.g. into the body of a lion or an ass. Albert is developing a point made by Averroes in his Long Commentary (*Sharḥ*) on Aristotle, *De Anima*, Latin translation probably by Michael Scotus (d. 1231?), ed. F. Stuart Crawford, Cambridge 1953, 74; tr. R.C. Taylor and T.-A. Druart, New Haven 2009, 67 (book I, 53): Averroes briefly says that Pythagoras spoke of reincarnation in order to correct the souls of the citizens.

170 He knew the idea from classical sources such as Cicero's *De natura deorum*, I, 118 ("some have said that the whole opinion about immortal gods was made up by wise men for the sake of the commonwealth"), which he cites without agreeing with it (see A. Brett (tr.), *Marsilius of Padua: The Defender of the Peace*, Cambridge 2005, 29n).

171 Brett, *Marsilius*, I, 5, 11–12 (pp. 28 f.).

172 Thus Girolamo Busale (d. 1541, probably of Marrano origin) in M. Firpo, *Tra alumbrados e "spirituali": Studi su Juan Valdés e il valdesianesimo nella crisi religiosa nel '500 italiano*, Florence 1990, 94 (drawn to my attention by Stefania Pastore). According to a Venetian Inquisitorial trial in 1553 (ASV, Sant'Uffizio, Processi, b. 159, f. II, f. 113r, made available to me by Stefania Pastore), a student of law by the name of Giulio Basalú passed from believing "only in that which tallied in the one and the other law, i.e. the Hebrew and the Christian", to the conviction that religion was no more than an "invention by humans for living well". Under the influence of a Spanish refugee in Italy, he came to hold that "Christ was purely human, but abundantly full of holy spirit", that the soul was mortal, that no religion was true, whether Christian, Jewish or other, and that "Christ was a good man who taught how to live well (*Christo era stato homo da bene che haveva insegnato el ben viver*)". He also held concubinage to be no sin, and laughed at everything. See further L. Addante, *Eretici e libertini nel Cinquecento italiano*, Rome 2010, 25–30 (drawn to my attention by Stefania Pastore).

173 S. Pastore, *Una herejía Española: Conversos, alumbrados e Inquisición*, Madrid 2010, 218, on Juan de Castillo, 1537.

174 C. Ginzburg, *The Cheese and the Worm*, Baltimore 1980, 11.

religion was invented for the enslavement of the masses appealed to Boccaccio (d. 1375) and was to play a major role in the radical Enlightenment as a thinly disguised attack on the Christian church, seen as manipulating and defrauding the common people, while a list of "articles in which modern heretics err" dismissed Easter observance, confession and penance as devices permitting the church to collect money.[175] Hell had been invented by priests in order to cheat people for the sake of money; it was an illusion created by the authorities so that they could rule as they liked.[176] The concept of religion as socially useful thus follows the same pattern as the impostor theme and the idea of pre-Adamites: well attested in many forms in the Islamic world from the third/ninth century onwards, it appears like a bolt out of the blue in the Latin West in the twelfth century, a bit earlier than the other themes, and surfaces from time to time thereafter until it takes off in the sixteenth century.

Conclusion

The three impostors illustrate a process that still has not received much attention, namely transmission from (and to) the Islamic world by word of mouth rather than by books. Where people live next to each other, they talk to each other, learn from each other and adjust to one another's positions, whether for purposes of living in peace or on the contrary to fight. We know a great deal about the relations between the Islamic world and Christian Europe in terms of war, political negotiations, polemics and translations, all of which left plenty of paper trails; but the same does not apply to oral contacts because they were not usually recorded, and on top of that they often took place at social levels that did not count from a high cultural point of view. Of such oral exchanges there must have been plenty, since Muslims and Christians were living cheek by jowl in the Mediterranean, with plenty of Jewish neighbours too. In fact, oral transmission must have played a major role even in connection with the translation of Arabic texts into Latin, for the collectors had to talk to (Muslim, Jewish or Christian) bearers of Islamic culture in order to acquire manuscripts, and the translators must have looked for informants to tell them how the texts

175 W. Wakefield, 'Some Unorthodox Ideas of the Thirteenth Century', *Medievalia et Humanistica*, NS, 4, 1973, 30.

176 Thus Christiern Pedersen (d. 1554) on "mad people" in Dinzelbacher, *Unglaube*, 70; the miller Pellegrino Baroni, nicknamed "Pighino" (1570), in Ginzburg, *The Cheese and the Worm*, 118; Costatino Saccardino in 1622 (in G. Schwerhoff, 'Die alltäglische Auferstehung des Fleisches', *Historische Anthropologie* 12, 2004, 309–337, at 332).

were to be understood. In fact, translations were often cooperative enterprises, and the middlemen were often Jews, who were more likely than others to master more than one high cultural language. But most exchanges will have taken place without the parties being aware of it, causing ideas to travel in imperceptible ripples from one community to the other and to display themselves in subtle adjustments to traditional ways of reading well-known material, for example in the new evaluation that John of Salisbury puts on King Numa or Alvarus Pelagius' accommodation of belief in pre-Adamites under the rubric of Aristotelianism. The impostor theme has unusual visibility in the sources because it was so scandalous, but it should be treated as symptomatic of a much broader process that we need to learn how to track; for we cannot otherwise know precisely what it meant for the development of Christian Europe that it had the Islamic world rather than some other civilisation as its neighbour.

CHAPTER 10

How the Field Has Changed in My Lifetime*

Let me start by telling you that there is one monumental change that I am *not* going to talk about even though it indisputably occurred in my lifetime, and that is the technological revolution that has given us computers, the web, databases and more besides. It is not that these changes have not affected me, far from it; but I don't feel they are really part of my scholarly history because they haven't shaped me. I use these gadgets, but only up to a point, and I still think as if I lived in a world of typewriters. So it is for the next generation to assess the effect that electronics have had on our field.

Back in the 1960s, when I started studying Islamic history, the field was still dominated by the work of the great Orientalists who had created the field. Most of them were Western Europeans working primarily in Germany, France, Britain and Holland. They usually came to Islamic studies from Biblical studies, but there were also many whose academic interest had been aroused by their work as colonial administrators. They all had Greek and Latin from school, they normally combined Arabic either with Persian and Turkish or with all the Semitic languages, and they often worked in many fields relating to Near East, not just Islamics. They were pretty impressive people. They edited the main texts and wrote the first scholarly accounts, started source-critical studies, and looked all set to raise the study of Islam to the level achieved in Biblical studies when the First World War broke out, soon followed by the second, and so everything changed.

The key characteristic of Orientalism was a sharp distinction between the subject and object of study. The Orientalists—the subject—were studying an alien world—the object—in order to explain it to a Western audience. They had no intention of converting the people they were studying, or of polemicising against them, or even of interacting with them in any way, except when they were colonial administrators or missionaries. Of course there were exceptions such as Goldziher, who studied at al-Azhar, or Edward Browne, to whom the study of Persian was intimately (if briefly) linked with interaction with Iranians.[1] But even when the Orientalists actually interacted with Muslims, their

* A version of this essay was presented as a lecture in Leiden on 9 February 2013 at a colloquium that marked the launch of *Ibn Ḥazm of Cordoba: The Life and Works of a Controversial Thinker*, edited by C. Adang, M. Fierro and S. Schmidtke (Leiden 2013).

1 Another exception is Bernard Lewis, who travelled extensively in the Muslim world through-

© KONINKLIJKE BRILL NV, LEIDEN, 2016 | DOI: 10.1163/9789004319318_011

approach was distinctive in that their aim was to explain them in terms intelligible to Westerners. In short, the Orientalists were doing much the same as Bīrūnī (d. c. 1050) had done in his India book. He wanted to explain Indian religions to a Muslim audience. He wasn't out to convert his object of study either, nor was he writing polemics against them; on the contrary, he complains that all earlier treatments of the subject were biased and partisan. He did collect information from them, and he was able to do so because his patron took him to India to assist his colonial expansion. But he was not interested in how the Indians would respond to his portrait of them—he didn't expect them to read it.

I shall have to leave Bīrūnī aside. The point I am trying to make is that the Orientalists studied Muslims as if they were distant stars, translating things Islamic or Indian into categories and patterns that their own people could understand, without regard for what the distant stars would make of it. Of course their writings were Eurocentric, partly because they were writing for Europeans using European concepts and categories, and partly because they assumed their own civilization to be superior. People usually do, especially when they are on top of the world. But the objects of study did not *remain* distant stars. Muslims were increasingly being schooled in Western languages and academic methods, and works written for Westerners began to look offensive when the audience came to include Easterners, who didn't like reading about themselves in translation and who disliked having to learn foreign categories in order to understand their own traditions. After WW2 they ceased to be colonial subjects whose opinion could be dismissed; they became independent and many of them moved to the West, where they acquired a voice in the universities and other elite institutions. So now you have the great drama whereby the subjects and the objects of enquiry begin to merge and have to work out new rules of intellectual coexistence. The landmark here is Edward Said's attack on Orientalism, which came out in 1978.

I grew up in that rather remote outpost called Denmark, and I had the Orientalist conception of Islamic studies. I originally wanted to study the ancient Near East, and I decided to do Islamic history instead without ever having set eyes on a Muslim or heard any Middle Eastern language spoken. I didn't think I would ever even *get* to the Middle East. To me, studying Sumerians and studying Muslims were much the same. Of course that changed when I

---

out his long career. But he moved in diplomatic, governmental and royal circles, so that his experience was quite different from that of younger specialists in Islamic studies (see B. Lewis (with B.E. Churchill), *Notes on a Century: Reflections of a Middle Eastern Historian*, New York 2012).

went to England, but even there the Orientalist conception only seemed to be frayed at the edges. That's fifty years ago, and things have *totally* changed since then, in our field as in Indian and Chinese studies. There is no Western study of the Orient anymore. The key distinction is no longer between West and East, but rather between Islamic (or Hindu or Confucian or whatever) history as done in the universities and as done in seminaries or madrasas or other traditional institutions of learning. This development has boosted our numbers, opened up new libraries in the Middle East, and led to the publication of a vast array of new sources. Islamic history is now a much bigger field with much better source material than it was in the fifties and sixties. It has also had some drawbacks, such as the intrusion of politicized history-writing, identity politics and victim culture, but overall it has been a good thing.

There are two further ways in which the end of colonialism has affected the field. One is what you might call the rise of post-colonial bad conscience, which became particularly pronounced after the publication of Edward Said's *Orientalism*. It is still with us and still rampant, and it requires you to denigrate Western civilization for its colonial and other sins whenever you can, whereas you may not say anything that could be construed as criticism of Islam. I could give many examples, but no doubt many others could too, and although some people seem to be unaware of the degree to which they are engaging in double-think, I prefer to say no more about it.

The second way is the degree to which intellectual developments in the Muslim world now affect Islamic studies in the West, which I think is not generally noticed. There is a good example in approaches to the Quran. When I started my studies, the general Islamicist view was that all interpretations of the Quran had to come out of the exegetical literature. All Islamicists were unwittingly subscribing to the rule that the tradition sat in judgement of the Quran, not vice versa: *al-sunna qāḍiya ʿalā ʾl-qurʾān*. But that's no longer the case, and the change started in the Islamic world, in Egypt in the 1950s, in Pakistan a bit later. Muslims were rebelling against the tradition because they wanted to adapt to modern ways, and they wanted the Quran to validate their views. So they started doing *tafsīr al-qurʾān biʾl-qurʾān*, and the results were startlingly different. In the west the first person to study the Quran on the basis of the Quran alone seems to have been Angelika Neuwirth, in her first book published in 1981. But now it is commonplace, and it has contributed to making Quranic studies a very live field. Everything has to be rethought. I shouldn't think Neuwirth was aware of following Muslim trends. I have found myself saying things which reflected modernist Muslim interpretations and which I myself was not aware of at the time. One thing I'd like to know is how these things spread. In the old days you called it *Zeitgeist*, now I think we have to come up with something better, such as some suggestions as to the mechanics, but I don't think anyone has worked on it.

To give you another example, when I started studying Islamic history, Arab nationalism was reigning supreme. And back then, Islamic history was studied in isolation from other fields, and with an overwhelming stress on the Arabs. Islam was seen as the fruit of a marriage between God and Arabia, and as having developed thereafter in accordance with its own internal needs, shaped by the Quranic spirit, and so on. Nobody paid any attention to the cultural traditions of the conquered peoples. Basically the Arab conquerors were assumed to have brought Islam as we know it to the Middle East, where it erased everything that went before it, except for a few so-called "foreign elements" that somehow slipped through. To suggest anything else was to detract from "the originality of the Prophet" or "the originality of Islamic civilization". Islamic history began in Arabia and ended with Arab nationalism, and it did so *because* Arab nationalism set the tone, yet we were not aware of being shaped by it.

Of course, other factors came into it too. In the 1950s and '60s it became fashionable to adopt a functionalist approach and to deride an interest in origins. There was much impatience with "diffusionism". This was a trend that affected all the humanities; I think it started in anthropology, and it is presumably also connected with the rise of the former colonies to independence. In any case, at a time when the whole world was being transformed by Western influence, academic orthodoxy required you to deny that there was any such thing as "influence" at all. All social and cultural transformations were allegedly due to "inner, organic" developments; foreign elements were only borrowed when people positively needed them and wanted them for their own internal reasons. That put a nice gloss on what was going on in the post-colonial world. It also did have some salutary effects, but like so many trends it became tyrannical.

There are still people who think that history-writing is about giving prizes for "originality" and "creativity", as if that was what people in the past were striving for, but Islamic studies have now been enormously affected by the developments inaugurated by Peter Brown. He put late antiquity on the map and made it so prestigious that now it is the height of fashion to connect Islam with developments in the Middle East outside Arabia and to stress the degree to which Islam originated as a late antique religion. In addition, globalization has caused people in just about every field to stress the porous nature of borders and the numerous ways in which neighbouring civilisations affected (and affect) each other. You still aren't allowed to speak of "influence", with the result that people sometimes resort to silly euphemisms to avoid it. It is true that it isn't a good word, but there are times when you need it, if only as a shorthand. But be that as it may, there can be no doubt that Islamic studies have come out of their isolation.

OK, so much for the aftermath of colonialism. Now for the changes internal to the West itself. The first big change to note here has been the rise and fall of the Soviet Union and, along with it, the rise and fall of socio-economic history, in Islamic studies as elsewhere. The interest in socio-economic history among Islamicists began in the late nineteenth century, but the big change came with the Russian revolution, and by the 1950s Islamicists were deeply into economic organization, social classes, the rise of capitalism and so on. Socio-economic history continued to reign supreme down to the eighties. My esteemed colleague, Michael Cook, started as an economic historian; it was his job description until he defected to America and he has published in that field as well. Though he has left it, there are still people in it, I am glad to say, for it *is* important, but it no longer plays a dominating role. It was replaced by questions to do with race, identity and gender. For some reason, the American preoccupation with race and slavery didn't have much of an impact on Islamic studies—the only one who took up the subject was Bernard Lewis. But identity was a different matter. For years after my move to the Institute for Advanced Study, the applications were dominated by questions of identity, and to a lesser extent gender. Gender is still going strong, but the favourite subjects are now porous boundaries along with agency (ascribed to everything, even inanimate objects).

The third big change has been the rise of Islamic studies in America together with the enormous expansion of the universities, which is still going on. Back in the '50s and '60s the only Americans who mattered in Islamic studies were immigrants from Europe, such as Rosenthal, Schacht or von Grunebaum. The field was dominated by Western Europe—especially England, France, Germany and Holland. Now America dominates the field. Lots of Islamicists are being produced there; and though many Europeans continue to be imported, there can be no doubt that America is setting the tone.

This has had both good and bad consequences. Among the good consequences is the sheer increase in our numbers. There just weren't enough of us before to get things moving—now there are. But the expansion of higher education has also resulted in a huge bottom of semi-educated people who are barely literate and whose entrance has introduced Gresham's law to Islamicist scholarship: the bad is driving out the good.[2] It is not sheer numbers alone that

2 As Lewis observes in his *Notes on a Century*, 193.

are at work here, though. All over the world, especially in the West, there has been a great wrench away from the tradition, including the traditional rules of how to write, spell and construe sentences and arguments, which were deliberately withheld from the next generation by teachers who were young in the '60s, so that the next generation reached maturity without the ability to express themselves and went on to teach their impoverished language skills to the next generation in their turn. Sheer numbers in combination with poor schooling and lack of interest in the tradition have also resulted in an increased number of people who only have one foreign language (in Islamic studies, usually Arabic), which condemns you to mediocrity.

Connected with this expansion is the rise of the publish or perish syndrome, which is something that did not affect me at all as a young scholar and which now dominates the lives of young scholars everywhere, partly thanks to increased competition and partly thanks to the victory of the business conception of academic output. It results in a lot of publications that are premature, hurried, second-rate and often much too long for what they have to say. It also means that certain types of enquiry simply don't get attempted any more because they would take too long. Or they get attempted only as part of big collaborative enterprises such as the ones that are funded by the European Union. All in all you could say that back in the '50s one thought of great scholars as geniuses toiling away in the attic—it was a Romantic conception of the scholar as the lone pursuer of the truth. But now it is the factory mode of production that prevails and the ideal great scholar now is not a genius in the attic, but rather an entrepreneur and broker. It has been accompanied by a huge increase in bureaucratic chores. All this is bad.

Another effect of the rise of American scholarship has been the rise of theory. Like most trends it has been both a good and a bad thing. The worst side effect has been the rise of pretentiousness. A lot of scholarship gets written in stilted Latinate jargon, almost beyond comprehension, and often very solipsistic. The only world that exists is the author's mind. It has also led to a sad contempt for philological skills, including those required to produce editions, which is a serious problem, for many of the standard editions we rely on are not proper editions, just printings of a particular manuscript, often without indication of variants, with lots of corruptions and so on. We desperately need better editions, but a graduate who decides to make one will not get a job. What people want is "originality". Every young person is trained to think that he is going to turn the field upside down. We have a situation in which people think that a healthy field is one in which there is nothing but paradigm shifts. It's the academic version of the doctrine of permanent revolution, and it is not doing anyone any good. But not all is lost. What could sound more philological than papyrology? Yet Petra Sijpesteijn has managed to make the topic sexy, and to integrate this formerly rather marginal field into mainstream historical studies.

Finally, there is a most positive effect. Americans take it for granted that people doing Islamic history belong in a history department, that those doing Arabic or Persian or Urdu literature belong in a literature department, and that those doing religion belong in a religion department. It may sound self-evident, but it is not at all how things were done back in England. There all Islamicists were put in faculties of Oriental studies, with a few in the faculty of divinity. The history faculty in Oxford, for example, did not recognize any non-European history as history, and believe it or not, that was a common attitude. It contributed to the isolation of our field. But over here Islamicists have been exposed to the ways of other historians, or literary scholars, or specialists in religion, and learned to ask the kind of questions that others ask, and it seems to me that the study of Islamic history, at least in the period that I tend work on, has become a lot more sophisticated.

There is no doubt that the Orientalists were amazing scholars. Somebody like Nöldeke puts us all to shame. But it has to be admitted that he was not a good historian, and that the same tended to be true of the other great Orientalists, though of course there were exceptions (e.g. Wellhausen). Most Orientalists practised what you might call the scissors and paste approach to history: first you separated fact from fiction—there was nothing in between: things were either true or fabricated, and if they were fabricated they were useless—and then you pasted the facts together, one piece here, another there, until eventually you had used them up, leaving you with a picture that had no depth, no perspective, no sense of real people interacting in a real world.[3] That's how Islamic history tended to be written when I started. You still see it today. But most Islamicists these days will treat information as just a tiny fragment of a lost world, an accidental survivor which is of value not only for what it explicitly says, but also, sometimes only, for what it presupposes, for the kind of beliefs and institutions it takes for granted, and for what it is trying to say even if every word is invented. A single potsherd can suffice to give you an idea of the whole vase. So we no longer insist on gluing all our sherds together. Rather, we will mount them the modern way, one here, one there, with a bit of conjectural metal to hold them together, so that what you see is a real, three-dimensional vase even though the actual fragments are tiny.

That has been a huge gain. The crude pictures with which the pioneers began are being discarded; there is a lot less "essentialism", a lot more sensitivity to

3 Nöldeke's *Sketches from Eastern History* is a good example.

changes over time and place and greater awareness of the different interests of competing groups, including women and children. There is also a much better understanding of how societies actually worked in the past, how social control was maintained, how politics were negotiated, how propaganda was shaped to dress it up, and so forth. We owe a lot to the social sciences here, but also of course to literary studies and deconstruction.

All in all, despite the loss of respect for philology, the excessive respect for originality, the tyranny of the factory model of academic work, the publish or perish syndrome, and other negative factors, the developments of the last fifty years strike me as largely positive.

List of Patricia Crone's Publications

Books

Hagarism: The Making of the Islamic World. Cambridge: Cambridge University Press, 1977 (with Michael Cook). Paperback edition, 1980. Unauthorized Arabic translation by Nabīl Fayyāḍ, *al-Hājariyyūn*, Damascus: n.p., 2003.

Slaves on Horses: The Evolution of the Islamic Polity. Cambridge: Cambridge University Press, 1980. Paperback edition, 2003.

God's Caliph: Religious Authority in the First Centuries of Islam. Cambridge: Cambridge University Press, 1986 (with Martin Hinds). Paperback edition, 2003.

Roman, Provincial and Islamic Law: The Origins of the Islamic Patronate. Cambridge: Cambridge University Press, 1987. Paperback edition, 2002.

Meccan Trade and the Rise of Islam. Princeton, NJ: Princeton University Press, 1987. Reprint, Piscataway, NJ: Gorgias Press, 2004. Arabic translation by Āmāl Muḥammad al-Rawabī, *Tijārat Makka wa-ẓuhūr al-islām*, Cairo: al-Majlis al-Aʿlā lil-Thaqāfa, 2005.

Pre-Industrial Societies. Oxford: Blackwell, 1989. Swedish translation by Birger Hedén and Stefan Sandelin, *Förindustriella samhällen*, Lund: Studentlitteratur, 1991. German translation by Marianne Menzel, *Die vorindustrielle Gesellschaft: Eine Strukturanalyse*, Munich: Deutscher Taschenbuch-Verlag, 1992. Second edition, Oxford: Oneworld, 2003. Revised edition, 2015.

The Book of Strangers: Medieval Arabic Graffiti on the Theme of Nostalgia. Princeton, NJ: Markus Wiener, 1999 (translated with Shmuel Moreh). Danish translation by Sune Haugbølle, *De fremmedes bog: Arabisk nostalgisk graffiti fra middelalderen*, Copenhagen: Vandkunsten, 2004.

The Epistle of Sālim ibn Dhakwān. Oxford: Oxford University Press, 2001 (with Fritz Zimmermann).

Medieval Islamic Political Thought. Edinburgh: Edinburgh University Press, 2004. Published in America under the title *God's Rule: Government and Islam; Six Centuries of Medieval Islamic Political Thought*. New York: Columbia University Press, 2004. Paperback edition, 2005. Turkish translation by Hakan Köni, *Ortaçağ İslam dünyasında siyasi düşünce*, Istanbul: Kapı, 2007. Persian translation by Masʿūd Jaʿfarī Jazī, *Tārīkh-i andīsha-yi siyāsī dar islām*, Tehran: Sukhan, 2011; chapter 13 reprinted as an article in *Bukhārā* 14, no. 80 (2011).

From Kavād to al-Ghazālī: Religion, Law and Political Thought in the Near East, c. 600–1100. Aldershot: Ashgate, 2005 (Variorum reprint of 12 articles).

From Arabian Tribes to Islamic Empire: Army, State and Society in the Near East, c. 600–850. Aldershot: Ashgate, 2008 (Variorum reprint of 12 articles).

The Nativist Prophets of Early Islamic Iran: Rural Revolt and Local Zoroastrianism. Cambridge: Cambridge University Press, 2012. Paperback edition, 2013.

Muqanna' wa sapīdjāmagān. Tehran: Māhī, 2013 (with Mas'ūd Ja'farī Jazī; four articles translated into Persian).

Collected Studies in Three Volumes (reprinted, revised and previously unpublished articles). Vol. 1: *The Qur'ānic Pagans and Related Matters*. Vol. 2: *The Iranian Reception of Islam: The Non-Traditionalist Strands*. Vol. 3: *Islam, the Ancient Near East and Varieties of Godlessness*. Edited by Hanna Siurua. Leiden: Brill, 2016.

Edited Volumes

Studies in Early Islamic History, by Martin Hinds, ed. Jere Bacharach, Lawrence I. Conrad and Patricia Crone. Princeton, NJ: Darwin Press, 1996.

The Greek Strand in Islamic Political Thought, ed. Emma Gannagé, Patricia Crone, Maroun Aouad, Dimitri Gutas, and Eckart Schütrumpf. *Mélanges de l'Université Saint-Joseph* 57. Beirut: Université Saint-Joseph, 2004.

Princeton Encyclopedia of Islamic Political Thought, ed. Gerhard Böwering with Patricia Crone, Wadad Kadi, Devin J. Stewart and Mahan Mirza. Princeton, NJ: Princeton University Press, 2013.

Articles

'Islam, Judeo-Christianity and Byzantine Iconoclasm'. *Jerusalem Studies in Arabic and Islam* 2 (1980): 59–96 (= *From Kavād to al-Ghazālī*, no. III).

'Jāhilī and Jewish Law: The *Qasāma*'. *Jerusalem Studies in Arabic and Islam* 4 (1984): 153–201 (= *From Kavād to al-Ghazālī*, no. IV).

'The Tribe and the State'. In John A. Hall (ed.), *States in History*, Oxford: Blackwell, 1986, 48–77. Revised version in John A. Hall (ed.), *The State: Critical Concepts*, London: Blackwell, 1994, vol. 1, 446–476 (= *From Arabian Tribes to Islamic Empire*, no. I).

'Max Weber, das islamische Recht und die Entstehung des Kapitalismus'. In Wolfgang Schluchter (ed.), *Max Webers Sicht des Islams: Interpretation und Kritik*, Frankfurt am Main: Suhrkamp, 1987, 294–333. Revised English version, 'Weber, Islamic Law, and the Rise of Capitalism', in Toby E. Huff and Wolfgang Schluchter (eds.), *Max Weber and Islam*, New Brunswick, NJ: Transaction Books, 1999, 247–272 (= *From Kavād to al-Ghazālī*, no. VI).

'Did al-Ghazālī Write a Mirror for Princes?' *Jerusalem Studies in Arabic and Islam* 10 (1987), 167–191 (= *From Kavād to al-Ghazālī*, no. XII).

'On the Meaning of the 'Abbasid Call to *al-Riḍā*'. In C.E. Bosworth, Charles Issawi, Roger

Savory and A.L. Udovich (eds.), *The Islamic World from Classical to Modern Times: Essays in Honor of Bernard Lewis*, Princeton, NJ: Darwin Press, 1989, 95–111 (= *From Arabian Tribes to Islamic Empire*, no. VII).

'Kavād's Heresy and Mazdak's Revolt'. *Iran* 29 (1991), 21–42 (= *From Kavād to al-Ghazālī*, no. I; = *Collected Studies in Three Volumes*, vol. 2, *The Iranian Reception of Islam: The Non-Traditionalist Strands*, art. 1).

'Serjeant and Meccan Trade'. *Arabica* 39, no. 2 (1992), 216–240.

'Tribes and States in the Middle East' (review article). *Journal of the Royal Asiatic Society* 3, no. 3 (1993), 353–376 (= *From Arabian Tribes to Islamic Empire*, no. II).

'"Even an Ethiopian Slave": The Transformation of a Sunnī Tradition'. *Bulletin of the School of Oriental and African Studies* 57, no. 1 (1994), 59–67 (= *From Kavād to al-Ghazālī*, no. VIII).

'Were the Qays and Yemen of the Umayyad Period Political Parties?' *Der Islam* 71, no. 1 (1994), 1–57 (= *From Arabian Tribes to Islamic Empire*, no. IV).

'Zoroastrian Communism'. *Comparative Studies in Society and History* 36, no. 3 (1994), 447–462 (= *From Kavād to al-Ghazālī*, no. II; = *Collected Studies in Three Volumes*, vol. 2, *The Iranian Reception of Islam: The Non-Traditionalist Strands*, art. 2).

'The First-Century Concept of *Hiǧra*'. *Arabica* 41, no. 3 (1994), 352–387 (= *From Arabian Tribes to Islamic Empire*, no. III).

'Two Legal Problems Bearing on the Early History of the Qur'ān'. *Jerusalem Studies in Arabic and Islam* 18 (1994), 1–37 (= *From Kavād to al-Ghazālī*, no. V).

'The Rise of Islam in the World'. In Francis Robinson (ed.), *The Cambridge Illustrated History of the Islamic World*, Cambridge: Cambridge University Press, 1996, 2–31.

'A Note on Muqātil b. Ḥayyān and Muqātil b. Sulaymān'. *Der Islam* 74, no. 2 (1997), 238–249 (= *From Arabian Tribes to Islamic Empire*, no. V).

'The 'Abbāsid Abnā' and Sāsānid Cavalrymen'. *Journal of the Royal Asiatic Society* 8, no. 1 (1998), 1–19 (= *From Arabian Tribes to Islamic Empire*, no. VIII).

'A Statement by the Najdiyya Khārijites on the Dispensability of the Imamate'. *Studia Islamica* 88 (1998), 55–76 (= *From Kavād to al-Ghazālī*, no. IX).

'The Early Islamic World'. In Kurt A. Raaflaub and Nathan S. Rosenstein (eds.), *War and Society in the Ancient and Medieval Worlds: Asia, the Mediterranean, Europe, and Mesoamerica*, Cambridge, MA: Harvard University Press and Washington, DC: Center for Hellenic Studies, 1999, 309–332 (= *From Arabian Tribes to Islamic Empire*, no. IX).

'The Significance of Wooden Weapons in the Revolt of al-Mukhtār and the 'Abbāsid Revolution'. In Ian Richard Netton (ed.), *Studies in Honour of Clifford Edmund Bosworth*, vol. 1: *Hunter of the East: Arabic and Semitic Studies*, Leiden: Brill, 2000, 174–187 (= *From Arabian Tribes to Islamic Empire*, no. VI).

'Ninth-Century Muslim Anarchists'. *Past and Present*, no. 167 (2000), 3–28 (= *From Kavād to al-Ghazālī*, no. X).

'The Khārijites and the Caliphal Title'. In Gerald R. Hawting, Jawid A. Mojaddedi and

Alexander Samely (eds.), *Studies in Islamic and Middle Eastern Texts and Traditions in Memory of Norman Calder*, Oxford: Oxford University Press, 2000, 85–91 (= *From Kavād to al-Ghazālī*, no. XI).

'*Shūrā* as an Elective Institution'. *Quaderni di Studi Arabi* 19 (2001), 3–39 (= *From Kavād to al-Ghazālī*, no. VII).

'A New Source on Ismailism at the Samanid Court' (with Luke Treadwell). In Chase F. Robinson (ed.), *Texts, Documents and Artefacts: Islamic Studies in Honour of D.S. Richards*, Leiden: Brill, 2003, 37–67 (= *Collected Studies in Three Volumes*, vol. 2, *The Iranian Reception of Islam: The Non-Traditionalist Strands*, art. 10).

'What Was al-Fārābī's "Imamic" Constitution?' *Arabica* 50 (2003), 306–321 (= *Collected Studies in Three Volumes*, vol. 2, *The Iranian Reception of Islam: The Non-Traditionalist Strands*, art. 11).

'The Pay of Client Soldiers in the Umayyad Period'. *Der Islam* 80, no. 2 (2003), 284–300 (= *From Arabian Tribes to Islamic Empire*, no. X).

'Al-Fārābī's Imperfect Constitutions'. *Mélanges de l'Université Saint-Joseph* 57 (2004), 191–228 (= *Collected Studies in Three Volumes*, vol. 2, *The Iranian Reception of Islam: The Non-Traditionalist Strands*, art. 12).

'Mawālī and the Prophet's Family: An Early Shīʿite View'. In Monique Bernards and John Nawas (eds.), *Patronate and Patronage in Early and Classical Islam*, Leiden: Brill, 2005, 167–194 (= *From Arabian Tribes to Islamic Empire*, no. XI).

'How Did the Quranic Pagans Make a Living?' *Bulletin of the School of Oriental and African Studies* 68, no. 3 (2005), 387–399 (= *Collected Studies in Three Volumes*, vol. 1, *The Qur'ānic Pagans and Related Matters*, art. 1). Danish translation in *Tidskrift for Islamforskning* 1 (2006), art. 2 (online).

'Post-Colonialism in Tenth-Century Islam'. *Der Islam* 83, no. 1 (2006), 2–38 (= *Collected Studies in Three Volumes*, vol. 3, *Islam, the Ancient Near East and Varieties of Godlessness*, art. 7).

'Imperial Trauma: The Case of the Arabs'. *Common Knowledge* 12, no. 1 (2006), 107–116 (= *From Arabian Tribes to Islamic Empire*, no. XII).

'Abū Saʿīd al-Ḥaḍrī and the Punishment of Unbelievers'. *Jerusalem Studies in Arabic and Islam* 31 (2006), 92–106 (= *Collected Studies in Three Volumes*, vol. 3, *Islam, the Ancient Near East and Varieties of Godlessness*, art. 4).

'Quraysh and the Roman Army: Making Sense of the Meccan Leather Trade'. *Bulletin of the School of Oriental and African Studies* 70, no. 1 (2007), 63–88 (= *Collected Studies in Three Volumes*, vol. 1, *The Qur'ānic Pagans and Related Matters*, art. 2).

'"Barefoot and Naked": What Did the Bedouin of the Arab Conquests Look Like?' *Muqarnas* 25 (2008), 1–10 (= *Collected Studies in Three Volumes*, vol. 3, *Islam, the Ancient Near East and Varieties of Godlessness*, art. 1).

'No Compulsion in Religion: Q. 2:256 in Medieval and Modern Interpretation'. In Mohammad Ali Amir-Moezzi, Meir M. Bar-Asher and Simon Hopkins (eds.), *Le*

Shīʿisme imāmite quarante ans après, Turnhout: Brepols, 2009, 131–178 (= *Collected Studies in Three Volumes*, vol. 1, *The Qur'ānic Pagans and Related Matters*, art. 13).

'The Muqannaʿ Narrative in the *Tārīkhnāma*' (with Masoud Jafari Jazi). Part I (Introduction, Edition and Translation), *Bulletin of the School of Oriental and African Studies* 73, no. 2 (2010), 157–177. Part II (Commentary and Analysis), *Bulletin of the School of Oriental and African Studies* 73, no. 3 (2010), 381–413. (= *Muqannaʿ wa sapīdjāmagān*, arts. 1 and 2 [in Persian]; = *Collected Studies in Three Volumes*, vol. 2, *The Iranian Reception of Islam: The Non-Traditionalist Strands*, arts. 6 and 7.)

'The Ancient Near East and Islam: The Case of Lot-Casting' (with Adam Silverstein). *Journal of Semitic Studies* 55, no. 2 (2010), 423–450 (= *Collected Studies in Three Volumes*, vol. 3, *Islam, the Ancient Near East and Varieties of Godlessness*, art. 2).

'The Religion of the Qur'ānic Pagans: God and the Lesser Deities'. *Arabica* 57, no. 1–2 (2010), 151–200 (= *Collected Studies in Three Volumes*, vol. 1, *The Qur'ānic Pagans and Related Matters*, art. 3).

'The Dahrīs According to al-Jāḥiẓ'. *Mélanges de l'Université Saint-Joseph* 63 (2010–2011), 63–82 (= *Collected Studies in Three Volumes*, vol. 3, *Islam, the Ancient Near East and Varieties of Godlessness*, art. 5).

'Abū Tammām on the Mubayyiḍa'. In Omar Alí-de-Unzaga (ed.), *Fortresses of the Intellect: Ismaili and Other Islamic Studies in Honour of Farhad Daftary*, London: I.B. Tauris and Institute of Ismaili Studies, 2011, 167–187 (= *Muqannaʿ wa sapīdjāmagān*, art. 4 [in Persian]; = *Collected Studies in Three Volumes*, vol. 2, *The Iranian Reception of Islam: The Non-Traditionalist Strands*, art. 5).

'Angels versus Humans as Messengers of God: The View of the Qur'ānic Pagans'. In Philippa Townsend and Moulie Vidas (eds.), *Revelation, Literature, and Community in Late Antiquity*, Tübingen: Mohr Siebeck, 2011, 315–336 (= *Collected Studies in Three Volumes*, vol. 1, *The Qur'ānic Pagans and Related Matters*, art. 4).

'Al-Jāḥiẓ on *Aṣḥāb al-Jahālāt* and the Jahmiyya'. In Rotraud Hansberger, M. Afifi al-Akiti and Charles Burnett (eds.), *Medieval Arabic Thought: Essays in Honour of Fritz Zimmermann*, London: Warburg Institute and Turin: Nino Aragno Editore, 2012, 27–39 (= *Collected Studies in Three Volumes*, vol. 2, *The Iranian Reception of Islam: The Non-Traditionalist Strands*, art. 8). Persian translation in *Bukhārā* 18, no. 108 (2015), 64–82.

'Buddhism as Ancient Iranian Paganism'. In Teresa Bernheimer and Adam Silverstein (eds.), *Late Antiquity: Eastern Perspectives*, n.p.: E.J.W. Gibb Memorial Trust, 2012, 25–41 (= *Collected Studies in Three Volumes*, vol. 2, *The Iranian Reception of Islam: The Non-Traditionalist Strands*, art. 9).

'The Quranic *Mushrikūn* and the Resurrection'. Part I, *Bulletin of the School of Oriental and African Studies* 75, no. 3 (2012), 445–472. Part II, *Bulletin of the School of Oriental and African Studies* 76, no. 1 (2013), 1–20. (= *Collected Studies in Three Volumes*, vol. 1, *The Qur'ānic Pagans and Related Matters*, arts. 5 and 6.)

'The *Book of Watchers* in the Qur'ān'. In Haggai Ben-Shammai, Shaul Shaked and Sarah Stroumsa (eds.), *Exchange and Transmission across Cultural Boundaries: Philosophy, Mysticism and Science in the Mediterranean*, Jerusalem: The Israel Academy of Sciences and Humanities, 2013, 16–51 (= *Collected Studies in Three Volumes*, vol. 1, *The Qur'ānic Pagans and Related Matters*, art. 7).

'Pre-Existence in Iran: Zoroastrians, Ex-Christian Muʿtazilites, and Jews on the Human Acquisition of Bodies'. *Aram* 26, no. 1 & 2 (2014), 1–20 (= *Collected Studies in Three Volumes*, vol. 2, *The Iranian Reception of Islam: The Non-Traditionalist Strands*, art. 13).

'Traditional Political Thought'. In Gerhard Böwering (ed.), *Islamic Political Thought: An Introduction*, Princeton, NJ: Princeton University Press, 2015, 238–251.

'Problems in Sura 53'. *Bulletin of the School of Oriental and African Studies* 78, no. 1 (2015), 15–23 (= *Collected Studies in Three Volumes*, vol. 1, *The Qur'ānic Pagans and Related Matters*, art. 12).

'Jewish Christianity and the Qur'ān'. Part One, *Journal of Near Eastern Studies* 74, no. 2 (2015), 225–253. Part Two, *Journal of Near Eastern Studies* 75, no. 1 (2016): 1–21. (= *Collected Studies in Three Volumes*, vol. 1, *The Qur'ānic Pagans and Related Matters*, arts. 9 and 10.)

'*Excursus II*: Ungodly Cosmologies'. In Sabine Schmidtke (ed.), *Oxford Handbook of Islamic Theology*, Oxford: Oxford University Press, 2016 (= *Collected Studies in Three Volumes*, vol. 3, *Islam, the Ancient Near East and Varieties of Godlessness*, art. 6).

Commentaries on Q 37:6–11, Q 43:81–83, Q 52 and Q 72. In Mehdi Azaiez, Gabriel S. Reynolds, Tommaso Tesei and Hamza M. Zafer (eds.), *The Qur'an Seminar Commentary: A Collaborative Study of 50 Qur'anic Passages*, Berlin: Walter de Gruyter, 2016.

'"Nothing but Time Destroys Us": The Deniers of Resurrection in the Qur'an.' *Journal of the International Qur'anic Studies Association* 1, no. 2 (2016).

'Tribes without Saints'. In *Collected Studies in Three Volumes*, vol. 1, *The Qur'ānic Pagans and Related Matters*, art. 15.

'Idrīs, Atraḫasīs and al-Khiḍr'. In *Collected Studies in Three Volumes*, vol. 3, *Islam, the Ancient Near East and Varieties of Godlessness*, art. 3.

'What Are Prophets For? The Social Utility of Religion in Medieval Islamic Thought'. In *Collected Studies in Three Volumes*, vol. 3, *Islam, the Ancient Near East and Varieties of Godlessness*, art. 8.

'Oral Transmission of Subversive Ideas from the Islamic World to Europe: The Case of the Three Impostors'. In *Collected Studies in Three Volumes*, vol. 3, *Islam, the Ancient Near East and Varieties of Godlessness*, art. 9.

'Pagan Arabs as God-Fearers'. In Carol Bakhos and Michael Cook (eds.), *Islam and Its Past: Jāhiliyya and Late Antiquity in Early Muslim Sources*, Oxford: Oxford University Press, forthcoming (= *Collected Studies in Three Volumes*, vol. 1, *The Qur'ānic Pagans and Related Matters*, art. 11).

Encyclopaedia Entries

A Companion to Samaritan Studies, ed. Alan D. Crown, Reinhard Pummer and Abraham Tal, Tübingen: Mohr Siebeck, 1993: 'Athinganoi'.

Encyclopædia Iranica, online edition (2011): 'Ḵorramis', http://www.iranicaonline.org/articles/korramis (= *Collected Studies in Three Volumes*, vol. 2, *The Iranian Reception of Islam: The Non-Traditionalist Strands*, art. 3); 'Moqanna'', http://www.iranicaonline.org/articles/moqanna (= *Muqanna' wa sapīdjāmagān*, art. 3 [in Persian]; = *Collected Studies in Three Volumes*, vol. 2, *The Iranian Reception of Islam: The Non-Traditionalist Strands*, art. 4).

Encyclopaedia of Islam, second edition: 'Kh̲ālid b. al-Walīd', 'Kh̲iṭṭa', 'Masāmiʿa', 'Maʿūna', 'Mawlā', 'al-Muhallab b. Abī Ṣufra', 'Muhallabids', 'Sulaymān b. Kat̲h̲īr', ''Ut̲h̲māniyya', 'Yazīd b. Abī Muslim'.

Encyclopaedia of Islam, third edition: 'Anarchism', ''Arīf', 'Atheism (Pre-Modern)', 'Bābak', 'Barāhima', 'Dahrīs', 'Dayṣanīs'.

Encyclopaedia of the Qur'ān: 'War' (= *Collected Studies in Three Volumes*, vol. 1, *The Qur'ānic Pagans and Related Matters*, art. 8).

Princeton Encyclopedia of Islamic Political Thought, ed. Gerhard Böwering with Patricia Crone, Wadad Kadi, Devin J. Stewart and Mahan Mirza, Princeton, NJ: Princeton University Press, 2013: 'Clients', 'Philosophy', 'Quraysh', 'Sunna', 'Traditional Political Thought'.

Other Writings

'Vom Studium vorindustrieller Gesellschaften'. *Börsenblatt* (1992), 78–80.

'The Rise of the Muslim Sects' [in Chinese]. In *Chung-tung yen-chiu tao-lun*, Taipei: Sino-Arabian Cultural and Economic Association, 1993.

'Til Paradis i lænker: Jihad i historisk perspektiv'. *Kritik* (Copenhagen) 36, no. 12/162 (2003), 37–43.

'What Do We Actually Know about Mohammed?' *Open Democracy* (online publication), 31 August 2006, available at https://www.opendemocracy.net/faith-europe_islam/mohammed_3866.jsp.

'"Jihad": Idea and History'. *Open Democracy* (online publication), 30 April 2007, available at https://www.opendemocracy.net/faith-europe_islam/jihad_4579.jsp. Reprinted (without the final section) in *Cosmopolis* 1 (2015), 99–104 [83–88]. Danish translation in *Weekendavisen*, 1–22 June 2007.

'Islam and Religious Freedom'. Keynote speech at the 30th Deutscher Orientalistentag, Freiburg im Breisgau, 24 September 2007, published at http://orient.ruf.uni-freiburg.de/dotpub/crone.pdf [no longer online] (= *Collected Studies in Three Volumes*, vol. 1,

The Qur'ānic Pagans and Related Matters, art. 14). Also published (without the beginning) under the title 'No Pressure, Then: Freedom of Religion in Islam' at *Open Democracy* (online publication), 7 November 2009, available at https://www.opendemocracy.net/patricia-crone/no-compulsion-in-religion.

'Remarks by the Recipient of the 2014 MEM Lifetime Achievement Award Written for the Annual Meeting of Middle East Medievalists and Read *in Absentia* by Matthew S. Gordon (November 22, 2014, Washington, D.C.)'. *Al-ʿUṣūr al-Wusṭā* 23 (2015), iii–vi (= *Collected Studies in Three Volumes*, vol. 3, *Islam, the Ancient Near East and Varieties of Godlessness*, XI–XV).

'Zandagīnāma-yi khūdniwisht'. *Bukhārā* 18, no. 108 (2015), 37–63.

'Safarnāma-yi Tirmiz'. *Bukhārā* 18, no. 108 (2015), 83–86.

'How the Field Has Changed in My Lifetime'. In *Collected Studies in Three Volumes*, vol. 3, *Islam, the Ancient Near East and Varieties of Godlessness*, Leiden: Brill, 2016, art. 10.

Festschrift

Behnam Sadeghi, Asad Q. Ahmed, Adam Silverstein and Robert Hoyland (eds.), *Islamic Cultures, Islamic Contexts: Essays in Honor of Professor Patricia Crone*. Leiden: Brill, 2015.

Index of Names and Terms

Note: The definite article (al- or 'l-) is ignored in alphabetisation.

ʿAbd al-Jabbār 84, 91, 169, 170, 205–206
ʿAbdallāh al-ʿĀdī/ʿAbdī 176–177
Abū 'l-Faraj al-Isfahānī XIII–XIV
Abū 'l-Hudhayl 131, 132
Abū ʿĪsā al-Warrāq 84, 92–93, 111, 174, 209, 217
Abū Qurra, Theodore 88–89, 90, 91
Abū Saʿīd al-Ḥaḍrī/Ḥaḍramī/Ḥuṣrī 82–83, 90–93, 111, 142
Abū Ṭāhir 224
accidents
  elementary qualities as 105, 114, 137
  motion as sole instance of 136, 140
  in prime matter/substance 131–132, 137–139, 206
  sides and magnitude of atoms as 130
Adam 86, 231–232
  humans before 230–233
Albright, W.F. 48
Alexander, Philip S. 47
Alexander Poem (Syriac) 67–68, 68–70
Alexander Romance 49, 66–67, 72
Alexander the Great 66–68, 72, 73
ʿAlī, lot-casting by 22, 30, 35
Andreas the cook
  in Alexander stories 66–68, 70, 72
  as Atraḫasīs 64, 67
  as Glaukos 67, 77
  as Idrīs/Enoch 49
angels
  demonic offspring of 54, 88
  demons posing as 89, 153, 195, 212
  fallen 78, 79, 86–87
  as subordinates of God 86, 87
animals, religion among 101, 191–192
anthropomorphism 106
anti-Arabism 163–166, 177–178
antinomianism
  among Ismāʿīlīs 157, 177–180, 222
  among Sufis 182–183
apostasy 106, 107–108, 112, 122
Arabs
  converts' resentments against 163–166, 177–178
  desert-dwelling, appearance of 1–16
  loss of political dominance by 159–160, 166–167, 169
  lot-casting among 22–24, 25–26, 29–32, 38, 42
  prejudice against non-Arabs of 163–164, 165, 168
  preserving Jewish customs 25
  role in Near Eastern history 41, 43, 81
  settled, sartorial norms of 2, 9–11, 16
Aramaeans
  as Arabs 41
  language and culture of 40, 54, 65, 75
Aristotle 119, 138, 139, 188n9, 230
Aṣamm, al- 127, 130, 136
astrology/astronomy
  among Dahrīs 108–109, 114, 122, 197, 205–206
  as esoteric knowledge 56, 75
  historical 232, 233, 234
  as philosophy/*kalām* 109, 115
  used by prophets 193, 194, 207, 208, 224n122
  See also *kalām*: as science/philosophy
atheism. *See* Dahrīs; *mulḥids*; Zindīqs
atoms 129, 130–132
Atraḫasīs
  as Andreas 67
  as Enoch 52–54, 55, 56, 59, 62–64, 78
  as flood survivor 49–52, 56–57, 62
  Idrīs as 49, 78
  as immortal 49, 51–52, 60–61, 62, 67
  al-Khiḍr as 75, 78
  as receiving revelations 56–57
  as taken by the gods 53, 61
  as Ūta-napishti 51–52, 53, 60, 62–63, 66–67, 78
  Yonṭon as 68
  as Zi(u)sudra/Xisouthros 50–52, 57, 60–61, 62–63, 78
Augustine 231

Babylonians, Jewish influence on view of Atraḫasīs of 53–54, 60–62

Bandahī, Fakhr al-Dīn b. al-Badīʿ al- 219
Bardesanes (Bar Dayṣān) 119, 128–129, 131
Bashshār al-Burd 124, 142
Bāṭinism 222, 223. *See also* Ismāʿīlīs
Battle of Siffin XI
Becker, Carl-Heinrich 151
Berossos 50, 60–61, 77
Bīrūnī, al- 240
"Brahmans" 207–208, 211
Brown, Peter 242
Buddhism 111, 113
Burzoē 121, 124, 176

Casanova, Paul 48
Christians
  Iranianised 119
  lot-casting among 17–18, 22, 28
  role in Near Eastern history 41
  and science 113–114
  views on Enoch 79, 80–81
  view of God and demons 87–89
circumcision 25
Clement of Alexandria 231
clothing, as marker of propriety 9, 16
consultative divination (*istikhāra*), as lot-casting 38
Cook, Michael 243
cosmology in late antiquity 118–119
Critias 189–190, 196

Dahrīs
  absence of community of 108–109, 114, 122
  as apostates 106, 107–108, 112, 122
  as *aṣḥāb al-hayūlā* 96, 138–139
  as *aṣḥāb al-ṭabāʾiʿ* 96, 108, 133–137
  belief in a creator of 141–142, 192–194, 206
  criticising scripture 99, 101–102, 103–104, 107
  denying God and prophethood 96, 98–99, 103, 104–105, 114, 118, 193, 206–207
  empiricism of 96, 103–105, 114, 206
  eternalism of 96, 98, 99, 111, 114, 139–140
  Greek influence on 113, 115, 136
  heavenly sphere for 98, 99–100, 104–105, 106, 114, 134, 142
  historical reality of 96–97, 115
  morality of 98–99, 100–101, 142
  as (former) pagans 120, 121
  reasons for becoming 106, 108, 109, 112, 121, 122
  role of reason for 96, 103, 107, 115
  and science 108–109, 110, 114–115
  social backgrounds of 112, 115, 122, 205–206, 215
  See also *mulḥids*; prime matter (*hayūlā*, *ṭīna*); *ṭabāʾiʿ* (elementary qualities); Zindīqs
Democritus 189, 190
demons
  deceiving prophets 89–90, 153, 195, 212
  as false prophets 89
  possessing/misleading people 85, 86–87, 88, 89, 91
  usurping divine prerogatives 87–89
design, argument from 100, 127, 142, 207
dhimmīs 167, 170
Dhū ʾl-Kifl 44, 48, 73, 78
Dhū ʾl-Qarnayn 72–73
disputation 109, 121–122, 123, 124
dualism 119, 128, 131, 132–133, 136. *See also* Manichaeans; Zindīqs
Durkheim, Émile 187, 188, 190

Elijah
  Idrīs as 46
  John the Baptist as 74
  al-Khiḍr as 46, 71
Elisha, Idrīs/al-Khiḍr as 73
empiricism 96, 103–104, 114, 124–127
Enki/Ea 18, 50, 56–57, 60
Enlil 18, 50, 56, 60, 62
Enmeduranki 52–53
Enoch
  association with flood of 55, 59
  as At(a)nabīsh 63
  Atraḫasīs as 52–54, 55, 56, 59, 62–64, 78
  books of 54–55, 79–81, 86
  Enmeduranki as 52–53
  as Hermes/Thoth 46–47
  Idrīs as 44, 46, 47–48, 78
  as Metatron 80
  taken away by God 44–45, 47, 53, 57–59, 61, 79–80
  as Ūta-napishti 63
  as visionary 56
equipollence of proofs (*takāfuʾ al-adilla*) 82, 90–91, 92, 126, 170, 173, 207–208, 210

Epicureanism
  atoms in 129–131, 132–133, 136
  on human nature 189
  influence on Dahrīs and Zindīqs 119
  on positive religion 192, 198, 211, 214
Erder, Yoram 48
Ess, Josef van 82–83, 84, 209, 210n49
eternalists. *See* Dahrīs

Fārābī, al- 174, 215
fire
  as elementary substance 105, 114, 132
  nature of 133, 140
  worship of 68
fish, in spring of life story 66–68, 69, 70n118, 71, 72–73
Frederick II 200, 225–229, 230, 233
Free Spirits 234
free will 106
Friedlaender, Israel 72n127, 76

Ghazālī, al- 175, 182–184, 195–196, 218–219, 223–224
giants
  in watcher story 54
  Manichaean Book of 63
  Qumran Book of 58–59, 63
Gil, Moshe 48
Gilgamesh
  Alexander the Great as 66–68
  in Book of Giants 59
  in magic incantations 65
  Moses as 69
  Nimrod as 68–69
  search for immortality of 51, 66–68
Glaukos 67, 76, 77
God
  as active principle 128
  denial of (*see under* Dahrīs; Zindīqs)
  fairness of 83, 90–92, 93–94
  likened to human king 82–83, 84–89, 188
  punishing infidels 83, 90–92, 94
gods, lesser 84–86, 87. *See also* demons
Grabar, Oleg 1–2
Greeks 40, 41
  lot-casting among 19–20, 27–28, 37
  as source of Dahrism 113–114, 115
  as source of "prophets as impostors" thesis 225–226
Gregory IX (pope) 200, 225, 227, 229

Ḥaddād, Abū Ḥafṣ al- 111, 142, 210
Hartmann, Richard 49
Hārūt and Mārūt 78, 79, 81
Ḥasan al-Baṣrī, al- 45, 59
heaven, ascent to
  by Atraḫasīs 61
  by Elijah 46
  by Enmeduranki 52–53
  by Enoch 44–45, 53, 56, 57–58
  by Idrīs 45–46, 47
  by martyrs 45–46
  by Utuabzu 52–53
heavenly sphere 98, 99–100, 104–105, 106, 114, 134, 142
Hermes 46–47, 48, 75, 134
Ḥīwī of Balkh 212–213
Huggins, Ronald V. 63

Ibn Khābiṭ 191
Ibn Mānūsh 130
Ibn al-Rāwandī
  on God 92–93
  on prophets 84, 143, 174, 179, 194, 208–209, 210
  reception of 198, 217
  scepticism of 207–211
  as unhinged Muʿtazilite 92–93, 111, 142
Ibn Rushd (Averroes) 34, 39, 176, 201
Ibn Waḥshiyya 232
Idrīs
  as Andreas/Andrew 48–49
  as Andreas the cook 49
  as Atraḫasīs 49, 78
  elevated by God 44, 45–46, 47, 59
  as Elijah 46
  as Elisha 73
  as Enoch 44, 46, 47–48, 78
  as Ezra/Esdras 48
  as Hermes 48
  as al-Khiḍr 46
  in the Qurʾān 44, 47, 81
Ikhwān al-Ṣafā 101, 174–175, 191–192
ilḥād. See *mulḥids*
imams (Ismāʿīlī) 157, 158, 184
immortality, search for 66–68, 70, 75
intentions, as determining salvation 90–91, 92, 94

interpenetration of bodies 128–130, 140
Iranians. *See* Persians
Īrānshahrī, Abū ʾl-Abbās al- 140, 174
irjāʾ (suspension of judgement) 125
Islamic empire
  post-colonialism in 158–162, 181
  tenth-century cultural fusion in 166–171, 183, 213–214
Ismāʿīlīs 152
  backgrounds of 172
  denounced as subversive 168–169, 223–224
  imams of 157, 158, 184
  on levels of religion 156–158, 182, 214, 222, 235
  messiah (Mahdī) of 157–158, 177, 178–180, 214, 222
  on prophets 154–155, 156, 172–173, 179–180, 222–224
  relationship to mainstream Islam of 177–180, 222–223

Jāḥiẓ, al-
  on Dahrīs 98–106, 107–108, 111–112, 113, 114–115
  on *kalām* 109–110, 113, 118
  on religion 100–101, 186–189, 190–192
Jesus 45, 128, 154, 230, 233–234
  as impostor 83, 179, 200, 203, 221, 223–227, 229, 233–234
  as possessed by a demon 85, 86, 89
Jews
  Christian polemics against 178
  disapproval of sciences of 109
  lot-casting among 19–22, 25–27, 28, 37, 42
  scriptural critics among 212–213
  views on Enoch of 53–54, 59–60, 61–62, 79–80
  view of God and demons of 86–87
jinn, eavesdropping in heaven 103–104, 127
John of Salisbury 235, 238
Jubilees 55, 59

kalām
  dangers of 110–111, 112–113, 115, 122
  as science/philosophy 109–110, 115, 118
  as theology 109, 115, 118, 126

Khiḍr, al-
  as Andreas the cook 72n127
  as Atraḫasīs 75, 76, 78
  as angel 72
  as Babylonian 74–76
  as Dhū ʾl-Qarnayn's commander 72–73
  as Elijah 46, 71, 74
  as Elisha 73
  as Enoch 74
  as Glaukos 76, 77
  as helpful wanderer 71
  as Idrīs 46, 73, 74
  as immortal 46, 70–72
  as Jeremiah 73–74
  name of 76–77
  as servant of God 71, 72, 73
  as servant of Moses 70–71
  as Son of Man 74
Khurramīs 234
kumūn (latency), doctrine of 139, 140

Lewis, Bernard XI, XII, 243
Lidzbarski, Mark 76, 77
lot-casting
  connecting ancient and Islamic culture 18, 41
  as contemporary political device 38–39
  to divide inheritances 17–18, 20–22, 23–25, 34
  as gambling 35–36, 38–39
  by gods 18–19, 21
  in Islamic law 34–36, 37–38
  as Islamic practice 18, 22–24, 25, 29–32, 38, 42
  in the Qurʾān 32–34
  to select people 26–32, 34–35, 39
  to share land and booty 18–20, 22–23, 24–26, 34
  as standard practice in the Near East 18, 24–25
  See also under ʿAlī; Arabs; Christians; Greeks; Jews; Muḥammad; Ottomans; Persians; Romans; Shīʿites

Maʿarrī, al- 175–176, 195, 198, 214–215, 221, 225, 226
Macdonald, Michael 7–9
Mahdī (Ismāʿīlī) 157–158, 177, 178–180, 214, 222

Maḥmūd Pasīkhānī 143
Malka 2–3
Manichaeans
  cosmology of 122, 129–130, 131, 138
  on Enoch 63, 81
  and Zandaqa 114, 119, 122, 123, 169, 206, 212, 217
Marcion 119, 179
Marcionites and Zandaqa 114, 119, 122, 128, 206, 212
Martān Farrūkh 91–92
martyrs, transfer to heaven of 45–46
Mary, chosen/assigned by lot 28, 32–33
Massignon, Louis 221–222, 224
Māwardī 175, 190–191
mawlā, status of 163
medicine 108–109, 110, 115, 124–125, 154, 176
metamorphosis (*maskh*) 102
Metatron 80, 86
Michael Scotus 227, 228
monotheism
  vs. Dahrism 105–105, 141
  vs. elementary qualities 109–110
Montgomery, James A. 49
Moses
  as false prophet 83, 89, 179, 200, 202–203, 221, 223–227, 229, 233–234
  as Gilgamesh 69–70
  servant of 69–71, 72–73 (*see also* Khiḍr, al-)
Muḥammad
  as deceived by demons 89–90
  as impostor 83, 179, 200, 204, 210, 221, 223–229, 233–234
  lot-casting by 22, 23, 30, 34, 35–36, 38
  as lawgiving sage 196, 211
  as leader 154, 155, 170–171, 187, 204
  See also prophets; three impostors thesis
*mulḥid*s
  backgrounds of 119, 121
  beliefs of 98, 99, 118
  converting others 112, 113
  empiricism of 124–125, 126–127
  and *kalām* 110, 113
  reasons for becoming 106
  as sceptics 99, 124–126
  See also Dahrīs; Zindīqs
Murji'ites 92, 125
Musil, Alois 25–26
"Muslim Enlightenment" 213–214. *See also* Islamic empire: tenth-century cultural fusion in
Muʿtazilites
  and Dahrism 97, 107, 111, 115, 123, 140, 142, 207
  God's justice for 91–93
  interest in science of 111

Naṣībī, Abū Iṣḥāq al- 142, 174, 210
nationalism, Arab 242
natural religion 101, 173–174, 183, 191–192, 213
natures. See *ṭabāʾiʿ* (elementary qualities)
Naẓẓām, al- 99, 101, 105, 123, 127, 139, 140
  Dahrī brother-in-law of 106, 123
Neoplatonism 119, 172, 176
Neuwirth, Angelika 241
Nimrod 68–69, 73
Noah 52, 55, 58, 59
Nöldeke, Theodor 48–49, 76, 245

Orientalism 239–241, 245
Ottomans, lot-casting among 30, 32, 34, 42

pagans, Near Eastern 84–85, 87, 120, 203–204
paramonē 42–43
Persians
  arabization of 160–161, 163–166
  lot-casting among 21, 28
Petra, papyrus finds in 17
philosophers 140, 172, 174, 211, 219–220
  as intellectual elite 176, 189–190, 214
  prophets as 197, 219, 227–228
  as source of three impostors thesis 179–180
  vs. theologians (*mutakallim*s) 118, 172, 211, 213
philosophy 109, 118–119, 153, 176, 182, 195, 213–214. See also *kalām*: as science/philosophy
Platonism 118–119, 128, 133, 137, 231
Polybius 189, 196
post-colonialism 151, 158–162, 181, 241–243
prime matter (*hayūlā*, *ṭīna*) 136, 137–138
  proponents of 137–140
prophets
  among animals 101, 191

in ancient Greek world 202–203
as bearers of divine law 155–157, 187, 190, 202–205, 218, 228, 233–234
as bearers of manmade law 156, 196–197, 211, 218, 220, 226
ceremonial cursing of 179
concept of 152–153, 158, 173–175, 187, 194, 205
deceived by demons/angels 89–90, 153, 195, 212, 220
deniers of (*see* Dahrīs; *mulḥids*; Zindīqs)
vs. imams 157, 158
as impostors 83, 84, 174–175, 179, 194, 200, 202–204, 208, 218, 223–229, 233 (*see also* three impostors thesis)
as leaders 154–156, 170–171, 202, 204–205, 233
non-Arabs among 165, 177
as philosophers 227–228
Protoevangelium of James 28, 32–33
"provincial law" 40–41, 42

Qarāmiṭa 178–179, 222, 224. *See also* Ismāʿīlism
qurʿa. *See* lot-casting
Qurʾān, interpretation of 241

Raspe, Heinrich 229
Rāzī, Abū Bakr al-
on prophets 89–90, 101, 152–153, 156, 158, 191, 195, 212, 214
on true religion 153, 194–195, 213–214
Rāzī, Abū Ḥātim al- 152, 154–155, 156–158, 171, 172–173
Rāzī, Fakhr al-Dīn al- 93–94
reason
as criterion of knowledge 96, 103, 107, 114, 118, 121–122, 174, 194, 208
limits of 90–91, 92, 170, 176, 184–185
as philosophy 153, 176, 195
vs. revelation 93, 114, 118, 122, 175, 207
Reeves, John C. 47, 63
reincarnation 136, 143
religion
expression of doubts on 112, 122, 198–199, 216–217, 227–228
higher vs. lower levels of 156–158, 176, 183–184, 214, 235
natural 101, 173–174, 183, 191–192, 213
and power 155–156, 169–171, 204–205
socio-political functions of 155–156, 176, 186–192, 196–197, 204–205, 211, 234–237
true vs. false 83, 88–89, 90–92, 153, 156, 170, 194–195, 196, 200, 214
as unnecessary 99–101, 174–175, 191–192, 194, 207–208, 211, 214
Roman empire, "Orientalisation" of 40–41
Romans 40–41
lot-casting among 20–21, 24, 25, 27–28, 37

Said, Edward 240, 241
Sarakhsī, al- 174, 179, 211, 217
ṣarfa, doctrine of 102–104, 107
scepticism 91, 124–126, 170, 173, 181, 207–209. *See also* equipollence of proofs (*takāfuʾ al-adilla*)
science 108–111, 113–114, 118. See also *kalām*; *ṭabāʾiʿ* (elementary qualities)
Shīʿites
criticising Companions 170
lot-casting among 38
and Zindīqs 123
Shuʿūbī movement 162–166, 181
Sijpesteijn, Petra 245
Sincere Brethren 101, 174–175, 191–192
Sirr al-khalīqa 131–132, 134–135, 137, 142
slaves, conditional manumission of 42–43
Solomon 102
spirit (*rūḥ*) as fifth nature 105, 133–134
Stoicism 119, 128–129, 133–134, 135–136, 137, 139, 231
Sufism
Dahrī views in 143
epistemology of 184–185
philosophical ideas about prophets in 219–220
role of law in 181–184, 196
Sūfisṭāʾiyya 124, 125
"Sunnī revival" 181
suspension of judgement (*irjāʾ*, *wuqūf*) 125–126

ṭabāʾiʿ (elementary qualities) 102, 105, 106, 114, 133–136
God as creator of 134–135
proponents of 96, 108, 131, 133–137
science of 109–111

takāfuʾ al-adilla 82, 90–91, 92, 126, 170, 173, 207–208, 210
taqiyya 198, 217
"tenth-century crisis" 166–171
theodicy motif 69, 72
Theodore of Antioch 228
theologians (*mutakallim*s)
  doubting religion 171, 173–174
  and philosophy/physics 109–110, 118, 126, 130, 170
  vs. philosophers 118, 172, 211, 213
  refuting *mulḥid*s 113, 123
  as tricksters 83–84
  See also *kalām*; Muʿtazilites
Thomas Scotus 229–230, 233
three impostors thesis
  in Islamic Near East 83, 224, 226–227
  among Ismāʿīlīs 221–224
  in medieval Europe 90, 200–201, 225–230, 233–234
  Muslims as source of 201, 225–227
  among philosophers 179–180
transmission
  as guarantee of content 107
  oral, of ideas 237–239
Turks 180–181, 192

ʿUmar Khayyām 93, 175, 185
Ūta-napishti
  as Atraḫasīs 51–52, 53, 60, 62, 66–67, 78
  as Enoch 63
  al-Khiḍr as 75, 78
  Yonṭon as 68
Utuabzu 52–53

Wansbrough, John xii
watchers, story of 54–55, 56, 57, 78, 79, 86, 88
water of life 49, 66–68, 69–70, 72
wuqūf (suspension of judgement) 125

Yazīd b. Unaysa 177
Yonṭon (son of Noah) 68–69

Zaninus 233–234
Zindīqs
  backgrounds of 119, 122, 206
  Christians as 114, 115, 119
  cosmology of 128–133, 139
  denying God and prophethood 111–112, 118, 120, 141–142, 206–207, 219
  persecution of 123, 217
  rationalism of 92–93, 142
  reasons for becoming 106, 107, 109, 110, 114–115, 122
  and science 109, 118
  Shīʿite view of 123
Zi(u)sudra/Xisouthros 50–52, 57, 60–61, 62, 77, 78
Zoroastrianism
  Islamic influence on 168, 169
  non-Persian forms of 120
  as source for Muslim heresies 122, 169, 177, 206